The Nature of Work

The Nature of Work

Sociological Perspectives

EDITED BY KAI ERIKSON
AND STEVEN PETER VALLAS

AMERICAN SOCIOLOGICAL ASSOCIATION

PRESIDENTIAL SERIES AND

YALE UNIVERSITY PRESS

NEW HAVEN AND LONDON

Published with assistance from the Kingsley Trust Association
Publication Fund established by the Scroll and Key Society of Yale
College.

Designed by Nancy Ovedovitz and set in Times Roman type by The
Composing Room of Mich., Inc. Printed in the United States of America
by Edwards Brothers, Inc., Ann Arbor, Michigan.

LIBRARY OF CONGRESS CATALOGING-IN-PUBLICATION DATA
The Nature of work : sociological perspectives / edited by Kai Erikson
and Steven Peter Vallas.
   p.   cm. — (American Sociological Association presidential series)
   Includes bibliographical references.
   ISBN 0-300-04520-4 (alk. paper) : $35.00
   1. Work. 2. Industrial sociology. I. Erikson, Kai T. II. Vallas,
Steven P. (Steven Peter), 1951– . III. Series.
HD4904.N347 1990
306.3′6—dc20   90-30425
                                                CIP

The paper in this book meets the guidelines for permanence and
durability of the Committee on Production Guidelines for Book
Longevity of the Council on Library Resources.

10   9   8   7   6   5   4   3   2   1

||||||| CONTENTS

| | | | | | | | Preface

The following is a gathering of papers originally presented at the annual meeting of the American Sociological Association in 1985 and then redrafted for publication by their authors.

The announced theme of the meeting was "Working and Not Working," and the scholars who came to Washington to address the theme were invited to consider the full range of issues that can be said to fit under that large canopy. Any call as general as that, obviously, encourages participants to spread out across a huge intellectual terrain, and the papers produced in response to it differed widely in topic and approach. That is what scholarly meetings are supposed to be, after all—a rich and varied discussion.

But that much diversity can pose a problem for editors who must later assemble that scatter of papers into some sort of package. The papers all stand alone. To arrange them in clusters, as we spent a good deal of time doing, is to make them part of a composition for which they were not originally intended. One is almost tempted in circumstances like that to shuffle the various papers like playing cards, send them off to the printer in the order fate had thus decreed, and let each of them announce their own place in the larger sociological project.

Books, however, are not made that way, and while we think the grouping and shaping we have done here makes good intellectual sense, we would like to note at the outset that the sociologists whose thought is represented here are among the reigning experts on work in this country. They are the ones who have been surveying the territory, drawing the maps; and the proper task of editors, once they have settled on an order, is to offer to serve as trail guides.

All of the papers in this volume, obviously, were once oral presentations, and they can be read that way now. Erikson was president of the American Sociological Association at the time of the meeting, so it was his responsibility to choose the theme, chair the Program Committee, and invite the principal speakers. His introduction to this volume, then, appropriately enough, is like the remarks a presider might make to open a session—a general prologue by way of getting things started. And Vallas's conclusion is like the remarks a discussant might make once the session nears its conclusion, commenting on

viii

the papers that have just been presented and speaking more generally about the state of the sociological art.

We spent a year together in academic 1987–88 talking about the nature of work when we were both Visiting Scholars at the Russell Sage Foundation, and our debt to that model of what a nonprofit organization ought to be is profound. Cynthia Fuchs Epstein and William Kornblum shared those conversations, and we want to acknowledge our debt to them as well. Above all, though, we would like to salute Gladys Topkis, our editor at the Yale University Press. She is wise and thoughtful, and her store of patience, inexhaustible when the times call for reflection and care, thins just the right amount when she senses the approach of sloth. We couldn't have asked for a better partner.

The Nature of Work

||||||| Introduction

KAI ERIKSON

Every author in this collection agrees that the nature of work in America is being transformed in important ways. Blue-collar factory jobs in such industries as steel and automobiles are being drained off into countries where lower wages are the rule, while the industrial center of gravity here, if one can speak of such a thing, is shifting toward the use of complex technologies, the provision of services, and the processing of information. The values and expectations of those who work, meantime, are shifting as well, and most of the familiar patterns of the world of work are at risk. Each of these transformations is connected to the others like the filaments of a huge circular web, a tissue without beginning or end. There is no logic to help one know where to enter that circularity for the purpose of opening discussion, so if we begin by asking how the modern workplace affects the people who are exposed to it, we are aware of choosing a place to start almost at random.

I

The first paper in this collection is far and away the hardest for me to introduce, since I was the one who wrote it. I have some idea what the author had in mind but hardly any of what the finished paper looks or sounds like; and that, of course, exactly reverses the way I experienced the other papers to be found here. Our opening section is on "Work and the Person." It is almost impossible to discuss that topic for more than a minute without bringing up the name of Karl Marx, since he is so closely identified with the view that industrial work in capitalist economies is doing real damage to the minds and spirits of workers. My contribution, the Presidential Address at the meeting at which all the pieces gathered here were originally presented, is an attempt to consider how Marx's concept of alienation—which I have always had a difficult time seeing clearly through the mists of debate that seem to surround it—may be

1

used to guide research. I refer to the essay as "a field-worker's reading" of Marx in recognition of the fact that I am less drawn to and familiar with the philosophical literature on alienation than I am to the anthropology—if that is the right word—of Marx's vision. Beyond that, I'll let the paper speak for itself.

Like so many others on the same general subject, my paper draws heavily on the research of Melvin L. Kohn. He and his associates have spent years exploring the relationship between work and personality, and the paper he offers here is a report on the present status of that developing body of data. Kohn begins by describing the relationships between work and personality that are more or less resolved, and he follows by suggesting what remains to be done.

What do we already know? Well, for one thing, we can say with considerable confidence that job conditions really do have an influence on personality, and, moreover, that they do so in strong measure. We can say, too, that the more autonomous and self-directed a person's work, the more positive its effects on personality; and the more routinized and closely supervised the work, the more negative its effects. And we can say, finally, that those results hold for both women and men and for workers in socialist as well as capitalist industrial economies.

What, then, are the important next steps? The unresolved issues? Our main need, says Kohn, now that we know that there *is* an effect, is to develop ways of examining the process in closer detail. What conditions of work seem to have the most influence on personality? And what parts of the personality—what nerve ends, so to speak—are most sensitive to the conditions thus identified? Are those sensitivities distributed evenly throughout the work force? Throughout the stages of a working career? We know the general contours of the problem, in short; we need now to adjust our lens so as to be able to focus on its texture and grain.

II

The papers by Kohn and myself consider how the conditions in which people work help shape the way they think and act—and, by extension, the way they participate in social life generally. Marx, of course, had no trouble at all envisioning how humors originating in the workplace might reach out and leave their mark on the rest of the worker's world. But he had little to say about the reverse flow, the ways in which values and perceptions from other social domains reach in and affect the character of work and the workplace—nor has there been much research on that subject since his time.

Cynthia Fuchs Epstein and Arthur L. Stinchcombe, each in a different way, go a long way toward making up that deficit. The workplace, they both suggest, cannot be understood properly as a contained space with its own norms and moods and patternings, but must be seen as a location on the larger social landscape across which the influences of culture flow easily and in all directions.

Epstein begins by noting that modern methods of research like the survey and modern theoretical approaches like labor process analysis have drawn sociological attention so narrowly to the workplace itself that they may have exaggerated its influence. When one's eyes are focused on the office or the assembly line, it is easy to see how the structure of that bounded world shapes the behavior and outlooks of the people who work there. But when one's eyes are focused on workers, so to speak, and remain so through the course of a workweek or even a work career, one can more easily see that places of work are stations through which they circle as they pursue the wider arcs of their lives. In order to understand what goes on in the workplace, then, one has to follow people across the boundaries of work into the families, neighborhoods, and communities in which they live the rest of their lives. It is a traffic that moves two ways. On the one hand, employees obviously move out of the workplace into other social worlds with a sense of self and a view of the world tuned by the rhythms of work. But on the other hand—and this is Epstein's main concern here—workers just as obviously bring to their place of work values and expectancies born elsewhere in the culture.

Stinchcombe takes a similar tack. The ways of the workplace, he argues, are governed both by a set of formal norms—rules, procedures, agreements—and by a set of semiconscious or even unconscious norms that are drawn from the larger culture and are used to deal with the more informal aspects of work life. The two sets of norms are like different languages or modes of discourse, and experienced workers, being fluent in both, switch from one to the other as they negotiate a working day—speaking in the more formal mode when discussing grievance procedures or technical matters, say, and drifting easily into the more informal one when discussing the personal, the emotional, the social.

Stinchcombe's point is that the informal modes of discourse issue from the culture in general rather than from the world of work itself, yet have a significant if not always visible effect on the workplace. The way work is apportioned in a given shop, for example, does not result just from bureaucratic design or an exercise of authority; it is greatly influenced by expectations of a more general sort about what is congruent and what is not, many of them outside the awareness even of those who draw on them the most decisively. They are like reflexes, acted on without calculation, and they involve such judgments as What kind of work is fitting for persons of this or that ethnic background or gender? What is the proper way for people to arrange themselves in space or to position themselves in conversation? To study the workshop, then, is, at least in part, to study the ways in which cultural currents reach in and mold the organization of work. Stinchcombe, in fact, once proposed an alternative title to the one his paper now bears: "How the reasonableness of everyday life shapes the rationality of work." Exactly.

The notion that modern workers increasingly turn to activities outside the sphere of paid work for a sense of meaning and identity appears a number of times in this collection and figures prominently in most sociological thinking about leisure. There is even a growing view that leisure may one day play the same part in human consciousness that Marx assigned to work. Let me digress for a moment to raise a point that will surface again: André Gorz, himself a Marxist, feels that the old working class has more or less disappeared, transformed into a "non-class of non-workers"—an amorphous mass of the chronically unemployed and underemployed, whose skills are no longer of any apparent use in the new workplace and who have little or no job security. This mass does not constitute some outer fringe, a group of people lurking around the edges of the social order. It embraces (or will soon embrace) a majority of the populace, and it drifts incoherently without any discernible sense of class identity or any organizational base.

A mass of people so inert can have no realistic hope of seizing the means of production, as Karl Marx had both hoped and predicted. But this does not dismay Gorz at all, for he thinks he sees the emergence of something better yet—a collection of individuals who repudiate the very idea of work, who free themselves from the notion that work enriches them and lends dignity to their lives, and who reject the work role and the work ethic altogether. Marx was horrified by the thought that people might have to measure their own worth by the way they spend their wages rather than by the way they spend their hours at work, but Gorz proposes that we regard that (inevitable) shift in focus as an opportunity for people to escape from the tyrannies of work altogether and to derive a sense of satisfaction and self from the way they consume their free time. We will pick up that thread again in pages to follow.

Rose Laub Coser is not dealing with the fortunes of a sinking proletariat here, but she is interested in a parallel connection between the workplace and the wider society. It has long been understood that the distribution of power within a family changes when the wife as well as the husband works for pay and contributes to the family's income. The husband loses a measure of control as a result of this shift in the center of economic gravity, as might be imagined; but, Coser points out, he may gain status as a result because the purchasing power of the family goes up, and those additional funds can be spent on the outer symbols of status.

Now this is obviously truer for the middle ranges of the class structure than for its highest and lowest strata. Among those persons who barely get by, women's work is a necessary contribution to subsistence, not a form of saved capital to be expended on the trappings of status. And in the upper reaches of the class structure, one income is sufficient to the purpose without requiring any kind of supplement.

Coser's observation fits the sardonic spirit of Thorstein Veblen far more than it does the views of Karl Marx, since it was Veblen, above all, who insisted that the satisfactions one gains from life and the stature one earns in the eyes of others are often derived from the way one consumes rather than from the way one relates to the means of production. Our culture's emphasis on consumer goods, then—so hard to justify in other ways—at least has the effect of changing the structure of opportunity for women. It moves them out into the market, gives them an additional measure of self-esteem, and increases their power within the family. And to that extent, the consumer society may be contributing in important ways to gender equality.

III

Work can take many forms. We use the word in conversation every day, taking it more or less for granted that we are speaking of the same universe of experience. Mostly, of course, we are thinking of "jobs" that are a part of the regular economy and supply an answer to the question What do you do for a living? People "do" many things, however, that qualify as work by any reasonable standard but belong outside the zone drawn by that definition.

There is a vast economic network out there in the world, for example, that is almost wholly hidden from sight because it is not registered anywhere by the official measuring instruments of society. It is known as the underground economy, the off-the-books economy, the hidden economy, the shadow economy, or, as Louis A. Ferman calls it here, the irregular economy. Transactions in the irregular economy involve the exchange of goods or services for money, as is the case in the regular economy, but they are not recorded and thus do not figure in any financial indices like the Gross National Product. The very notion of an underground or irregular economy, as Ferman notes, sounds a bit sinister and even hints vaguely of vice. But a child's lemonade stand belongs in the irregular economy every bit as much as an illicit distillery, the services of a babysitter as much as those of a prostitute; and, in fact, a large part of the irregular economy involves exchanges of the sort most often found in communities or in villages. If I sell something to a friend without using the services of a broker, or pay cash to a local teenager for mowing my lawn, or repair my neighbor's furnace for the price of a case of beer, I am participating in the irregular economy. It is a wide, shadowy, fascinating world, and Ferman's paper offers a wise and thoughtful introduction to it.

If Ferman is concerned with work that remains hidden from the official sensors of society, Eliot Freidson and Stanton Wheeler are concerned with work that people do as an occupational sideline simply because they like it or feel called to it.

Most commentators on work, Freidson notes, seem hostile to it. The Christian tradition of the Fall, for instance, has it that human beings must work as a penalty for the presumption of their ancestors, and the Marxian tradition, as my paper points out, describes work—in the industrial age, anyway—as a source of pain and alienation. Freidson wants to turn a spotlight on what he calls labors of love: voluntary work, for the most part, that draws on creative energies, produces intellectual and sensory satisfaction, and enriches the person who engages in it. If alienated labor can be conceptualized as belonging at one end of an axis or continuum, labors of love would belong naturally at the other.

What are labors of love? The activities of hobbyists and amateurs, for one thing. Most of the poetry composed, the music performed, the art done in our society—in most societies, for that matter—is the work of people who earn their livings in other occupations, and, in a like way, quite a few of the people who keep parishes alive and hospitals humane are volunteers who want to participate in the life of the community as well as to occupy their time. Such activities as these are often gathered together under the heading leisure, but Freidson thinks they ought to be regarded as unpaid or very lightly paid work.

They often require heavy expenditures of energy and, like other activities that belong in the irregular economy, involve the production of goods or the performance of services. Labors of love also share with work hidden in the shadows of the society that they go unrecorded. They are work, though, even if done in the hours economists classify as leisure time, and it is very important for specialists to view them as such. When we talk about the ways in which work leaves its imprint on the human soul, then, we clearly need to have labors of this kind very much in mind.

Wheeler picks up that theme exactly and even draws on many of the same examples Freidson uses. An increasing number of people, he notes, express their true selves not in the day-to-day work by which they earn their bread but in activities that occupy their hours away from the workplace. These activities cannot be understood as play, pastime, hobby, avocation. Wheeler joins Freidson in insisting that they, too, are a form of work, though he proposes to call them preoccupations rather than labors of love. At the celebrated end of the scale, we find poets like Wallace Stevens and William Carlos Williams, the one an insurance adjustor and the other a pediatrician. At the other end we find all those people who derive their main sense of vocation and calling from the way they collect, create, play, repair, learn, compose, care for, compete, attend, and, in general, engage in activities that pay them little or nothing but provide them with their most significant investments of self, their most meaningful forms of work, their principal niches in life.

Double lives, Wheeler calls them, and he thinks, as does Freidson, that they are becoming an ever more prominent feature of modern life. To begin with, the demands of everyday work for large numbers of people are not so consuming as was once the case, leaving time and energy for other projects. And, too, the decline of a sense of craft, the increase of routinized work in the office and on the shop floor, take from everyday work some of its meaning, its creativity, its communality, its ability to provide identity. That is André Gorz's point, too.

Some of those preoccupations are secluding in the sense that they draw individuals into their own envelopes of privacy—to compose music or work on collections, say. But they can create openings into new social worlds, too, supplying new contacts and new sources of fellowship. Those who climb mountains, collect antique cars, watch birds, share a passion for Gustav Mahler or the Grateful Dead, or (as happens to be the case with Wheeler himself) make music derive from membership in such groups a kind of support and collegiality the workplace often lacks. They are neighborhoods.

To move from labors of love to work in concentration camps is to make a leap in subject that all the transitional sentences in the world could not smooth. But the very fact that one section of a book on work can contain such wildly diverse topics as writing poetry, sitting babies, and forcing labor on inmates—so far apart on the scale of human horror—at least illustrates how wide a range the term *work* encompasses.

Lewis A. Coser writes of a social order turned upside down, one in which everything is reversed. The occupational structure of a concentration camp, obviously, is very unlike that of any other social world, certainly unlike the worlds from which the inmates came. The skills of a carpenter or mechanic, say, are far more valuable to the keepers of an inmate population than are those of a lawyer or philosopher, and the people who can adjust to the rhythms of hard labor and who approach tasks with a certain obstinacy of mind and spirit—not talents accorded high status in the rest of the world—are greatly rewarded. The dregs of outside society ("the brutal, the vile, the unscrupulous, the sociopaths") are often given special privileges and special responsibilities precisely because their cruelty and barbarity equip them so well for doing the work of their keepers.

The notion of alienation has no place in such a context as this. Work is meaningless by definition, and even those who by virtue of old skills are given a chance to express some sense of craft can gain no satisfaction from it. Status does not matter. Pay does not matter. The only reward the system can supply is survival itself, and there, too, the camp is a world turned on its head, for the inmates most likely to make it are the ones whose qualifications in a sane world would have been regarded as the most marginal. The camp is an almost perfect instrument of degradation in Harold Garfinkel's sense, and to call what happens there work may even be to stretch the term beyond its natural range. It is difficult to think of concentration camps sociologically under the best of circumstances: the concepts we normally employ seem to shrink before the enormity of the facts they are being asked to help organize.

IV

We turn now to the problem of unemployment and to measures that have been proposed at one time or another to make sure that work is available to those persons who want it. The meeting at which these papers were originally given was entitled "Working and Not Working," as was noted earlier, and its organizers had in mind that contributions would address both halves of that whole—not only what happens to people who are fortunate enough to find employment on a more or less regular basis, but what might be done on behalf of those who do not.

Seymour Bellin and S. M. Miller are interested here in the by now familiar question: Is our society becoming increasingly polarized into a two-tiered labor market, one in which a portion of those who work find well-paid, clean, skilled, secure jobs, especially in high technology and service industries, and another portion find themselves stuck in dead-end, poorly paid, unskilled, insecure jobs? Or is the postindustrial society, as so many hoped, providing increasing numbers of good jobs near the middle of the economic range? Is the labor market shaped like an hourglass—that is, with masses of people at the upper reaches of whatever scale measures "good" jobs and masses of the underemployed at the bottom? Is it shaped like a diamond with an ever-expanding middle? Or is it shaped like a pyramid, with a tiny working elite emerging from a massive base of what Gorz called the "non-class of non-workers"?

The data appear to be mixed on that score, but it is evident at present that the lower levels of the class structure—the bottom portion of whatever figure one draws to represent the labor market—are expanding. Unemployment is on the rise, disproportionately so for youth in general and for black and Hispanic youth in particular, and, likewise, for women in general and for women heads of households in particular. In addition, there are reasons to suspect an increase in jobs with poor pay, low benefits, and dim prospects.

But such drifts are subject to the influence of government. The major argument of the article, in fact, is that patterns of stratification are *manufactured* by the machinery of government. They are *willed* into being. And so the question becomes, How might the economy be shaped so as to avoid that imbalance in the lower tiers? Bellin and Miller have a number of suggestions in that regard. It

is important, first, to reject the widespread notion that some level of unemployment is normal or inevitable. That, too, is a matter of choice. And if we choose
to reduce the level of unemployment, the government has any number of
devices at its disposal. It can adjust its expenditures in such a way as to promote
employment—investing in activities like education that create jobs, for example, rather than in activities like military research and development that do not.
A government can use its power to subsidize and to protect in such a way as to
enhance employment. And a government can regulate: it can reduce the hours
of work, raise the minimum wage, reform the tax structure, provide medical
insurance, and in a hundred other ways create a diamond-shaped labor market
even when other currents in the economy appear to be pressing it into an
hourglass or a pyramid.

The United States, as it happens, has tolerated a remarkably high rate of
unemployment over the past fifty years or so, larger by quite a margin than in
any of the other democracies in Europe and the rest of the world. Yet, as Theda
Skocpol argues, it was not always thus. The original architects of the New
Deal, which is to say the prime movers of America's version of the welfare
state, were mainly interested in assuring full employment, not in providing
relief. Whether that goal was to be achieved by manipulating the economy in
some way or by the simpler expedient of creating jobs, it was understood to be
one of the most important priorities of the new administration. There have been
a fair number of efforts since to mandate full employment, but not very much
has come of them. Why? The idea of making jobs available to those who want
them, Skocpol points out, is very much in the American grain: most of us
regard work as the natural way for people to realize their promise and to assert
their independence, and most of us, too, regard relief as demeaning and degrading. One might reasonably suppose, then, that full employment measures
would be as popular here as they are, say, in Sweden. But no. Relief is a burden
the nation has for the most part accepted, if not gracefully, while high rates of
unemployment are thought to be not only inevitable but natural.

All of this has something to do with the peculiar species of democracy found
in America, and the main thrust of Skocpol's article is to describe some of those
peculiarities. American business has been opposed to everything smelling even
faintly of the welfare state, for one thing, and the people who would benefit
most from such measures have been too weak and too poorly organized to
mount much in the way of pressure. Our experience as a nation with the politics
of patronage and with the graft that so frequently accompanied it has made us
wary of the notion that jobs can be created by the machinery of the state. And
the strangely ambivalent structure of the Democratic party, in which for fifty
years liberal impulses from the urban North have been stalled by tough old
congressional chieftains from the rural South, and in which the employed

working classes have opposed efforts to make room for the disadvantaged in their ranks, has played a part as well.

Among the efforts that have been made to open spaces for the unemployed are the various job-training programs that began in the early years of the New Deal and have received sporadic support since. Elijah Anderson, an experienced field observer of urban black communities, reports on the history and prospects of such programs as they affect ghetto youth. During the years of the New Deal, Anderson points out, and in the decade or two following, employment programs for the young generally involved on-the-job training— almost like traditional forms of apprenticeship—in which linkages of family and community and ethnic group loomed very important. Craftspersons in the program would find openings for cousins, neighbors, landsmen, ethnic fellows from local lodges and parishes. As a result, supervisors met trainees in a cultural context familiar to both, and blacks, being without the kind of opening wedge provided by older and more seasoned craftspeople, were for the most part excluded.

In the 1960s, though, during the Kennedy and Johnson years, job-training programs became a good deal more formal and bureaucratic. Mentors tended to be ethnic whites with a deep sense of craft and a respect for discipline, while trainees tended to be urban blacks and Puerto Ricans with quite different expectations and manners. White met black. The work ethic met the culture of the ghetto. And in those meetings very different concepts of punctuality and demeanor collided. Black trainees, street tough and sensitive to racial slights, appeared to white instructors as belligerent, arrogant, touchy, unwilling to bend to even the most elementary disciplines of work. This tended to be the case, moreover, even when the instructors were themselves black, since they had been conditioned by the values and disciplines of another time. So the programs were characterized by a good deal of tension and distrust.

The situation becomes worse when, as often happens, young men and women leave the programs out of frustration or anger because that only proves to already skeptical instructors that the people of the ghetto lack the necessary motivation or discipline, and it only proves to the withdrawing youth as well as the rest of the community that the instructors are surly if not racist and the programs a waste of time. A poor record of success thus becomes poorer yet— as clear an instance of self-fulfilling prophecy as can be found. And the failed trainees become all the more likely to drift into patterns of dependency or to become absorbed into the rough and irregular economies of the ghetto streets— dealing drugs, say, or engaging in any number of other illegalities.

If it is true, however, as many commentators suppose, that the job market will not produce enough hours of work for all the people who want to be employed, then job-training programs, even at their best, are a means of redistributing opportunity rather than a means of increasing employment. The question then becomes not simply how to prepare people for the work that needs to be done, but how to divide up the available hours of work among those who present themselves as candidates for them.

The answer we have been living with in this society for two generations or more is to divide the work up into forty-hour weeks, hire people to fill in those established time units, and then accept the considerable burden of allowing the people left over to remain unemployed. We have lived for so long with that procedure for parceling out labor that most of us think of it as natural. A work week lasts forty hours, a work year lasts fifty weeks, a working career lasts thirty, forty, maybe even fifty years.

But nature did not decree that division, and among the most logical ways of finding employment for larger numbers of people is to allot each of them a smaller share of the hours available. How about a shorter workweek? A shorter work year? A shorter career? How many new jobs could be created if four persons were to take on the work assignments now performed by three, which is more or less what would happen if the conventional workweek shrunk to thirty hours?

This is the issue addressed in the papers by Fred J. Best and Herbert J. Gans. They both speak of work sharing, meaning the strategy of redistributing the available working hours among a larger work force. The strategy itself has a long history. Best quotes Samuel Gompers: "As long as we have one person seeking work who cannot find it, the hours of work are too long."

Best's contribution here is to disassemble the concept of work sharing and to set forth the practical options it contains. He sees seventeen such options altogether, but they fall into four general groupings. The first would be to provide inducements to employees for reducing the number of hours they work over a career span—something that might be accomplished by retiring from the work force earlier, entering the work force later, or taking more time off in-between. The second would be to impose limits on the amount of work a person can do by simple fiat—restricting overtime, reducing the standard workday or workweek, requiring longer vacations, and the like. The third would be to create long-term tradeoffs in which workers forfeit future pay raises or promotions for present reductions of workhours—in effect buying current hours of leisure by borrowing on future earnings. And the fourth, an extension of the third, would be to create short-term tradeoffs in which employees elect to buy free time from current earnings—taking a reduction in pay, for example, in return for longer vacations or shorter workdays.

Bellin and Miller, as I noted a moment ago, argue that governments have the power to balance unemployment and employment in any way they see fit. Thus stratification patterns are political, not economic, and Best's main point here is to describe a set of ways in which full employment could be realized if the power of the government were brought to bear on it. The paper by Gans, written as a companion piece to the one by Best, considers in further detail those options outlined by Best that are voluntary and egalitarian in nature (as distinct, say, from forced retirement or work reductions imposed by mandate).

Work-sharing schemes have been tried in a number of other countries, according to Gans, and although the evidence on their success has to be seen as inconclusive so far, they help us see what questions need to be asked about prospects in this country.

Who supports work sharing, for example? The unemployed and the underemployed do, presumably, although no one will ask their opinion or pay attention to it if by some miracle an effort *is* made to find out what it is. The trade union leadership can be counted on, too, for the good reason that work sharing is likely to increase potential membership. But the rank and file can be expected to regard the unemployed as competitors for the hours of work that are available and to treat work sharing itself as a calamity.

Suppose, however, that some form of work sharing does come into play. What will people do with the extra time? Are we ready to move into a world where the way one plays, the way one consumes, the way one volunteers or helps out or raises children can supply identity and a feeling of usefulness? Gans raises the question without answering it, but in doing so he touches on a matter we have had several occasions now to consider. One virtue of work sharing, clearly, is to distribute opportunity more evenly throughout the working ranks. If that project results in reducing the amount of time workers must spend in routine, numbing jobs, is that not a good in itself? That is Gorz's view, in any event, and it would presumably appeal as well to Freidson and Wheeler. If automated work has the potential of influencing the human personality negatively, as Kohn's data seem to indicate, then the less one is exposed to it— or, rather, the less one measures oneself by it—the better off one is.

V

The final three papers in this gathering deal with the shape of the future. Imagining worlds yet to come is not done by gazing into crystal balls, of course, but by sorting through trends evident in the present and identifying the ones most likely to gain momentum in the years to come. Many of the issues raised here, then, are by now fairly familiar.

For example, the idea that modern conditions of work are dividing people into a class of skilled, secure, reasonably affluent workers, on the one hand, and a class of relatively unskilled workers who live in a state of almost constant insecurity, on the other, has surfaced several times so far.

The workers who fall into that first and fortunate class, as Rosabeth Moss Kanter suggests, are of a different breed in several respects. They are better educated on the whole; they tend to be more distrustful of authority in general and of autocratic forms of management in particular; they want to participate in the design of the work setting as well as in the decisions that bind them. They adhere to a "work ethic" quite unlike the one known to their parents, and they operate on the basis of a different set of moral and cognitive reflexes.

It follows, then, that the forms of industrial bureaucracy left behind by the passing age of mass production are not very well suited to the expectations of a newer generation of worker. The older pattern was characterized by levels of command, superimposed one on another like the layers of a cake, in which each stratum monitored and supervised the activities of the strata below. Even if this hierarchical arrangement lent itself to the coming age of automated tech-nology—and the experiences of countries like Japan and Sweden suggest that it does not—it surely does not fit the temper of the new work force.

So there has been a pronounced shift in the past few years, Kanter says, toward a more participative kind of workplace, one in which consultation and sharing replace fixed hierarchies as a way of distributing responsibility. The hope has been that these new forms of involvement, in which workers are listened to and share at least some measure of control, will not only create higher levels of job satisfaction—a good in its own right, of course—but tap hidden creativities and even increase productivity.

Kanter sees several potential sources of tension emerging from these efforts to increase worker participation—all of them verging on the ironic. To begin with, the wish of employees to participate and to *matter* will sooner or later conflict with what, after all, are the prevailing aims of industrial bureaucracy: to command, to control, to hold things in place. When one welcomes innova-tion at the employee level, one is promising a kind of flexibility and fluidity that the old hierarchies, dependent as they are on fixed rules and traditional forms of authority, cannot afford. They are too obdurate and brittle for the new tasks being asked of them.

For example, worker involvement is apt to create a feeling on the part of employees that they should be rewarded for the work they do rather than for the positions they occupy. Not so revolutionary a proposal, one might think. But in fact it is. Most employees are paid according to grade—craftspeople being grouped on one wage scale, first-level supervisors on another, second-level managers on a third—rather than according to the volume of work they turn out or the value of the contribution they make. It is almost impossible to imagine the old structure accommodating with any grace to a change of that sort. It would be like an energetic and productive corporal being paid more than his commanding officer.

The new workplace, Kanter adds, promising a higher level of involvement and maybe even a token reallocation of reward, may have the effect of narrowing the range of opportunity for women. The new arrangements require both an increased commitment to and an increased absorption in work, and this may turn out to be a price that women, who (still) do a disproportionate share of the work of the family, find hard to pay.

The paper by Amitai Etzioni and Paul Jargowsky, too, draws together a number of threads that have appeared earlier. One of the most prominent theses on the changing nature of work, associated with the name of Daniel Bell and others, is that the future is likely to bring a drastic decline in basic manufacturing and a rise in high technology industries. A society long tuned to the production of goods will soon be replaced by a society tuned to the processing of information; blue-collar workers will soon be replaced by technical and clerical personnel wearing neat white collars. A lot can be said for that notion. There has been a clear drop in steel and automobile production, the two best known of the basic smokestack industries, as a result of plant obsolescence, competition from low-wage countries, and so on. And there has been a clear increase in the number of jobs being created in high technology industries, too. But these trends are deceptive and can lead to an easy form of exaggeration. The decline of basic industries, if it is generally true at all, is so gradual as to mean a good deal less than appears on the surface, and the growth of high tech industries, though it seems steep when described as a proportion, is based on numbers so small that the actual volume of change is quite modest.

Etzioni and Jargowsky predict that American society of the future will be two-track, with basic industries remaining strong and running on a parallel course with high technology, service, and information industries. The two tracks may fuse and overlap in places, since high tech is itself moving into basic industries, automobile manufacturing being a good case in point. But the American economy will run on both of those complementary tracks for quite some time to come.

The work force called upon to staff both tracks, writes William Form, or at least that portion of it that has been traditionally drawn to trade unions, is moving into the final years of the century with diminished organizational resources, fewer sources of support, and a rather diffuse sense of direction. There was a time, says Form, particularly during the early years of the New Deal, when organized labor and the American species of welfare state were virtually of a piece. Labor regarded itself as occupying a rung near the bottom of the class structure and supported such measures as unemployment insurance, minimum wages, and old age pensions on the theory that it was promoting its own interests in doing so. And those wings of the Democratic party concerned with welfare legislation, meantime, were protective of the interests of labor in other domains as well.

In recent years, though, that natural partnership has more or less dissolved. Welfare legislation of the past two decades—Johnson's War on Poverty being a good example—has for the most part been aimed at minorities, women, the nonworking poor, and a number of other constituencies that do not belong in the ranks of organized labor at all, and it has been a long time, moreover, since Congress has offered any legislative comfort to trade unions. And that is not the worst of it. The shrinking of basic industries and the relocation of jobs from the urban North (strong union country) to the suburban South and Southwest have helped erode labor's base of support, and there has been a real decline of public sympathy for trade unions themselves, at least in part because the work force seems so much more affluent.

The very success of organized labor, then, has brought it into a new relationship with the economy and set it very sharply apart from the poorer and less organized portions of the working class. Form shares the by now familiar suspicion that we may be on the verge of seeing two working classes: organized labor, which has lost a good measure of its political clout and can no longer be counted on even to deliver votes, and a growing underclass of the poor, the underemployed, and the underorganized. The gulf between the two is large, not only because unions are more and more interested in protecting their members from the demands of less organized workers pressing up from underneath, but also because the less organized part of the working class, in its turn, quite sensibly views the unions as adversaries. This is a development that Form deeply regrets, since he does not see how organized labor can resume its place in American political life without the affection and energy and passion of those loosely organized constituencies.

Can anything be said at the last minute to draw all these diverse offerings into a simple frame? Not easily, anyway. And, in any event, the job of an introducer is to describe the fare yet to come and then leave the task of wrapping up the package to our discussant.

PART ONE • WORK AND THE PERSON

I I I I I I I   On Work and Alienation

KAI ERIKSON

My intention in the paragraphs to follow is to consider once again the familiar concept of alienation. I do not plan to report on a completed piece of research here or to argue for any particular way of doing sociological work on the subject. I hope, rather, to engage in the kind of aerial reconnaissance sociologists often undertake before they move on foot into a new research terrain.[1] This will mean that I cannot help being more attentive to the broader contours of the subject than to its finer grains and textures; and it will mean, too, that in sweeping across so wide a surface I am bound to skim past scholarly contributions of crucial importance to the sociology of work. Scouting expeditions are like that.

My remarks are in three parts: first, a field-worker's reading of Karl Marx's views on the nature of human alienation; second, a few thoughts on alienation in the increasingly automated and computerized workplaces of today; and third, a note of vaguely methodological intent on how one can know when one is in the presence of alienation.

When done, I hope to have demonstrated that the idea of alienation, despite the heavy philosophical and ideological cargo it is often asked to carry, can

I owe a special debt to the generosity of Marvin Bressler, Cynthis Fuchs Epstein, William Form, Richard H. Hall, David Montgomery, and especially, Steven Peter Vallas. I have more than the usual reasons, though, for wanting to make clear that I alone am to blame for errors of fact, tone, and imagination.

1. The new research terrain in my case is a study of workers in the telecommunications industry. The working title of the project is "The Culture of the Workplace." Cynthia Fuchs Epstein and I serve as principal investigators, and support has been provided by a grant from the Russell Sage Foundation.

serve as a sensitive conceptual device for helping us understand the way people relate to the work they do.[2]

The very term *alienation* is so closely identified with the work of Karl Marx that one is almost required to begin a reconnaissance with him. The genealogy of the concept, of course, can be traced past Marx to Feuerbach, Hegel, Fichte, and a number of others, so it had been toughening for years in the heavy brine of German metaphysics before Marx turned to it; and, moreover, he may have eyed the concept more warily in his later writings than in his earlier ones. I do not want to enter the ongoing discussions about these matters here, even supposing that I knew enough to do so. But it may be useful (to borrow a wonderful image from Jaroslav Pelikan) to pass a magnet lightly across Marx's writings on alienation in the hope of drawing out from them those scraps of metal, those filings, that may have special value to sociologists trying to find grounding in the world of work.

Human beings, says Marx, are, quite literally, made for work. This is not because we are doomed to toil as a result of the Fall ("Cursed is the ground for thy sake . . . in the sweat of thy face shalt thou eat bread"), but, on the contrary, because working is in our bones, in the very tissues of our being. The human animal emerged as a species from an environment in which laboring already played a prominent evolutionary part, and to that extent humankind is shaped by work, molded by it. The human hand, the human eye, the human brain have all evolved in response to the nature of work, and so, of course, have the human nervous system and the human imagination.[3] Hannah Arendt (1958:86) called this "the seemingly blasphemous notion of Marx that labor (and not God) created man or that labor (and not reason) distinguishes man from other animals."

Human beings reach out, gather the materials of nature, and fashion them into objects of one kind or another. We collect an armful of wood, pick up a piece of flint, extract a stone from a quarry—or, for that matter, capture a sight or a sound that happens to move us. The true character of humankind is reflected in the objects we produce as a result of that process: a campfire, an axe, a cathedral, a sonnet. Work of that kind is necessary for humans to fulfill their true nature. That is how, Marx said, they "develop" their "slumbering powers" ([1906] 1967:177). Now the energy and skill invested in the object are the very stuff of the person who created it, a part of his life's blood. And in a

2. See Archibald, 1978, for a good review of some of the issues involved in even so gentle a claim as this.

3. "Thus the hand is not only the organ of labour, it is also the product of labour," wrote Frederick Engels in a section of *Dialectics of Nature* entitled "The Part Played by Labour in the Transition from Ape to Man" (1987:453).

very real sense, he sees himself, evaluates himself, measures himself—even knows himself—by the things he makes. He "sees his own reflection in a world which he has constructed," Marx put it (1964:128). The producer, then, and the thing he produces are of the same flesh. Or at least that is the way nature intended it to be.

In the age of industrialization and capitalism, however, three developments have conspired to disturb that natural arrangement. The first is the institution of private property. Both the means by which objects are produced and the objects themselves are owned by somebody else in a functioning capitalist system, with the result that the worker is drawn apart from the work itself. They are of a flesh, the worker and the work, but that flesh is severed by the cruel wedge of private ownership.

The second is the development of a more and more complex division of labor. Workers play a reduced role when a task is broken up into minute segments; they apply but a fraction of their skill and knowledge to the task at hand and often lose their sense of the larger logic of the productive process in the bargain.

The third is the process by which human labor becomes a commodity like all other commodities. Workers in a capitalist economy do not ordinarily manufacture things for their own consumption, nor, presumably, do they do so for the joy of it. They manufacture things for money, for cold tender. Their experience and ability—their very selves, in fact—are sold at market prices in much the same way as a side of beef or a sack of onions, and in that sense they become commodities themselves. They are objects, things of a measured worth, without any greater value than the denomination of the coin used to purchase them.

Alienation, then, is disconnection, separation—the process by which human beings are cut adrift from their natural moorings in the world as the result of unnatural, alien work arrangements. And, Marx thought, it can take a number of forms.

For one thing, people can be said to be alienated when they lose contact with the product of their own labor. The things people fashion become an extension of their persons, a part of themselves, because they have breathed life into them. In the process of shaping a bowl or working a piece of leather or stitching a garment, they have poured some of themselves into it—a portion of their inventiveness, energy, humanity. And when the objects they have created are taken away to be stored in someone else's warehouse or sold on someone else's terms, the qualities they had invested in those objects are simply lost to them. They are reduced in stature, diminished in spirit. And as this raid on their personalities is repeated every day of their working lives, they become more and more incomplete human beings, facing life with dulled moral reflexes, blurred perceptions, and an impaired ability to think matters through.

People can also be said to be alienated when they lose their involvement in the activity of working itself and no longer experience it as a meaningful act of creation. This can happen, for example, when a worker feels dominated by the machinery with which she works. It can happen when the work of the hand is separated from the work of the brain, when the rhythms of a particular set of tasks are choreographed by a planner in some distant office and carried out with wooden compliance by workers on the shop floor. It can happen when a person's working hours are sharply differentiated from the other hours of the daily round: most modern workers can draw the line between the hours that belong to work and the hours that belong to them with a fierce precision, punching in and punching out on the dot of the minute. And it can happen, finally, when a person comes to see work as a means to an end, as an instrumentality. It does not nourish the worker's spirit but depletes it, and he becomes like a machine, senselessly grinding out something for the food it will bring to his table. "From being a man," said Marx somewhat starchily, "he becomes merely an abstract activity and a belly" (1964:72).

People can also be said to be alienated when they become estranged from their fellow creatures, as, says Marx, is inevitable in capitalism. Being commodities for sale, people are always in competition with one another, and that understandably helps reduce whatever feelings of comradeship and communality might otherwise emerge. Workers tend to be so brutalized and depleted by the experience of work, moreover, that they are largely incapable of authentic relations with others anyway.

And, finally, people can be said to be alienated when they find themselves separated from their own nature as members of the human species. Since they are not engaged in creating life but are merely earning the wherewithal to stay alive, they are no longer an active part of nature, no longer participants in its rhythms. They are, then, less than human, alienated even from themselves. (That thought has always had a good deal of appeal to critics like Erich Fromm, who want to talk about the existential crisis of modern times, but I will abandon it here, a bit prematurely, with the observation that, whatever its other virtues, it will not yield our magnet many scraps of the sort we need for a venture into the field.)

So all of the methods devised under capitalism to increase production, said Marx with a fine flourish,

mutilate the labourer into a fragment of a man, degrade him to the level of an appendage of a machine, destroy every remnant of charm in his work and turn it into a hated toil; they estrange from him the intellectual potentialities of the labour-process to a despotism the more hateful for its meanness; they transform his lifetime into a working-time, and drag his wife and child beneath the wheels of the Juggernaut of capital. (1906:708)

Whew! Thus the views of Karl Marx on alienation—or a version of them anyway.

Now suppose for a moment that we were to take those views with us into the new research terrain and use them to inform our inquiry. From what regions of the modern workplace should we most expect alienation to emerge? Where should we look for those sensitive zones in the structure of work that seem most capable of inducing it?[4]

If he followed his own texts as closely as those who now think themselves his heirs, Marx's belief would presumably be that alienation is most likely to issue from those overlapping spheres in the workplace (a) where workers are separated both from the products of their labor and from the means of production, (b) where people contributing to the overall production process do not have a clear sense of the pattern of the whole and are not really sure what their own role is in it, (c) where the work process is controlled by an external force or condition to which the worker has to adapt her own movements, and (d) where the work task has been splintered into so many specialties that only a fraction of the worker's intelligence and skill is required for its completion.

The first of those considerations has a rather antique sound in this day and age. Workers in industrialized countries everywhere can be said to have lost whatever claim they might otherwise have had to the product of their own labor, even if we knew what *product* meant in an economy increasingly devoted to service; and few persons can be said to own the means of production, except in the somewhat remote sense that they are among "the people" in whose name the title has been drawn up.[5] The main issue in any event is not whether workers have legal claim to the equipment they use but whether they exercise some real measure of control over it, as Braverman (1975), among others, has been at pains to point out. So the first and third considerations really collapse into one. And, in a like way, the second and fourth considerations overlap so greatly that they, too, can merge.

The key sources of alienation, then, from this point of view, reduce to two— first, those structures in the modern workplace that subdivide labor into narrower and narrower specialties, and, second, those structures in the modern workplace that limit the amount of control workers exercise over the conditions in which they work.

4. I do not want to commit myself to an awkward new term here, so I will duck into the nearest footnote to point out that if "pathogenic" refers to conditions that appear to induce pathology, then "alienogenic" could serve as a way to refer to those zones of sensitivity that seem to induce alienation.

5. The thinning but still sturdy ranks of the "self-employed" provide an exception, of course, and owning the means of production in their case really seems to matter. See Archibald 1981 for one view.

II

To the extent that Marx's observations were meant to serve as notes on the history of capitalism, he was asking us to envision a transformation from the gentler rhythms and more intimate scales of the artisanal past to the clatter and brutality of the industrial present. It is a story of the ways in which a system of production based on craft is replaced by a system of production based on a finely calibrated division of labor.

If we were to try to portray that transformation as drama, our first scene would almost have to take place in a craft workshop, where a cobbler or spinner or barrel maker fashions an object, invests something of himself in it, and either figuratively or literally leaves his signature on it; and our last scene would almost have to take place in a modern factory, especially one engaged in line assembly. Those are the images, after all, around which most of us organize our sense of that critical passage. The song of the craftsman would be drawn from such testimony as this (Sturt 1923:78):

> But no higher wage, no income, will buy for men that satisfaction which of old—until machinery made drudges of them—streamed into their muscles all day long from close contact with iron, timber, clay, wind and wave, horse-strength. It tingled up in the niceties of touch, sight, scent. The very ears unawares received it, as when the plane went singing over the wood, or the exact chisel went tapping in (under the mallet) to the hard ash with gentle sound. But these intimacies are now over. Although they have much for leisure men can now taste little solace in life, of the sort that skilled handwork used to yield to them. . . . In what was once the wheelwright's shop, where Englishmen grew friendly with the grain of timber and with sharp tool, nowadays youths wait upon machines.

And the song of the factory operative would be drawn from any of the hundreds of interviews that abound in contemporary social studies. "God, I hated that assembly line," a mechanic says to Lillian Breslow Rubin (1976:155): "I hated it. I used to fall asleep on the job standing up and still keep doing my work. There's nothing more boring and more repetitive in the world. On top of it, you don't feel human. The machine's running you, you're not running it." And another operative says to Charles Walker and Robert Guest (1952:54): "The assembly line is no place to work, I can tell you. There is nothing more discouraging than having a barrel beside you with 10,000 bolts in it and using them all up. Then you get a barrel with another 10,000 bolts, and you know every one of those 10,000 bolts has to be picked up and put in exactly the same place as the last 10,000 bolts."

The problem with that way of portraying the transformation is that the craft workshop and the assembly line can hardly be understood as much more than symbols. To speak of handicrafts in the preindustrial age is to speak of the economy of the towns and the occupations of a select few, not of the vast stretches of farmland in which most of the population scratched out a living. To speak of the assembly line in our own time is to speak of a rather special form of manufacture. For all the celebrity of the automobile industry among social scientists, a decreasing number of workers are involved in manufacturing of any kind, and even at its moment of glory, no more than a fraction of manual workers in the United States were engaged in line assembly. Nor can we take for granted that even that minority has been as abused by the ways of the workplace as is often supposed (Form 1976, 1987). The world we have lost is a world of agriculture; the world we are in the process of becoming is a world in which manufacture is yielding to service and both are becoming automated.

It is hard to know how to speak of the toil of the peasant when our subject is alienation. It is a form of craft work, to be sure, conducted at one's own pace and involving an intimate association with tools and materials; and to the extent that one extracts a living from the land one works, one can be said to be retaining at least a portion of the product of one's labor. There is personality in a good thatch, presumably, craft in a well-fashioned harness, art in a clean furrow. Ferdinand Toennies (1963:164) thought, "The Gemeinschaft, to the extent that it is capable of doing so, transforms all repulsive labor into a kind of art, giving it style, dignity, and charm, and a rank in its order, denoted as a calling and an honor." Well, maybe; but how many peasants, gnarled and leathery and bent to the hoe after decades in the fields, knew of that charm and honor? Somehow we need a different conceptual vocabulary than the one from which the term *alienation* comes to deal with the preindustrial countryside.

It is also hard to know how to speak about alienation as workers leave the satanic mills and move into the automated workplaces of our own period. There have been many expressions of hope in the last two or three decades that the coming of automation would reduce the amount of alienation in the modern workplace by replacing labor of the most mechanical and mindless kind with activities that require skill, judgment, and a sense of craft. Workers in charge of automated equipment, so the argument goes, rely on quick intelligence and sure perceptions rather than on raw strength, are freed from the unrelenting rhythms of a machine, can wander around the larger workplace and develop some feeling for what the whole enterprise is about, and, in general, escape from the pinched and narrow niches into which a complicated division of labor would otherwise have confined them. These expressions of hope have been nourished by just enough empirical evidence to make it one of the more important hypotheses under consideration in the sociology of work (see, for example, Bell 1973; Blauner 1964; Shepard 1971).

There is a contrary position, however, also nourished by enough data to protect its standing in the field. For if it is reasonable to point out, as Blauner and others have, that the division of labor is likely to become less problematic in automated work settings because more aspects of the productive process are gathered into a single set of hands, then it is also reasonable to note that automation may have a pronounced potential for sharpening other aggravations in the workplace that appear to induce alienation (for example Braverman 1974; Burawoy 1979a; Edwards 1979; Glenn and Feldberg 1977; Feldberg and Glenn 1983; Noble 1984; Wallace and Kalleberg 1982; Zuboff 1988). Let me review some of those reasons, moving lightly across the surface.

To begin with, the work required in most automated settings, though largely free of muscular exertion, can replace the boredom that comes from endlessly repeating the same rote activity ("then you get a barrel with another 10,000 bolts") with the boredom that comes from doing nothing at all. That is sometimes a blessing, to be sure. "When the machine is working," said one operative happily, "I am not" (Shaiken 1984:134). His job is to attend the machine, to be at its service. He is, as David Halle (1984) puts it, "on guard duty." But monitoring the workings of some machine can be profoundly tedious when things go right, which is most of the time; and if the worker finds other things to engage her mind—reading, musing, telling tales—the activity itself is clearly alien from the substance of the work.

Even when the process is complex and demanding, however, the skills called for in many automated procedures are really a quickness of reflex, a sureness of eye, and, maybe most important, an ability to pay attention—not the mastery of materials and the command of pace that is usually implied by the work *craft*. In such settings, the finer tunings of the human body—its deftness, artistry, cunning, versatility—are simply not brought to bear at all.

Nor, for that matter, are most of the human senses. The day is clearly long past when more than a handful of workers actually sight down the grain of the wood, feel the texture of the weave, or otherwise remain in touch with the materials they use by listening, smelling, tasting; but it should be noted that those who work with certain kinds of automation become yet another step removed from things they are shaping. In continuous process plants, for example, it is not uncommon for workers to never see or touch the raw materials that come in one end of the cycle or the finished products that come out the other. And in computerized offices, similarly, it is not uncommon for workers to see nothing but the images on a screen or to touch nothing but the keys on a keyboard, rarely coming into physical contact with the letters they type, the files they prepare, and so on.

Moreover, information flows both back and forth along the circuits of a computer. They send programmed instructions out to the office or the shop floor, and, at the same time, they bring intelligence back. In the process, they have the capacity to drain workers of what may well have been their most important lever of control—the wisdom and lore that come from years of seasoning. "Any self-respecting machinist," says Harley Shaiken (1984:54), "has a legendary 'black book' that records the problems encountered and the short cuts discovered on the previous jobs." It is a special kind of knowledge, "enriched over time." The same is true, of course, though less formally so, of coal miners, short order cooks, filing clerks, salespeople, and anyone else who becomes more skilled with experience. Computers, though, can appropriate such experience and store it permanently, and they can do so for every worker who enters a computer network. So the computer's black book can easily contain the lore of thousands of minds, and as all that information is sorted out, experience becomes a matter of formula, intuition and judgment become matters of computation. It is almost as if the computer's black book does for human workers what genetic codes do for social insects: give creatures the accumulated experience of generations without asking from them so much as a trace of thought.

In a sense, then, computerized procedures can draw away most of the faculties that are the stuff of humanhood. People have been operating machines since the beginning of the industrial era, of course, and under the right circumstances the largest of them is like a hand tool, an extension of the person. It clearly makes a huge difference, though, in the almost organic relationship between person and machine whether you master it or it masters you. When the machine is yours to command, you turn it on and thereby give it life; you adjust it and thereby make it an annex of your hand; you instruct it and thereby make it an expansion of your brain. But when it does its own calculations, monitors its own performance, consults its own immense bank of experience, applies its own logics, reviews its own thinking, makes its own decisions, and even turns itself on and off, then it is like a willful creature with its own motives whom you must serve. It is an unrelenting, massively stubborn, inexhaustible intelligence.

So the operator of a really smart machine enters the process only in the sense that she occupies a work station. Her intelligence is not engaged, her motor skills are not engaged, her fund of past experience is not engaged, her sense organs are not engaged. She is hardly there at all. "Lobotomized" is Harry Braverman's word for her condition (1975:25), but that is not quite right: the properties of her humanhood have been absorbed by the machine, and in that sense she has been emptied of content. It is a kind of evisceration, a kind of decortication, and that, surely, comes close to what Marx meant by alienation (cf. Zuboff 1988).

For all of the reasons just cited, then, automated processes in general and computerized processes in particular can become an almost perfect instrument of control over *process*. If the goal of the old Scientific Management movement was to control the muscle activity of the worker from the distant removes of the front office, to eliminate flourish and personality and lazy rhythms from the doing of everyday tasks, then it should be noted that the computer can program not only the behavior of the machine, but, in a very real sense, the behavior of the operator.

And, for all the reasons just cited, automated procedures in general and computerized processes in particular can become an almost perfect instrument of control over *persons*. This is true not only in the sense that automation offers a means of programming almost everything that happens in the workplace, but also in the sense that it makes possible a remarkably efficient system of surveillance. A computer can count and measure and time virtually everything its operator does, down to the number of keys he strikes in any given quarter minute; and it can keep a record of his performance for as long a stretch of time as the most curious of managers could ask. "Once computers are linked," Barbara Garson (1988:205) notes, "anyone who touches the keyboard is automatically reporting on himself." It is a continuous, tireless time and motion study.

Now I need to pause for a moment before the momentum of these thoughts carries me beyond the sight of shore to repeat that I am not talking here about *inevitable properties* of the smart new machines but of *potentialities* that seem often to be taken advantage of. The computer *need* not behave in the manner I have been suggesting, but it *can;* and its capacity to monitor the activities of the persons who monitor it, to keep a running log of their performance, is likely to prove irresistible.

It may really matter, too. If the grinding pace of the assembly line, say, makes one into a kind of motor, a torpid technical instrument, so can supervision. At its rawest, in fact, supervision can feel like a kind of automation, if only in the sense that when it is too mechanical, too automatic, too relentless, it becomes machinelike. Harry Braverman complains that clerical workers are too often

> subjected to routines, more or less mechanized according to current possibilities, that strip them of their former grasp of even a limited amount of office information, divest them of the need or ability to understand and decide, and make of them so many mechanical eyes, fingers, and voices whose functioning is, insofar as possible, predetermined by both rules and machinery. (1974:340)

The dominion of the machinery to which Braverman refers has been remarked any number of times; the dominion of the rules less often. Yet workers who are pressed in on all sides by quotas, indices, routines, and all those forms of monitoring that managers can turn to when they are under pressure themselves are, for all practical purposes, being exposed to a major source of alienation. To be reproved for minor lapses, to have every working minute measured and evaluated, to be paced by routines wholly unresponsive to the realities of the moment, to be judged against quotas of someone else's making, to need to ask permission to leave a work station for even a moment—these can feel demeaning and infantilizing. The logic of supervision (at its worst, anyway) is the logic of childhood. So it scarcely ranks as good news to those who work at the nonmanagement level that the number of supervisors seems to be growing at a much faster rate throughout the labor force than other employees and that the tools of their trade are becoming ever more sensitive and precise.

My own fledgling study, for what it may be worth at this early stage, suggests that supervision may be a key element in this kind of routinization, and there are quite a few studies in the literature, the work of Melvin L. Kohn and his associates being prominent among them, that alert us to expect as much (Kohn 1976, 1985; Kohn and Schooler 1973, 1978, 1982, 1983; Mortimer and Lorence 1979; Mottaz 1981; Walsh 1982).

There is no easy answer, then, to the question as to whether automation serves to restrict the range of a worker's skill and autonomy or serves to free him from the old tyrannies of work (for a balanced view see Form 1981, 1987; Spenner 1979, 1983). There is every reason to suppose, however, that the effects of automation are spread very unevenly throughout the workplace, not only from industry to industry or from occupation to occupation, but from one work station to another (see Vallas 1988).

III

I have been trying to review here some of the structural conditions of the modern workplace that may be especially productive of alienation. But in order for that to be a useful contribution to the sociology of work, we need to consider another matter. Where does alienation reside? How does one know when one is in its presence? That is a tougher question than might appear on the surface, because so many different currents of thought have converged on it from so many different ideological directions.

Joachim Israel (1971) distinguishes between "estranging processes"—those conditions in the structure of the workplace that induce alienation—and "states of estrangement"—those psychological dispositions that result. I have been speaking more or less of the former; I am turning now—more or less—to the latter.

There are those who argue that one ought to be able to determine when a person is alienated by taking a look at the objective conditions in which she works. The worker exposed to estranging conditions is alienated almost by definition, no matter what she says she thinks or even what she thinks she thinks. Harry Braverman, for example, would accuse us of doing the work of the personnel administrator if we dealt with "the reaction of the worker" rather than with the nature of the work (1974:29), by which he means, apparently, that certain forms of work can be understood as alienating no matter how that condition is registered in the person of the worker.[6] That view, whatever else one might want to say about it, has the effect of closing off sociological investigation rather than inviting it. Alienation, in order to make empirical sense, has to reside somewhere in or around the persons who are said to experience it.

Yet it sounds rather naive to assume, as many sociologists have, that a state like alienation can be discerned by so simple a procedure as asking people about their degree of job satisfaction—which is essentially what Blauner, for all the other riches of his analysis, actually did. People can think themselves satisfied by work that degrades them in countless ways, and, of course, they can grumble incessantly about work that would appear on the face of it to be enhancing. Michel Crozier (1971), for instance, discovered in his study of Parisian office workers that the employees who expressed the most interest in their work were often the ones who complained the most about it, an observation others have made as well; and in general, there are many reasons to suppose that the relationship between expressions of satisfaction and the facts of the workday is, to say the least, an inexact one (see, for example, Kahn 1972).

Robert Blauner and Harry Braverman, as a matter of fact, mark the two poles very well. Virtually all of Blauner's data come from surveys on job satisfaction conducted by Elmo Roper, while Braverman reports no data at all on the way workers *feel* about work, how they experience it, or what it does to them.

So we need something in between. The concept alienation, let's say, has a limited number of uses for sociology unless it refers to a condition that is registered somewhere in the person's mind or spirit or body and is reflected in actual behavior. On the face of it, at least, that would seem like easily defended ground, but in fact it cuts off friends on both ends of the conceptual continuum. On the one hand, we have to jettison the idea that situations rich in the kinds of detail that appear degrading by some external standard or another can be assumed to generate alienation. That must be shown, not taken as given. Otherwise we would be in much the same logical position as a physician prepared to diagnose malaria on hearing the news that someone passed through an especially virulent swamp. On the other hand, we have to jettison a lot of what we think we have learned from surveys, for we dare not assume that the effects of alienation are readily apparent even to those who experience it. The kinds of questions we ask in the usual survey on job satisfaction would seem

6. In the "usage" of "official sociology and popular journalism," Braverman writes elsewhere with evident scorn (1975:20), "alienated labor is understood to mean the worker who suffers from a feeling of distress, a malaise, a bellyache about his or her work."

like rather frail instruments for probing into all those layers of emotional scar tissue which, if Marx is even half right, can be formed over the injuries of work.[7] I would argue, in fact, that qualitative field studies, for all their widely advertised imprecisions, offer by far our best opportunity to understand how the ways of work are impressed on the persons exposed to them.

If alienation is a state of being, it is not a creature of the workplace alone, and that raises other questions. How do the degradations of the workplace bleed into the larger fabric of a person's life? How do the activities people engage in outside the realm of work aggravate or compensate for whatever dissatisfactions are generated in the workplace? Karl Marx obviously thought of work as near the core of a person's moral life, the forge in which the self is tempered. And much depends, as I have been suggesting, on the way a worker's mind and spirit are affected by the logics, the cadences, the pressures of the workplace. But it should be noted, if only in passing, that while the structures of modern life make it easy to distinguish between the world of work and the world of leisure, the structures of the human mind do not operate in the same way. The moods of the workplace are carried across the threshold into the rest of life, and, of course, the moods of the rest of life are carried back, and the ways in which the two are played off in the organization of a person's life are a critical piece of the larger puzzle.

Within the narrower confines of the work station itself, moreover—cubicle, cab, desk, compartment, niche—one can decorate and improvise, become involved in acts of passive resistance or outright sabotage, and in a thousand other ways introduce a sense of self in settings that would otherwise seem to exclude it. The wider communalities of the workplace, too, from informal kinds of camaraderie to more formal associations like trade unions, have a major impact on the character of work. And, obviously, persons who enter the office or shop floor for scheduled hours of work bring with them imaginations that have been nourished and lives that have been given meaning by activities engaged in elsewhere. These are all ways in which personality, intelligence, playfulness, and whim are brought to bear on the workplace, and more important, they are all means of coping with, drawing insulation around, or making an argument against the pains of work.[8]

Keeping in mind the larger wholes of human life, then, one notes there are many forms of behavior that might alert an observer to the possibility that

7. For a helpful and wise discussion, see Archibald 1978.
8. A good reading list on this general subject could begin (but ought not end) with Burawoy 1979a, Garson 1977, Halle 1984, Molstad 1986, Moorhouse 1987, Nash 1976, and the papers in this volume by Epstein, Freidson, and Wheeler. The opening pages of Moorhouse's article are particularly instructive.

alienation is lurking somewhere below the surface. One can begin, as sociologists traditionally have, with the standard indices of dissatisfaction: calling in sick, filing grievances, and quitting altogether have long been regarded as hidden protest votes on the quality of work life, and most of the available data seem to indicate that such votes are cast far more often in the kinds of work setting that can reasonably be described as alienating. One can try to assess the long-range effects of various working conditions on the personalities of those exposed to them, as Kohn and his associates have been doing for years. Then one can attend to the things people do—and the things that happen to them—outside the immediate precincts of work: we have every reason in the world to think, for example, that taking drugs and drinking too much and sinking into a kind of numbed depression are correlated with alienating work conditions.

All of which raises a darker point as I bring these remarks to a close. We have to assume, as I noted a moment ago, that alienated work leaves some sort of mark on the persons affected by it, and that those marks are at least in principle detectable by the right kind of geiger counter. We also have to assume—this too is repetition—that the persons so marked are not usually the ones best equipped to understand what has happened to them. Indeed, it is one of Marx's major contributions to our thinking that lack of insight into one's true condition can itself be a consequence of alienation. The condition furnishes its own camouflage.

We are, then, engaged in a haughty business, for we are declaring for all practical purposes that trained and thoughtful observers can see traces in the conduct of fellow human beings of something they are not aware of and, in fact, cannot be aware of. That prospect did not bother Marx for one moment. His language crackles with feeling when he describes what he thinks the capitalist mode of production does to a worker exposed to it. It "mortifies his body and ruins his mind," said he, leaving "idiocy" and "cretinism" in its wake. It makes of the worker "a crippled monstrosity"—"mutilated," "degraded," "stunted," "broken," "emasculated," "stupefied," "debased."

Now that is a sharp diagnosis by any standard, and I, for one, do not plan to walk onto a shop floor somewhere and ask hulking operatives whether the conditions under which they work have stupefied them or made idiots of them. But there may be an important world to be discovered there as soon as we learn to ask the right questions about it. The work of Melvin Seeman in particular gives us a secure place to stand when we consider the anatomy of alienation (see 1959, 1972, 1975, and especially 1983). But being raised now is the question of what it does to the human spirit in other ways. Do the conditions that Marx encouraged us to think of as alienating add in any appreciable way to the sum of human indifference, brutality, exhaustion, cruelty, numbness? Is there any relationship between alienation and the passion with which capital punishment is promoted, guns and other weapons cherished, insults to national honor resented, people of other kinds demeaned? I have no idea. I only know that such questions are important, sympathetic, and, in principle, answerable.

REFERENCES

Archibald, W. Peter. 1978. "Using Marx's Theory of Alienation Empirically." *Theory and Society* 6:119–32.

Archibald, W. Peter, Owen Adams, and John W. Gartrell. 1981. "Propertylessness and Alienation: Reopening a 'Shut' Case." In *Alienation: Problems of Meaning, Theory and Method*, edited by R. Felix Geyer and David Schweitzer. London: Routledge and Kegan Paul.

Arendt, Hannah. 1958. *The Human Condition*. Chicago: University of Chicago Press.

Bell, Daniel. 1973. *The Coming of Post-Industrial Society*. New York: Basic Books.

Blauner, Robert. 1964. *Alienation and Freedom*. Chicago: University of Chicago Press.

Braverman, Harry. 1974. *Labor and Monopoly Capital*. New York: Monthly Review Press.

———. (1975). "Work and Unemployment." *Monthly Review* July: 18–31.

Burawoy, Michael. 1979a. *Manufacturing Consent: Changes in the Labor Process under Monopoly Capitalism*. Chicago: University of Chicago Press.

———. 1979b. "The Anthropology of Industrial Work." *Annual Review of Sociology* 8:231–66.

Crozier, Michel. 1971. *The World of the Office Worker*. Chicago: University of Chicago Press.

Edwards, Richard. 1979. *Contested Terrain: The Transformation of the Workplace in the Twentieth Century*. New York: Basic Books.

Engels, Frederick. 1987 [1896]. "The Part Played by Labour in the Transition from Ape to Man." Karl Marx and Frederick Engels, *Selected Works*, vol. 24, pp. 452–63. New York: International Publishers.

Feldberg, Roslyn L., and Evelyn Nakano Glenn. 1983. "Technology and Work Degradation: Effects of Office Automation on Women Clerical Workers." In *Machina Ex Dea: Feminist Perspectives on Technology*, edited by Joan Rothschild. Oxford: Pergamon.

Form, William. 1973. "Auto Workers and Their Machines: A Study of Work, Factory, and Job Satisfaction in Four Countries." *Social Forces* 52:1–15.

———. 1976. *Blue-Collar Stratification: Auto Workers in Four Countries*. Princeton: Princeton University Press.

———. 1981. "Resolving Ideological Issues on the Division of Labor." In *Theory and Research in Sociology*, edited by Hubert M. Blalock, Jr. New York: Free Press.

———. 1987. "On the Degradation of Skills." *Annual Review of Sociology* 13.

Gerson, Barbara. 1977. *All the Livelong Day*. London: Penguin.

———. 1988. *The Electronic Sweatshop*. New York: Simon and Schuster.

Glenn, Evelyn Nakano, and Roslyn L. Feldberg. 1977. "Degraded and Deskilled: The Proletarianization of Clerical Work." *Social Problems* 25:52–64.

Halle, David. 1984. *America's Working Man*. Chicago: University of Chicago Press.

Howard, Robert. 1985. *Brave New Workplace*. New York: Viking.

Israel, Joachim. 1971. *Alienation*. New York: Allyn and Bacon.

Kahn, Robert L. 1972. "The Meaning of Work: Interpretation and Proposals for Measurement." In *The Human Meaning of Social Change*, edited by Angus Campbell and Philip E. Converse. New York: Russell Sage Foundation.

Kohn, Melvin L. 1976. "Occupational Structure and Alienation." *American Journal of Sociology* 82:111–30.

———. 1985. "Unresolved Interpretive Issues in the Relationship between Work and Personality." Paper presented at the annual meeting of the American Sociological Association. Washington, D.C.

Kohn, Melvin L., and Carmi Schooler. 1973. "Occupational Experience and Psychological Functioning: An Assessment of Reciprocal Effects." *American Sociological Review* 38:97–118.

———. 1978. "The Reciprocal Effects of the Substantive Complexity of Work and Intellectual Flexibility: A Longitudinal Assessment." *American Journal of Sociology* 84:24–52.

———. 1982. "Job Conditions and Personality: A Longitudinal Assessment of Their Reciprocal Effects." *American Journal of Sociology* 87:1257–86.

———. 1983. *Work and Personality: An Inquiry into the Impact of Social Stratification.* Norwood, N.J.: Ablex Publishing.

Marx, Karl. 1906 [1867]. *Capital,* volume 1, edited by Frederick Engels, translated by Samuel Moore and Edward Aveling. London: Charles H. Kerr.

———. 1964 [1844]. "Economic and Philosophical Manuscripts." In *Karl Marx: Early Writings,* edited and translated by T. B. Bottomore. New York: McGraw-Hill.

Molstad, Clark. 1986. "Choosing and Coping With Boring Work." *Urban Life* 15:215–36.

Moorhouse, H. F. 1987. "The 'Work Ethic' and 'Leisure' Activity: The Hot Rod in Post-War America." In *The Historical Meanings of Work,* edited by Patrick Joyce. Cambridge: Cambridge University Press.

Mortimer, Jeylan T., and Jon Lorence. 1979. "Work Experience and Occupational Value Socialization: A Longitudinal Study." *American Journal of Sociology* 84: 1361–85.

Mottaz, Clifford J. 1981. "Some Determinants of Work Alienation." *Sociological Quarterly* 22:515–29.

Nash, Al. 1976. "Job Satisfaction: A Critique." In *Auto Work and Its Discontents,* edited by B. J. Widick. Ann Arbor: University Microfilms International.

Noble, David F. 1984. *Forces of Production: A Social History of Industrial Automation.* New York: Knopf.

Roy, Donald F. 1960. "Banana Time: Job Satisfaction and Informal Interaction." *Human Organization* 18:158–68.

Rubin, Lillian Breslow. 1976. *Worlds of Pain: Life in the Working-Class Family.* New York: Basic Books.

Seeman, Melvin. 1959. "On the Meaning of Alienation." *American Sociological Review* 24:783–91.

———. 1972. "Alienation and Engagement." In *The Human Meaning of Social Change,* edited by Angus Campbell and Philip E. Converse. New York: Russell Sage Foundation.

———. 1975. "Alienation Studies." In *Annual Review of Sociology,* edited by Alex Inkeles, James Coleman, and Neil Smelser, 1:91–123.

————. 1983. "Alienation Motifs in Contemporary Theorizing: The Hidden Continuity of the Classic Themes." *Social Psychology Quarterly* 46:171–84.

Shaiken, Harley. 1984. *Work Transformed.* New York: Holt, Rinehart and Winston.

Shepard, Jon M. 1971. *Automation and Alienation: A Study of Office and Factory Workers.* Cambridge: MIT Press.

Spenner, Kenneth I. 1979. "Temporal Changes in Work Content." *American Sociological Review* 44:968–75.

————. 1983. "Deciphering Prometheus: Temporal Change in the Skill Level of Work." *American Sociological Review* 48:824–37.

Sturt, George. 1923. *The Wheelwright's Shop.* Excerpted in *Work and Community in the West,* edited by Edward Shorter. New York: Harper and Row, 1973.

Toennies, Ferdinand. 1963. *Community and Society.* Edited and translated by Charles P. Loomis. New York: Harper Torchbooks.

Vallas, Steven Peter. 1988. "New Technology, Job Content and Worker Alienation: A Test of Two Rival Perspectives." *Work and Occupations.*

————. 1989. "Computers, Managers and Control at Work." *Sociological Forum* 4:291–303.

Walker, Charles R., and Robert H. Guest. 1952. *The Man on the Assembly Line.* Cambridge: Harvard University Press.

Wallace, Michael, and Arne L. Kalleberg. 1982. "Industrial Transformation and Decline of Craft: The Decomposition of Skill in the Printing Industry." *American Sociological Review* 47:307–24.

Walsh, Edward J. 1982. "Prestige, Work Satisfaction, and Alienation." *Work and Occupations* 9:475–96.

Zuboff, Shoshana. 1988. *In the Age of the Smart Machine.* New York: Basic.

IIIIIIII Unresolved Issues in the Relationship between Work and Personality

MELVIN L. KOHN

My intent in this essay is to address the principal unresolved interpretive issues in research on work and personality. Such an enterprise presupposes that there are resolved issues, as I think there are. So I shall also discuss what I consider to be the principal resolved issues. In so doing, I shall unabashedly rely most heavily on research that my collaborators and I have done, bringing in the work of others insofar as that work is pertinent to confirming or disconfirming our findings, suggesting alternative approaches, or shedding light on issues we have ignored. I begin with some fundamental presuppositions.

PRESUPPOSITIONS

First, I take it as an underlying premise that, in attempting to disentangle the complex interrelationships between work and personality, it is fruitful to base one's analyses on dimensions of work—job conditions such as

Earlier versions of this essay were presented at a conference on work and personality held at the Max Planck Institut für Bildungsforschung, West Berlin, May 10–12, 1984; at the Academy of Sciences of the German Democratic Republic, East Berlin, May 15, 1984; and at the Eighth Biennial Meeting of the International Society for the Study of Behavioural Development, Tours, France, July 1985. One earlier version has been published in German (Kohn 1985), another in English (as chapter 13 of Kohn and Schooler 1983). I am indebted for critical readings of preliminary drafts of the essay to Carmi Schooler, Carrie Schoenbach, Karen A. Miller, Kazimierz M. Slomczynski, Jeylan T. Mortimer, Wolfgang Lempert, Ernst-Hartmut Hoff, Lothar Lappe, Aaron Antonovsky, and Douglas A. Parker.

heaviness, time-pressure, job complexity, and closeness of supervision. This may seem so obvious as not to be worthy of notice. Yet, if one looks at the history of research on work and personality, one soon discovers there have been two predominant approaches, neither of which provides a method for distinguishing which dimensions of work are pertinent to which dimensions of personality. One approach has been case studies of named occupations: railway men, teachers, taxi drivers. These studies have been invaluable for sensitizing us to the multidimensionality of occupations and thus have been very useful for generating hypotheses; but since any given occupation represents a package of interlocked job conditions, case studies of named occupations do not provide a way to examine the psychological impact of any particular dimension of work apart from all the other aspects of work with which it is interlocked. A diametrically opposite approach has been to reduce the multidimensionality of occupation to a single dimension, ignoring all others. Thus, for example, sociologists have often seemed not to be aware that there could be anything important about a job other than the status it confers, just as economists have often seemed not to be aware that there could be anything important about a job other than the income it yields. In terms of impact on personality, however, occupational status serves mainly as a gross indicator of a job's location in the hierarchical organization of the economic and social system. The status of the job is closely linked to such structural conditions of work as how substantively complex it is, how closely it is supervised, and what sorts of pressures it entails. It is these structural realities, not status as such, that affect personality (Kohn and Schooler 1973; Slomczynski et al. 1981; Kohn and Schoenbach 1983).

My collaborators' and my strategy for disentangling the intercorrelated dimensions of work has been to secure a large and representative sample of workers from varied occupations, to inventory their job conditions, and then to differentiate the psychological concomitants of each facet of work by statistical analysis. Even though job conditions are intercorrelated, they are not perfectly intercorrelated. Thus, substantively complex jobs are likely also to be time-pressured; but there are enough jobs that are substantively complex yet not time-pressured, and enough that are substantively simple yet time-pressured, to make it possible to examine the relationship between the substantive complexity of work and, say, anxiety, while statistically controlling time pressure. One can also examine statistical interactions, asking whether the impact of substantive complexity on, let us say, anxiety is different for people whose work is more time-pressured and for people whose work is less time-pressured.

Admittedly, there are serious limitations to securing occupational data by interviewing a representative sample of employed workers. One is that workers' descriptions and evaluations of their job conditions may be biased—a problem with which I shall deal later. Another is that workers may have only

limited information about some aspects of their jobs, such as the overall structure of the firm or organization in which they are employed. Similarly, the
method is not well adapted for studying the industrial and technological contexts in which jobs are embedded—information that many workers do not
have. Moreover, a sample of workers scattered across many occupations and
many workplaces does not contain enough people in any particular occupation
or any single workplace to trace out interpersonal networks and belief systems.
The method is useful, though, for studying the immediate conditions of workers' own jobs—what they do, who determines how they do it, in what physical
and social circumstances they work, to what risks and rewards they are subject.
The advantages of this research strategy are considerable, but one must keep the
disadvantages in mind in weighing the evidence—and in deciding what issues
remain unresolved. Other research strategies are possible, each with its own
advantages and disadvantages. My point is not that ours is the only possible
strategy or even the best one, but that any strategy should deal with dimensions
of work. This is true even for case studies of named occupations, one of whose
principal uses is to suggest previously overlooked dimensions of work.

My second presupposition is that insofar as possible analyses of the relationship between work and personality should begin with objective conditions
of work—what workers do, who determines how they do it, in what physical
and social circumstances they work, to what risks and rewards they are subject—rather than with workers' subjective appraisals of those job conditions.
Granted, it is difficult to measure job conditions objectively, especially when
relying on survey data, but I think it imperative that we define job conditions
objectively and that we attempt to measure them as objectively as possible,
recognizing it to be a limitation of the research when, and in the degree to
which, we fall short of this ideal. Not all students of work and personality agree
with me on this issue (see, for example, Hackman and Lawler 1971). An
alternative approach employed by many investigators deliberately begins with
subjective appraisals of job conditions, on the rationale that job conditions
become important for psychological functioning only as they enter into the
perceptions of workers. Investigators using this approach measure boredom
rather than routinization, interest in the work rather than its substantive complexity, and "alienation in work" rather than actual working conditions. I
believe that this approach ignores the possibility that there may be a gap
between the conditions to which workers are subject and their awareness of
those conditions. The presence or absence of such a gap is itself problematic
and may be structurally determined. Moreover, conditions felt by workers to be
benign may have deleterious consequences, while conditions felt to be onerous
may have beneficial consequences.

Clearly, it would be desirable to design research to include measures both of objective working conditions and of workers' subjective appraisals of those conditions. This would make it possible to assess empirically how objective conditions become transformed into subjective experience and how objective conditions and subjective perceptions of those conditions together affect personality and behavior. Such an assessment would not be simple to carry out, but it would be feasible. Short of this ideal research design, though, I would maintain that it is the objective—not the subjective—that forms the social-structural reality that is a sine qua non of meaningful inquiry into the relationship between work and personality.

My third presupposition is that any analysis of the relationships between work and personality should allow for the possibility of reciprocal effects—that work may both affect and be affected by personality. It was not always evident that it is necessary or even desirable to allow for this possibility. When Schooler and I began to plan our 1964 cross-sectional survey of employed men in the United States, we were astonished to learn that both the occupational psychologists and the occupational sociologists whose advice we solicited thought the relationships unidirectional, but that their opinions stemmed from fundamentally incompatible premises: Occupational psychologists generally assumed that the relationship between work and personality results solely from selective recruitment, selective retention, and job molding—that is, personality affects the job. Occupational sociologists, to the contrary, generally assumed that the relationship between work and personality results solely from job affecting personality. Neither side acknowledged the possibility that the other side might be even partly correct. We concluded that it would be foolhardy to assume that the relationship results from a unidirectional effect in either direction—a point of view for which we cannot claim originality, since Weber came to the same conclusion in 1908 (see Eldridge 1971:104). All of our research has been premised on the assumption of reciprocity. One important methodological implication is that it is highly desirable that research on work and personality be longitudinal, for only in longitudinal research can one definitively assess reciprocal effects.

Finally, I hold it an article of faith that it is possible to establish reasonably firm evidence as to whether job conditions affect personality (and vice versa) without having to do controlled experiments—which means, crucially, without having to assign workers randomly to specified job conditions. Granted, controlled experiments are the ultimate in scientific proof; but realistic experiments are exceedingly difficult to conduct in this field, and experiments that only partially simulate the reality of actual job conditions impacting on people's actual lives over a substantial length of time fall too far short to be definitive. Longitudinal data provide a much better basis for drawing inferences about work and personality. Recently developed methods for analyzing such data—

namely, confirmatory factor analysis and linear structural-equations causal modeling—give the investigator the means of taking account of measurement error and of modeling reciprocal effects. Together with the standard analytic techniques for statistically controlling the effects of other pertinent variables, these methods make possible rigorous analysis of work–personality relationships. Admittedly, even these methods leave a modicum of uncertainty, for there is always the possibility of an alternative model that would be theoretically appropriate and would fit the data better. Nevertheless, short of our having the power and ability to conduct realistic, long-term experiments, these methods, applied to longitudinal data, are quite good enough to enable us to draw reasonably firm conclusions.

These, then, are my principal presuppositions: that analyses of the work–personality relationship should be based on *dimensions* of work; that investigators should define and measure job conditions as *objectively* as possible; that any assessment of the relationships between work and personality should allow for the possibility of *reciprocal* effects; and that one can draw reasonably firm conclusions about the work–personality relationship on the basis of *nonexperimental* data. Now for some empirical generalizations, based on these presuppositions. These are the resolved issues, or so I think. I state them baldly, leaving for later discussion the amplifications and reservations that should also be understood—for around every resolved issue are numerous unresolved ancillary issues.

RESOLVED ISSUES

1. *Work does affect adult personality.* Only longitudinal studies can demonstrate an actual causal effect of job conditions on personality, and there have been relatively few such studies. But these studies uniformly support the proposition that the conditions of work experienced by gainfully employed men and women affect their values, self-conceptions, orientations to social reality, and cognitive functioning (see Kohn and Schooler 1983; Mortimer, Lorence, and Kumka 1986; Andrisani and Abeles 1976; Andrisani and Nestel 1976; Brousseau 1978; Lindsay and Knox 1984; Spenner and Otto 1984). Moreover, the effects of job conditions on personality are far from trivial in magnitude, particularly considering how very stable are the dimensions of personality studied in these inquiries (Kohn and Schooler 1978, 1982). To take a prime example: The substantive complexity of work has an effect on the intellectual flexibility of adult men fully one-fourth as great as that of their own prior levels of intellectual flexibility, measured ten years earlier (Kohn and Schooler 1978).

Although cross-sectional studies cannot be definitive on the crucial issue of directions of effects, their results are entirely consonant in showing consistent relationships between conditions of work—variously conceptualized and in-dexed—and one or another aspect of personality. All studies that meet even minimal research standards show that job conditions are meaningfully related to adult personality. (For reviews of this literature, see Kohn and Schooler 1983, chap. 12; Mortimer, Lorence, and Kumka 1988; Frese 1982, 1983.)

In short, the empirical findings of the past two decades add up to a striking confirmation of Sorokin's (1927:321) prescient assertions of a half-century ago, when he wrote, "All the psychological processes of any member of an occupation undergo modification, especially when one stays for a long time in the same occupation. The processes of perception and sensation, attention, imaginative reproduction, and association bear the marks of a corresponding occupation. . . . Still greater is the occupational influence on the processes and on the character of one's evaluations, beliefs, practical judgments, opinions, ethics, and whole ideology."

2. Although it is premature to rule out any particular job conditions as having no effect on personality, *we do know enough to characterize a set of fourteen job conditions that decidedly do affect personality,* independent of each other and independent of education (Kohn and Schooler 1982). Together, they identi-fy a worker's place in the organizational structure, opportunities for occupa-tional self-direction, the principal job pressures to which the worker is subject, and the principal extrinsic risks and rewards built into the job. Specifically, the aspects of a worker's place in the organizational structure that have been shown to be pertinent to personality are ownership, bureaucratization, and hierarchical position. The principal facets of occupational self-direction are the substantive complexity of the work, closeness of supervision, and degree of routinization. The job pressures are time-pressure, heaviness, dirtiness, and the number of hours worked in the average week. The extrinsic risks and rewards are the probability of being held responsible for things outside one's control, the risk of losing one's job or business, job protections, and job income. I call these fourteen conditions the *structural imperatives* of the job. They are structural in two senses: they are built into the structure of the job and they are a function of the job's location in the structures of the economy and the society. These job conditions are imperatives in that they define the occupational realities that every worker must face.

Of all the structural imperatives of the job, those that determine how much opportunity, even necessity, the worker has for exercising occupational self-direction are the most important for personality. For this reason, I shall focus on these job conditions in all that follows. Occupational self-direction—by which I mean the use of initiative, thought, and independent judgment in work—is greatly facilitated by some job conditions and constrained by others. Three job conditions, in particular, are critical in determining the degree to which workers are able, or even required, to exercise self-direction in their work: the *substantive complexity* of work is at the very center of occupational self-direction. Substantively complex work—work that requires thought and independent judgment—by its very nature requires making many decisions that must take into account ill-defined or apparently conflicting contingencies. *Closeness of supervision,* on the other hand, is a limiting condition: workers cannot exercise occupational self-direction if they are closely supervised, although not being closely supervised does not necessarily mean that one is required or even free to use initiative, thought, and independent judgment. Highly *routinized* (repetitive and predictable) jobs restrict possibilities for exercising initiative, thought, and judgment, whereas jobs with a variety of unpredictable tasks may facilitate or even require self-direction.

Exercising self-direction in work—doing work that is substantively complex, not being closely supervised, not working at routinized tasks—is conducive to favorable evaluations of self, an open and flexible orientation to others, and effective intellectual functioning (see, generally, Kohn and Schooler 1983; see also Mortimer, Lorence, and Kumka 1986). People thrive in meeting occupational challenges.

3. *Although the evidence on which the foregoing generalizations are based comes mainly from studies of men in the United States, the evidence for employed women in the United States is entirely consonant* (J. Miller et al. 1979; Spade 1983; Spenner and Otto 1984; Kohn et al. 1986), *as is the evidence for employed men in other industrialized societies.* The cross-national evidence is particularly strong for Poland and Japan, where precise replications of Schooler's and my U.S. studies have been carried out (Slomczynski et al. 1981; J. Miller et al. 1985; Naoi and Schooler 1985; Kohn et al. 1986; Kohn 1987; Schooler and Naoi 1988; Kohn et al. 1990). The Polish and Japanese studies conclusively show that the work–personality relationship is not limited to the United States, to capitalist societies, or to Western societies. There is evidence as well (see the extensive review in Kohn and Schooler 1983, chap. 12) from studies done in the Federal Republic of Germany (Hoff and Gruneisen 1978; Gruneisen and Hoff 1977), Canada (Coburn and Edwards 1976; Grabb 1981a,b), Norway (Dalgard 1981), Italy (Pearlin and Kohn 1966), and Ireland (Hynes 1979).

4. There is accumulating evidence that *job conditions affect adult personality mainly through a direct process of learning and generalization*—learning from the job and generalizing what has been learned to other realms of life. Although such indirect processes as compensation and reaction-formation may also contribute to the effects of work on adult personality (K. Miller and Kohn 1983; Staines 1980), the learning-generalization process is of predominant impor-

tance (but see House 1981). Thus, people who do intellectually demanding work come to exercise their intellectual prowess not only on the job but also in their nonoccupational lives (Kohn and Schooler 1978, 1982; J. Miller et al. 1979, 1985); they even seek out intellectually demanding activities in their leisure-time pursuits (K. Miller and Kohn 1983). More generally, people who do self-directed work come to value self-direction more highly, both for themselves and for their children, and to have self-conceptions and social orientations consonant with such values (Kohn 1969; Coburn and Edwards 1976; Hoff and Gruneisen 1978; J. Miller et al. 1979; Mortimer, Lorence and Kumka 1986; Slomczynski et al. 1981; Grabb 1981b; Naoi and Schooler 1985; Kohn and Schooler 1983; Bertram 1983). In short, the lessons of work are directly carried over to nonoccupational realms. All these findings are consistent with the theoretical expectation that "transfer of learning" extends to a wide spectrum of psychological functioning (Gagne 1968; see also Breer and Locke 1965). The findings also are consistent with the fundamental sociological premise that experience in so central a domain of life as work must affect orientations to and behavior in other domains as well (Marx 1964, 1971).

Admittedly, I stretch the term *learning* when I apply the concept "learning-generalization" to the processes by which job pressures and uncertainties lead to distress; but even here the crux of the matter is that job experiences have straightforward psychological effects. In any case, it certainly does not stretch the meaning of *learning* to speak of learning from the experience of occupational self-direction and applying these lessons to nonoccupational realities.

5. Consonant with the presupposition that the relationship between work and personality may well be reciprocal, the empirical evidence is that *job conditions not only affect but also are affected by personality*—even after people are well into their occupational careers. Our longitudinal analyses (Kohn and Schooler 1982) show, for example, that over time personality has important consequences for the individual's place in the job structure: both intellectual flexibility and a self-directed orientation lead to more responsible jobs that allow greater latitude for occupational self-direction. So far as I can judge from limited evidence, the personality-to-job effects—particularly the effects of personality on the most objectively measured conditions of work—are mainly lagged rather than contemporaneous. The implication is that job conditions are not readily modified to suit the needs or capacities of the individual worker. Over a long enough period of time, though, many workers either modify their jobs or move to other jobs more consonant with their personalities. Thus, the long-term effects of personality on conditions of work are considerable.

6. Finally, *job conditions do not exist in a social-structural vacuum* but are inextricably bound up in the class and stratification systems of industrial society. The most directly pertinent evidence for this generalization comes from

studies conducted in the United States, Poland, and Japan (Kohn 1969; Slomczynski et al. 1981; Kohn and Schoenbach 1983; Naoi and Schooler 1985; Kohn et al. 1986; Kohn 1987; Kohn et al. 1990). There is supportive evidence from studies conducted in other countries as well (see Kohn and Schooler 1983, chap. 12). That we have such evidence for both capitalist and socialist societies and for both Western and non-Western societies indicates that we are dealing with a social-structural phenomenon not limited to any one type of political or economic system or to Western cultures, but very likely true of industrial societies generally. Job conditions are not only structurally interrelated, they are systematically built into the larger class and stratification systems of industrial society.

The foregoing summary of resolved issues constitutes a rather substantial body of knowledge. Yet, many important issues remain unresolved. I shall therefore reconsider, in turn, my characterization of the pertinent job conditions, my conceptualization of personality, and my treatment of the processes by which work affects personality. Then I shall discuss the critical question of the utility for social policy of our knowledge about work and personality. Can our knowledge be utilized for purposive social change? Can job conditions be modified to increase opportunities for occupational self-direction? To anticipate: perhaps, but not readily.

CHARACTERIZATION OF JOB CONDITIONS

Objective Job Conditions and Subjective Appraisals of the Job

Although my approach to work and personality deliberately focuses on objective job conditions, I have not always succeeded in measuring job conditions as objectively as I should like. Unfortunately, other investigators have not done much better. My measures are based on interview reports, not on observations by trained analysts; moreover, even for indices based on interview reports, some are more subjective than need be. (Consider, by contrast, the rigorous attempts by German occupational psychologists to obtain truly objective measures of job conditions; see Hacker 1984; Volpert et al. 1983; Oesterreich 1984; Resch et al. 1983.)

Still, my collaborators and I have made strenuous efforts to validate interview-based indices with other sources of information. We have, for example (Kohn and Schooler 1973), assessed all named occupations for which our cross-sectional sample of 3,100 men contains at least 30 incumbents, ranking these occupations in terms of the median rating their incumbents give to each specified job condition. Our purpose in this exercise was to see whether these rank orderings are consonant with our knowledge of occupational realities. Insofar as they are, this provides assurance that respondents' reports about their job conditions are essentially unbiased. In fact (Kohn and Schooler 1973, table 2), these evaluations—over a range of job conditions—conform closely to what we should expect them to be. Thus, it is improbable that systematic biases in respondents' reports about their jobs distort our understanding of the relationships between job conditions and psychological functioning.

For the central job condition in all of our analyses, the substantive complexity of work, we have been able to do much more to validate the interview reports. Using U.S. data for men, we (Kohn and Schooler 1973) compared our index of substantive complexity, which is based on each worker's description of his own work with data, with people, and with things, and thus is precisely tailored to the specifics of the worker's own job, to the assessments given in the *Dictionary of Occupational Titles* (U.S. Department of Labor 1965), for every occupation in the U.S. economy. The *Dictionary*'s ratings of the complexity of work with things, with data, and with people are averages for entire occupations, so they lack the specificity of ours; they also are imperfect in important respects (Cain and Treiman 1981); but since they are based on observations by trained occupational analysts, they can nevertheless serve as a source of external validation. We found the multiple correlation between our index of the substantive complexity of work and the independently coded *Dictionary* ratings of complexity of work with data, with things, and with people, to be 0.78— sufficiently high to give assurance that our appraisals of substantive complexity accurately reflect the realities of our respondents' work. If the correlation were much higher, we would wonder whether it is necessary to go to the trouble and expense of securing job-specific information about the substantive complexity of work, rather than setting for the crude approximation provided by occupational-level data.[1]

Using Polish data, also for men, and a Polish variant of the *Dictionary of Occupational Titles*, Janicka et al. (1983) repeated this analysis, with similar

---

[1] Few studies have had the requisite descriptive data for a job-level index of substantive complexity. To fill the gap, several approximate measures of substantive complexity have been developed, using occupational-level data (Kohn and Schooler 1973; Temme 1975; Spenner 1980; and Cain and Treiman 1981). All of these indices extrapolate from the *Dictionary of Occupational Titles* (U.S. Department of Labor 1965) classifications of the average level of complexity of work with data, with things, and with people for an entire occupation to the substantive complexity of a particular job. Used cautiously, such indices provide serviceable approximations for use in studies that lack precise data about the substantive complexity of particular jobs. It must be kept in mind, though, that such approximate indices seriously underestimate the magnitudes of the relationships of substantive complexity with other variables.

results—a multiple correlation of 0.81. They then went on to further assess the validity of the index of substantive complexity used in both the original U.S. study and the Polish and Japanese replications. On the rationale that relatively brief descriptions of what a respondent does in his work with data, with things, and with people may be subject to an unknown amount of subjective distortion, they reinterviewed subsamples of their national sample in two industrial cities, Lodz and Wloclaw, securing much more detailed descriptive information about job content than would be possible in any broader survey. Using a number of alternative coding schemes, they consistently found high correlations (in the 0.90s) between the index of substantive complexity based on brief descriptions of the work and indices based on much more detailed descriptions.

Finally, there is limited but highly reassuring evidence from a study of skilled metalworkers conducted in West Berlin by Lempert, Hoff, and Lappe (see Hoff et al. 1983). Theirs is an intensive study of twenty-one young, apprenticed workers whom they followed into their occupational careers. They observed the men at work, using precisely calibrated methods of observation, supplemented by interviews with the men's supervisors. At my request, their collaborator, Manfred Moldaschl, coded this information according to Schooler's and my scheme for rating the overall complexity of work (Kohn and Schooler 1983, appendix B). He then independently rated this same dimension of complexity, this time using only such information as had been secured from interviews with the men themselves—interviews that focused not on job conditions, but on psychological functioning. The correlation between the observation-based and interview-based ratings of complexity is 0.75. Considering that we are dealing with an extremely narrow range of job conditions, that the interviews were not designed to provide systematic descriptive information about work complexity, and that the reliability of a single indicator of substantive complexity must inevitably fall considerably short of the reliability of a multi-indicator measurement model, a correlation of 0.75 is indeed encouraging. It implies that a correlation based on a representative sample of workers, systematic data, and multiple indicators would be much higher.

Multiple Indicators of Job Conditions

Closely related to the issue of objectivity is another issue of measurement: the desirability, especially when using interview-based information, of having *multiple indicators* of job conditions. No matter what method of index creation one uses, multiple indicators of a concept provide much greater assurance that you really are measuring what you mean to measure. If one uses confirmatory factor analysis to create indices of job conditions—as I think is generally desirable, particularly in longitudinal analyses—then multiple-indicator measurement models provide the further considerable advantage of enabling one to create indices shorn of measurement error (measurement error being defined for this purpose as variance in any of the indicators not shared with the other indicators of the underlying concept). This gives a powerful advantage to variables based on multiple indicators, to the corresponding disadvantage of variables measured by single indicators. I have no doubt that such well-measured job conditions as the substantive complexity of work really do matter for personality; what remains unresolved is whether less well-measured job conditions might be more powerful than our analyses have shown them to be.

Interpersonal Context and Interpersonal Relations

In my emphasis on the structural imperatives of the job, I may have underestimated the importance of the interpersonal contexts of work and of interpersonal relationships on the job; as already noted, cross-sectional surveys of the employed population are not optimal for studying such phenomena. Insofar as we have been able to measure on-the-job interpersonal relationships, however, we have found little evidence that they affect off-the-job psychological functioning (Kohn and Schooler 1973). The exceptions, of course, are interpersonal relationships that directly enter into occupational self-direction, that is, closeness of supervision and complexity of work with people. Such other aspects of interpersonal relatedness as whether one works alone or in company with others, whether one is part of a work "team," and the competitiveness of one's relationships with coworkers seem to have little bearing on off-the-job personality. I must quickly add that this negative evidence is much too limited to be definitive.

It is also possible that my central concept, the substantive complexity of work, underestimates the importance of interpersonal relatedness by combining complexity of work with people with complexity of work with data and with things into a single overarching concept, the substantive complexity of the work, rather than treating work with people as a separate domain. I find the complexity of work with people to be no more important for personality than is complexity of work with data or with things (see Kohn 1969:155–58). Of primary importance is complexity; of only secondary importance is whether complex work is done with people, with data, or with things. An alternative approach (Coser 1975) sees complexity of work with people—more precisely, complexity of role-sets—as having pivotal importance, with other aspects of complexity being only ancillary. From that point of view, the substantive complexity of work is a proxy for what is really important about work—the complexity of one's role relationships. Until we have a precise measure of complexity of role-sets, it is not possible to assess that assertion empirically.

Time as a Parameter in the Effects of Job on Personality

The longitudinal analyses that have thus far been done tell us little about the timing of the effects of job on personality, because most such analyses are locked into research designs that measure change only once, generally after a long time interval—in the case of my own research, an interval of ten years. From information based on such research designs, we can properly infer that job conditions do affect personality, but we cannot say when these processes begin, whether they are continuous or discontinuous, or whether they taper off after some time or cumulate indefinitely (see Frese 1983). Yet, timing is a crucial parameter of the work–personality relationship and should be explicitly built into our formulations. It may be that some effects of job on person occur even before the individual actually experiences new working conditions, in anticipation of conditions that will be encountered or of what a new job will signify. For example, a promotion might lead to an increase in self-esteem even before—or, perhaps, especially before—the individual actually begins a new job. Other job conditions might have their impact early on, diminishing as the individual grows accustomed to the conditions of work. It is possible, for example, that tasks that seem at first to be challenging will in time become old hat. The opposite might also happen: some job conditions—one thinks of noise and time-pressure—might become more onerous as one endures them longer. There are other obvious possibilities, all of them requiring that we regard present findings as representing the net outcome of many processes, some of which may have run their course long before the follow-up interviews, others of which may still be ongoing, and still others barely having gotten under way.

What implications would it have for our conclusions if the psychological effects of job conditions were not relatively constant, but instead increased or decreased over time? In all probability, our estimates of magnitudes of effects would thereby be affected: If the effects of occupational self-direction, for example, actually decrease over time, our ten-year assessments probably have underestimated the magnitudes of effects; if the effects of occupational self-direction actually increase over time, we probably have overestimated the magnitudes of these effects. It is hard to believe that the degree of exaggeration or underestimation can have been very great. In any case, it is unquestionable that occupational self-direction does have substantial effects on personality; what is not certain is whether we have measured those effects at their maximum, at their average, at some point after they were at their maximum, when there were in decline, or perhaps differently for different psychological consequences. Distinguishing the many strands of the actual processes requires a much more fine-grained analysis than we or any other investigators have done, using data collected at closer intervals. Here is a crucial place where small-scale, intensive studies can yield knowledge that no extensive study could possibly yield.

Both job conditions and personality are generated by dynamic processes; but our models are structural, not dynamic (Spenner 1988). Fortunately, Schoenberg (1977) has demonstrated that a static model of what in actuality is a dynamic process will underestimate the magnitudes of the parameters but will not otherwise be misleading. Here again, it is hardly likely that our models are grossly inaccurate in giving an overview of the total process; but they are certainly limited, in that they summarize total effects rather than specifying the dynamics of the process.

Threshold Effects

There is a distinct possibility that the effects of (at least some) job conditions on (at least some) facets of personality might depend on a particular job condition exceeding some critical threshold. Closeness of supervision, for example, might increase authoritarian conservatism only when the degree of supervisory control reaches a particular level. No analyses of which I am aware have dealt with this possibility; it would require a very intensive study over a long period of time to do so. We must allow the possibility, though, that job conditions may affect personality only when some threshold level is reached.

Interactions among Job Conditions

It might also be that job conditions have differential impact depending on the presence or absence of other job conditions. House (1980), for example, finds that workers who have positive, supportive relations with their coworkers and supervisors are less affected by stressful job conditions than are workers who do not perceive their coworkers and supervisors to be supportive. While the evidence is less than fully convincing, the hypothesis is certainly tenable. Alternatively, Karasek and his collaborators, in analyses of the occupational precursors of "mental strain" (Karasek 1979) and of cardiovascular disease (Karasek et al. 1981), find that the critical element is the interaction between "job demands" and "job decision latitude"—the latter explicitly analogous to my occupational self-direction, albeit with a greater emphasis on routinization and freedom from close supervision than on the substantive complexity of work. Unfortunately, their conceptualization of both job demands and job decision latitude is imprecise, and their measures, particularly of job demands, are subjective; it is therefore difficult to evaluate their findings. Yet the idea clearly has merit and is worth pursuing.

A little-explored but theoretically appealing possibility is that job conditions may affect personality differentially, depending on the organizational structure or the location in the economy of the firm or enterprise in which these conditions are experienced. It might well be that job conditions have differential impact in bureaucratized and nonbureaucratized firms and organizations. It might also be that job conditions have differential impact in the primary and secondary sectors of the economy in capitalist societies—that, for example, occupational self-direction has a greater effect on the personalities of workers employed in the primary sector of the economy, where they are better paid and more secure, while job risks and job uncertainties are of greater consequence for the personalities of workers employed in the secondary sector. On all these matters we know almost nothing.

Equivalents to Occupational Self-Direction

It is possible that other conditions of life may serve as equivalents to occupational self-direction, providing opportunities for self-direction either in job-related activities or in nonoccupational spheres of life. House has speculated (1981:552), for example, that "workers may also have other occupational experiences that modify or compensate for the degree of self-direction in their particular job. Workers in non-self-directed jobs may . . . participate in union activities or organizational decision making in ways not captured in Kohn's measures." Perhaps so, but our (admittedly incomplete) analyses (Kohn and Schooler 1973; Kohn 1976) give little indication that other occupational involvements can compensate for lack of opportunity to be self-directed in one's work.

I do think, though, that there are nonoccupational equivalents to occupational self-direction. My collaborators and I (Schooler et al. 1983) have shown, for example, that the conditions of work experienced in housework are equivalent to those experienced in paid employment in their effects on women's psychological functioning. We have also found (K. Miller et al. 1985, 1986) that there is a direct analogue between the experience of self-direction experienced by adults in their paid employment and the experience of self-direction experienced by adolescents and young adults in their schoolwork. Educational self-direction, as indexed by the substantive complexity of schoolwork and closeness of supervision by teachers, enhances intellectual flexibility and self-directedness of orientation while decreasing feelings of distress, just as does occupational self-direction.

CONCEPTUALIZATION OF PERSONALITY

Which facets of personality are implicated in the work–personality relationship and how should personality be conceptualized? There are three basic approaches to these issues. The first and to my mind least strategic approach is to begin with a single facet of personality and ask, How is this facet of personality influenced by, and how does it influence, conditions of work? In looking from the vantage point of any single facet of personality back to its social-structural underpinnings one always runs the risk of emphasizing variations on theme while failing to see the main theme—the main theme in this instance being that the effects of job conditions extend to many facets of personality (see Kohn 1989). As a case in point, consider the research literature on job conditions and perceived "locus of control," that is, feeling in control of one's life versus feeling subject to external control. These studies, almost all of them based on one or another variant of Rotter's (1966) conceptualization and index, are altogether consonant with my own and with other studies of job conditions and personality (see, for example, Andrisani and Nestel 1976; Andrisani and Abeles 1976; Hohner and Walter 1981; Spector 1982; O'Brien 1984, 1986; Hoff and Hohner 1986). Yet, in their preoccupation with this one facet of personality, many investigators ignore the parallel findings of other studies that the job conditions that affect [perceived] locus of control also affect such other, related facets of personality as fatalism, self-directedness of orientation, standards of morality, and self-confidence. Similarly, research on the occupational concomitants of self-esteem has been so focused on this one facet of personality that rarely have investigators noted that self-esteem is affected by the same job conditions as are other facets of self-conception and social orientation. Focusing on any single aspect of personality results in much too narrow interpretations of the work–personality relationship.

The problem is ameliorated by beginning with a multifaceted conceptualization of personality (for example, Holland 1966). But even then, a serious problem must be faced: no matter how adequate one's conceptualization of personality, beginning with personality and reaching back to job conditions seems inevitably to lead to an overly psychologized picture of job conditions. To my mind, beginning with personality, even a multifaceted conceptualization of personality, is an unstrategic way to get at actual job conditions.

An obvious alternative approach is to start with job conditions and study whichever facets of personality may affect or be affected by those job conditions—which is what I mainly have done. This approach, too, may distort our understanding of the job–personality relationship because it may yield too partial a picture of the personality side of the work–personality relationship. In particular, this approach may lead one to overemphasize those aspects of personality that either decidedly affect or are decidedly affected by those job conditions in which one has a particular practical or theoretical interest. Worse yet, beginning with job conditions may lead one to emphasize those aspects of personality that are most closely related to those aspects of the job that are most easily studied or most effectively measured. Still, I think the dangers of starting with job conditions are considerably less and the strategic advantages considerably greater than beginning with personality.

A sensible way to overcome the limitations of both approaches (see Frese 1982; Hoff et al. 1982) is to employ a conceptualization that starts neither with personality nor with job conditions but attempts to deal with them jointly. The classic illustration, of course, is Marx's concept alienation, which refers both to conditions of work and to the psychology of the worker (Kohn 1976; and Erikson, in this volume). For all the confusion and dispute engendered by the two-sidedness of this concept, I believe that a major reason Marx's formulation has been so valuable is precisely because it has dramatized the intimate connection between work and personality. The limitation of the approach, though, is that in attempting to make a single overarching generalization about the work–personality relationship, it necessarily deals with only some of the many aspects of work that bear on personality and only some of the aspects of personality that bear on work. I think multidimensional approaches to both work and personality are needed, at least at this stage of our understanding.

My own provisional attempt to conceptualize personality as it relates to work (Kohn and Schooler 1982; Kohn and Schoenbach 1983) is admittedly tentative and incomplete; in no sense does it purport to be a model of personality in all its ramifications. What I do attempt is a partial conceptualization of those facets of personality that are central to the work–personality relationship. In so doing, I deal with three fundamental dimensions of personality: intellectual flexibility; self-directedness of orientation; and a sense of well-being or distress.

Intellectual flexibility is measured by the respondents' intellectual performance in the interview situation itself. Our appraisals are based on a variety of indicators—including the respondents' answers to seemingly simple but highly revealing cognitive problems, their handling of perceptual and projective tests, their propensity to agree when asked agree–disagree questions, and the impression they make on the interviewer during a long session that requires a great deal of thought and reflection (Kohn and Schooler 1978). None of these indicators is assumed to be completely valid; but we do assume that all the indicators reflect in substantial degree the respondents' flexibility in attempting to cope with the intellectual demands of a complex situation. That the index is not artifactual and that it measures an enduring characteristic are attested to by its remarkably high stability—a ten-year over-time correlation of 0.93.

Self-directedness of orientation is, in my usage, an underlying dimension of orientation to self and society. It implies the beliefs that one has the personal capacity to take responsibility for one's actions and that society is so constituted as to make self-direction possible. Our index of self-directedness of orientation is based on a second-order confirmatory factor analysis (Kohn and Schooler 1982: fig. 3). Self-directedness is reflected in not having authoritarian/conservative beliefs, in having personally responsible standards of morality, in being trustful of others, in not being self-deprecatory, in not being conformist in one's ideas, and in not being fatalistic.

Self-directedness of orientation is a cumbersome expression, but I have been unable to find a simpler term that does full justice to the range of phenomena encompassed. Antonovsky's (1979, 1987) term *sense of coherence* is a possible alternative, but it does imply a somewhat different emphasis. Another possible alternative is [perceived] *locus of control*. This concept may have a narrower focus than mine (Hoff 1982). Other characterizations of personality development, although not exactly equivalent to my conceptualization, are in important respects analogous. The stage theories of moral development of Piaget (n.d.), Kohlberg (1976; Kohlberg and Gilligan 1972), and Habermas (1979) certainly have much in common with what I mean by conformity to external authority versus self-directedness, even though mine is decidedly not a stage theory. Pertinent, too, is Bernstein's (1971, 1973) sociolinguistic distinction between the restricted code of the working class and the elaborated code of the middle class.

Distress versus a sense of well-being constitutes another underlying dimension of orientation to self and society. Schooler and I strove to measure not only people's sense of personal efficacy, but also their feelings of comfort or pain; self-directedness and conformity may each have distinct psychic costs and rewards. In our second-order measurement model, distress is reflected in anxiety, self-deprecation, lack of self-confidence, nonconformity in one's ideas, and distrust.

When one considers how broad a range of orientations is encompassed in this measurement model, it is clear that self-directedness and distress summarize a great amount of information about personality as it relates to work. The inclusion of intellectual flexibility in the overall conceptualization increases the scope of our depiction of personality even further, encompassing in three dimensions a parsimonious summary of many important facets of personality that are directly implicated in the work–personality relationship. Nevertheless, I must again emphasize that this is not a full conceptualization of personality, but only a partial conceptualization of those facets of personality that are most directly involved in the work–personality relationship. Unquestionably, the full conceptualization of personality remains a major unresolved interpretive issue in the work–personality relationship.

THE PROCESSES BY WHICH WORK
AFFECTS PERSONALITY

I stated above that the research evidence points to learning-generalization as the principal process by which job conditions affect personality. Some would disagree with that statement and would regard the processes by which work affects personality as still an unresolved issue (House 1981). Be that as it may, five major questions about these processes certainly do remain unresolved: (1) Do job conditions affect all people exposed to those conditions similarly, or are their effects dependent on the needs, values, and abilities of the worker? (2) Is the process of learning from the job and generalizing those lessons to off-the-job reality similar for all segments of the work force? (3) Do job conditions impinge on personality differently at different stages of life-course or of career? (4) Is it possible that job conditions affect workers' off-the-job psychological functioning indirectly through job conditions affecting workers' subjective feelings about the job and these feelings, in turn, affecting workers' orientations to nonoccupational social realities? (5) What are the actual processes of learning and generalization?

The Fit Hypothesis

My summary of the resolved issues implies that job conditions have generally similar effects on the personalities of all workers. An alternative formulation is offered in the fit hypothesis, which holds that job conditions have differential effects, depending on how the demands of the job fit the needs, values, and capacities of the individual worker (see, for example, Lofquist and Dawis 1969; Hackman and Lawler 1971; Coburn 1975; but see Mortimer 1979; O'Brien 1986). Substantively complex work, for example, might be stimulating to most workers, yet be more burden than challenge to those workers who value extrinsic over intrinsic qualities of work. The fit hypothesis is appealing, in part because—at a sufficiently detailed level of analysis—it must be true. It is inconceivable that all workers react to all job conditions the same way. The real issue, though, is, What are the relative magnitudes of the main effects and the interaction effects? If the main effects are substantial and the interaction effects insubstantial, then our formulations have been sensible, our statistical models appropriate, and our conclusions justified; the fit hypothesis (and other interaction-based hypotheses) may well be true, but for purposes of general analysis only a variation on the principal theme. If the interactions are substantial, however, then our formulations have been erroneous, our statistical models inappropriate, and our conclusions suspect.

Our analyses of the interaction of occupational values and job conditions (Kohn and Schooler 1973; Kohn 1976) cast considerable doubt on the fit hypothesis. These analyses suggest, for example, that occupational self-direction is related to such basic needs and values as to be important to all workers, at least under the conditions of working life generally experienced in the United States. The analyses, however, have been far from definitive. Analysis of (linear) interactions does not exhaust the possibilities of subgroup variations. And we have not considered many other aspects of fit—for example, the relationship between aspirations and job conditions or between physical stamina and job conditions. Fit may yet be shown to play a part in the process, if not as the main theme, at least as a secondary theme.

The analytic problem is that it is exceedingly difficult to deal with reciprocal effects and statistical interactions in the same analyses. We have therefore done fewer such analyses than we should have liked to do.

Subgroup Variations in the Effects of Job on Person

The effects of work on personality could be essentially invariant for all segments of the work force or they could be more pronounced for some segments of the work force than for others. If the latter, the learning-generalization hypothesis should be refined and the conditions under which it holds specified much more precisely.

At many points in our analyses, my collaborators and I have considered whether the observed relationships between job conditions and psychological functioning hold, not only on the average for the entire population of employed people, but specifically for particular segments of the work force: for both men and women (J. Miller et al. 1979), for women who have young children and for those who do not (J. Miller et al. 1979), for both manual and nonmanual workers (Kohn and Schooler 1973), for people employed in profit-making firms and for those employed in nonprofit organizations (Kohn 1971), and (when examining housework) for women who are employed outside the home and for full-time housewives (Schooler et al. 1983). In general, we have found the impact of job conditions on personality to be more or less invariant for all segments of the work force. But, although we have repeatedly done comparative analyses of strategic segments of the work force, we have done many fewer such analyses than we should have liked—primarily because of the difficulty of doing such analyses when using linear structural-equations measurement and causal modeling. The possibility of subgroup variations in the impact of work on personality remains an unresolved issue.

Considerations of Life-Course and Career

Conspicuously lacking in my own and also in other investigators' analyses is any systematic attention to issues of life course and career. We have implicitly treated all sequences of jobs as if they were equally continuous or discontinuous along some meaningful career line. A more realistic conceptualization would have to take account that some job changes represent logical progressions in a meaningful sequence, while others represent shifts out of one career sequence, perhaps into another. I know of no really satisfactory way of dealing with this issue, despite early efforts by Wilensky (1961) and more recent efforts by others (for example, Spilerman 1977) to classify career patterns. Nor have investigators given sufficient attention to the possibility that the relationships of job conditions to personality might change over the life-course. (For pertinent discussions of *life-course*, see Elder and Rockwell 1979; Baltes 1982; and Spenner 1988.) Instead, we have mainly assumed that processes of learning and generalization are essentially invariant at different stages of life-course and career.

Recent work in developmental and social psychology does suggest that learning, particularly as represented in crystallized (or synthesized) intelligence, continues throughout the life span (see Baltes and Labouvie 1973; Baltes et al. 1984). In principle, since "transfer of learning" is "an essential characteristic of the learning process" (Gagne 1968:68), not only initial learning but also the generalization of what has been learned should continue as workers grow older. It is nevertheless possible that learning-generalization does not occur at the same rate or to the same extent at all ages and all stages of life-course or of career. The process may be especially pronounced in younger workers, at early stages of their occupational careers, before they are preoccupied with family responsibilities, but may diminish as workers grow older, advance in their careers, and have changing family responsibilities. It is also possible that either learning or generalization diminishes as workers grow older simply because of biological decrements (Horn and Donaldson 1980:476–81; Jarvik and Cohen 1973:227–34; but see Labouvie-Vief and Chandler 1978; Riley and Bond 1983). On the other hand, as Spenner (1988) imaginatively argues, the very processes by which occupational self-direction and personality reciprocally affect one another may result in increased effects of job on personality at later stages of life-course and career.

To see whether learning and the generalization of learning continue unabated throughout adult life requires analyses of how job conditions affect the psychological functioning of workers at different ages, different stages of career, or different stages of life-course. My collaborators and I (J. Miller et al. 1985) have done one such analysis: a cross-national analysis for the United States and Poland designed to assess whether occupational self-direction has as great an effect on intellective process for older workers as for younger and middle-aged workers. This analysis unequivocally shows an undiminished effect of occupational self-direction, particularly of the substantive complexity of work, on intellective process for the oldest segment of the work force. This argues strongly for the continuity of the learning-generalization process, regardless of the age of the worker and—by extrapolation—regardless of stage of career and stage of life-course. Still, one analysis, even when done comparatively for the United States and Poland, is hardly definitive, particularly because our analysis could not differentiate age-groups from cohorts defined on the basis of stage of career or of life-course.

Subjective Feelings about the Job as Mediators

It may be that job conditions do not affect personality through a direct process of learning and generalization, but rather through an indirect process, with the effects of job on off-the-job psychological functioning mediated by workers' subjective feelings about the job itself. (The issue here is not objective or subjective indices or even appraisals of job conditions, but subjective *feelings* about the job, such as satisfaction or dissatisfaction with the job.) Two such subjective feelings—job satisfaction and stress—have been the focus of extensive research.

The rationale for believing that job satisfaction may be an intervening link between job conditions and off-the-job psychological functioning is that people who are satisfied with their jobs may transfer such favorable orientations to their appraisals of self and of the larger world; correspondingly, people who are dissatisfied with their jobs may transfer their dissatisfaction to their appraisals of self and of the larger world. Our data, though, refute the assumption of a close connection between job satisfaction and orientations to self or to nonoccupational social reality. The correlations between job satisfaction and the several facets of values and orientations that we have measured are neither strong nor entirely consistent with the assumption that positive feelings about the job are related to positive feelings about self and the nonoccupational world (see Kohn 1969:178–80). Moreover, for job satisfaction to play an important intervening role in the relationship of job conditions to off-the-job psychological functioning would require job satisfaction to have a considerably stronger relationship to job conditions than it does (Kohn and Schooler 1973; J. Miller 1980; Kahn 1972). There is no reason to accord to job satisfaction the role of intermediary; job satisfaction (or dissatisfaction) is simply one of many psychological consequences of work—and, to my mind, not the most important.

Another, more plausible candidate for the role of intervening link in the processes by which job affects personality is stress. The hypothesis is that job conditions affect personality, in whole or in part, because they induce feelings of stress, which in turn have longer-term psychological consequences, such as anxiety and distress. The hypothesis is not merely an assertion that some job conditions result in workers' feeling subjective stress. Neither is it limited to the assertion that felt stress is one of the psychological consequences of work. The hypothesis asserts much more: that feelings of stress are a necessary intervening variable between job conditions and off-the-job psychological functioning. Were it not that job conditions produce feelings of stress, they would not affect off-the-job psychological functioning. A weaker version of the hypothesis would say that, absent stress, job conditions would have substantially smaller or less general effects on personality.

I know of no research, with the partial exception of House's (1980), that adequately tests the stress hypothesis, for no study includes measures of all the necessary elements: objective job conditions, felt job stress, and pertinent aspects of off-the-job psychological functioning. Most studies addressed to the stress hypothesis fail to measure actual job conditions. In the absence of information about actual job conditions, though, it is impossible to say whether what appear to be the psychological consequences of stress actually result from stress or from the job conditions themselves.

Studies that do measure job conditions, on the other hand, typically do not measure whether they are felt to be stressful, hence can only infer that some job conditions are stressful and that stress plays the role of intervening link between these particular job conditions and off-the-job psychological functioning. The list of putatively stressful job conditions is endless, including even the lack of opportunity for occupational self-direction. It seems to me that when stress is imputed to job conditions without direct measurement of whether the conditions are felt to be stressful, the argument is tautological. The evidence is not improved by what purports to be a validation, namely, that job conditions deemed by the investigator to be stressful correlate with such psychological phenomena as anxiety and depression.

Since my own research does not measure whether job conditions are felt by the workers to be stressful, it cannot provide direct evidence about the validity of the stress hypothesis. Schooler's and my findings (Kohn and Schooler 1982) do, however, cast some doubt on stress interpretations, for they indicate that purportedly stressful job conditions do not have uniformly deleterious psychological consequences—as implied by most stress interpretations (but see LaRocco et al. 1980; Karasek 1979). Still, there is evidence in our research that some job conditions generally thought to be stressful—close supervision, dirty work, a lack of job protections—do lead to feelings of distress. Thus, even though stress is probably not of any great importance for such facets of personality as intellectual flexibility and self-directedness of orientation, stressful job conditions may result in feelings of distress. To this limited but important extent, the stress hypothesis is consonant with our data.

In general, though, the evidence suggests that what people do in their work affects their cognitive functioning, their values, their conceptions of self, and their orientations to the world around them "directly"—in the sense that the effects of job on personality are not mediated by feelings about the job itself, such as job satisfaction or felt stress. I see no need to posit that subjective feelings about the job necessarily play an intermediary role in this process; the structural imperatives of the job can directly affect all aspects of people's thinking and feeling. But, since existing research does not rule out alternative interpretations of psychological process, the evidence is not definitive.

The Actual Processes of Learning and Generalization

The simple explanation that accounts for virtually all that is known about the effects of job on personality—save, perhaps, vis-à-vis distress (see Kohn 1987)—is that the processes are direct: learning from the job and extending those lessons to off-the-job realities. But how does this occur? On this central question, neither my collaborators' and my research nor that done by any other investigator has much to offer (see the discussion in Spenner 1988). Perhaps the answer to this critical question requires other types of data and other types of analyses than those provided by studies of representative samples of employed workers; it may require extended observational studies or even experimental studies. Or perhaps it will require, not a different method of inquiry, but much more detailed information, collected at more frequent intervals. In any case, I have every reason to believe that learning-generalization is the central psychological process by which job affects personality, even if research has thus far not done much to elucidate this process.

THE MODIFICATION OF JOB CONDITIONS

The final unresolved issue I shall address in this essay is the modification of job conditions: whether it is possible to modify job conditions purposively and systematically; and whether the modification of job conditions would affect the personalities of job incumbents. These issues are pertinent to the work–personality relationship for two distinct reasons. The actual modification of job conditions would provide the ultimate "experimental" test of whether job conditions actually do have the hypothesized effects on personality. Ultimately, the true utility of understanding the work–personality relationship is purposive social change.

The Historical Process

In one sense, the historical processes by which any society's job structure developed are irrelevant to whether it is possible to change conditions of work in that society by deliberate design. Yet, knowledge of the historical processes might provide insight into what forces would facilitate and what forces would impede attempts to change job conditions. Unfortunately, the historical record is not at all clear. It has been argued that the main trend of the past fifty years in advanced capitalist societies has been ever-increasing complexity of work, a result of ever-increasing technological requirements (Blauner 1964). This reading of history sees the industrial economy as having required an increasingly educated work force and as having had less and less need for semiskilled and unskilled workers capable of doing only routinized tasks. Another reading of the same evidence is that there has been a relentless process of breaking jobs down into simple components, not because this necessarily makes for a more efficient productive process, but because it has enabled management to gain control over workers (Braverman 1974; Goldman and Van Houten 1980a,b).

Undoubtedly, contradictory processes have operated and continue to operate (see Wallace and Kalleberg 1982; Spenner 1983; Form 1987). I am not able to assess the partial and conflicting evidence as to which process has predominated. For present purposes, it may be sufficient to note that any effort to change job structure may require contending not only with the technological requirements of the work, but also with political and economic constraints.

Modifying Job Conditions

It seems a reasonable extrapolation from the body of research I have reviewed in this essay to hypothesize that deliberately instituted change in pivotal job conditions would affect people's values, orientations, and intellectual functioning. We should not necessarily expect dramatic changes in job conditions to bring about equally dramatic changes in the personalities of the workers. On the other hand, the research suggests that even small changes in job conditions may have modest but enduring—and therefore, in the long run, important—psychological consequences.

When one looks for actual experimental evidence, though, one finds surprisingly little that is pertinent. Although experiments in the restructuring of work have been conducted in several countries, I know of none that adequately assesses the consequences of changes in job conditions for the personalities of affected workers (see Berg et al. 1978). Many such experiments seem not even to recognize that the most important work conditions are embedded in larger social and economic structures. Other experiments—perhaps most—deal only with job conditions that I see as having only secondary or even trivial importance for personality. Unless experiments give workers meaningful opportunities to exercise occupational self-direction, there is little reason to expect much effect on workers' off-the-job psychological functioning (see Kahn 1975). One important question is how large a measure of individual control or how significant a role in group decision making is required for workers to believe they have sufficient command over their essential occupational conditions that it really matters.

An even more critical issue is whether the pertinent job conditions can be substantially modified, not just as an experiment but as a regular practice (see Berg et al. 1978; Cole 1979). If so, can this be done within the structure of capitalist enterprise or does it require worker ownership of the enterprise or even worker control over the means of production generally? For that matter, is substantial modification of job conditions possible even under conditions of worker ownership? Despite considerable research and much discussion of the issues, the answers to these questions are largely unknown. The evidence about worker-owned companies within capitalist economies is equivocal (see Stern and Whyte 1981), the most general finding being that no real effort has been made in most such companies to appreciably alter job structure. The evidence from socialist countries is not at all clear either. The efforts to change job structure in Yugoslavia are well known (see Taylor, Grandjean, and Tos 1987), but it is far from certain how much change has actually occurred in job conditions as such. As for the socialist countries of Eastern Europe, their modal form of industrial organization seems to offer their workers no greater, and quite possibly less, opportunity for occupational self-direction than do most firms and organizations in capitalist countries. (On this see Wesolowski and Mach, 1986. Their conclusion, based mainly on Poland, has been confirmed for other East European countries by many informed observers with whom I have spoken.)

In short, I know of no answers to the question of whether and, if so, how it is possible to modify job structure so as to increase workers' opportunity for occupational self-direction. That it is desirable to do so seems to me to be unequivocal. Translating this eminently desirable goal into a plan for social change, though, will be an immensely difficult task.

RESOLVING THE UNRESOLVED ISSUES

How can we resolve the unresolved interpretive issues? I think it is apparent in my discussion of the issues that I do not think any single type of study can answer all the important questions. There is a critical need for a range of studies: case studies, experimental studies, longitudinal studies of the entire work force and of particular segments of the work force. There is a special need for longitudinal studies using repeated measurement at relatively closely spaced intervals, for intensive studies of individual firms or organizations, for systematic observation of workers' immediate conditions of work, and for systematically collected information about the technological and organizational contexts of work. Quantitative researcher though I am, as a former worker in automobile and train factories, cattle ranch-hand, and participant-observer of industrial relations in a printing plant, I also recognize the great importance of intensive, *qualitative* research for studying process. If ever there was a realm of social-scientific inquiry where the great range of interpretive issues called for an equally great range of methodological approaches, this is it.

This makes the field tremendously exciting, but it also puts limits on what we can hope to accomplish in any one type of inquiry. I think that we are likely to do best by designing any one study, not to answer as many of the unresolved issues as possible, but to address one or another of them as thoroughly as possible. The ideal research design for deciding whether the stress hypothesis has general validity, for example, is not the ideal design for studying the timing of effects of job on personality or for determining whether interview-based measures of job conditions are valid, in comparison to observation-based indices of those same job conditions. There is a sufficient diversity of important unresolved issues to call for all the research approaches in our armamentarium and all the ingenuity at our command.

REFERENCES

Andrisani, Paul J., and Ronald P. Abeles. 1976. "Locus of Control and Work Experience: Cohort and Race Differences." Paper presented at annual meeting of the American Psychological Association. Washington, D.C., September 3–7.

Andrisani, Paul J., and Gilbert Nestel. 1976. "Internal-External Control as Contributor To and Outcome of Work Experience." *Journal of Applied Psychology* 61:156–65.

Antonovsky, Aaron. 1979. *Health, Stress, and Coping.* San Francisco: Jossey-Bass.

———. 1987. *Unravelling the Mystery of Health.* San Francisco: Jossey-Bass.

Baltes, Paul B. 1982. "Life-Span Developmental Psychology: Observations on History and Theory Revisited." In *Developmental Psychology: Historical and Philosophical Perspectives,* edited by R. M. Lerner. Hillsdale, N.J.: Erlbaum.

Baltes, Paul B., Freya Dittmann-Kohli, and Roger A. Dixon. 1984. "New Perspectives on the Development of Intelligence in Adulthood: Toward a Dual-Process Conception and A Model of Selective Optimization with Compensation." In *Life-Span Development and Behavior,* edited by Paul B. Baltes and Orville G. Brim. New York: Academic Press.

Baltes, Paul B., and Gisela V. Labouvie. 1973. "Adult Development of Intellectual Performance: Description, Explanation, and Modification." In *The Psychology of Adult Development and Aging,* edited by Carl Eisdorfer and M. Powell Lawton. Washington, D.C.: American Psychological Association.

Berg, Ivar, Marcia Freedman, and Michael Freeman. 1978. *Managers and Work Reform: A Limited Engagement.* New York: Free Press.

Bernstein, Basil. 1971. *Class, Codes and Control.* Vol. 1, *Theoretical Studies toward a Sociology of Language.* London: Routledge and Kegan Paul.

———. 1973. *Class, Codes and Control.* Vol. 2, *Applied Studies toward a Sociology of Language.* London: Routledge & Kegan Paul.

Bertram, Hans. 1983. "Berufsorientierung erwerbstatiger Mutter." *Zeitschrift fur Sozialisations-forschung und Erziehungssoziologie* 3(1):29–40.

Blauner, Robert. 1964. *Alienation and Freedom: The Factory Worker and His Industry.* Chicago: University of Chicago Press.

Braverman, Harry. 1974. *Labor and Monopoly Capital: The Degradation of Work in the Twentieth Century.* New York: Monthly Review Press.

Breer, Paul E., and Edwin A. Locke. 1965. *Task Experience as a Source of Attitudes.* Homewood, I L.: Dorsey Press.

Brousseau, Kenneth R. 1978. "Personality and Job Experience." *Organizational Behavior and Human Performance* 22:235–52.

Cain, Pamela S., and Donald J. Treiman. 1981. "The *Dictionary of Occupational Titles* as a Source of Occupational Data." American Sociological Review 46:253–78.

Coburn, David. 1975. "Job-Worker Incongruence: Consequences for Health." *Journal of Health and Social Behavior* 16:198–212.

Coburn, David, and Virginia L. Edwards. 1976. "Job Control and Child-Rearing Values." *Canadian Review of Sociology and Anthropology* 13(3):337–44.

Cole, Robert E. 1979. *Work, Mobility, and Participation: A Comparative Study of American and Japanese Industry.* Berkeley: University of California Press.

Coser, Rose Laub. 1975. "The Complexity of Roles as a Seedbed of Individual Autonomy." In *The Idea of Social Structure: Papers in Honor of Robert K. Merton,* edited by Lewis A. Coser. New York: Harcourt Brace Jovanovich.

Dalgard, Odd Steffen. 1981. "Occupational Experience and Mental Health, with Special Reference to Closeness of Supervision." *Psychiatry and Social Science* 1:29–42.

Elder, Glen H., Jr., and Richard C. Rockwell. 1979. "The Life-Course and Human Development: An Ecological Perspective." *International Journal of Behavioral Development* 2:1–21.

Eldridge, J. E. T., ed. 1971. *Max Weber: The Interpretation of Social Reality.* New York: Charles Scribner's Sons.

Form, William. 1987. "On the Degradation of Skills." *Annual Review of Sociology* 13:29–47.

Frese, Michael. 1982. "Occupational Socialization and Psychological Development: An Underemphasized Research Perspective in Industrial Psychology." *Journal of Occupational Psychology* 55:209–24.

———. 1983. "Der Einfluss der Arbeit auf die Personlichkeit: Zum Konzept des Handlungsstils in der beruflichen Sozialisation." *Zeitschrift für Socializationsforschung und Erziehungssoziologie* 3:11–28.

Gagne, Robert M. 1968. "Learning: Transfer." In *International Encyclopedia of the Social Sciences,* vol. 9, edited by David L. Sills. New York: Macmillan and Free Press.

Goldman, Paul, and Donald R. Van Houten. 1980a. "Uncertainty, Conflict, and Labor Relations in the Modern Firm. I: Productivity and Capitalism's 'Human Face.'" *Economic and Industrial Democracy* 1:63–98.

———. 1980b. "Uncertainty, Conflict, and Labor Relations in the Modern Firm. II: The War on Labor." *Economic and Industrial Democracy* 1:263–87.

Grabb, Edward G. 1981a. "Class, Conformity and Political Powerlessness." *Canadian Review of Sociology and Anthropology* 18(3):362–69.

———. 1981b. "The Ranking of Self-Actualization Values: The Effects of Class, Stratification, and Occupational Experiences." *Sociological Quarterly* 22:373–83.

Gruneisen, Veronika, and Ernst-Hartmut Hoff. 1977. *Familienerziehung und Lebenssituation: Der Einfluss von Lebensbedingungen und Arbeitserfahrungen auf Erziehungseinstellungen und Erziehungsverhalten von Eltern.* Weinheim, W. Germany: Beltz Verlag.

Habermas, Jurgen. 1979. *Communication and the Evolution of Society.* Boston: Beacon Press.

Hacker, Winfried. 1981. "Perceptions of and Reactions to Work Situations: Some Implications of an Action Control Approach." In *Toward a Psychology of Situations: An Interactional Perspective,* edited by David Magnusson. Hillsdale, N.J.: Erlbaum.

Hackman, J. Richard, and Edward E. Lawler III. 1971. "Employee Reactions to Job Characteristics." *Journal of Applied Psychology Monograph* 55:259–86.

Hoff, Ernst. 1982. "Kontrollbewusstsein: Grundvorstellungen zur eigenen Person und Umwelt bei jungen Arbeitern." *Kolner Zeitschrift fur Soziologie und Sozialpsychologie* 34:316–39.

Hoff, Ernst-Hartmut, and Veronika Gruneisen. 1978. "Arbeitserfahrungen, Erziehungseinstellungen, und Erziehungsverhalten von Eltern." In *Familiare Sozialisation: Probleme, Ergebnisse, Perspektiven,* edited by H. Lukesch and K. Schneewind. Stuttgart: Klett-Cotta.

Hoff, Ernst, Lothar Lappe, and Wolfgang Lempert. 1982. "Sozialisationstheoretische Uberlegungen zur Analyse von Arbeit, Betrieb, und Beruf." *Soziale Welt: Zeitschrift fur Sozialwissenschaftliche Forschung und Praxis* 33:508–36.

———. 1983. *Methoden zur Untersuchung der Sozialisation Junger Facharbeiter. Materialien aus der Bildungsforschung.* no. 24, parts 1, 2. Berlin: Max Planck Institut für Bildungsforschung.

Hoff, Ernst-H., and Hans Uwe Hohner. 1986. "Occupational Careers, Work, and Control." In *The Psychology of Control and Aging,* edited by Margret M. Baltes and Paul B. Baltes. Hillsdale, N.J.: Erlbaum.

Hohner, H. U., and H. Walter. 1981. "Ursachenzuschriebung (locus of control) bei Arbeitern und Angestellten. Einige empirische Befunde." *Psychologische Beitrage* 23:392–407.

Holland, John L. 1966. *The Psychology of Vocational Choice: A Theory of Personality Types and Model Environments.* Waltham, Mass.: Blaisdell.

Horn, John L., and Gary Donaldson. 1980. "Cognitive Development in Adulthood." In *Constancy and Change in Human Development,* edited by Orville G. Brim, Jr. and Jerome Kagan. Cambridge: Harvard University Press.

House, James S. 1980. *Occupational Stress and the Physical and Mental Health of Factory Workers.* Report on NIMH Grant No. 1R02MH28902. Research Report Series: Institute for Social Research, University of Michigan.

———. 1981. "Social Structure and Personality." In *Social Psychology: Sociological Perspectives,* edited by Morris Rosenberg and Ralph H. Turner. New York: Basic Books.

Hynes, Eugene. 1979. "Explaining Class Differences in Socialization Values and Behavior: An Irish Study." Ph.D. diss., Southern Illinois Univ.

Janicka, Krystyna, Grazyna Kacprowicz, and Kazimierz M. Slomczynski. 1983. "Zlozonosc pracy jako zmienna socjologiczna: Modele pomiaru i ich ocena." (Complexity of work as a sociological variable: Measurement models and their evaluation.) *Studia Socjologiczne* 3:5–33.

Jarvik, Lissy F., and Donna Cohen. 1973. "A Behavioral Approach to Intellectual Changes with Aging." In *The Psychology of Adult Development and Aging,* edited by Carl Eisdorfer and M. Powell Lawton. Washington, D.C.: American Psychological Association.

Kahn, Robert L. 1972. "The Meaning of Work: Interpretation and Proposals for Measurement." In *The Human Meaning of Social Change,* edited by Angus Campbell and Philip E. Converse. New York: Russell Sage Foundation.

———. 1975. "In Search of the Hawthorne Effect." In *Man and Work in Society: A Report on the Symposium Held on the Occasion of the 50th Anniversary of the Original Hawthorne Studies, Oakbrook, IL, November 10–13, 1974,* edited by Eugene L. Cass and Frederick G. Zimmer. New York: Van Nostrand Reinhold.

Karasek, Robert A., Jr. 1979. "Job Demands, Job Decision Latitude, and Mental Strain: Implications for Job Redesign." *Administrative Science Quarterly* 24:285–308.

Karasek, Robert, Dean Baker, Frank Marxer, Anders Ahlbom, and Tores Theorell. 1981. "Job Decision Latitude, Job Demands, and Cardiovascular Disease: A Prospective Study of Swedish Men." *American Journal of Public Health* 71:694–705.

Kohlberg, Lawrence. 1976. "Moral Stages and Moralisation: The Cognitive-Developmental Approach." In *Moral Development and Behavior*, edited by T. Lickona. New York: Holt, Rinehart, and Winston.

Kohlberg, Lawrence, and Carol Gilligan. 1972. "The Adolescent as a Philosopher: The Discovery of the Self in A Post-Conventional World." In *Twelve to Sixteen: Early Adolescence*, edited by Jerome Kagan and Robert Coles. New York: Norton.

Kohn, Melvin L. 1971. "Bureaucratic Man: A Portrait and An Interpretation." *American Sociological Review* 36:461–74.

———. 1976. "Occupational Structure and Alienation." *American Journal of Sociology* 82:111–30.

———. 1977. *Class and Conformity: A Study in Values*, 2d ed. Chicago: University of Chicago Press.

———. 1985. "Arbeit und Personlichkeit—ungeloste Probleme der Forschung." In *Arbeitsbiographie und Personlichkeitsentwicklung*, edited by Ernst-H. Hoff, Lothar Lappe, and Wolfgang Lempert. Bern: Verlag Hans Huber.

———. 1987. "Cross-National Research as an Analytic Strategy: American Sociological Association 1987 Presidential Address." *American Sociological Review* 57:713–31.

———. 1989. "Social Structure and Personality: A Quintessentially Sociological Approach to Social Psychology." *Social Forces* 68:26–33.

Kohn, Melvin L., Atsushi Naoi, Carrie Schoenbach, Kazimeierz M. Slomczynski, and Carmi Schooler. 1990. "Position in the Class Structure and Psychological Functioning in the United States, Japan, and Poland." *American Journal of Sociology* 95.

Kohn, Melvin L., and Carrie Schoenbach. 1983. "Class, Stratification, and Psychological Functioning." In *Work and Personality: An Inquiry into the Impact of Social Stratification*, Melvin L. Kohn and Carmi Schooler. Norwood, N.J.: Ablex Publishing.

Kohn, Melvin L., and Carmi Schooler. 1973. "Occupational Experience and Psychological Functioning: An Assessment of Reciprocal Effects." *American Sociological Review* 38:97–118.

———. 1978. "The Reciprocal Effects of the Substantive Complexity of Work and Intellectual Flexibility: A Longitudinal Assessment." *American Journal of Sociology* 84:24–52.

———. 1982. "Job Conditions and Personality: A Longitudinal Assessment of Their Reciprocal Effects." *American Journal of Sociology* 87:1257–86.

———. (in collaboration with Joanne Miller, Karen A. Miller, Carrie Schoenbach, and Ronald Schoenberg). 1983. *Work and Personality: An Inquiry into the Impact of Social Stratification*. Norwood, N.J.: Ablex Publishing.

Kohn, Melvin L., Kazimierz M. Slomczynski, and Carrie Schoenbach. 1986. "Social Stratification and the Transmission of Values in the Family: A Cross-National Assessment." *Sociological Forum* 1:73–102.

Labouvie-Vief, Gisela, and Michael J. Chandler. 1978. "Cognitive Development and Life-Span Developmental Theory: Idealistic versus Contextual Perspectives." In

Life-Span Development and Behavior, vol. 1, edited by Paul B. Baltes. New York: Academic Press.

LaRocco, James M., James S. House, and John R. P. French, Jr. 1980. "Social Support, Occupational Stress, and Health." *Journal of Health and Social Behavior* 21:202–18.

Lindsay, Paul, and William E. Knox. 1984. "Continuity and Change in Work Values among Young Adults: A Longitudinal Study." *American Journal of Sociology* 89:918–31.

Lofquist, Lloyd H., and Rene V. Dawis. 1969. *Adjustment to Work: A Psychological View of Man's Problems in a Work-oriented Society*. New York: Appleton-Century-Crofts.

Marx, Karl. 1964. *Early Writings*, edited and translated by T. B. Bottomore. New York: McGraw-Hill.

———. 1971. *The Grundrisse*, edited and translated by David McLellan. New York: Harper and Row.

Miller, Joanne. 1980. "Individual and Occupational Determinants of Job Satisfaction: A Focus on Gender Differences." *Sociology of Work and Occupations* 7:337–66.

Miller, Joanne, Carmi Schooler, Melvin L. Kohn, and Karen A. Miller. 1979. "Women and Work: The Psychological Effects of Occupational Conditions." *American Journal of Sociology* 85:66–94.

Miller, Joanne, Kazimierz M. Slomczynski, and Melvin L. Kohn. 1985. "Continuity of Learning-Generalization: The Effect of Job on Men's Intellective Process in the United States and Poland." *American Journal of Sociology* 91:593–615.

Miller, Karen A., and Melvin L. Kohn. 1983. "The Reciprocal Effects of Job Conditions and the Intellectuality of Leisure-time Activities." In *Work and Personality: An Inquiry into the Impact of Social Stratification*, edited by Melvin L. Kohn and Carmi Schooler. Norwood, N.J.: Ablex Publishing.

Miller, Karen A., Melvin L. Kohn, and Carmi Schooler. 1985. "Educational Self-Direction and the Cognitive Functioning of Students." *Social Forces* 63:923–44.

———. 1986. "Educational Self-Direction and Personality." *American Sociological Review* 51:372–90.

Mortimer, Jeylan T. 1979. *Changing Attitudes toward Work*. Work in America Institute Studies in Productivity, vol. 2. Scarsdale, N.Y.: Work in America Institute.

Mortimer, Jeylan T., Jon Lorence, and Donald Kumka. 1986. *Work, Family, and Personality: Transition to Adulthood*. Norwood, N.J.: Ablex Publishing.

Naoi, Atsushi, and Carmi Schooler. 1985. "Occupational Conditions and Psychological Functioning in Japan." *American Journal of Sociology* 90:729–52.

O'Brien, Gordon E. 1984. "Locus on Control, Work, and Retirement." In *Research with the Locus of Control Construct*. Vol. 3, *Extensions and Limitations*. New York: Academic Press.

———. 1986. *Psychology of Work and Unemployment*. Chichester: Wiley.

Oesterreich, Rainer. 1984. "Zur Analyse von Planungs- und Denkprozessen in der industriellen Produktion—Das Arbeitsanalyseinstrument VERA." *Diagnostica* 216–34.

Pearlin, Leonard I., and Melvin L. Kohn. 1966. "Social Class, Occupation, and Parental Values: A Cross-National Study." *American Sociological Review* 31:466–79.

Piaget, Jean. (n.d.). *The Moral Judgment of the Child*. Glencoe, Ill.: Free Press.

Resch, M., W. Volpert, K. Leitner, and T. Krogoll. 1983. "Regulation Requirements and Regulation Barriers—Two Aspects of Partialized Action in Industrial Work." In

Design of Work in Automated Manufacturing Systems with Special Reference to Small and Medium Size Firms, edited by T. Martin. Oxford: Pergamon Press.

Riley, Matilda White, and Kathleen Bond. 1983. "Beyond Ageism: Postponing the Onset of Disability." In *Aging in Society: Selected Reviews of Recent Research,* edited by Matilda White Riley, Beth B. Hess, and Kathleen Bond. Hillsdale, N.J.: Erlbaum.

Rotter, Julian B. 1966. "Generalized Expectancies for Internal versus External Control of Reinforcement." *Psychological Monographs,* 80(1), whole no. 609.

Schoenberg, Ronald. 1977. "Dynamic Models and Cross-Sectional Data: The Consequences of Dynamic Misspecification." *Social Science Research* 6:133–44.

Schooler, Carmi, Melvin L. Kohn, Karen A. Miller, and Joanne Miller. 1983. "Housework as Work." In *Work and Personality: An Inquiry into the Impact of Social Stratification,* edited by Melvin L. Kohn and Carmi Schooler. Norwood, N.J.: Ablex Publishing.

Schooler, Carmi, and Atsushi Naoi. 1988. "The Psychological Effects of Traditional and of Economically Peripheral Job Settings in Japan." *American Journal of Sociology* 94:335–55.

Slomczynski, Kazimierz M., Joanne Miller, and Melvin L. Kohn. 1981. "Stratification, Work, and Values: A Polish-United States Comparison." *American Sociological Review* 46:720–44.

Sorokin, Pitirim. 1927. *Social Mobility.* New York: Harper and Brothers.

Spade, Joan Z. 1983. "The Nature of the Work Activity: Its Impact on the Family." Ph.D. diss., State University of New York/Buffalo.

Spector, Paul E. 1982. "Behavior in Organizations as a Function of Employee's Locus of Control." *Psychological Bulletin* 91:482–97.

Spenner, Kenneth I. 1980. "Occupational Characteristics and Classification Systems: New Uses of the *Dictionary of Occupational Titles* in Social Research." *Sociological Methods & Research* 9:239–64.

———. 1983. "Deciphering Prometheus: Temporal Change in the Skill Level of Work." *American Sociological Review* 48:824–37.

———. 1988. "Occupations, Work Settings, and the Course of Adult Development: Tracing the Implications of Select Historical Changes." In *Life-Span Development and Behavior,* vol. 9, edited by Paul B. Baltes, David L. Featherman, and Richard M. Lerner. Hillsdale, N.J.: Erlbaum.

Spenner, Kenneth I., and Luther B. Otto. 1984. "Work and Self-Concept: Selection and Socialization in the Early Career." In *Research in Sociology of Education and Socialization,* vol. 5, edited by Alan Kerckhoff. Greenwich, Ct.: JAI Press.

Spilerman, Seymour. 1977. "Careers, Labor Market Structure, and Socioeconomic Achievement." *American Journal of Sociology* 83:551–93.

Staines, Graham L. 1980. "Spillover versus Compensation: A Review of the Literature on the Relationship between Work and Nonwork." *Human Relations* 33(2): 111–29.

Stern, Robert N., and William F. Whyte, eds. 1981. "Economic Democracy: Comparative Views of Current Initiatives." *Sociology of Work and Occupations* 8: Special Issue.

Taylor, Patricia A., Burke D. Grandjean, and Nico Tos. 1987. "Work Satisfaction under Yugoslav Self-Management: On Participation, Authority, and Ownership." *Social Forces* 65:1020–34.

Temme, Lloyd V. 1975. *Occupation: Meanings and Measures*. Washington, D.C.: Bureau of Social Science Research.

United States Department of Labor. 1965. *Dictionary of Occupational Titles*, 3d ed. Washington, D.C.: U.S. Government Printing Office.

Volpert/Oesterreich/Gablenz-Kolakovic/Krogoll/Resch. 1983. *Verfahren zur Ermittlung von Regulationserfordernissen in der Arbeitstatigkeit (VERA). Analyse von Planungs- und Denkprozessen in der Industriellen Produktion. Handbuch*. Cologne: Verlag TUV Rheinland.

Wallace, Michael, and Arne L. Kalleberg. 1982. "Industrial Transformation and the Decline of Craft: The Decomposition of Skill in the Printing Industry, 1931–1978." *American Sociological Review* 47:307–24.

Wesolowski, Wlodzimierz, and Bogdan W. Mach. 1986. "Unfulfilled Systemic Functions of Social Mobility." *International Sociology*. Part 1: "A Theoretical Scheme" 1:19–35. Part 2, "The Polish Case" 1:173–87.

Wilensky, Harold L. 1961. "Orderly Careers and Social Participation: The Impact of Work History on Social Integration in the Middle Mass." *American Sociological Review* 26:521–39.

‖‖‖‖‖‖ **PART TWO • WORK AND THE WIDER SOCIETY**

I I | | | | | | Power Lost and Status Gained: A Step in the Direction of Sex Equality

ROSE LAUB COSER

Where wives are gainfully employed, husbands lose power and gain status. This is the finding of an empirical study of middle-class couples in Israel by Ruth Katz and Yochanan Peres (1983).

As I have written elsewhere with Lewis Coser, power depends on resources, and women who have relatively few resources are in a poor position to share it equally with their husbands (Coser and Coser 1974; see also Scanzoni 1972, 1979). Conversely, the fact that the distribution of power in the family changes in favor of the wife wherever she contributes financial means to the household has been amply demonstrated. Blood and Wolfe (1960:40–41) and others (Scanzoni 1970; Mortimer and Sorensen 1984) have shown this to be true for the United States, and Hyman Rodman (1972) examined this for all countries for which data are available—Belgium, Denmark, Finland, France, Germany, Ghana, Greece, Japan, the United States, and Yugoslavia—and found it to be true throughout.

SOCIAL STATUS AND THE SOCIAL ROLE OF WIVES

Scholars of the subject agree that, with minor variations, husbands are likely to hand over some of their familial power to their wives when the latter work outside the home. What has been less emphasized as a conse-

An earlier version of this paper appeared in German in *Kölner Zeitschrift für Soziologie und Sozialpsychologie* 39 (1987): 1–14. The paper is a revised version of two papers read at consecutive annual meetings of the American Sociological Association: "In Defense of Consumption," read at the 1984 meetings in San Antonio, and "Power Lost and Status Gained," read at the 1985 meetings in Washington, D.C.

quence of a wife's monetary contribution to the household is the fact that in losing power the husband gains something in return, namely, social status in the eyes of the community.

Max Weber (1978) has defined status groups as being based on consumption (in contrast to social classes, which he defines as being based on life chances determined by people's place in the production process) for the maintenance and improvement of styles of living. This takes place largely through the selection of residence and the purchase of education, objects of art, and other valued goods—all items that are visible to a community of peers.

Visibility is a precondition for status maintenance in Weber's definition. Consumption that serves the perquisites of status must be conspicuous, whether in Veblen's (1953) or Weber's (1958) understanding of the term. Consumption items can be symbols of individual status attainment, as in Veblen's sense, for the purpose of staking a claim to belongingness, or they can, as in Weber's formulation, serve collective status maintenance and closure to access. Lest it be objected that I am belaboring the by now well-known observation that behavior that makes a claim of normative conformity must be made visible to other members of the group, let me state that it gives me pleasure to contribute no matter how little to the systematization of sociological theory by integrating Weber's and Veblen's theories of social status with Merton's theory of reference group behavior (1968: chap. 10).[1]

Opportunities for enhancing living styles through consumption have vastly increased in our society with the growth of the middle class and the rapid development of technology for consumption goods. Much of this enhancement has been due to the efforts of women, who usually have contributed to the status of their husbands, as Veblen has also noted in his early writing on the subject

---

1. In his masterful development of the concept of observability Merton deals mainly with observability as a means of social control as well as with the benefits deriving from insulation from observability (1968:373ff). He is, of course, aware of the usefulness of observability for other purposes as well. He says, "The property of observability is necessarily implied if not expressly taken into account in reference group theory" (1968:375). He goes on to say that "this can be more appropriately considered later" (1968). He fulfills this promise some fifteen pages later when he states that individuals who compare themselves to others must have some knowledge of the latter's behavior (1968:390). To this one should add that individuals who compare their own lot to that of others also want to have their own behavior be known. They *have the desire* to make their behavior visible. This came to me—although I should have remembered the by-now familiar concept of *conspicuous consumption*—while I was analyzing interviews of immigrant Italian women. One of them reported the pleasure she took in promenading on the street with her manly looking grown son; another told of her husband's pride when taking his well-clad little daughters to church. (From a study of the social roles of immigrant women, see note 4 below.)

(1953). It has been obvious in the upper classes, where a wife's contribution would consist not only of inheritance (achieved, expected or *inter vivos*), but also of status symbols such as her family name (cf. Rosenfeld 1974). Traditionally, wives have helped enhance a valued style of living, whether through cultivation and support of the arts, officeholding in museums, or active participation in philanthropy. As David Riesman (1964) has suggested, in the traditional upper classes men have been too busy living up to and enhancing their achieved status outside of the family to get involved in prestige-giving cultural activities. Their wives' cultural activities would constitute a resource for furthering their status and even their power in the outside world.

Cultural activities can be considered part of what more generally Hanna Papanek (1984) has called "status-production work" in the middle and upper classes. It consists of the wife's support of her husband's career (see also Mortimer and Sorensen, 1984), the training of children, and what Papanek calls the "politics of status maintenance," such as gossip, gift exchange, and management of feasts. To this list I would add entertainment generally as well as work in the community, which, while serving the public good, also helps maintain and increase family status. I have in mind all sorts of volunteer work, for example, in women's auxiliaries, in PTA and scout groups, in political campaigns and philanthropic fund-raising as well as through membership in associations from the League of Women Voters to the Daughters of the American Revolution (Rosenfeld, 1974). Through such activities women have increased the status of the family and, since he is considered head of household, of the husband. In return for such prestige-giving activities and attributes husbands seem to be willing to relinquish some of their familial power. Blood and Wolfe (1960:38–39) found that where women participate in organizations (including church attendance) the husbands' power decreases.

As Peter Blau (1964:133) has written, "Status can be considered as capital, which an individual can draw on to obtain benefits, which is expended in use, and which can be expanded by profitably investing it at interest." Similarly, the French sociologist Pierre Bourdieu (1977) has suggested the concept of "cultural capital" to denote the symbolic wealth that is being appropriated and accumulated and that by itself generates additional privileges. That such capital is being transmitted mainly by women has been supported in an empirical study by Paul DiMaggio (1982). He provided striking evidence that cultural capital is positively related to scholastic grades in high school. More important for the point I am making here is the fact that "women in the sample expressed substantially more interest and reported greater participation in high cultural activities than did the men." DiMaggio further suggests that "cultural interests and activities [are] culturally prescribed for teenage girls, while for adolescent boys they were less strongly prescribed. . . . High cultural involvements may have been part of an identity kit that academically successful high-status girls, but not similar boys, possessed."

Typically, cultural interests and activities are more prevalent among higher- than among lower-status girls. DiMaggio concludes that "women who wish to be recognized as eligible partners for men from high-status backgrounds may need cultural capital to a greater extent than men who wish to achieve in the world of work." In contrast, for the boys from "high-status families it may be more important to develop a taste for women who appreciate culture than to develop a taste for high culture [themselves]" (DiMaggio 1982).

Women's task of taking charge not only of culture but of consumption of all sorts became widespread with the development of capitalism, concomitant with urbanization, when women were removed from production on the land. Max Weber (1978) insisted that capitalist development owes much of its vigor to the fact that, in his words, the productive unit became separated from the budgetary unit, by which he meant that the place of work became separated from the home. This, he said, established in the realm of production the impersonal, that is, the rational nature of economic activities. When we apply this notion of the separation between activity systems to his definition of status groups as collec- tivities that can be identified by styles of consumption, it will become clear that the separation of the two spheres is being upheld through gender-role differ- entiation between production and consumption, with men by and large taking charge of the former, and women who stay at home taking over the manage- ment of consumption.

In the transformation from rural to urban life, and with the separation of the home from the place of work, women changed their position of junior part- nership with their husbands to a condition in which, as Judith Blake has noted (1974), they have become dependent for their livelihood on their husbands' work while the latter have become independent of their wives in their productiv- ity. Yet, while this helped diminish the status of women, it gave them some autonomy in that they were freed from the control of their husbands during the day. In their husbands' absence they gained much leeway in the use of their time and in deciding how the money their husbands earned was to be spent—at least in those social strata where the husbands' income was not limited to the dire necessities of physical survival.

I note in passing that, probably because of the loss of male power, women's management of consumption has earned them the hostility of men—if writings from those by Philip Wylie (1942), Geoffrey Gorer (1948), and Christopher Lasch (1967) are indicators of an ambivalent cultural trend that derogates women for doing what they are expected to do. I venture to speculate that the objections of would-be upper-class traditionalists and would-be intellectual sophisticates to what they derogatorily call a "consumption culture" (the advantages of which they gladly share) is due at least in part to the fact that it is women who are in charge of it.

In general, women who have taken charge of maintaining and enhancing the husbands' and the families' status through consumption have depended on their husbands for providing the money for their status-enhancing activities, including their self-grooming. Many men actually encouraged their wives to do so because of the status advantages they themselves gained from this. A husband's pride often has consisted in showing that he makes enough money to enable his wife to enhance the glamor of self and home. The husband gained status through the consumption pattern that his wife managed. As consumption goods multiplied through technological advances and refinement in taste—after radio, television; after cars, family boats; houses, cameras, camping equipment, travel by air, and gourmet food—the taste developed further for possession and use of goods not only for the practicalities of everyday life but also for the filling of leisure time, to a point where their conspicuousness would make even a Veblen stand aghast.

I would like to show in the rest of this paper that our "consumption culture" is not all for the bad; that, on the contrary, it has improved the status of families and has helped women on the long road to emancipation and equality, especially among the middle and the working classes, by providing cultural legitimacy for women to enter the labor market, that is, to take part in production for the sake of increasing the family's consumption.

THE GIVE AND TAKE OF POWER AND STATUS

Even before the recent massive influx of women into the labor force and before the postwar growth in the demand for women's labor (Oppenheimer 1974), middle-class women took jobs, temporary or part-time, usually not to gain occupational status but to provide what they called the extras for family living: Christmas presents, a trip abroad, college tuition for Johnny. Such jobs were not meant to lead to a career, nor were they meant to indicate that their husbands did not sufficiently provide for the family's daily needs. They were meant to allow an increase in the family's consumption of status-enhancing objects. This has been much of the motivation for women's employment ever since. As Papanek (1979) notes in her aforementioned paper on "status-producing work," "increasingly, middle-class families in many societies opt for the returns of . . . women's paid employment outside the home," which is "replacing status-production work as means of social mobility." As ever more status-enhancing goods have become available and as, correlatively, people's taste has expanded, informal means for status attainment have become insufficient to meet ever-growing expectations. This has encour-

aged women to seek work outside the home. The women who meet this challenge increase their power in regard to the management of the family budget.

It has been shown that specifically in regard to economic decisions gainfully
employed wives are likely to gain power (Blood and Wolfe 1960). Nye (1963)
also found that, compared with their power in other areas, wives have gained
power in regard to purchases and living standards. In the same vein, writing
about the loss of a husband's authority in Greece and in France as a result of the
wife's employment, Constantina Safilios-Rothschild (1967) examines the
kinds of decisions the working wife usually makes. "They are those concerning
child-rearing, the purchase of clothes for the entire family, the purchase of
furniture and other household items" as well as "the budgeting of money."

She reports further that men continue to make decisions about relations with
in-laws, choice of friends, and the use of leisure time. Since keeping up
relations with kin and friends offers the opportunity to make one's acquisitions
visible, these findings mean that women manage consumption and men decide
to what status group they belong or aspire to belong. Indeed, in this process the
husbands gain status. Tamara Hareven (1982:204) writes, "The men [whose
wives worked] admitted that a second job was essential for the purchase of a
home, a car, or even smaller amenities." One of her interviewees, a woman,
explained, "We wanted a car like everybody else." Another respondent, a
male, stated, "First of all, if she hadn't worked, we'd never been able to build a
house." A skilled worker stated that, with his wife working, he "could afford a
lot of things which only with *my* pay we couldn't afford."

Cynthia Epstein reports (in a personal communication) that the working
wives of skilled blue-collar workers whom she interviewed said their husbands
tend not to feel alienated by the routine of their work since with two incomes
they are able to enjoy the status that comes from the comfortable use of leisure
time. As C. Wright Mills (1951:237) observed some four decades ago, "Each
day men sell little pieces of themselves in order to try to buy them back each
night and weekend with the coin of fun." But today the coin of fun is largely
derived from their wives' gainful activities, and it serves as a signal of status.
As Valerie Oppenheimer (1977) concluded from her empirical study of wom-
en's economic role in the family, "Although wives earn considerably less, on
the average, than husbands, wives' economic contribution to their families can
still be highly important—enough, in many cases, to provide a functional
substitute for upward occupational mobility on the husband's part, or to compensate for a husband's relatively low earnings compared to other men in his
occupational group."

As women help increase their husbands' status, the latter are willing to grant
their wives a measure of equality, as Nye (1963:264) found. The skilled worker
who was reported by Hareven to have said that with his wife's income he could

afford a lot of things went on to indicate how he and his wife were sharing household activities: "I like to help her wash the floors. . . . She found time to take the kids to a show, and we bought a car."

To be sure, some men and women may already be predisposed in their egalitarian values to have wives take jobs in the first place. However, once a wife works, the ensuing advantages may help strengthen such predispositions. Ferber (1982) has concluded from her careful analysis of empirical data that the husband's attitudes regarding his provider role are indeed influenced by the fact that his wife works outside the home. Spitze and Waite (1981) found in a longitudinal study that "controlled for the husband's perceived attitude four years earlier, the wife's taste for work and her sex-role attitudes at that time and her work experience in the intervening years all had a large impact on the husband's perceived attitude toward his wife working." These authors further note that "husbands may approve of their wives working if it is necessary to reach whatever financial level they deem appropriate for the family" (see also Oppenheimer 1977).

By a curious twist, then, through a trick played by socioeconomic development, the mandate for women to be in charge of consumption has pushed them into the sphere of production.

In spite of the fact that the idea of *separate spheres* made so much of in the nineteenth century helped keep women in their place at the same time as it devalued their household activities (note that what they did at home was no longer called work), it gave women the opportunity to develop a sense of individual self. As Jane Hood (1983:139) has observed, "A wife's bargaining power improves by the mere fact of her gaining self-esteem and obtaining increased social support."

The ever-increasing desire for consumption goods and the power to take charge of consumption, at the same time as the economy increased the demand for female labor (Oppenheimer 1974), helped to pull women into the production process. Women started working "for the family" and continued working for consumption, which brought honor by providing better living conditions, more comfort, and education for children.

Industrialization had a twofold impact on women. While it lowered their status by depriving them of partnership in production, it freed them from being observed by their husbands most of the day and from much of the control that husbands had exercised in the past.[2]

Thus, in addition to putting women in charge of consumption, the separation between home and work had the unanticipated consequence of awakening,

2. On observability as a means of social control among spouses, see Rose Laub Coser and Gerald Rokoff (1971).

even if only dimly at first, women's sense of self, their awareness that they are distinct individuals who are not tied to the land and not tied full-time to the household. They also became increasingly aware of the discrepancy between the promise of equality in the value system of our society and the reality of their subordination to men.

A similar process had taken place in the working class. The change that industrialization brought about in the position of wives is comparable to the impact the factory system had on workers. They lost the security of bondage— that is, the security that comes from being dependent yet protected—but they gained some degree of freedom by no longer being tied to the land. Having become free to sell their labor even if, as Anatole France quipped, they were equally free as the rich to sleep under bridges, workers developed a consciousness of their ability to engage in united action for the betterment of their lot. Similarly, women gained something in return for losing the security they enjoyed in preindustrial society. At the same time they lost much of their husbands' protection they escaped from much of their husbands' supervision during most of the day and developed some awareness of their individual capabilities. It was an important step toward liberation into that state of consciousness that made them consider themselves individuals with equal rights in accord with the promise of the foundation of the Republic (cf. Inkeles 1984). When the demand for female labor increased, first during World War II and then again after the war (Oppenheimer 1974; Chafe 1972), together with renewed pressures for consumption, women continued in their roles of status producers by entering the labor market, thus taking another giant step toward autonomy.

VARIABILITY BY SOCIAL CLASS

So far I have been talking mainly about the middle classes. Not in all strata of society is there an equal willingness by husbands to let their wives work and thus to relinquish some of their power. A brief examination of these exceptions will confirm the general rule of exchange I have been talking about, for it will turn out that when no status can be gained, husbands are less willing to encourage their wives to seek gainful employment.

At a low level of economic conditions a wife's resources deriving from gainful employment are likely to be low as well. For example, Mary Van Kleeck (1913) has shown that among immigrants at the beginning of the century, the lower a husband's income, the lower was the wife's income for piecework done at home. This is because the poorer the family, the worse its members' bargaining position on the labor market.

Under conditions of poverty or near-poverty the few resources a wife can add to the household don't achieve more than patchwork: a little essential food, a little essential clothing, some money for rent or utilities. Her wages will help make ends meet but will hardly lead to the type of consumption that is likely to increase social status. Consumption at the subsistence level is not visible to the community. By having a working wife the husband loses familial power without gaining status in the eyes of his peers, and his masculine self-image is diminished rather than enhanced in a community that measures a man's worth by his ability to support his family.

As a result there should be a high rate of marital disruption among the very poor when the wife goes out to work—and this is indeed the case; alternatively, the husband will resist his wife's employment no matter how poor the family. Such resistance is perhaps not as frequent in the United States as in some other countries, for example, Israel, where, even if they live in abject poverty, Arabs and some Oriental Jews may not let their wives work outside the home.

In some well-to-do households as well there are few incentives for husbands to relinquish some power in exchange for their wives' financial contributions. This happens often when men have sufficient income to afford the purchase of status-enhancing goods without additional income from their wives. High-level professionals like physicians offer a convenient example. Martha Fowlkes (1980) has shown that in many medical families men are more attached to their authority than they are in most academic families in the same community, and that, in contrast to most wives in academic families, those in medical families do not prepare to take up an occupation after the children are grown. This is so, I believe, because by the time these women are through raising their children, their husbands' status is so high that nothing the wife can earn will help improve it. Moreover, a physician in private practice would fear that his wife's gainful employment will diminish him in the eyes of a lay community in which his prestige is measured by his ability to make money, as the visible prestige of the physician on Park Avenue in New York City or Beacon Street in Boston or Harley Street in London amply testifies.

Within the strata of the well-to-do there is, however, a countervailing trend that mainly concerns those who do not derive most of their prestige from the power they exercise in the family but rather from the status they derive from the outside, for example, from a community of peers. If a husband's status is located in his occupation, his wife's employment may be more or less indifferent to his status among his colleagues. It is also unthreatening to his sense of masculinity, especially as his wife's occupational status and earnings are unlikely to be—at least visibly—superior to his own.

THE COMMUNITY AS A SOURCE OF STATUS

I continue to use the medical profession as a useful example of the trend I have just described. The prestige-grading in that profession is undergoing significant changes. As physicians increasingly derive prestige from appointments in hospitals and medical schools rather than from their private practice, and as their salaries are being bureaucratically leveled, they may well be willing to give up some of their power at home. Rather than their ability to make money, which is being judged by the lay community, it is their competence in giving service, which is being judged by their colleagues (Hall 1946), that will be the source of their social status. It is therefore to be expected that medical families will become more egalitarian in the future, although the change may be slow. Some evidence of this trend is already contained in Martha Fowlkes' research. She finds that physicians who work in hospitals insist less on exercising authority at home than do physicians in private practice. I hope that some survey researchers will put my prediction to the test.

The traditional East European Jewish family provides another example of the fact that, when a man's social status derives from his position in a community of peers, he may be more or less indifferent to his power at home. The status of the orthodox Jew was anchored in the community of the faithful. Religious activities, which were carried out by males only, took place in a collective of at least ten men—the *minyan*. Talmud readers were highly esteemed, and *Yeshiva Bokhers,* the apprentice Talmud readers, were supported by all. They were invited to share the Sabbath meal, and they were considered desirable grooms. It was not uncommon—indeed, it was acceptable—for wives to support the family while husbands spent their days reading the Talmud. Their wives' gainful activities did not diminish their social status. The Jewish husband derived prestige from his position in the religious community. As a consequence, he had little interest in who made decisions at home as long as his wife did not violate religious law. Only such violation, not her gainful employment, would diminish him in his social world.

Let us not be misled into believing that this family structure was not patriarchal. On the contrary, in the Jewish tradition a man has a covenant with God while his wife does not; her task is to support him in his efforts to maintain the covenant. In traditional Jewish culture the man's power is firmly established in the community and in tradition, and the woman's powerlessness is firmly established in the lack of expectations regarding religious activities. Her religious obligations are limited to serving her husband and her family according to prescriptions for the preparation of food, the lighting of candles for the Sabbath, and the observing of rules for her own bodily care. She does not have to take part in communal prayer and is not permitted to read from the Torah. If the religious Jewish man thanks God every morning for not having been born a woman, it is not for escaping a fate of powerlessness at home. He gives thanks for being privileged with a religious existence. His wife's powerlessness comes from being deprived of it. Her domain is the household. To this she is indeed able to contribute, adding to her husband's and her own social status if she is able to have a nice table and to show hospitality, that is, if, like most American middle- and upper-class wives, she does status-enhancing work. She can improve on this if she makes money. The Jewish husband feels no ambivalence about this because he is not thereby diminished in the sense he has of his masculinity.

As Jewish immigrants in the United States became secularized, consumption was seen as an important link between them and the host society. Although there was much poverty among Jewish immigrants, the very poor did not compose the vast majority as they did in other immigrant groups.[3] Many of the men were middle class—traders, artisans, low-level professionals—before they came here. They tolerated, even encouraged, their wives to seek jobs and to get educated in order to be qualified for filling jobs, especially since in their tradition it was perfectly acceptable to let women provide for the family.

With the secularization of Jewish culture, men tended to anchor their status in communal groups—from political movements to philanthropic organizations—and to attach importance to consumption as a means for status enhancement. In this they continued to rely on their wives, who put their traditional skills for supporting a family to good use in a society in which the emphasis was being shifted from production to consumption (Lowenthal 1961, chap. 4). The success of Jews in assimilating to American culture owes much to the fact that their women were relegated to the sphere of consumption in order that the family might rise in status, which was promised in a society in which there was a trend toward emphasizing consumption.[4]

Indeed, in the American middle class the modern American husband–father derives his prestige from his occupation, as Talcott Parsons (1949:20) has shown so well. Structurally, this is similar to deriving social status from one's religious or communal activities in that the source of prestige is extrafamilial peers. By becoming visible, a state that is being achieved through consumption, the family signals its prestige to the community. And a man's interest in achieving communal prestige can be served through the wife's gainful employment, but not through power over her. This is because his interest as well as the interest of the community in occupational prestige, and the man's interest in this being transmitted to the community, puts the emphasis on consuming rather than on controlling.

3. Of Jewish immigrants arriving in the United States between 1899 and 1910, 68 percent were skilled (including professionals), 31.7 percent unskilled—figures that compare with 21.6 percent and 78.4 percent, respectively, for all immigrants (computed from U.S. Immigration Commission III, 130–78, in Thomas Kessner [1977:33–34]). See also Andrea Tyree (1981).

4. The preceding pages are part of a preliminary analysis of research on the social roles of immigrant women, sponsored by the Russell Sage Foundation.

It is largely in the middle class—or in other strata that share middle-class aspirations—that husbands are likely to gain status if their wives are gainfully employed. If the family lives above the poverty level, any resource the woman brings in from her gainful employment increases the family's status visibly. New furniture can be bought and neighbors invited in to admire it, with some display and consumption of baked goods thrown in for good measure. Moreover, if a wife's monetary contribution causes some loss of familial power for the husband, this will be gradual, whereas the gain in social status through consumption is immediate and immediately visible.

DEVELOPING SOCIETIES

The fact that the exchange of power for status is likely to vary by social class has some implications worldwide. In a recent lecture, Kingsley Davis stated that the population growth in the world could be slowed down, if not stopped, if women were given employment because wherever women work outside the home they prefer this to having many children. If this slowing is to be achieved, we need family structures in which the men are willing to exchange some of their familial power for social status in the community. According to my reasoning this is more likely to happen on a large scale where there is a relatively large middle class. If a society remains polarized between rich and poor, the rich would not need the wives' monetary gains for an increase in social status, and the poor will hardly gain enough resources for status enhancement through a wife's work. Therefore men will see no need to give up some of their familial power.

It would be useful to examine some developing countries from this perspective. Since I am not a student of developing societies, I rely on the scholarly competence of Hanna Papanek for providing illustrations from South Asia in her comprehensive review article (1984). She points out that, according to research done by Leela Gulati (1981), "deploying female labor . . . requires that a household have sufficient resources to invest some of them in future payoffs," because in poorer neighborhoods it is "the household which can afford *not* to send their women to work [that] gains in social esteem" (emphasis supplied). However, with the development of a middle class, this seems to change. There seems to be "a shift in middle-class perceptions of consumption needs and status aspirations. As the contents of the 'status basket' change, so do family strategies for obtaining what it takes to fill it," and so "educated women take modern-sector jobs that bring in needed income." As a consequence, "in middle-class households . . . women's paid employment outside the home may provide them with resources and influence." Papanek quotes the work of Asok Mitra and associates (1980), according to which "women's participation in socioeconomic development becomes a global political and economic problem and lies at the very center of equity and distributive justice."

Papanek's remarks and citations—as well as the hypothesis I have formulated in these pages about a husband's loss of power (at least in the middle class) when his wife is gainfully employed—do not detract from the fact that conjugal equality has not been achieved even under the best of circumstances—and most circumstances are not the best. If we were to measure men's loss of familial power only by their willingness to share in household chores and child care, my hypothesis could be refuted, even though today in the American middle class husbands are more willing than they were yesteryear to do some part of housework; yet on the average their contribution has remained minimal. However, husbands of gainfully employed wives have lost some of their power, mainly in the economic realm. They no longer have the power to tell their wives not to go out to work; their provider role has been seriously curtailed, and it is mainly this role, after all, that legitimizes their domination, as the Norwegian sociologist Erik Grønset (1970) showed several decades ago.

We learn from a study of female immigrants that Haitian men in the United States grumble that the women "are not as submissive as in Haiti because, they reason, women here learn the power of money." Women "realize that their increased earning capacity, regular jobs, and the centrality of their income to the household give them more leverage and power with respect to their husbands" (Stafford 1984:184). It is to be noted that these immigrants no longer live in dire poverty after having come to North America.

True, as Goody (1984, passim) also points out in her introduction to the special issue of *Anthropologica* in which this and other studies of female immigrants are reported (Gilad and Meintel 1984), the division of labor in the household, and the domination of husbands in this sphere, has hardly changed. Yet, Gilad (1984:211) reports about Yemeni couples in Israel that "since moving to Israel, Yemeni women have gained in wealth, power, and privileges both inside and outside of their homes" and "domestic life has been . . . detrimental to men."

Further, writing about immigrant women workers in Montreal, Meintel et al. (1984:162) find that "whenever a shift [in conjugal power relations] occurs, it is likely to be found in the economic domain; i.e., some wage-earning women take part in major financial decisions from which they were formerly excluded." These immigrants from Latin America and the Caribbean not only entered a different culture, but also came from extreme poverty to more comfortable conditions where money can buy status-enhancing goods. One Colombian woman explains the change in relationships: "I used to give the money to my husband and he would take care of everything. . . . Now he has his account, and me, too, I have mine. . . . I do the food shopping. . . . For bigger things we decide together" (Meintel et al. 1984:156). The quote says it all: the woman is still in charge of the food but no longer leaves the big decisions to her husband alone.

From her empirical study of conjugal relations in seven cities—Detroit, Tokyo, Paris, Louvain, Athens, Los Angeles, and Calgary—Ruth Katz (1983) concludes that "overall . . . the modern urban family, as it has developed in several societies, is close to achieving an equal allocation of power between marital partners." She adds, however, that "a second general finding is that even though power allocation tends towards equality, the traditional division of roles and responsibilities between the spouses survives. In other words, husbands have relinquished their overall dominance over almost every sphere of conjugal interaction except over those areas closely related to male roles" in the household.

Be this as it may, today some men do share in taking care of household routines. And what is more important, those who do, even if they are a small minority, are no longer subject to ridicule. While the norms as to women's cultural mandate may not have changed much,[5] the symbolism of what is to be considered masculine or feminine has changed to some extent. The glass may not be even half full, but the low level of its content is—ever so slowly—rising.

I believe that the equality of women, including but not limited to their freedom to seek employment and their consciousness that it is in their interest to seek employment and to have fewer children, depends to a large extent on the interests that women *and* men have in their level of consumption and in the level of consumption they aspire to for their children. Perhaps this is not a nice thing to say. Perhaps it would be nicer to be able to say that gender equality depends on insight of what is decent. To be sure, equality can be fostered more easily where a more egalitarian value system favors more egalitarian family relationships (Rodman 1967; Katz and Peres, 1985). And there are plenty of decent men—but more than individual decency is needed. The importance of the structural interests of men and women in generating such social change in family relations should not be underestimated. As the philosopher Vico said more than 250 years ago, it is out of "ferocity, avarice and ambition" that the

5. I can only speculate (feebly, for that matter) about some reasons why the sphere of the household is the most resistant to sex equality. One reason could be that this sphere, more than any other, attacks the cultural mandate that women's major commitment be to the family. Another reason could be that this realm is the last bastion, so to speak, of what men consider male strength. Suzanne Keller (1988) believes that in spite of all the changes that have taken place in the status of women in American society in the last two decades, the basic gender definitions have not changed. I believe that what is at stake in the household division of labor is that men simply have no interest in changing it—there is nothing in it for them.

"strength, riches and wisdom of commonwealths [have been created]" and "narrow ends [were] employed to preserve the human race upon earth" (Vico 1925).

REFERENCES

Blake, Judith. 1974. "Changing Status of Women in Developed Countries." *Scientific American* 231:24, 1136–47.

Blau, Peter M. 1964. *Exchange and Power in Social Life*. New York: John Wiley and Sons.

Blood, Robert O., Jr., and Donald M. Wolfe. 1960. *Husbands and Wives: The Dynamics of Married Living*. New York: Free Press.

Bourdieu, Pierre. 1977. *Reproduction in Education, Society, and Culture*. Beverly Hills: Sage Publications.

Chafe, William H. 1972. *The American Woman: Her Changing Social, Economic, and Political Roles, 1920–1970*. New York: Oxford University Press.

Coser, Rose Laub, and Gerald Rokoff. 1971. "Women in the Occupational World: Social Disruption and Conflict." *Social Problems* 18 (Spring):535–52.

Coser, Rose Laub, and Lewis A. Coser. 1974. "The Housewife and Her Greedy Family." In *Greedy Institutions*, edited by Lewis A. Coser. New York: Free Press.

Davis, Kingsley. 1983. "Development without Progress: The Economic Demography of the Third World." SUNY-Stony Brook University Lecture, March 17.

DiMaggio, Paul. 1982. "Cultural Capital and School Success: The Impact of Status Culture Participation on the Grades of U.S. High School Students." *American Sociological Review* 47:189–201.

Ferber, Marianne A. 1982. "Labor-Market Participation of Young Married Women: Causes and Effects." *Journal of Marriage and the Family* 44:457–68.

Fowlkes, Martha R. 1980. *Behind Every Successful Man: Wives of Medicine and Academia*. New York: Columbia University Press.

Gilad, Lisa. 1984. "The Transformation of the Conjugal Power Base: Yemeni Jewish Couples in an Israeli Town." In Gilad and Meintel 1984:191–215.

Gilad, Lisa, and Deirdre Meintel, eds. 1984. *Female Migrants and the Work Force: Domestic Repercussions*. *Anthropologica* (Special Issue) 26.

Goody, Esther. "Introduction" to Gilad and Meintel 1984:123–34.

Gorer, Geoffrey. 1948. *The American People: A Study in National Character*. New York: W. W. Norton.

Grønset, Erik. 1970. "The Dysfunctionality of the Husband Provider Role in Industrialized Societies." Paper for the Seventh World Congress of Sociology, Mimeo.

Gulati, Leela. 1981. *Profiles in Female Poverty: A Study of Five Poor Working Women in Kerala*. Oxford: Pergamon Press.

Hall, Oswald. 1946. "The Informal Organization of the Medical Profession." *Canadian Journal of Economics and Political Science* 12:30–41.

Hareven, Tamara. 1982. *Family Time and Industrial Time*. Cambridge: Cambridge University Press.

Hood, Jane C. 1983. *Becoming a Two-Job Family*. New York: Praeger.

Inkeles, Alex. 1984. "The Responsiveness of Family Patterns to Economic Change in the United States." *The Tocqueville Review* 6:5–50.

Katz, Ruth. 1983. "Conjugal Power: A Comparative Analysis." *International Journal of Sociology of the Family* 13:79–101.

Katz, Ruth, and Yochanan Peres. 1985. "Is Resource Theory Equally Applicable to Wives and Husbands?" *Journal of Comparative Family Studies* 16:1–10.

Keller, Suzanne. 1988. "Women in the 21st Century: Summing Up and Going Forward." Paper presented at the Radcliffe Conference *Defining the Challenge*.

Kessner, Thomas. 1977. *The Golden Door*. New York: Oxford University Press.

Lasch, Christopher. 1967. *The New Radicalism in America 1889–1963*, New York: Random House.

Lowenthal, Leo. 1961. *Literature, Popular Culture, and Society*. Englewood Cliffs: Prentice-Hall.

Meintel, Deirdre, Micheline Labelle, Genevieve Turcotte, and Marianne Kempeers. 1984. "Migration, Wage Labor, and Domestic Relationships: Immigrant Women Workers in Montreal." In Gilad and Meintel 1984:135–69.

Merton, Robert K. 1968. *Social Theory and Social Structure*. New York: Free Press.

Mills, C. Wright. (1951). *White Collar: The American Middle Classes*. New York: Oxford University Press.

Mitra, Asok, Lalit P. Pathak, and Shekhar Mukherji. 1980. *The Status of Women: Shifts in Occupational Participation, 1961–1971*. New Delhi: An ICSSR/JNU Study. Abhinav Publications.

Mortimer, Jeylan T., and Glorian Sorensen. 1984. "Men, Women, Work, and Family." In *Women in the Workplace: Effects on Families,* edited by Kathryn M. Borman, Daisy Quarm, and Sarah Gideonse. Norwood, N.J.: Ablex Publishing Corp.

Nye, F. Ivan. 1963. "Marital Interaction." In *The Employed Mother*, edited by F. Ivan Nye and Lois W. Hoffman, Chicago: Rand McNally.

Oppenheimer, Valerie Kincade. 1974. "Demographic Influences on Female Employment and the Status of Women." In *Changing Women in a Changing Society*, edited by Joan Huber. Chicago: University of Chicago Press.

———. 1977. "The Sociology of Women's Economic Role in the Family." *American Sociological Review* 42:387–406.

Papanek, Hanna. 1979. "Family Status Production: The 'Work' and 'Nonwork' of Women." *Signs: Journal of Women in Culture and Society* 4:775–81.

———. 1984. "False Specialization and the Purdah of Scholarship—A Review Article." *Journal of Asian Studies* 44:127–48.

Parsons, Talcott. 1949. *Essays in Sociological Theory Pure and Applied*. Glencoe, Ill.: Free Press.

Riesman, David. 1964. "Two Generations." *Daedalus* 93:711–35.

Rodman, Hyman. 1967. "Marital Power in France, Greece, Yugoslavia, and the United States: A Cross-National Discussion." *Journal of Marriage and the Family* 29:320–24.

———. 1972. "Marital Power and the Theory of Resources in Cultural Context." *Journal of Comparative Family Studies* 3:50–67.

Rosenfeld, Jeffrey. 1974. "Inheritance: A Sex Related System of Exchange." In *The Family, Its Structures and Functions*, edited by Rose L. Coser. New York: St. Martin's.

Safilios-Rothschild, Constantina. 1967. "A Comparison of Power Structure and Marital Satisfaction in Urban Greek and French Families." *Journal of Marriage and the Family* 27:345–52.

Scanzoni, J. 1970. *Opportunity and the Family*. New York: Free Press.

———. 1972. *Sexual Bargaining*. Englewood Cliffs: Prentice-Hall.

———. 1979. "Social Processes and Power in Families." In *Contemporary Theories about the Family,* vol. I, edited by W. R. Burr, R. Hill, F. I. Nye, and I. L. Reixx. New York: Free Press.

Spitze, Glenna D., and Linda J. Waite. 1981. "Wives' Employment: The Role of Husbands' Perceived Attitudes." *Journal of Marriage and the Family* 43:117–24.

Stafford, Susan H. Buchanan. 1984. "Haitian Immigrant Women: A Cultural Perspective." In Gilad and Meintel 1984:171–89.

Tyree, Andrea. 1981. "Comments on the Observed and Predicted Economic Success of Immigrants." In *Gateways,* edited by Barry Chiswick. Washington, D.C.: American Enterprise Institute.

Van Kleeck, Mary. 1913. *The Artificial Flower Makers*. New York: Russell Sage Foundation, Survey Associates, Inc.

Veblen, Thorstein. 1953. *The Theory of the Leisure Class*. New York: New American Library.

Vico, Giovanni Battista. 1925. *La Scienza Nuova Seconda,* edited by F. Nicolini, translated by T. G. Bergin and M. H. Fisch. Ithaca: Cornell University Press, 1948. Paragraphs 132 & 1108, in Karl Lowith, *Meaning in History*. Chicago: University of Chicago Press, 1949, p. 126.

Weber, Max. 1958. "Class, Status and Power." In *From Max Weber,* edited by H. H. Gerth and C. W. Mills. New York: Oxford University Press.

———. 1978. *Economy and Society,* edited by Guenther Roth and Claus Wittich. Berkeley: University of California Press.

Wylie, Philip. 1942. *The Generation of Vipers*. New York: Rinehart.

I I I I I I I The Cultural Perspective and the Study of Work

CYNTHIA FUCHS EPSTEIN

The current interest in the culture of the workplace is regarded by many as new, but sociological research linking culture and social structure has a long history. Rich and textured accounts of the lives and beliefs of working people were written in the early days of our discipline. Not long after the turn of the century, the Russell Sage Foundation published volumes reporting research on artificial flower makers (Van Kleeck 1913) and women munitions workers (Hewes 1917), and later, a volume on relations between employees and management in Filene's Department Store (LaDame 1930). Members of the Chicago School produced fine-grained studies of a wide range of occupations, both "respectable" and deviant (Cottrell 1940; Hughes 1958; Polsky 1971). Scholars associated with the Human Relations school of organizational behavior studied shop floor relationships, noting the interaction between the social needs and ties of workers and their productivity at work (Roethlisberger and Dickson 1939; Roy 1952). In the 1950s a generation of organizational sociologists (for example, Gouldner 1954a, 1954b; Lipset, Trow, and Coleman 1956, and many others) enriched classical theories of bureaucracy and oligarchy with their observations and insights on work life in factories and print shops.

Since midcentury, some researchers have continued this emphasis on the patterns of community and identity that workers forge while at work (for example, Chinoy 1955; Garson 1977). But the discipline's mainstream has moved it in other directions, as methodological and theoretical developments have led researchers away from the cultural or human side of work—that is,

The author wishes to acknowledge the support of the Russell Sage Foundation in the preparation of this paper, and the critical comments and editorial suggestions of Steven Vallas and Howard Epstein.

concerns with workplace culture and the formation of occupational communities and identity. As a result, much of the richness that characterized earlier generations of occupational research has been lost, as sociologists have neglected to inquire into the specific meanings workers bring to bear on their work and the link between work values and the wider culture. Drawing on existing case studies and on current research conducted by Kai Erikson and myself on the workplace and community culture of communications workers, this essay will illustrate the rewards of paying greater attention to these cultural themes and the irreducibly human side of work.

MISPLACED MATERIALISM IN THE SOCIOLOGY OF OCCUPATIONS

Three intellectual trends are especially noteworthy in the sociology of work during the past quarter-century: the growth of survey research on work attitudes (especially job satisfaction); the increasing influence of Marxist theory; and the rise of a "new structuralism," focused on how the characteristics of firms affect the distribution of job rewards. While these developments have made important contributions, they have not addressed a number of important issues related to the dynamics of inequality.

Survey research that blossomed from the 1950s through the 1970s particularly influenced the ways in which working people were studied by focusing on problems amenable to the method. It neglected other types of problems and sometimes resulted in a skewed understanding of the issues explored. Surveys tended to focus on social psychological attributes reported by workers, especially job satisfaction without regard to context.[1] Thus, for example, the responses to surveys have been accepted as accurate without consideration of the norms that prescribe certain answers to questions or of discrepancies between attitudes and the actual behavior of respondents. Furthermore, surveys permit analysis of only those factors that lent themselves to identification by questionnaire.

Theoretical work also affected the ways in which research on the workplace was conducted.[2] Issues such as the impact of technology and alienation were addressed with models that provided a historical, macrostructural framework but that simultaneously limited discussion of workplace behavior. Labor pro-

1. For a thorough review of the job satisfaction literature, see Locke 1976. See also Kalleberg 1977 and Mottaz 1985.

2. This focus on the labor process drew special inspiration from Braverman's *Labor and Monopoly Capital* (1974) and is reflected in the work of Friedman (1977), Edwards (1979), Burawoy (1979, 1985), and the studies in Zimbalist 1979. For discussion see Wood 1982 and Salaman 1986.

cess theorists have emphasized the role of class power and economic exploitation—valid concerns, to be sure—but in ways that have often yielded wooden models of the wage–labor relation, divorced from the actual experience of work in people's everyday lives. Remarkably few of the major concerns that workers bring to their jobs—security, conviviality, tradition, and opportunity, to say nothing of pay—are given much room in the models of labor process theorists.

A third and more recent development in the sociology of work has been called the new structuralism (Baron and Bielby 1980; Kalleberg and Berg 1987). As with labor process studies, the power of this strand of research derives from its macrosocial view of firms, industries, and occupations. Yet, by focusing on such matters as industrial variations in income inequality and labor market structures, analysis of the workplace is further removed from concrete patterns of culture and the community at work. To be sure, these analysts speculate insightfully about the forces that create such a phenomenon as sex segregation in organizations (Bielby and Baron 1986), but the type of statistical data they use does not permit explanation from the point of view of workers and their employers. Hence, questions of meaning are inferred rather than described, leading one critic to ask, "Where have all the workers gone?" (Simpson 1989).

Although surveys of the workplace have provided important findings about the work attitudes among particular categories of people—managers, foremen, union members—we have not learned much about the feedback processes between individuals and their wider cultural environments. And while neo-Marxist and new structuralist studies have sharpened our understanding of economic inequality, we have learned remarkably little about the place of work in people's lives. In our quest for hard, measurably facts concerning work, we have forgotten to ask what conceptions people hold about work, whether or how people may identify with their jobs, and how the boundaries between the workplace and other spheres of life are experienced. In short, the concepts of workplace culture and occupational communities and identities have been gathering dust, and our craft is the poorer for it.

Once these conceptual tools are put to use, however, it becomes possible to address a set of intriguing questions and paradoxes about workplace behavior. We can begin to ask, for example, why factory and clerical workers sometimes express satisfaction with or even choose repetitive jobs, and how they cope with boring work (Molstad 1986). We can inquire into the ways in which men and women are attracted or recruited to different kinds of work. We can explore the processes that maintain salient boundaries at work, demarcating skilled from nonskilled labor, clean tasks from "dirty" work, and "manly" jobs from "women's work." We can begin to investigate the nature of the work ethic in our culture as well as the varied conceptions of work held by different groups and classes in our society (Morse and Weiss 1955; Joyce 1987).

The renaissance of research on the workplace that does not treat it as an isolated domain has begun to reveal the complex relationship of work to all aspects of our lives. Such research is an attempt to "breach the wall of demarcation" (McCloskey 1986) and to "blur genres," as Clifford Geertz (1984) suggests. The identification of the culture of work is part of the process—exploring the beliefs that people hold about their jobs and the organizations in which it is performed and their beliefs about the kinds of people suited to work with them. Such a perspective reminds us that jobs have mystiques, auras—and, sometimes, stigmas—attached to them that go well beyond the content of their tasks. Jobs bring their occupants prestige or dishonor, a sense of being manly or womanly, and sometimes of being sacred or profane. At the same time, wider cultural beliefs assign value to the way work is organized: by sex, by group, in a circle or on a line, defining its organization as critical or, in some cases, improper.[3] The wider culture establishes rules that specify how people ought to think and act about their work, and consequently about themselves. It encourages some groups to aspire to certain jobs, while requiring other groups to accept others. To tear the workplace out of the cultural context that gives it meaning is to substitute simplistic models for the complex richness of human life.

IN SEARCH OF THE CULTURE OF THE WORKPLACE

Among the sociologists whose work is important in providing textured accounts of work life is the scholar Sallie Westwood (1982), whose study of women textile factory workers shows how these people sought to "domesticate" their workplaces, drawing on their roles in the family to gain a measure of freedom from their male overseers in the factory. One finds a similar emphasis on the nature and sources of workplace culture in the research of Lamphere (1985), Yarrow (1987), Kimeldorf (1985), and several others. Their rich descriptions and analyses have shown that workers are not passive, obedient creatures but active beings who imbue their work situations with meanings and who respond to organizational demands in ways that often reflect their involvements outside the sphere of work.

3. Cultures vary with respect to these matters. In a study of occupational sex segregation in twelve industrial countries, Roos (1985) found considerable differences among them. Japan, for example, exhibited the greatest discrepancy in the average prestige of men's and women's jobs—women's jobs having significantly lower prestige.

In much of this developing literature one finds a sense of optimism or despair present in the culture seeping into the workplace and affecting the way workers view their work roles. Workers I have interviewed during my research on the communications industry often know this better than sociologists. The fact is sometimes evident in the popular culture, where at least one modern balladeer, Bruce Springsteen, has chronicled the changing lives and expectations of workers in lyrics such as these:

> Seems like there ain't nobody wants to come down here no more
> They're closing down the textile mills across the railroad tracks
> Foreman says these jobs are going, boys
> And they ain't coming back to your hometown.

As Springsteen's songs remind the listener, the passing of steel mills and automobile factories (and of many manual crafts in the communications industry) represents more than a loss of jobs. New jobs have come to replace some of those lost by the fading of old methods and industries. But people are hurt in the process, and the loss of certain types of jobs creates a change in ethos as well; a change also brought about by other forces—in style of life, in the relations between the sexes, in parenting, and in the definition of the meaning of work in their lives.

For those with a stake in an older ethos, and even those who merely view it with nostalgia, a kind of mourning goes on. These sentiments are important in their own right, but they are also important because they constitute a potential agenda for public policy issues. The young worry, along with their rock hero, about a loss of opportunity; residents of factory towns sense the loss of the axis that has held their communities together; and groups ranging from the fundamentalist far right to the sentimental left mourn the passing of old traditions, regardless of their views. These attitudes and fears have serious consequences for public policy and legislation.

What does this threatened ethos consist of? In some ways it is a caricature. In spite of the steady decline in their numbers, in the popular culture the blue-collar worker is conceived as the prototypical American. He is the independent Marlboro man, a spiritual cowboy in a Ford or Chrysler, a car with a big engine. His wife is the little woman who takes care of the dream house—something detached with a bit of a yard, especially nice if near water or the woods. Blue-collar workers often are immersed in ethnic ties and networks, and their work and home communities are characterized by strong group boundaries and hearty prejudices that have kept some people together and excluded others; have made access to some jobs predictable and dependable and have kept strangers out (Shostak 1969; Kornblum 1974).

The things one valued in this ethos were doing a good job and trying to get ahead, devoting oneself to traditional family life, and deriving comfort from performing these roles. Another aspect seemed to be the creation of identity through work; the Marlboro man was defined by his occupation, and the little woman by her man's. Whatever the reality, these stereotypes were an important part of the American dream. As Alice Rossi (1980) and others have pointed out, this ethos emanated from a generation that grew up in the Depression and went through World War II. But it did affect other generations and social scientists as well. Of course, these beliefs have begun to falter as times and the realities of working-class life change, and we worry as a nation that there is no longer a good fit between work and people's values.

Many social scientists have noted that the production goals of large corporations today often are at odds with the goals of the working person, although workers certainly do care about having jobs. Social scientists also have idealized some workers and belittled the jobs of others. Until recently, they have focused mainly on white, male workers; their concern about the alienation felt by white men has crowded out concern for the alienation women might feel in jobs usually more routinized and pedestrian (including domestic work) than those of men. In this, social scientists have reflected the wider cultural bias that exhibits little concern about how women fare in the workplace because women are not supposed to be there or because their work involvements are alleged to be a subsidiary part of their lives (Feldberg and Glenn 1979).

Yet even this research on male workers has often generated narrow observations because social scientists have failed to understand how the interplay among work, community and family ties tempers not only women's, but also men's involvements at work. Perhaps even more important, when their focus is on white, male work communities, social scientists have been slow to observe that the practices that make the workplace so warm and secure for some inflict alienation and punishment on others, those who are denied admission into the occupational spheres dominated by white men. The channeling of opportunity to sons of workers who hold favored occupations comes at a heavy cost to those who lack the proper attributes, a fact largely unobserved by many social researchers. Save for research on the structure and functioning of labor markets (for example, Bonacich 1976), and the work of Kornblum (1974) one looks in vain for sensitive accounts of the social processes that underlie racial segregation and boundaries within the workplace itself.

In our research on communications workers we found ample evidence of communal behavior among workers, with all the gemeinschaft relations celebrated by students of workplace solidarity. The formation of occupational identity was especially pronounced among cable splicers, who repair and maintain heavy lines atop poles and underground. Some splicers suggested to us that they could distinguish members of their craft at large union meetings just by looking at them. "We've all come from the same place," one splicer told us. Another recalled,

> There used to be a commercial on television. It was a family decorating a Christmas tree and then it was good night time. The husband and wife had gone to bed, the children in bed, now the lights are out and the phone rings. The guy answers the phone and he gets up and gets dressed. He goes out to his car and he drives to a Telephone garage. He gets in his truck and he clears a failure. He was a splicer. . . . The idea was that we, the telephone company, are willing to work under any conditions at anytime to give you, the people, service. I appreciated that commercial. I don't think too many other people really remember it, but I do because that's what we do. *Being a splicer is us.*

However, another, less innocent aspect of this occupational community must be stressed. While the culture of the splicers provides a source of solidarity for members of the group, such solidary relations come at the direct expense of other workers—especially women—who are discouraged from entering the fold.

While splicers and other craft workers suggested in conversations that women would be welcome in their trade, they infuse their work with an ethos of manliness that is an all but physical barrier to women. Their occupational culture emphasizes the physical strength, endurance, and toughness required to deal with dirty and dangerous work. The splicers have taken the ethos of manliness well beyond what might reasonably be viewed as natural in manual work, and it serves to defend their craft against potential interlopers. Some splicers questioned the character of male workers in a rival craft—installation and repair technicians—asserting they were too delicate to be good at cable work.

When we asked splicers what made them different from other craft workers, one replied, "We're not afraid to get down in the mud and get dirty like they are. An installer would call for help if he has to carry a twenty-eight-foot ladder. A splicer would carry the ladder himself and wouldn't think about it." Equipped with this ethos of manliness, splicers have staked out an occupational terrain as uniquely their own. Not coincidentally, despite efforts to dissolve gender boundaries, the splicer's craft remains more than 95 percent male.

The nature and dynamics of workplace culture are thus vital determinants of workers' career paths. Yet my research repeatedly suggested that the workplace is not an island, separated from other institutional spheres. Home and work overlap; they interrelate and affect one another. Workers bring into the workplace values and expectations from home and community that have bearing on their involvements and aspirations while at work. Conversely, from the workplace the worker takes to the family a self altered by frustration or a sense of efficacy that affects his or her role as father or mother or member of the community. To view work behavior in isolation from other role relationships is to tear it out of the normative context that sustains it and gives it meaning.

In some cases Erikson and I found that patterns of authority in the home affected workers' view of career opportunities. The rumination of one telephone operator was representative of many others. Asked how she felt about the prospect of promotion and the notion of a career, she said, "I worry about what would happen if I work my way up and become a supervisor. . . . Some women can do that. They figure, well, women's lib: they worked their way up. . . . *I don't think I could do that to him* [her husband] *as a man.* . . . Every week my paycheck is a little more than his because of all the time he takes off. I know it aggravates him—if I make a dollar or two more, he's frustrated that I'm making more than him."

In cases such as these, the normative order outside the workplace actively discourages women from aspiring to managerial careers. In other cases, cultural values can have a different effect: they can define lines of work as unacceptable for men and inflict real pain on those who dare to transgress. This was plainly true for male telephone operators, whose masculinity was assaulted virtually every day by the wider culture's perspective on their jobs. As one male operator told us, "I got people calling me a 'tinker bell,' and 'oh, you're one of them gay bastards. . . .' They figure I'm in a female office so I must be queer. I've had a guy a couple of times—six months later he remembers me. He's coming out here to take me out *to tea*." In some cases, gender ideology was so entrenched as to cause male workers to refuse operators' jobs. As one operator told us, "I have a twenty-three year-old son, and last year he lost his job. I said to him, 'Why don't you fill out an application for the phone company?' He said, 'Ma, I think if they offered me $1,000 a week tax-free, I wouldn't take that job. When I go up with you now [to visit the telephone company] and I see those guys sitting in there I wonder *what's wrong* with them. Are they pansies or what?' "

Thus the wider culture encourages some to pursue particular occupations while discouraging others. To say this is not to embrace a simple cultural determinism, for the effect of cultural values on workers may often depend on the specific organizational settings in which they are employed. For example, the wider culture exalts the notion of getting ahead—the "tradition of opportunity," as Ely Chinoy termed it (1955). Yet people can interpret this value in many ways and can at times—as when they are denied opportunity at their jobs—look outside the employment setting for their attainments. For a man, it might mean fixing up a boat or a car; for a woman, it might be having another baby (Gerson 1985).

While men in craft and professional positions may derive their identities from their work—and so too may women workers—it is all but impossible to identify oneself on the basis of work that is segmented and unskilled, such as routine, repetitive clerical or production work. Not surprisingly, many of the workers we have spoken to define themselves not in terms of their jobs, but on the basis of their community and kin: where they come from and where they live is who they are. For such workers, the prospect of moving to a new location (whether owing to a promotion or an involuntary transfer) implies a loss of ties that are far more important than the tie to work. Even if some were able to relocate, they would find it difficult to reproduce their lives and their identities. This point is of broader relevance to organizational change, for persons who have learned to look outside their jobs for fulfillment may be loath to embrace changes in the workplace—even changes that promise to improve their working lives—if they fear there will be a concomitant cost to the other spheres of their lives. Thus the roles workers play in the various spheres of their lives form a whole constellation of activities that are closely intertwined. What happens at the workplace is only part of the picture.

The last several decades of occupational sociology have added to our knowledge of the organizational bases of work attitudes. We have gained an understanding of the varied forms of control over work that have developed under industrial capitalism and of the role of firms and industries in fostering economic and social inequalities. Less well developed are certain older themes involving the meaning of work and patterns of workplace culture and identity. Indeed, these issues—once the central objects of social research—have been severely neglected. In this paper I have illustrated some of the ways in which these themes might be addressed, and why. The logic of my argument should by now be clear. The sociology of work is not likely to advance unless we attend to the meanings workers attach to their jobs and to the myriad links among these meanings, the nonwork spheres of life, and the wider culture of our society.

REFERENCES

Baron, James N., and William T. Bielby. 1980. "Bringing the Firms Back In: Stratification, Segmentation and the Organization of Work." *American Sociological Review* 45:737–65.
Bielby, William T., and James N. Baron. 1986. "Men and Women at Work: Sex Segregation and Statistical Discrimination." *American Journal of Sociology* 91:759–99.
Bonacich, Edna. 1976. "Ethnic Antagonisms under Advanced Capitalism: A Split Labor Market Approach." *American Sociological Review* 41:34–51.
Braverman, Harry. 1974. *Labor and Monopoly Capital: The Degradation of Work in the Twentieth Century*. New York: Monthly Review Press.

Burawoy, Michael. 1979. *Manufacturing Consent: Changes in the Labor Process under Monopoly Capitalism*. Chicago: University of Chicago Press.

———. 1985. *The Politics of Production: Factory Regimes under Capitalism and Socialism*. London: Verso.

Chinoy, Ely. 1955. *Automobile Workers and the American Dream*. Garden City, N.Y.: Doubleday.

Cockburn, Cynthia. 1983. *Brothers: Male Dominance and Technological Change*. London: Pluto.

Cottrell, W. F. 1940. *The Railroader*. Stanford: Stanford University Press.

DiFazio, William. 1985. *Longshoring: Community and Resistance on the Brooklyn Waterfront*. South Hadley, Mass.: Bergin and Garvey.

Dubin, Robert. 1956. "Industrial Workers' Worlds: A Study of the Central Life Interests of Industrial Workers." *Social Problems* 3.

Edwards, Richard C. 1979. *Contested Terrain: The Transformation of the Workplace in the Twentieth Century*. New York: Basic Books.

Feldberg, Rosyln, and Evelyn Glenn. 1979. "Male and Female: Job vs. Gender Models in the Sociology of Work." *Social Problems* 26(5).

Friedman, Andrew. 1977. *Industry and Labor: Class Struggle at Work and Monopoly Capital*. London: Macmillan.

Garson, Barbara. 1977. *All the Livelong Day: The Meaning and Demeaning of Routine Work*. New York: Penguin.

Geertz, Clifford. 1984. *Local Knowledge: Further Essays in Interpretive Anthropology*. New York: Basic Books.

Gerson, Kathleen. 1985. *Hard Choices: How Women Decide about Work, Career and Motherhood*. Berkeley: University of California Press.

Gouldner, Alvin. 1954a. *Patterns of Industrial Bureaucracy*. New York: Free Press.

———. 1954b. *Wildcat Strike*. Yellow Springs, Ohio: Antioch Press.

Halle, David. 1984. *America's Working Man: Work, Home, and Politics among Blue-Collar Property Owners*. Chicago: University of Chicago.

Hewes, Amy. 1917. *Women as Munitions Makers: A Study of Conditions in Bridgeport, Connecticut*. N.Y.: The Russell Sage Foundation.

Hughes, E. C. 1958. *Men and Their Work*. New York: Free Press.

Joyce, Patrick. 1987. "Introduction." In *The Historical Meanings of Work*, edited by P. Joyce. Cambridge: Cambridge University Press.

Kalleberg, Arne. 1977. "Work Values and Job Rewards: A Theory of Job Satisfaction." *American Sociological Review* 42:124–43.

Kalleberg, Arne, and Ivar Berg. 1987. *Work and Industry: Structures, Markets and Processes*. New York: Plenum.

Kimeldorf, Howard. 1985. "Working Class Culture, Occupational Recruitment and Union Politics." *Social Forces* 64(2).

Kornblum, William. 1974. *Blue Collar Community*. Chicago: University of Chicago Press.

LaDame, Mary. 1930. *The Filene Store: A Study of Employees' Relation to Management in a Retail Store*. N.Y.: The Russell Sage Foundation.

Lamphere, Louise. 1985. "Bringing the Family to Work: Women's Culture on the Shop Floor." *Feminist Studies* 11:519–40.

Lipset, S. M., Trow, M., and Coleman, J. 1956. *Union Democracy: The Internal Politics of the International Typographers' Union*. Glencoe, Ill.: Free Press.

Locke, Edwin A. 1976. "The Nature and Causes of Job Satisfaction." In *Handbook of Industrial and Organization Psychology,* edited by M. D. Dunnette. Chicago: Rand McNally.

McCloskey, Donald. 1986. "The Post-Modern Rhetoric of Sociology." *Contemporary Sociology* 16:815–18.

Molstad, Clark. 1986. "Choosing and Coping with Boring Work." *Urban Life* 15(2):215–36.

Morse, Nancy, and Robert S. Weiss. 1955. "The Function and Meaning of Work and the Job." *American Sociological Review* 20:191–98.

Mottaz, Clifford. 1985. "Relative Importance of Intrinsic and Extrinsic Rewards as Determinants of Work Satisfaction." *Sociological Quarterly* 26(3):365–85.

Polsky, Ned. 1971. *Hustlers, Beats and Others.* Hammondsworth: Penguin.

Roethlisberger, F. J., and W. J. Dickson. 1939. *Management and the Worker.* Cambridge: Harvard University Press.

Roos, Patricia. 1985. *Gender and Work: A Comparative Analysis of Industrial Societies.* Albany: State University of New York.

Rossi, Alice. 1980. "Life-span Theories and Women's Lives." *Signs* 6(1):4–32.

Roy, Donald. 1952. "Quota Restrictions and Goldbricking in a Machine Shop." *American Journal of Sociology* 57.

Salaman, G. 1972. *Community and Occupation: An Exploration of Work/Leisure Relationships.* Cambridge: Cambridge University Press.

———. 1986. *Working.* London: Tavistock.

Shostak, Arthur. 1969. *Blue-Collar Life.* New York: Random House.

Simpson, Ida Harper. 1989. "The Sociology of Work: Where Have All the Workers Gone?" *Social Forces* 67(3).

Van Kleeck, Mary. 1913. *Women in the Bookbinding Trade.* N.Y.: Russell Sage Publications.

Westwood, Sallie. 1982. *All Day, Every Day: Factory and Family in the Making of Women's Lives.* Chicago: University of Illinois Press.

Wood, Stephen, ed. 1982. *The Degradation of Work? Skill, Deskilling and the Labour Process.* London: Hutchinson.

Yankelovich, Daniel. 1974. "The Meaning of Work." In *The Worker and the Job,* edited by Jerome Rosow. New York: Prentice-Hall.

Yarrow, Michael. 1987. "Gender and Class in the Developing Consciousness of Appalachian Coal Miners." Paper presented at the Fifth Annual Conference on the Labour Process, University of Manchester Institute of Science and Technology, Great Britain.

Zimbalist, A., ed. 1979. *Case Studies on the Labor Process.* New York: Monthly Review Press.

I I I I I I I I Work Institutions
and the Sociology of
Everyday Life

ARTHUR L. STINCHCOMBE

The purpose of this chapter is to outline new research opportunities in the sociology of work that grow out of the "sociology of everyday
life," as practiced by Goffman, Garfinkel, and Lévi-Strauss (for example,
Goffman 1963; Garfinkel 1967; and for an application of Lévi-Strauss, Stinchcombe 1982). In particular I want to address the ancient problem of the relations
between formal and informal organization in work life and to include in the
informal organization the place of work in the family and community.

I take it that the central focus of the sociology of everyday life tradition is the
detailed analysis of discourse, including nonverbal communication, for what it
shows about the semiconscious or unconscious norms governing social interaction. That is, many of the norms analyzed by Goffman, Garfinkel, and Lévi-
Strauss are like the norms of grammar or phonetics, unconsciously applied
except in a few contexts, as phonetics is used in courses teaching the language
to foreigners. When one observes with Goffman how strangers meeting on the
street look away after they are within the distance where looking is staring, we
all recognize that we have followed the norm without ever formulating it. And
we certainly followed it without ever relating it to semiconscious norms that are
part of the same structure, such as not making a scene. Making a scene means
making it hard for others to follow the norm of civil inattention. We obviously
learned the norm and the structure of norms in which it is embedded through
socialization (perhaps, if Chomsky and others are right about where linguistic

Allen Grimshaw gave extensive, detailed, and relevant comments. I have sometimes
used them to sharpen the formulation of our differences, sometimes to improve my
thought.

normative structures come from, with some substantial contribution from the unconscious), but equally obviously we would not give good explanations of it and would have to learn its deep structure from a professional like Goffman.

My first argument below will be that informal organization, which we learned twenty years ago to talk of as a matter of social organization, of primary and secondary relations, is actually a matter of a style of discourse, a matter of when certain unconscious norms of switching between formal and informal modes of talking have application. We did not understand our own norms of when we talk to people the way we talk in "informal organization" at work, and so we mistook a cultural form for a social organizational form.

One thing I want to complain about that is relevant to this point is that too few people are doing field observation of work institutions. Only in the British section of the sociology of science is it routine to collect ethnographic data about social action, social interaction, and various kinds of discourse that happen in work institutions. We have tended in recent years, first, not to do ethnography, and, second, to confine what little we did to the informal part of the old dichotomy of formal and informal. Except for the "strong programme" sociology of science, then, ethnographic accounts of work in our discipline tend to be about such topics as what happens in families when women take their careers seriously (for example, Gerstel and Gross's study *Commuter Marriage* [1984]) or what happens in slums when the men do not have any work or don't take what work they have seriously (for example, in Liebow 1967).

INFORMAL ORGANIZATION AS A STYLE OF DISCOURSE

My first argument is that the old literature on informal organization mistakenly conceived it to be a matter of social organization, while in reality it is cultural. That is, we identified the informal organization of, say, workers as that which went on in primary groups, defined by the character of the social relations between them. But a bit of attention to the findings of Gilbert and Mulkay in *Opening Pandora's Box* (1984) on scientists shows that the same pair of scientists talk or write to each other in the formal language of their science (the language of positivism, of the facts speak for themselves) part of the time, but in the restricted code of loyalty, of helpfulness, of judgments of individuals, of hopes and fears and ambitions another part of the time. The informality, then, is a matter of *the character of discourse* rather than of the character of the relation between scientists, in the sense that the relationship stays the same while the degree of informality varies.

Similarly, Michael Burawoy's machinists in *Manufacturing Consent* (1979) talk the language of the game of making out (of arranging work so as to overachieve by just the right amount) on the shop floor and use that language across racial barriers that divide workers at lunchtime, talk to the foreman in that language, but switch to a formal language of trade union contracts and grievance procedure when dealing with the same subjects with the same people in a context of formal claims against management. The game of making out, then, is a way of talking about the incentive system, a way people use, whatever their formal status may be and whatever the formal relationship between them, when they want to talk about ambition, about other people getting in a worker's way, or about the motives of the other side in bargaining about the rates that are central components of the formal *and* the informal system.

In both cases, one is more likely to use the personalistic or restricted code when talking to people one is close to, but that is because one is more likely to discuss the subjects of emotions, personalities, illegitimate or sub-rosa arrangements, and the like when talking to people one trusts. But we see from Burawoy's account of his own induction into the culture of the machine shop and from Halle's account in *America's Working Man* (1984) of the introduction of new workers into the culture of operators in a chemical plant that strangers are, under the appropriate circumstances, obliged to learn the rules that make up the personalistic, working-class way of talking about work rules; they learn faster, of course, if they have previously learned similar ways of talking by working elsewhere. They are obliged to learn by virtue of their formal status as workers, because people in that formal status are obliged to participate in the informal as well as the formal system. Further, it is clear from Halle's account that people in different parts of the plant who do not work together and have no well-developed friendly relations used this informal mode of discourse among themselves in arranging the informal social life of the plant across work group boundaries.

Much of what is discussed in the informal or personalistic or restricted code mode of discourse is the formal system itself. The rate for a job in Burawoy's shop is formally discussed in industrial engineering terms and in a series of formal documents without reference to persons and in the collective contract. But those same rates are discussed also in the informal system, both by the foremen and by the workers, in terms of easy and tight or hard rates.

Gilbert and Mulkay's scientists are sometimes very explicit about how the same thing looks different in the formal and the informal discourse: "If the purpose of the [scientific] literature is to describe what you did, why in scientific terms you did it—I mean, not because you want to do some bloke down or you want to advance your own career or get a quick paper out just because there's a grant application coming up soon. All these are valid reasons, but they're never admitted to" (Gilbert and Mulkay 1984:60). My point here is that these are not only valid reasons, but that there are contexts in which it is perfectly appropriate for scientists to say that these matters of judgment of persons and of hopes and ambitions are the reasons for writing a paper.

So it is not a particular social structure that talks one way, another social structure that talks another way. By conceptualizing these different modes of discourse as a contrast of formal organization with informal organization, we are making the same mistake that Gumperz in *Discourse Strategies* (1983) points out about groups of bilinguals. Bilinguals often believe, for example, that they talk Spanish at home and in groups of Chicanos, English at work and in groups with English monolinguals present. But Gumperz shows that when talking to other bilinguals they mix Spanish and English in the same sentences, using the subordinate language to express emotions, to formulate hopes and ambitions, to speculate, and in general to express that sort of thing that one uses the subjunctive or imperative to express in French or Spanish. Like voluntary bilingualism, the informal or restricted code communication tends to be discourse in the subjunctive or imperative.

And that means that all those people who use subjunctives or imperatives to each other are likely to participate, to some degree, in the informal cultural mode of any given social structure. But they will also use the indicative mode in that same structure, the formal language of matter of fact and consensus and legal or formalized grievances. Further, they will talk about the same subjects sometimes in the indicative or formal, sometimes in the subjunctive or informal, mode.

To put it another way, informal versus formal is a matter of context, of what sorts of things are relevant at a given time in a given type of discourse; informal discourse involves verbs such as "like," "hope," "would if I had the chance," "must," and other highly affectively toned verbs, while formal discourse involves verbs such as "is," "did," "report," "testify," or "conclude." The difference shows up in the pronouns used as well, that informal discourse often uses the first person singular "I" and the second person "you," and when it is deadly serious perhaps the first person plural "we," or "your mother and I." Linguists generally discuss such variations in language use as a matter of context (for example, Gumperz 1983), and the communicative purpose of using such language is often the purpose of communicating what context the talk is to be referred to. Pronouns are, of course, also crucial in communicating context.

Most of the conversation about work that goes on in the family, as reported in studies like that of Gerstel and Gross about commuter marriage (1984), has first person pronouns in it and verbs such as "like," "hope," or "can't stand." But it is also about incidents and dynamics of the formal system, about such things as pay, promotions, assignments of responsibilities, and measurements of worker productivity. Think of the sick detail about the formal process of decision that characterizes the conversation about one's own academic promotion among family and friends.

I would not of course argue that the family is not a different social structure than work organization; when one comes home from work, the relationships change from colleague to kin, which is related to the change in discourse from matter-of-fact to matter-of-hopes-and-fears. What I want to emphasize instead is that the substance of discourse about work in the family has much the same form and content as the discourse about the same things in the work setting. And I also want to emphasize that many times there is nothing informal about the subject of the discourse, about the baroque structure that makes decisions about tenure, for example; it is only that one would not put that kind of discourse on one's vita, the formal document in which you plead and hope to be promoted in the language of opaque matter of fact.

Perhaps the best way I can summarize this section is to say that if you want to do the sociology of work, you should read Gilbert and Mulkay's *Opening Pandora's Box* (1984), on how scientists choose the mode of discourse they use about the same scientific subject matter, and then try to imagine how to apply that to the work setting you are interested in.

CONSENSUS AND MATTER-OF-FACT DISCOURSE

Discourse in the indicative mode, in which one talks of matters of fact, makes an implicit assertion that there is consensus (or at least consensus among all right-thinking people) on what one is saying. People who have the right to speak on behalf of a social group, people in authority, tend to formulate whatever they think as a matter of consensus. De Gaulle, for instance, used to state his opinions about what the government should do in a sentence with the subject "*La France.*" "France will not tolerate. . . ." This is an extreme form of a strategy of exercising power, the "of-course-you-can't-disagree-with-such-a-sensible-thing-as-this" tone, well beloved of teachers and professors as well as presidents of France. Two of the central points of the sociology of everyday life are that the definition of the situation is a contested matter and that the formal mode of discourse is a way of asserting that what one believes is and ought to be the consensus. Personalistic discourse often involves statements about consensus, such as, "You know," but they are generally directed at particular partners in interaction expected to be on the speaker's side, rather than assuming the consensus of everyone, as the matter-of-fact tone does.

For example, Gilbert and Mulkay show that scientists with contrasting opinions often assert *whatever they believe* as the consensus of the field, a consensus believed by all except a few people with motives of ambition, with character faults such as thickheadedness, or whatnot. When they are asserting such character faults under considerable evidence to the contrary, such as the leader of an opposing view of biochemical mechanisms getting a Nobel Prize, they formulate the consensus in very vague, general terms and then use more informal language to describe the "matters of detail" on which they happen to disagree with the Nobel Prize winners. Consensus is not some sort of amateur General Social Survey that shows that 90 percent of the people believe that people should be able to have a legal abortion if the baby will be born deformed, but is instead a way of talking about what they would hope they could assert in public in a matter-of-fact tone, because they believe it to be true. In short, it is the sort of thing I did above when I asserted it as a matter of fact that informal organization was not social organization at all but rather a mode of discourse within all organizations. The matter-of-fact style of that assertion is of course a persuasive or rhetorical strategy that people who have been teaching sociology for twenty-five years fall into so naturally that they catch themselves giving lectures at cocktail parties. My style says that although the readers may not have thought of it up until now, they will if they are right-thinking people obviously agree with me. By taking it out of the matter-of-fact tone in *this* paragraph, I may well remind the reader that he or she does not agree.

Much of the work on this persuasive strategy in conversations has been done in the field of sex roles (Fishman 1978). The finding is essentially that men tend to formulate the consensus as being whatever they happen to think, while women tend to listen—or at least to listen to men—and that the mode of discourse men use is essentially the authoritative mode; men no more expect to be interrupted (at least not by a woman) with a correction or a notice of disagreement than de Gaulle expected to be interrupted when he was telling us what France's opinion was.

Given this fact, it is of course wisdom not to take matter-of-fact statements as formulations of an actual consensus, of a culture in the sense of a consensus. But what it does more interestingly is to provide sensitive clues to points of tension and dissensus. And furthermore, with such sensitive indicators we are sure to find out that *different folks see different points of tension and dissensus.* If a person drops out of the formal mode of discourse into one reflecting dissensus, this says he or she has just got into a situation in which he or she cannot expect to get away with formulating his or her own opinion as a matter of fact. This gives an indication not only of there being a tension, but of the situations in which the tension is relevant, to whom it is relevant, and who, in that situation, is expected to be in a position to define the matter of fact.

An example of an application of such an indicator of possible disagreement occurred in some work I did on consulting engineering organizations in the Norwegian North Sea, in my and Carol Heimer's *Organization Theory and Project Management* (1985). A consulting engineering organization provides proposed technical and economic decisions to the client organization. The product is defined by whether or not the client organization takes the decision proposed by the consulting engineer; if it is not approved by the client, the work is not finished. So in order to find out whether one is getting one's work done, one needs to find out what will be acceptable to the client. But for the consulting engineer to get an authoritative opinion about a plan only after it is completed is expensive, because if some element of that plan is not acceptable then everything that depends on that element will have to be done over. And it is further expensive in terms of the reputation of the consulting engineering organization with the client; the consultant wastes our money chasing chimeras. So a complicated informal structure, much like that described by Peter Blau in his classic study of the enforcement agency in *The Dynamics of Bureaucracy* (1963), allows engineers working for the consulting engineer to consult psychologically and administratively cheaper sources of information about what will be acceptable before finally submitting the recommended decision formally to the client.

The way this shows up in the discourse is that verbal or situational markers are attached to the element of the solution proposed by an engineer working for the consultant to show that it is just an inquiry about what would be all right. Some of these are obvious markers, such as consulting colleagues within the consulting engineer's own organization who have had more experience with the client; no one would believe this was a formal request for an approval. Some are, for example, telephone calls to the relevant technical expert in the client organization's project engineering crew, noted in the diary of the consulting engineer who is inquiring so that he or she can defend that element later on if it is questioned. Some are meetings of committees that have representatives from both the client and the consultant, whose minutes are circulated and taken as authoritative unless someone specifically challenges them. The differences asserted here, from informal to formal discourse, are based on reports by engineers about what they do, not on the collection of a sample of texts. We are, of course, here turning the informality versus formality of discourse from a dichotomy to a continuous variable.

The point is that all of these markers are points of contact between an informal system of originating proposals marked as tentative and the more formal system, with a result that moves the proposals a bit farther up toward formal approval. Of course formally, even with the unchallenged minutes of a committee meeting in the record, the client can refuse to make the decision recommended by the consulting engineering organization and send it all back to the drawing boards.

From a formal point of view, all the intermediate stages are not decisions or approvals of the work of the consultant, but rather information. They are not authoritative. But as they progress toward a more matter-of-fact mode of discourse and appear in contexts with more of the markers of formal discourse (for example, at the extreme, in the minutes of a committee meeting with authoritative representatives), they take on more and more the character of piece of discourse indicating consensus, and so appear more and more reliable as a basis for making decisions about how to draw in the other parts which technically depend on the thing about which information has been received.

This informal process of consensus formation reflects differing perceptions by people differently situated of whether their own opinions are matter-of-fact, consensual, and authoritative. Senior engineers make less intensive use of this informal system than junior engineers before submitting their work—they often start at a higher level, such as directly calling a meeting of a committee to deal with a question rather than conferring extensively within the consulting engineer organization and with the client's engineer in his or her specialty first. Conversely, senior engineers are consulted by junior engineers and tell them, when appropriate, that they will bring it up in a committee meeting with the client, so they take charge of moving a junior engineer's proposal up to a more formal level of discourse. At the last stage the proposal is formulated in very formal language and is sent over as a proposed decision by the project manager in the consulting engineer to the project director in the client, for formal approval by the client, from the most senior consultant to the most senior manager in the client organization.

Numerous variables besides seniority affect the intensity of use of the more informal levels of discourse. Another example is the complexity of the decision the client will have to make: more engineering decisions have to be made for a custom designed system of rotating equipment, such as motors and generators or for a computerized, automatic control system than for procuring more or less standard equipment "off the shelf," such as a lifeboat, or for procuring structural steel shapes that are more or less standard. The less room there is for lack of consensus, the less use there needs to be of the informal system, so off-the-shelf purchases or structural steel specifications will use less of the informal modes of discourse than will procurements of rotating equipment or computerized control systems.

THE CULTURAL DIVISION OF LABOR

In a paper with a marvelous title and somewhat confused substance, Michael Hechter (1978) introduced the notion of "the cultural division of labor," though it turned out to mean the disproportionate locations of some ethnic groups in particular occupations. The phrase suggests that there is a definition in the general culture of features of various occupations and also a definition of people's ethnic, sexual, educational, and other features which fit them for those occupations. Thus we see nurse as a nurturant role, though nurses in fact mainly do administration and management on behalf of physicians; we think of women as nurturant. We therefore see women as appropriately nurses. We see automobile factory worker as a job for strong men, unless we work in automobile factories (see Duncan, Duncan, and McRae 1978:81; this sentence is a guess about the explanation of the facts given there) and know that most hard work is done nowadays by power tools. Black or white people running a Chinese or (worse) a Thai restaurant offend our sense of the fitness of things, though naturally restaurants serving midwestern bland (what I have also heard called the North Atlantic boiled potato complex) should be run by Greeks.

The classification of occupations from the point of view of their symbolic structure has a number of dimensions that are symbolically related to the classification of people. These cultural distinctions form a structure whose elements enter into the norms that define situations and whose distinctions form the analysis of reality in everyday life (and in revolutions—see Stinchcombe 1982). Cultural characteristics of work relevant to the classification of people by sex (see Ortner 1974) include:

Male	*Female*
requiring strength	requiring delicacy
dangerous	safe
night work	day work
involves traveling	fixed locations, especially near home
coarse, vulgar	refined
sexually approachable	respectable
managing money	managing interpersonal relations
authoritative	subordinate
impersonal	nurturant
violent	peaceable
no segregation of toilets and sleep from work	segregation of work from care of the person
work in solidary male group	work in mixed or female group
work in shaping metal	work with soft goods
high culture producers	high culture consumers

My general argument here is that such a list as the above, patterned on the discussions in Lévi-Strauss about the contrasts in distinctive features that make up the meanings of symbols in a mythical system, gives a set of semiconscious or unconscious norms by which a system of classification of jobs is related to classification by sex. Insofar as jobs can be classified by those dimensions, the semiconscious norms come into play in conceiving who is appropriate for the jobs.

The advantage of a general structural analysis of women such as that advanced by Ortner (1974) is that it allows us to predict what features of jobs are likely to give rise to sex segregation in the occupational system. Since the investigations of Baron and Bielby (1985) show that quite often the index of segregation by sex between occupations within a firm runs near 100 percent (that is, there are no men in any occupation in which there are any women and vice versa—see also Francine Blau 1978:42–46, esp. 45), and since formal provisions that occupations be segregated by sex are not common, the formal act of appointment evidently develops out of informal and semiformal ideas of what jobs go together with what sex. In some cases these informal and semiconscious norms merely specify that women in an occupation with the specified characteristic are not entirely ideal women, that jobs in which one must work at night in revealing clothes are not jobs one would want one's wife working in.

Thus, while in modern society most clerical work is done by women, one can use the cultural structure as outlined above to predict which clerical jobs are likely to be filled by hiring men: clerks in roles that are likely to exercise authority (even on someone else's behalf) over male workers, such as time clerks on construction sites; clerks at the company level in the military services, especially for companies in the field; clerks managing tool cribs or supplying maintenance parts in factories; clerks on the night shift in telegraph offices. The argument, then, is that the cultural division of labor between the sexes has not only a general injunction that women should be oppressed; one can predict which jobs will be given high wages and given to men by the cultural definitions defining the symbolic place of women in everyday discourse. We do not analyze such discourse here, except insofar as the list of contrasts above is an analysis of informal discourse that we would be unlikely to see enacted officially or written down in a formal organization. A comparison of informal and formal texts should show more use of symbols laden with the above contrasts in informal discourse.

One might also use such a system of cultural contrasts to predict which salespeople in department stores are likely to be men rather than women, which shifts will have special provisions for protecting the nurses and medical technicians from exposure to presumed risks outside the hospital, which sorts of jobs provide a cultural degradation of the women who work in them and so form part of that gray world between legitimate society and crime from which prostitutes are recruited, and the like. It should also enable us to analyze which occupations on a vocational interest inventory are likely to differentiate most between the sexes, what classes in secondary schools are likely to have an all-male enrollment, and so on. Those infamous counselors who did not encourage girls to take physics were not trying to maintain the wage levels of engineers; they were just trying to keep male things from polluting females and females from polluting male things.

The cultural system is thus made up of a fairly fixed system of contrasts associated with sex, which also are associated with occupations; and discrimination against women in the occupational system is at least in part not a direct exercise of power politics but instead a system of half-conscious judgments about cultural congruence between people and roles. Further, we would expect that the less formal a given piece of discourse, as measured by markers such as those suggested in previous sections, the more prominent such contrasts as those suggested by Ortner would be. Such an analysis would enable us to understand the phrase in *The Economist* (1984:3) "professional women are as rare in the Square Mile [of the financial center of The City of London] as at a Texas oil jamboree" by sensing the commonness of the cultural process that produced the sex segregation of these very different occupations. What they have in common is that handling money in fiduciary roles and handling heavy and dangerous drilling apparatus occupy roughly the same place in the structure of symbols defining women and men in the society.

CULTURAL DEFINITIONS OF ETHNICITY

Ethnic segregation in the occupational world is presumably a combined product of processes of members of a given ethnicity who dominate a given occupation choosing to recruit and train people culturally similar to themselves (this presumably explains the predominance of Greeks in restaurants in the United States not serving Greek food) and processes involving other people's notions of the fitness of ethnic groups for an occupation (which presumably partly explains why Thais dominate the work force of Thai restaurants). In turn, some of the distinctions by which jobs are culturally classified by ethnicity are specific to the defining features of the ethnicity (teachers of French conversational skills should have French as a mother tongue or people who run Thai restaurants should know what Thai food should taste like). Others are more in the nature of ethnic stereotypes. For example, the typical courtroom scene in the Northeastern United States has an Anglo-Saxon Protestant judge, an Irish prosecutor managing the testimony of an Irish policeman, and a Jewish psychiatrist explaining why the defendant is not responsible enough to be culpable—the cultural stereotypes involved in the differential recruitment emphasize integrity, political skill, and sensitivity or sympathy with oppression, respectively.

The ethnic stereotypes may be strongly hierarchical, as the traditional American race prejudices that confined blacks or Slavs and Italians to low status manual work were, or mere horizontal distinctions, as the identification of black musicians with jazz and white musicians with country and western music seem to be.

In general each ethnicity will be associated in the culture with a series of distinctive features, much as a phoneme in the structural analysis of the phonology of a language has its distinctive features. Not all of the dimensions that distinguish people in the culture will be relevant to any given ethnicity, just as not all possible dimensions distinguishing phonemes are relevant to distinguishing particular ones (for example, in French only vowels, not consonants, are contrasted with other vowels only by being nasalized; in Russian only consonants, not vowels, are distinguished by hard versus soft or palatalized). Not all jobs are contrasted with other jobs by ethnically relevant cultural characteristics, and of course not all pairs of people are contrasted by ethnicity.

Some part of ethnic discrimination no doubt involves the mere use of an ethnic boundary, regardless of its associated culturally validated stereotype, in the service of interests—if the main cheaper labor available in the labor market is Slavic, we should find jokes about Polish stupidity and skilled worker discrimination against Poles, but if the main cheaper labor is black, we should find skilled workers who previously supported the Civil War and Reconstruction to enfranchise blacks developing race prejudice. In these cases we would expect the culture to develop as a dependent variable, to be explained by the independent variable of labor market interest. The boundary gets distinguishing features associated with it because those features justify a discriminatory labor market policy.

Other cases are likely to be ambiguous. For example, symphonic and chamber music are considered high culture, so the general presumption that musical competence in that kind of music is found among whites (especially whites from Eastern Europe) is invidious and denigrates blacks. Yet even people who prefer jazz to classical music associate jazz competence with blacks, symphonic competence with East European whites. Thus the straightforward presumption that high prestige positions will tend to exclude blacks does not explain the cultural psychology of those who would give higher esteem to jazz. In these cases it is not clear whether overall the cultural system is a rationalization of self-interested discrimination or whether its basic dynamics are fundamentally autonomous parts of the cultural system.

Sometimes a cultural distinction that was not much involved with the definitions of interests in the economic system, that provided only horizontal classifications of people, changes its meaning with developments in the economy. For example, fifty years ago pizza was not the popular way to fix a hot cheese sandwich (it is hard to imagine now that there were once grilled cheese sandwiches), so the putative association (insofar as there was one) between Italian ethnicity and familiarity with pizza had no economic force. At first, pizza was generally sold in Italian restaurants run by Italians; this was not economic discrimination, however, but only the operation of cultural definitions. But when pizza turned out to be a really good thing economically, it came to be exploited by chains of fast food places, some of which are completely detached from Italian ethnicity.

The system of ethnic stereotypes that combines with economic interests to produce the system of ethnic segregation in the labor market tends to be distinctive to each country, even each subculture within a country. In Finland, Swedes are strongly stereotyped, whereas in the United States they are merely Protestant North Europeans, just like Finns, and Americans do not know that many Swedes live in Finland. Puerto Ricans occupy a distinctive place in the firmament of cultural distinctions of New York City; Cubans occupy a distinctive place in the culture of Miami; neither occupies a place in the system of stereotypes of Dubuque, Iowa.

Further, this set of cultural distinctions among people and among jobs develops over time, pushed by interests and by cultural reform movements with a civil rights overtone as well as by whatever processes determine the structure of culture generally. Since the phonetic structure changes over time, though surely subject to less powerful forces than the classification of people and jobs, it is certain that the ethnic stereotype space of a culture must change over time and have corresponding effects on the evolution of ethnic segregation in the labor market. Because we have not studied the complete system of subjective categories and distinctions in which ethnic discrimination is embedded, we have overemphasized the dynamics of oppressive interests as a determinant and underemphasized the role of cultural, subjective factors.

The general point here is that there is a spotty and irregular mapping of the distinctive features of ethnicity onto the distinctive features of occupations. While this mapping varies rapidly in historical time and is distinctive to different national and regional cultures, it often appears to have strong effects of ethnic occupational segregation. Ethnicities are ranked not only from high to low, but also from less to more appropriate for restaurants serving pasta, less to more likely to be able to play jazz or symphonic music. And again, the more informal the discourse, the more we would expect people to use ethnicities and occupations as sets of symbols with many such symbolic contrasts.

COMPETENCE IN ETHNOMETHODOLOGY AS AN OCCUPATIONAL QUALIFICATION

Consider the used car salesperson (almost always a man, for various reasons hinted at above) who keeps a customer from going across the street to investigate competitive prices by giving him or her a package of ice cream as a gift. The sensible thing for the customer to do is to ask the salesperson to keep it in the refrigerator while the customer goes across the street and to come back for it later. The salesperson knows, however, that there is a norm that one does not ask someone who has just done one a favor to do another; it is because this norm is not conscious that the used car clients do not realize that the norm is being used to manipulate them (Browne 1973; see also Robert Cialdini 1984). Only because the whole process is unconscious can the used care salesman use the norm to modify the behavior of the client at the cost of a couple dollars' worth of ice cream.

Without presumably being able to formulate in any general way why the customer will not ask him to keep the ice cream while checking the competitive prices, the salesperson has developed a feel for what is socially possible under various circumstances and built it into his or her interpersonal routines. Such salespeople develop a conscious lore about devices that work, but not ordinarily, apparently, a conscious analysis of the norms that make them work. The extroverted personalities recruited to used car sales positions are unlikely to be very reflective about unconscious norms—they would not make good ethnomethodologists. But a part of their competence is a reliable use of those norms to get the interaction to go the way they want. A large number of roles do not seem to have any formulable or certifiable competences, yet a large number of aspirants fail to perform in them. Those who succeed in them may have competences in the unconscious use (use without generalized knowledge) of unconscious norms. Too delicate a sense of manners, of what decent folks owe the social situation, probably prevents the accumulation of knowledge of how such unconscious norms can be used—they are not supposed to be used by well-mannered people, but followed.

A generalization in the ethnomethodology of work life, then, might be that highly paid occupations with indefinite and uncertified requirements may have their competences in the mastery of the use of unconscious norms.

VARIABILITY IN THE CAUSAL FORCE
OF UNCONSCIOUS NORMS ABOUT SPACE

Many unconscious norms have to do with the use of space on a very small scale. The barrier between the incoming throngs of students and the departmental clerical staff establishes an area behind the barrier which belongs to the secretaries. Belonging to is not a category in the formal arrangements of the University, and it regulates details of the use of the body in other people's space that Goffman or Garfinkel, but not Parsons or Marx, would be likely to analyze.

The letter on the parking sticker on an American college campus is a more persistent reminder of the status order than the now-defunct differences in dress;

professors give up their dignified dress a lot sooner than their F (or A) privileges in the parking lot.

Walker and Guest (1952:69–70) in their classic study of social life on the assembly line note the peculiarity of the GM assembly line that workers did not even have enough control over their bodies to be able to form a boundary around a conversational group. The social relations of each position on the assembly line were distinct from the social relations of its neighbors because control over the boundaries of interaction was not in the hands of the group (contrast this with the description of ordinary conversational body positioning as described in Goffman 1963:98–104).

In many organizations the offices occupied by women normatively have their door kept open, communicating that anyone may make requests of the occupant of the office, while the doors occupied by men have their doors closed.

The general point is that control, status, solidarity, accessibility, and other central aspects of the obligations and duties of a role, the contingencies to which the occupant will be forced to respond, and the like have their expression also in the physical setting. Norms about physical access and orientation are normally unconscious ways of controlling social life.

The ordinary experience of all but very privileged workers is that all re-organizations of space threaten their control, status, chances of friendship and solidarity, and access to people they need. And all formal reorganizations of roles may sometimes be subverted or modified by the use of informal control over space. Because the norms expressing control, status, solidarity, and access in the physical setting are unconscious (or at most semiconscious), they are often not incorporated into the organizational plans. Hence the physical planning goes on separately from the planning of social organization, and social organization is often replanned without corresponding changes in the physical arrangements. Then low status people modify the physical space to shape access, status, and solidarity.

What this in turn means is that people are ordinarily advantaged by individually hoarding space within the organization, by supplying organizationally unplanned barriers to perception and movement and by generally making radically "suboptimal" use of space. In some organizations (such as universities), most of the space is unoccupied most of the time. Universities have few other mechanisms to make them go except a status system, and the self-control of research and learning that that system makes possible—they have no overall plan of production. University decision making is radically decentralized so that the hoarding and barrier building cannot be controlled hierarchically. In a situation of no hierarchical planning of activities and very little real control over the use of space, we would expect luxuriant growth of spatial arrangements controlled by ethnomethodological principles. Similarly, we would predict that craftsmen who control their work would have a lower rate of utilization of any space under their control, that high executives would have separate spatial settings for the variety of interactional settings they have to work in, most of which would be unoccupied most of the time.

The other end of the dimension is that people whose roles are most planned in the light of higher organizational purposes by their superiors would make the most efficient use of space, because crowding them and making them work in a fishbowl is simply another form of their oppression.

When there is no hierarchically imposed plan of production but people have minimal control over space and accessibility, as at conventions, we would expect them to use their hotel bedrooms in creative ways to support their control, status, solidarity, and access. But people who rely more on control over physical space to protect their private lives from invasion by coworkers, such as women, may be particularly exposed in such situations.

My purpose here has been to connect two traditions, the tradition of analysis of unconscious norms in social interaction pioneered in recent years by Goffman, Garfinkel, and Lévi-Strauss and the older tradition of the ethnography of work pioneered by people like Everett Hughes (1958), William Foote Whyte (1948, 1961), and Theodore Caplow (1964). Many of the examples I have used to illustrate the operation of unconscious norms in work life will sound familiar to people who studied with Hughes, Whyte, or Caplow. As Michael Schudson has pointed out about Goffman, much of the fieldwork on which the new tradition is based is not about the parts of life which involves us deeply, work and the family, but instead about superficial interaction in public places (1984).

At the same time, there is now very little ethnography of any kind about social interaction at work. Our general inclination nowadays is to summarize all a person's activity at work in an occupational name, sum up occupational names in four or five dimensions of social standing, work with things, people, and data, or core versus periphery, and so to miss the normative complexity that interaction at work involves. It takes a social movement, such as that happening in the strong program of the sociology of science, to get us to look at the social organization of work in any rich detail. There are some fine examples of throwbacks to the old tradition, such as Halle's book (1984) or Sabel's ingenious mixture of historical, comparative, and ethnographic work on the politics of the workplace (1982; see also Epstein 1981; Coser, Kadushin, and Powell 1982; Hochschild 1983; Faulkner 1983). Presumably part of the reason is that Hughes, Whyte, and Caplow do not provide us with currently fashionable theoretical frameworks to make their work seem sufficiently professional. The gift they had was to make social life at work juicy and interesting, an area in which a gifted observer could provide materials for Homans in both *The Human Group* (1950) and *The Elementary Forms of Social Behavior* (1961).

But those of the ethnographer's observations that fit uncomfortably with the Homans sort of theory need to be recovered now by the new theories of social interaction. And that also gives new reasons to do ethnography in the work-place.

REFERENCES

Baron, James, and William Bielby. 1985. "Organizational Barriers to Gender Equality: Sex Segregation of Jobs and Opportunities." In Rossi 1985:233–49.

Blau, Francine. 1978. "The Data on Women Workers, Past, Present, and Future." In Stromberg and Harkess 1978:29–62.

Blau, Peter. 1955. *Dynamics of Bureaucracy*. Chicago: University of Chicago Press.

Browne, Joy. 1973. *The Used Car Game: A Sociology of the Bargain*. Lexington, Mass.: D. C. Heath.

Burawoy, Michael. 1979. *Manufacturing Consent: Changes in the Labor Process under Monopoly Capitalism*. Chicago: University of Chicago Press.

Caplow, Theodore. 1964. *The Sociology of Work*. New York: McGraw-Hill.

Charlton, Joy. 1983. "Secretaries and Bosses." Ph.D. diss., Northwestern University.

Cialdini, Robert. 1984. *Influence: How and Why People Agree to Things*. New York: Morrow.

Coser, Lewis, Charles Kadushin, and Walter Powell. 1982. *Books: The Culture and Commerce of Publishing*. New York: Basic Books.

Duncan, Beverley, and Otis D. Duncan with James A. McRae, Jr. 1978. *Sex Typing and Social Roles: A Research Report*. New York: Academic Press.

The Economist. 1984. "Survey: The City of London," July 14–20.

Epstein, Cynthia. 1981. *Women in Law*. New York: Basic Books.

Faulkner, Robert R. 1983. *Music on Demand: Composers and Careers in the Hollywood Film Industry*. New Brunswick, N.J.: Transaction Books.

Fishman, Pamela M. 1978. "Interaction: The Work Women Do." *Social Problems* 25:397–406.

Garfinkel, Harold. 1967. *Studies in Ethnomethodology*. Englewood Cliffs: Prentice-Hall.

Gerstel, Naomi, and Harriet Gross. 1984. *Commuter Marriage: A Study of Work and Family*. New York: Guilford Press.

Gilbert, G. Nigel, and Michael Mulkay. 1984. *Opening Pandora's Box: A Sociological Analysis of Scientists' Discourse*. Cambridge: Cambridge University Press.

Goffman, Erving. 1963. *Behavior in Public Places: Notes on the Social Organization of Gatherings*. New York: Free Press.

Gumperz, John Joseph. 1983. *Discourse Strategies*. New York: Cambridge University Press.

Halle, David. 1984. *America's Working Man: Work, Home, and Politics among Blue-Collar Property Owners*. Chicago: University of Chicago Press.

Hechter, Michael. 1978. "Group Formation and the Cultural Division of Labor." *American Journal of Sociology* 84(2):293–318.

Hochschild, Arlie. 1983. *The Managed Heart*. Berkeley: University of California Press.

Homans, George Caspar. 1950. *The Human Group*. New York: Harcourt Brace Jovanovich.

———. 1961. *Social Behavior: Its Elementary Forms*. New York: Harcourt Brace Jovanovich.

Hughes, Everett C. 1958. *Men and Their Work*. New York: Free Press.

Leidner, Robin. 1985. "Clerical Home Work." Unpublished paper, Northwestern University.

Liebow, Elliott. 1967. *Tally's Corner: A Study of Negro Street-Corner Men*. Boston: Little, Brown.

Ortner, Sherry B. 1974. "Is Female to Male as Nature Is to Culture?" In *Women, Culture, and Society,* edited by Michelle Zimbalist Rosaldo and Louise Lamphere. Stanford: Stanford University Press.

Rossi, Alice S., ed. 1985. *Gender and the Life Course,* New York: Aldine.

Sabel, Charles F. 1982. *Work and Politics: The Division of Labor in Industry.* Cambridge: Cambridge University Press.

Schudson, Michael. 1984. "Embarrassment and Goffman's Idea of Human Nature." *Theory and Society* 13(5):633–48.

Stinchcombe, Arthur L. 1982. "The Deep Structure of Moral Categories, Eighteenth-Century Stratification, and the Revolution." In *Structural Sociology,* edited by Ino Rossi. New York: Columbia University Press.

Stinchcombe, Arthur L., and Carol A. Heimer. 1985. *Organization Theory and Project Management: Administering Uncertainty in the North Sea.* Bergen: Norwegian University Press; New York: Oxford University Press.

Stromberg, Anne, and Shirley Harkess, eds. 1978. *Women Working: Theories and Facts in Perspective.* Palo Alto: Mayfield Publishing.

Walker, Charles, and Robert H. Guest. 1952. *The Man on the Assembly Line.* Cambridge, Mass.: Harvard University Press and New York: Arno Press.

Whyte, William Foote. 1961. *Men at Work*. Homewood, Ill.: Dorsey Press.

———. 1948. *Human Relations in the Restaurant Industry*. New York: McGraw-Hill.

|||||||| **PART THREE • FORMS OF WORK**

ⅠⅠⅠⅠⅠⅠⅠ Participation in the Irregular Economy

LOUIS A. FERMAN

The totality of economic activity in any given society is not encompassed in estimates of employment, unemployment, and Gross National Product. These estimates are based on information recorded by the economic measurement techniques that are available and form the basis for policy development and administration. Yet a certain amount of economic activity goes on that is not monitored or recorded. Part of this activity is based on money as a medium of exchange. This is the irregular economy.

Economic activity, the production and distribution of services and goods, can be conceptualized as belonging to one of three classes on the basis of two criteria:

1. Enumeration by the economic measurement technique of the society.
2. Use of money (whether currency, coin, bank draft, credit card, or other credit extended as a stated value of reckoning) as a medium of exchange.

Exchanges can be categorized into one of three modes of economic activity, social, irregular, or regular, according to the presence or absence of these features. For expedience we shall refer to each type of economic activity as a distinct economy.

Types of Economic Activity	Enumeration by Economic Measurement Techniques	Money as a Medium of Exchange
Social	−	−
Irregular	−	+
Regular	+	+

The *social economy* is that sector of economic activity not registered by the economic measurement techniques of the society and which does not use money as a medium of exchange. Social exchanges are those in which there is no monetary payment for services of goods produced or exchanged. The *irregular economy* is that sector of economic activity that is not registered by the economic measurement techniques of the society and that uses money as a medium of exchange. Irregular exchanges are monetary transactions in which the services or goods rendered are not recorded by the economic measurement techniques of the society. The *regular economy* is that sector of economic activity that (1) is registered by the economic measurement techniques of the society and (2) uses money as a medium of exchange. Regular exchanges are transactions that are both monetary and recorded by the economic measurement techniques of the society.

Regular, irregular, and social economic activities combine forces in the process of provisioning the society. While most of the services and goods that are crucial to the maintenance of the economic level of the society, as measured by the Gross National Product, are produced and distributed to a mass market through the regular economy, the day-to-day process of distribution operates through social or irregular channels. Services and goods are exchanged with relatives, neighbors, friends, and acquaintances daily. While any one exchange may be small and of little consequence on a macroeconomic scale, taken as a whole they may become important both in the provision of goods and services that are unavailable or difficult to obtain through the regular economy and in the distribution of products produced in the regular economy to local or marginal markets.

In 1977 we surveyed 284 households in Detroit, Michigan, focusing on the households' use of irregular and social sources as an option in attaining common home-related and personal services (Ferman, Berndt and Selo 1978). Sixty percent of the services households reported using were secured through the social economy: either produced within the household itself or provided by friends, relatives, neighbors, or coworkers without monetary payment; 10 percent of the services were purchased through the irregular economy; and 30 percent through regular suppliers. Of all the services we asked about fully 25 percent of those for which payment was made were purchased through the irregular economy. Over half of the households surveyed (51 percent) had purchased at least one service through irregular sources. For our sample there was no significant variation in the use of the irregular economy based on income level. Participation in the irregular economy is widespread throughout all levels of society.

RANGE AND NATURE OF IRREGULAR
ECONOMIC ACTIVITIES

The range of services and goods represented in the irregular economy is very broad, extending from a child's lemonade stand to the empires of organized crime. We have isolated seven types of activities that characterize the irregular economy:

Sale and/or production of goods
Home related services provided to consumers
Personal services provided to consumers
"Off-the-books" employment by a regular establishment
Rental of property
Provision of entertainment
Criminal activities

Each of these types encompasses a wide range of variation in terms of the size and scale of the activity, the levels of investment in time or money, the relationships between providers and users, the levels of return for work done, the frequency of the activity in terms of provision or use, and the relative availability of the service or goods through regular sources.

The *sale and/or production of goods* include such diverse enterprises as church-sponsored bake sales, garage sales, lemonade stands run by neighborhood children, production of arts and crafts, door-to-door peddling, resale of automobiles, sewing, and furniture making. All can be termed irregular if they involve an exchange of money and are unrecorded. Yet the nature of the enterprise even within one activity type can differ radically. The homemaker who decorates and sells five ashtrays a year to her friends for $2 each and the potter who earns over $10,000 annually at art fairs and through galleries without reporting the income are both engaged in the irregular economy.

Similarly, diversity extends through each of the remaining categories. *Home related services* range from a child mowing an elderly neighbor's lawn for $10.00 to a crew of unlicensed builders constructing a new house or garage. *Personal services* include such items as running an errand for a quarter, weekly housecleaning, or long-term nursing care. *"Off-the-books" employment* by a regular establishment covers a teenager sweeping the floor once a week for $5, a waitress working for cash at a bar while receiving government aid for her dependent children, and a dispatcher working for a trucking firm and depositing his cash income in an out-of-state bank while receiving total disability payments. *Rental of property* might be the rental of one's automobile to a local funeral home for infrequent use or the rental of a room or apartment in one's home. *Provision of entertainment* runs from an unrecorded $2 bet on a baseball game to a band working regularly for cash payments they do not report. *Criminal activities* also extend from the relatively minor and insignificant, such as a teenager selling marijuana cigarettes to his buddy, to large-scale, high-profit enterprises such as wholesale importing and distributing of heroin.

Almost every type of economic activity found in the regular economy is probably found in the irregular economy: goods are manufactured and distributed, services are provided, people are employed by others, and income is earned from capital investments. While the types of activities in the irregular economy reflects those in the regular economy, the nature of the activities is probably somewhat different. The size and scale of activities in the irregular economy may be generally much smaller than in the regular economy. On the whole, levels of investment of time and money in the irregular activities may be substantially less than in regular economic enterprises. With the notable exception of organized crime and similar overtly illegal activities, irregular enterprises and exchanges are generally small, frequently involving only one person acting as an entrepreneur; seldom do more than three or four individuals work together on any ongoing basis. The scale of irregular enterprises is likewise small. Producers and consumers of goods and services generally meet face-to-face and arrange the terms of their own transactions (usually within a limited geographical setting). Irregular exchanges are characterized by direct distribution of product and little or no specialized division of labor within the producing unit.

Levels of investment in most irregular activities are low in terms of operating capital and investment in equipment and supplies. Frequently the irregular entrepreneur utilizes his or her regular employment for access to necessary tools. A clerical worker who types manuscripts on the side may depend on her regular employer to supply not only the typewriter, but also the paper, ribbon, and office space. Most irregular enterprises are intermittent. The general low level of capitalization does not allow for ongoing activity when there is no demand for products. Few irregular activities allow full-time, year-round employment. More often they are engaged in as part-time pursuits, either intensively for short duration, such as a garage or yard sale or a roofing job over the weekend, or as a sideline for one or two hours at a time on a more regular schedule.

The levels of return for work done in the irregular economy may vary more widely than in the regular. Certainly the irregular economy is more integrated than the regular, with fewer intermediate transactions between production and final consumption and substantially less overhead cost. However, these factors do not necessarily translate into lower costs for the consumer *or* higher rate of return for the producer. Although, as a whole, our respondents did pay less for the services they obtained through the irregular economy than through the regular economy, there is no evidence that the same services are cheaper in the irregular economy. The specific services more likely to be purchased from irregular producers may be, in general, less costly than those purchased from firms or businesses. Pricing in the irregular economy is idiosyncratic and often particularistic, depending in part on the nature of the relationship between parties involved in the exchange.

The relations between providers and users of irregular services and goods are frequently grounded in personal ties, which in some cases override the economic content of the exchanges. Many exchanges that are irregular and involve an unrecorded exchange of money are virtually indistinguishable from similar transactions that do not involve overt payment. Money is a general purpose commodity—the mere fact of its changing hands does not delimit a market relationship. Gifts can be cash or in kind; international business can be conducted by barter as well as bills of exchange. In the irregular economy the price often depends as much on the nature of the relations between the parties involved as on the "market" value of the service or goods exchanged. An irregular auto mechanic might rebuild his mate's engine for free, his in-law's for parts and a discount, and his neighbor's for the going hourly rate. Certainly factors other than human capital, supply, and demand mediate the cost of the product.

Technological constraints on manufacture, division of labor, overhead, distribution, capitalization, licensing laws, and other regulations act in concert to limit the irregular manufacture of durable goods in highly industrialized economies. Although letting out piecework to unregistered shops or employees has not been entirely eradicated, we suspect that the manufacture of consumable or specialty goods and the production of services are more characteristic of irregular activities in North America. While we do not have systematic survey data support, our research strongly suggests that the provision of services is more prevalent in the irregular economy than is the manufacture or distribution of goods. The services most frequently obtained through the irregular economy generally demand a higher level of technical expertise and more capital investment in equipment than similar services provided by the social economy. They are usually less complex and capital intensive than services produced in the regular economy. In our sample, a remarkably high rate of services was produced without monetary payment, either by the respondents themselves or through their social networks. But as the skill level necessary for a service, the amount of money required to produce it, or the degree of complexity involved in the task increased, there was greater likelihood of a monetary transaction. For example, three types of kitchen cabinet work were reported: new cabinets were built and installed, prebuilt cabinets were installed, and existing cabinets were repaired. The installing of prebuilt cabinets accounts for 64 percent of irregular work, 35 percent of social, and only 18 percent of regular work; the building of new cabinets accounts for 56 percent of regular work, 40 percent of social, and 36 percent of irregular work. No cabinets were repaired by irregular workers. The skill level involved in irregular work is intermediate. People who do not install cabinets for free through their social channels tend to pay irregular workers to install prebuilt cabinets, but to go to regular sources to build and install cabinets.

The services for which the irregular producers were used most frequently were lawn care, exterior painting, interior painting, paneling, carpentry, babysitting, and child care. These services were secured for free by the majority of the respondents. If purchased, they were more often secured from irregular sources than from established firms or businesses. The irregular economy was generally utilized for services that most people secure without monetary payment and that are usually not provided by regular firms and businesses. The irregular sector seems to function as an alternative service provider in instances where the household is unable to perform the service or unable to have it done without payment. In this sense it fills an intermediate position between the regular market economy and do-it-yourself activities.

INTERDEPENDENCE OF THE IRREGULAR
AND REGULAR ECONOMIES

The irregular economy is highly dependent on the regular economy as a source of goods distributed through irregular channels. The regular economy provides the source for manufacture and initial distribution of most new goods for the society. Even those goods most likely to be produced in the irregular economy are dependent for the most part on materials procured through the regular economy. An artist may paint a picture and sell it irregularly, but the materials used—the canvas, brushes, oils, and turpentine—will probably be purchased through regular sources. The raw materials used to produce goods in the irregular economy, whether furniture, baked goods, clothing, or art, are almost invariably purchased from regular outlets and manufactured or processed by regular firms. Irregular producers of goods are steady consumers of regular products. In this sense the irregular economy is part of the market of the regular economy. Persons who produce goods in the irregular economy are consumers of goods produced in the regular economy.

The irregular economy serves as a means of distribution of regular products through their transformation into new goods that are sold irregularly, through resale of used goods originally produced and sold in the regular economy, through irregular sale of goods purchased from regular sources, and through products purchased from regular sources and used in providing services irregularly. The role of the regular economy in providing raw materials for irregular manufacture or processing has been described above. The regular economy is also the source for used and new goods resold through the irregular economy. The merchandise sold at garage sales through want ads was usually purchased from regular sources. Its subsequent sale in the irregular economy is a continuing means of redistributing regular goods. Door-to-door and street peddlers who do not report their income usually purchase their wares from suppliers whose profits are monitored and recorded. Services provided through the irregular economy frequently include the installation of new goods manufactured by and purchased from regular sources. An irregular plumber who installs a new faucet acts as a distributor for regularly produced goods.

Many products produced in the regular economy may be dependent on the irregular economy for repair and maintenance. For example, chimneys are built from bricks manufactured in the regular economy and are constructed by regular workers—there are, however, very few regular chimney sweeps working in this country. Small appliance repair is another area in which maintenance services are often obtained through the irregular economy. It is unlikely that one can find a repairman employed by an established business who will fix a broken toaster for a cost that is less than the replacement price of the appliance.

The irregular economy also acts as a producer of goods and services that are distributed through the regular economy. A worker who is employed off-the-books produces profit for the regular employer. A painting that is produced and sold irregularly by an artist may be distributed quite regularly by a gallery. A seamstress who sells her product to a store may not report her income, but the store will record their purchase and sale of the irregular clothing as a regular transaction.

The irregular economy serves four basic functions with respect to the regular economy. It is a *consumer* of products produced in the regular economy; a *distributor* of products produced in the regular economy; a *maintainer* of products produced in the regular economy; and a *producer* of products sold in the regular economy.

DISTINCTION BETWEEN FORMAL AND INFORMAL SECTORS OF THE ECONOMY

Although there is a close interdependence between the formal and informal sectors of the economy, we should not gloss over the fact that sharp differences occur in the conditions, values, and structures that underpin the two sectors. In table I, we have spelled out some of these differences based on our field observations in the Detroit study.

Size/scale. The informal sector is characterized by small operating units (usually less than six workers) while the formal sector is characterized by much larger units. Two basic values underpin the small size of units in the informal sector: (1) remain inconspicuous and (2) keep it simple. Size is obviously a factor in avoiding monitoring and regulation by official agencies. Large economic units are more likely to be observed and regulated. Beyond this is the notion that the work organization should be simple with a low investment in technology; both factors place limits on size of unit.

Table 1. Distinction between Formal and Informal Sectors

Characteristics	Formal Sector	Informal Sector
Size/Scale	large/generally more than 6 employees	small/generally less than 6 employees
Levels of Investment		
capitalization	high capital investment	low capital investment
access to capital	high probability	low probability
Institutional Requirement		
credentials	license mandatory	licence not required
degree of regulation	high	low
Internal Organization/Labor		
division of labor	fixed	flexible
formal organization	high degree of hierarchical control	low–high hierarchical control
acquisition of skills/work experience	important/formal	not important/formal and/or informal
Business Operation		
ease of entry	difficult	easy
acquisition of customers	open market	social networks and/or location of activity
Levels of Return		
price of determination return for investment	structured/universalistic	unstructured/particularistic
time	predictable/fixed	unpredictable/flexible
money	determinate	indeterminate
manpower	predictable	unpredictable
Institutional Protection		
protective legislation	sheltered	unsheltered
contractual sanctions	legal	social
element of risk	low	high
Norms of Exchange	market rules	personal and reciprocity values

Levels of investment. The formal sector is far more likely to have a high capital investment and high access of institutional capital (for example, from banks). Units in the formal sector are regulated and credentialed, leaving a paper trail of economic legitimacy. It is this legitimacy that is the basis of bank loans. Units in the informal sector, lacking this legitimacy, have low access to institutional capital and thus must minimize capital investment or obtain financial support from kin and friendship networks.

Institutional requirements. Formal sector units require licensing both as a means of quality control and for tax accountability. The emphasis is on the standardization of performance and thus the producers as well as the end-product must fulfill certain specified criteria. In the informal sector, standardization of performance is not a dominant norm. Operations may be performed with unconventional techniques and tools on an unpredictable time line. The criteria for quality control are not rigidly spelled out and regulation is low.

Internal organization/labor. Units in the formal sector follow certain rules of internal organization. This internal organization stresses hierarchical relationships, a fixed division of labor, and credentialed or certified workers. The major focus in such an organization is to reduce variance in production through a tight span of control and standardization of performance. For this reason, there is limited flexibility in such work systems. In contrast, units in the informal economy stress flexibility, nonhierarchical relationships, and the acquisition of skills through unconventional channels. Since work opportunities are unpredictable, emphasis is placed on adapting to unforeseen contingencies imposed by the work task and the conditions of work. Job switching in such situations is frequent, making a rigid division of labor almost impossible. The emphasis is on workers who can perform many different tasks as the work demands and not on specialization.

Business operation. The establishment of a unit in the formal sector is fraught with difficulties. Rigid rules of the game are imposed by licensing requirements, financial accountability, and state agency regulation. Entry into the informal sector is relatively easy—one puts up a sign and does business. An operational plan may well be developed as the business progresses since no initial approval is required by any entity other than those workers who are engaged in the enterprise. There is also the matter of recruiting customers. In the formal sector, such recruitment is through formal channels of communication—newspapers ads and radio or television commercials. These efforts are costly. In the informal sector, a business unit recruits its customers through social networks, word-of-mouth, and notices on local bulletin boards. Such units may not get started unless they are responding to the needs of local social networks so that a customer cohort may be ready-made.

Levels of return. Price determination for work is different in the formal and informal sectors. In the formal sector, price is structured and, except for unusual situations, is the same for all customers. Market factors are of paramount importance. Not so in the informal sector. Price is unstructured and may vary considerably depending on the social relationship between producer and buyer. This is more likely to be so if both parties are conjoined in some kinship or friendship relationship. In such situations, the norm of reciprocity is more apt to be the determinant of price than market factors.

The return for the work investment is more predictable and fixed in the formal sector. Time, money, and frequently manpower are usually features of the work contract making the investment and its return highly predictable. Since unit time, cost, and manpower are standardized concerns, not varying from one job to another, a calculus for return from investment can easily be determined by the producer and made known to the customer. The situation is quite different in the informal economy. Time investment may vary depending on other work or nonwork obligations of the producer, so that strict time schedules or deadlines are problematic. Financial return may vary from job to job depending on the social and interpersonal relationships between seller and buyer. Manpower investment can fluctuate widely depending on the obligations and availability of key work people for the job. In many cases, the work crew is composed of pickup people who come together for a single job. Given that these people have other work and nonwork obligations, their availability and turnover is questionable.

Institutional protection.   Workers in the formal sector are covered and protected by a myriad of state and federal social programs (social security, unemployment insurance, health and safety regulations, and workmen's compensation). Medical coverage is usually provided by corporate-contributed programs. Thus, participation in the formal economy brings with it a great measure of worker protection. Workers in the informal sector are not protected by these programs. Whatever protection they do have must be provided by themselves through some pay-in system or public welfare system.

Contractual sanctions between buyer and seller also vary between the two sectors. A very well developed system of contract law governs relations between the producer and purchaser in the formal sector. The ultimate recourse for relief is legal action. This does not mean that exchanges in the informal sector are without recourse. Since most exchanges are initiated and occur within a social network, the major sanction is social. This is especially true if the exchange has been initiated by a referral agent who is known and respected both by the buyer and the seller. These social sanctions may in many cases have as strong an influence as legal sanction.

We conclude that the element of risk is greater in the informal sector than in the formal sector. The protective measures put in place by state and federal governments offer a high degree of security not found in the informal sector.

Norms of exchange.   Economic exchanges and transactions are highly impersonalized within a framework of market rules and regulations in the formal sector. Every effort is made to depersonalize transactions. In contrast, transactions in the informal sector are for the most part highly personalized and reciprocity-oriented. The informal sector is underpinned by personalistic values, characteristic of social networks. Some transactions approach market norms but even these are tinged with emotive tones. Frequently, as a condition of exchange, personalistic values must be honored.

THE WORK FORCE OF THE INFORMAL ECONOMY

The work force of the informal economy is composed of people from all walks of life. The informal labor force includes workers employed full time and part time in the regular economy; persons currently unemployed in the regular economy; new entrants into the labor market; people not officially in the labor force; children, students, homemakers, retired individuals. There is no one type of irregular worker. Some depend on transfer payments for basic income; others are financially secure. Irregular work is not dominated by any racial, ethnic, social, or occupational grouping. Anyone who derives any unreported income from any source is a member of the irregular economy.

A work force typology based on participation in the formal and/or informal sector of the economy (table 2) gives us some clues (but not numbers) as to the worker groups that constitute the irregular work force. Our field observations in the Detroit study in 1977 indicated a group of workers who participated in both the informal and formal sectors of the economy, and we labeled them *moonlighters*. These workers acquired their skills through conventional training and were employed in licensed and regulated work organizations. They utilized these skills and the tools/technologies that were part of their regular employment for work opportunities in the irregular economy. Their work in the irregular economy was episodic and flexible, being fit around the demands of

Table 2.   Work Force Typology Based on Participaton in the Formal and/or Informal Sectors of the Economy

	Participation in the Formal Sector	
	High	*Low*
Participation in the Informal Sector		
High	Moonlighter	Transfer payment recipients
		• welfare clients
		• disabled
		• social security recipient
		• insured unemployed
		Young children
		New labor force entrants
		Discouraged workers
Low	"Straight-arrow worker"	Economic retreatist

the regular job and social obligations at home. The work organization was very flexible and included other workers who also had regular employment. There was no sense of permanency to these informal work organizations; most lasted for the duration of a job or a limited number of jobs. As a rule, prices for work were about one-third or one-half less than regular market prices. Motivation for participation in both the formal and informal sectors varied; the majority of these moonlighters felt that a stable source of income was necessary for their life-style but that irregular income offered them an opportunity to raise their standard of living. In addition, the regular job offered certain protection (health coverage, unemployment insurance) that were not available in irregular employment. These workers craved resource stability but also wanted the option of added income. Many of these workers had established skills to begin with.

A second group of respondents did not participate in the formal sector of the economy but were active in the informal sector. The largest group in this category were *transfer payment recipients* (welfare clients, the disabled, social security recipients, and the insured unemployed). The motivation was to supplement what was regarded by them as meager social payments. Some in this group also used informal activity to try out new job skills or businesses that they felt had long-run possibilities for work careers. Children were also represented in this category; the youngest was eight and the oldest was fifteen. Their activities ranged from gardening and baby-sitting to the manufacture and door-to-door distribution of jewelry. These children, excluded by child labor laws from participating in the formal sector of the economy, sought income gathering for a variety of reasons in the informal sector. Another group of workers that was active in the informal sector but not in the formal sector was drawn from *new labor market entrants*. Large numbers of youths (ages seventeen to twenty-one) were engaged in a variety of irregular economic activity. Lacking specialized skills and/or an established work history, these young workers found it difficult to become attached to employment in the formal sector. Many of them described their work activity as temporary until they could get regular employment, but others saw irregular work as a necessary, long-term alternative to jobs in a labor market in which they felt locked out. A similar picture existed for some of the workers who were recent *immigrants* to this country. Facing language barriers and a lack of skill coupled with large-scale discrimination, these immigrants sought some relief in informal sector employment. Finally, there were the *discouraged workers,* who had given up the search for employment in the formal sector. The age range here was from sixteen to sixty-five years of age. Their abandonment of the search for regular jobs was the result of a complex set of psychological, social, and economic factors, ranging from a burned-out worker syndrome to the lack of fair wage employment opportunities. They sought the recourse of irregular employment.

A third group of workers did not participate in the informal sector but rather, earned all of their income in the formal sector—*straight arrow workers*. They professed to have sufficient resources for their standard of living and were wary of the difficulties and problems that could arise if they were caught participating in irregular work. Some of them felt that "it was morally wrong to make money and not report it to IRS."

Finally, there were the *economic retreatists,* who did not participate in either the formal or informal sector of the economy. They appeared to be beset by emotional problems of different types and not to have much interest in economic exchanges and trading. Many of these were homeless—the vagrant and the bag lady. They explored the environment for sustenance but did not appear willing or able to undertake the social and psychological commitments required for participation in the formal or informal sectors of the economy.

From this brief sketch, two conclusions can be drawn. First, the work force of the informal sector is not uniform but represents a variety of workers in different circumstances. Consequently, a complex of motives underpins participation in the informal sector. Second, the informal sector itself must be seen as a conceptual umbrella under which a variety of economic systems operate. The informal sector can be understood only if we accept these perspectives.

FEMALE PARTICIPATION IN THE
IRREGULAR ECONOMY

Thus far, we have sketched the contours of the irregular economy, the values/norms that underlie it, and the nature of its work force. We turn now to some description of how it actually operates for a category of workers. We have elected to focus on female workers and their participation in the irregular economy.

Previous analyses of the irregular economy have focused on male rather than female workers. There are no precise data on sex differences in irregular economy participation, but the study of the irregular economy in nine Detroit neighborhoods in 1975 reveals a mosaic pattern of female participation in irregular work, both as suppliers and consumers. A number of social conditions would push females toward the irregular economy. First, the occupational structure of the society is inequitable in terms of jobs available or offered, the content of the jobs, and the compensation offered. The regular opportunity structure offers far less to women than to men, which suggests that women would seek alternatives to work in the regular economy. Second, the social infrastructure of our society is far less supportive of women than of men. Lack of specialized skill training, absence of child-caring facilities, and lack of employer allowances for female obligations in the family impose considerable barriers for females in the regular market. Work cannot easily be restructured to make it compatible with the family obligations of many women. Third, there is a lack of a highly developed formal and informal support system for women in work. Access to risk capital from lending institutions and to information about techniques and work methods still follow well-worn Indian pathways trod previously by men. Even access to high opportunity jobs tends to be restricted to social networks dominated by male gatekeepers. Since the majority of jobs in our society are passed on through such networks, many women do not get to know about these jobs, much less compete for them. Given these barriers posed by formal and informal institutions of the society, many women are put in the position of devising strategies about how to overcome such inequities or how to expand job options to mitigate some of the barriers.

We can classify female participation in the irregular economy into five overlapping categories:

cottage industry
transfer payment supplements
flexible job holding
nontraditional jobs
service jobs

Cottage Industry

According to the Small Business Administration, in 1981 there was a record increase in new business starts: 580,607 compared to 533,520 in 1980. The Internal Revenue Service (IRS) reports that from 1975 to 1981 the number of self-employed on its records rose 23.4 percent from 5.6 million to slightly more than 6.9 million. And these numbers do not reflect new entrepreneurs working in the underground economy. What has happened during recent recessions is what usually happens in hard times: more people go into business for themselves, using the home as a locus of work operations.

For a variety of reasons, women have been prominent in irregular economy entrepreneurship. In many cases, the advent of unemployment for the male spouse has triggered the need for income gathering activity on the part of the female spouse. Faced with inadequate preparation for regular jobs in the labor market, these women have often turned to the marketing of home production products and services. Such services and goods include housecleaning, shopping and transportation services, interior decorating, food catering, jewelry making, baking goods, and crafting of porcelain products. Home-based entrepreneurship may combine the talents and services of a number of family members; requires minimal capital and labor investment; optimizes profit since tax and license costs are nil; and offers an opportunity to honor family obligations without being absent from home.

Home-based businesses in the irregular economy offer other advantages for women. First, the avoidance of complicated, often time-consuming licensing and certification procedures. Being outside the regular market, women entrepreneurs can acquire knowledge and information (administrative and technical) in unconventional, informal ways: through social networks of friends and acquaintances, short courses of instruction, reading, and instruction in the college of practical experience. Most preparation scenarios for regular businesses require a lengthy mix of supervised book learning and practical experience. All of this can be shortcut in the irregular economy. Second, the opportunity to try out work scenarios without an extensive capital and time investment. These cottage-based businesses provide an opportunity to test out work options without extensive financial risk or legal entanglements if they fail. Third, risk capital becomes available not through formal lending institutions, but through the resources (financial and material) of social networks of friends, relatives, and consumers. One does not need collateral for these loans, and one need not pay an exorbitant rate of interest. These circumstances permit small business development that would not be possible in the regular economy.

Cottage industry is also helped by societal advances in technology. Office equipment and machinery have become increasingly compact and portable so that they can be installed and operated in the home. The typewriter, the paper copier, and the calculator no longer need be operated and maintained in an office setting. The advent of the word processor has carried this physical divorcement between office setting and technology to an extreme. An operator at home can receive instructions and assignments through a phone connection, making it unnecessary to leave the home setting for any reason. This cottage entrepreneurship can have favorable consequences both for the employer and the home operator. The employer can hand out assignments on a piece rate basis and avoid expensive fringe benefits by not adding the operator to the company payroll. The free-lancing becomes a cheap way to get the work done. The employer can also maintain quality control by checking the printed output of the operator on the office terminal, avoiding the necessity for bringing him or her into the office. The operator, on the other hand, obtains more control over the work environment and the pace of work. Compensation for the operator may also be higher since he or she can trade off the fringe benefits, inherent in a regular job, for a higher hourly rate of pay. This cottage entrepreneurship may indeed be perceived as a favorable circumstance both to the company and the home-based entrepreneur.

Transfer Payment Supplements

A second instance of female participation in the irregular economy is found among those women who receive one form or another of transfer payment. The receipt of payment benefits usually excludes work activity in the regular economy. To engage in such work is to face the prospect of penalty, usually the reduction or loss of benefits. Such benefit payments include disability payments under Social Security, Aid to Families with Dependent Children (AFDC), and Veterans Disability Payments. Given the inadequacy of many transfer payment systems, there is a strong temptation to earn money "off-the-books."

This category of participation covers a broad category of irregular work activities: baby-sitting, home repair, decorating, the production of goods (food, jewelry, furnishings). Many of these workers are unskilled or have no formal credentials for work. The jobs they take are usually episodic, short-term, and low paying. In and of itself, the irregular job does not yield sufficient income to maintain an adequate life style. This income must be combined with transfer payments to meet a minimum standard of living. These activities are not only income producing but therapeutic, and in some cases they are used as testing situations for regular employment.

We can explore the set of circumstances involved in the irregular employment of AFDC mothers by reviewing several cases from our 1975 study of Detroit neighborhoods. These cases suggest work motivations and work rewards that may stimulate movement of aid recipients into the irregular economy. What is important is that such recipients engage in risk-taking behavior to improve or stabilize their living situations. The notion of irregular income in these cases must be framed as problems of economic existence, not as moral problems of welfare cheaters.

A mother and one dependent child living in Detroit received about $324 per month in direct cash assistance in the summer of 1975. The work incentive plan allowed an AFDC mother to earn up to $100 per month before losing any of her allotment. If she earned more than this amount and reported it, she would end up with a lower total income than she could accrue by earning only $100, since a large amount would be deducted from the assistance check. In order to match the amount of money she could get from public welfare, we estimate—taking account of the costs of child care, taxes, and increased food costs in the absence of food stamps—she would have had to earn at least $700 a month in a regular job. When one then considers the physical and psychological stresses that might accompany her work (that is, separation from children, housekeeping after a full workday, job pressures), the income earned from full employment would probably have to be much greater in order to prompt most AFDC recipients to leave the rolls. Further, many AFDC mothers do not possess the skills or work experience to qualify for these relatively high-paying jobs. Others are not physically able to hold down a full-time job.

Mrs. Scruth is an example of someone who needs the unreported income for economic survival and is unable to earn a living through regular employment:

Mrs. Scruth is fifty-three years old, divorced, unemployed, and ill. She is receiving AFDC and public assistance. She is physically unable to care for her home, and a housekeeper is provided once a week through a social service agency. She has housed at least two roomers over the last five years. They are charged monthly rent for room and board and the income is not reported for tax purposes. Mrs. Scruth requires her tenants to pay their rent promptly, as this income is vital to her.

If she were cut off public assistance because of this unreported income, it is hard to know how Mrs. Scruth would survive, since any other money-making activities are essentially blocked by her health problems.

Our other three AFDC informants were younger than Mrs. Scruth and did not have severe health problems, but there were other reasons for their irregular activities. Mary Lou Jones needed the money to finance the future education of her children:

Mary Lou Jones is in her early thirties and receives AFDC and some child support for her two daughters ages eleven and twelve. She works as a barmaid in a nearby tavern four days a week, from 2 to 10 P.M. She is paid in cash weekly and does not report this income. She does not possess any clerical or secretarial skills and has no desire for factory work despite the higher wages she might earn from it. She feels compelled to work in order to finance her daughters' future educations, as both are excellent students. For the most part she enjoys her work and the opportunity to be around people. By working irregularly, she is able to maintain a decent standard of living, hold a job which is both flexible and rewarding, and save for her daughters' educations.

In choosing the type of irregular activity she did, Mary Lou Jones gave great importance to the fact that she enjoyed the work. This was also true for Linda Geary, who was engaged in child care in her own home:

Linda Geary is twenty-five years old, has a six-year old daughter, and is getting a divorce from her second husband, from whom she has been separated for four years. Linda quit school in the eighth grade and first got married when she was sixteen. She receives AFDC and she and her daughter live with her brother and his wife. She cares for their house and their child while they both work in exchange for her rent. She earns additional unreported income by caring for several other children in her home. She advertises on local bulletin boards and charges from $30 per child per week for day care and lunch. By taking a number of children, she claims she "can earn as much per hour as working in a restaurant, but the work is easier." Linda has had a varied work career, having been employed at different times as a waitress, short-order cook, cosmetic salesperson, telephone solicitor, clerical in a gas station, and even as an employee in a chicken factory for $2.25 an hour. She prefers caring for children in her own home because "there are not as many pressures and children are more honest. If the kid likes you, you know it immediately." Linda is studying for her GED [General Equivalency Diploma] and has applied to the WIN program for training in writing. Her dream is to become a journalist, as it is something she could do at home with no fixed hours. Barring this, she would like to work with children, perhaps with crippled children in an institution.

To some extent, the work Linda Geary is doing in the irregular economy can be viewed as a way of preparing herself for regular employment when her circumstances change. Though it has economic benefits for her at the present time, this irregular activity may actually be more important in its long-term consequences for conventional employment. The benefits of irregular activity in developing the basis for regular employment are even clearer in the case of Mary Jane Folkers:

> Mary Jane Folkers is 28 and has two children in elementary school. She has been divorced for five years after marrying at the age of 17. Mary Jane is a high school dropout but operates a full-time irregular interior decorating business out of her home. She had never regarded her skill as a seamstress as a potential income source until a neighbor asked her to make a slip cover for her sofa. The neighbor was so pleased with her work that she then requested Mary Jane to make drapes as well. The business developed gradually as word spread and people began to consult her about colors and choice of fabrics as well as her sewing. Today she is doing "quite well" and has hired a friend to assist with the sewing. She says she eventually plans to open a regular shop but is not anxious to do so at the moment since she would then lose her eligibility for AFDC.

In the transition between irregular work and regular employment, it is probably necessary for most of these single parents with dependent children to rely on AFDC payments for basic financial support. But if the transition is successful, we can probably expect them to leave the roles and become self-supporting. It is thus important to look at the irregular economy as a means by which at least some AFDC mothers can provide a few extras for their families and/or as a way to begin to sever their ties with public assistance.

Many public welfare recipients, however, are unskilled and lack work experience, and the irregular economy cannot be viewed as the major avenue for movement into well-paying conventional employment. Other types of manpower training and career development options must be made available to them, and these services must be planned with the special needs of these mothers in mind.

Flexible Job Holding

Another group of female participants in the irregular economy could be classified as flexible jobholders. Among these women, there was a well-developed norm that a desirable work situation was one in which they had control over working conditions and work schedule. A substantial number of these women stated this preference because they had family obligations, while others stated it as an "anti–time clock punching" value. These women found little to attract them to regular jobs with fixed hours, centralized control, and fixed work scenarios. They viewed the irregular economy not only as an alternative income opportunity structure, but also as another option for work flexibility. They were willing to forego the fringe benefits of a regular job to achieve this flexibility.

We can identify three types of jobs that permit work flexibility. The first is employment that the worker can choose to fit her schedule (for example, baby-sitting assignments or telephone soliciting). The worker has some choice in the hours to be worked. The second is employment that is made possible by assignments to be completed at the discretion of the worker (for example, word processing or typing). The machine may be located at home or in the office, but the worker decides the hours to be worked and the pace of work. Finally, there is the sales job, usually door-to-door, with no fixed schedule of work. In all three instances, the worker is able to write her own ticket regarding flexibility.

Nontraditional Jobs

The elite jobs in a blue-collar society are in the skilled crafts: electrician, plumber, and carpenter. They are high-paying and offer prestige and union protection. Entry into these jobs is highly controlled, and they have remained male-dominated; few women gain access to apprenticeship training, much less participation in the trades. Further, the skilled crafts are characterized by a highly controlled learning structure and licensing procedure under state supervision.

In the irregular economy, women have participated in such craft jobs. Techniques and knowledge about the job are acquired in unconventional ways. Frequently, they receive personal instruction from a relative or friend. Some women have gained technical information by attending how-to hobby classes. The proliferation of how-to books has also been a source of information. Obviously these women work without license and confine themselves to tasks that are simple and need no official permit from local authority. In a few cases, this work experience has been recognized by the union and made the basis of apprenticeship status, but this is the exception rather than the rule. These craftswomen attract a clientele by offering bargain rates and by confining themselves to job assignments that skilled craftsmen consider insignificant. Without doubt, given the opportunity for training, these women could become full members in the trade.

Service Jobs

Another category of job held by women in the irregular econo-my is in service employment: waitressing, car washing, domestic work, and sales. Most of these jobs are also found in the regular economy. They are low-paying, offer little protection, and carry few benefits. The issue for most women in these jobs is survival. They bargain with employers for higher wages by permitting the employer to forego payment into social insurance programs (social security, unemployment insurance). The employer is willing to pay more because the job is off-the-books, and he realizes a considerable saving in payments into the social insurance funds. In many cases these are the jobs of last resort for women, and hence they have little bargaining power. The tragedy is that they receive no insurance credit for their work and are vulnerable since they are not covered by health insurance, unemployment compensation, or social security benefits.

SIGNIFICANCE OF THE IRREGULAR ECONOMY

As Eric Wolf has said, complex societies are "not as well organized or tightly knit as their spokesmen would on occasion like to make people believe" (1966:1). Official economic statistics are generally assumed to measure accurately the real production of the society and the current deployment of the labor force. Our immediate response to news briefs announcing the government's latest estimates of Gross National Product, employment or unemployment betrays our acceptance of the official models as true reflections of economic activity. But our research has shown that there is a widespread irregular economy that is ignored in official estimates of economic activity. The magnitude of the economic activity that escapes enumeration in the national accounts is unknown, but recent estimates based on slippages in macroeconomic statistics for 1976 vary from $176 billion (Gutmann 1977) to $369 billion (Feige 1979). That is, the size of the irregular economy in the United States in 1976 may have equaled up to 19 percent of the regular, enumerated Gross National Product. Furthermore, both Gutmann and Feige assert that the irregular economy is continuing to grow and that its expansion is at the expense of the regular economy. If this is so, the success of monetary and employment policies and programs based on official statistics may be doomed from the onset.

Our study of the irregular economy points up the fact that there are alternative informal activities that generate paid work. Quite apart from the large blocks of unpaid work in the social economy and the block of recorded paid work in the regular economy, there are mechanisms in the economy whereby flexible work arrangements for pay are available. The importance of these arrangements is that they offer some workers an opportunity to cope with life situations that require new sources of income; for example, layoffs, inadequate transfer payments, inflation—any pressures on prices. What should be recognized here is that this form of income support is controlled by relationships between buyers and sellers in the irregular economy and not by public agencies. In this sense, it may be a more flexible income-producing tool than institutionalized aid programs in which eligibility rules play a prominent role.

Conventional constructs of labor force analysis must be revised to account for unconventional patterns of work. The conventional categorization of the work population into "employed," "unemployed," and "not in the labor force" has to be recognized as an analytical distinction not wholly in step with real labor force behavior. Some employed workers in our study did more work than was officially recognized or recorded. Some officially unemployed workers actually worked during their period of unemployment and some workers who were officially "out of the labor force" actually did some work and were actively seeking work in the regular labor market. Conventional constructs obscure the actual operations of the labor force and the economy.

We need new models to more adequately represent work careers. Most careers are described in terms of job changes from one regular job to another; or shifts from a regular job to a period of unemployment; or in shifts from a work or unemployment status to a "left the labor force" status. Certainly we must now add to career analyses some concern with periods of irregular employment and the function that it plays in the total organization of the career. Adding this information may be made more difficult by the fact that irregular activities can co-exist with other labor force statuses. This means that some theories of the neat stages of labor market behavior may have to be revised to include an overlay of various kinds of irregular activity.

Finally, we speculate that the rules and regulations, the entire bureaucratic apparatus that has been built up to protect and nurture the regular economy, have created an environment where informal mechanisms of production and distribution are actually necessary. The regular economy is increasingly dominated by large concerns whose products are geared toward mass markets and mass profits. Regulations designed to protect workers and consumers and the bureaucratic red tape involved have tended to create an atmosphere antithetical to regular production for a localized or specialized market unless there is some guarantee of profit margin. The irregular economy is not merely a stepchild of recession and high unemployment. Nor is it simply the bastard of excessively high tax rates and general inflation. The irregular economy is the legitimate child of the marriage of business and the state, an elegant economic and social welfare structure which sets context for an irregular economy and is dependent on informal processes to continue operation.

REFERENCES

Dow, Leslie M., Jr. 1977. "High Weeds in Detroit." *Urban Anthropology* 6(2):111–28.

Feige, Edgar L. 1979. "The Irregular Economy: Its Size and Macroeconomic Implications." Social Systems Research Institute, University of Wisconsin, mimeo.

Ferman, Louis A., Louise Berndt, and Elaine Selo. 1978. "Analysis of the Irregular Economy: Cash Flow in the Informal Sector." A report to the Bureau of Employment

and Training, Michigan Department of Labor, Institute of Labor and Industrial Relations, University of Michigan–Wayne State University, Ann Arbor, Michigan.

Gutmann, Peter. 1977. "The Subterranean Economy." *Financial Analysts Journal,*
November/December, pp. 26, 27, 34.

Newcomber, Mabel. 1961. "The Little Businessman: A Study of Business Proprietors
in Poughkeepsie, New York." *Business History Review* (Winter): 477–531.

Weeks, John. 1975. "Policies for Expanding Employment in the Informal Urban Sector
of Developing Countries." *International Labour Review* (January): 1–13.

Wolf, Eric R. 1962. "Kinship, Friendship, and Patron-Client Relations in Complex
Societies." In *The Social Anthropology of Complex Societies,* edited by Michael
Banton. A.S.A. Monographs 4. London: Tavistock Publications.

| | | | | | | | Double Lives

STANTON WHEELER

"His failures as a reporter and a practicing attorney were behind him, and he found his vocation in the insurance world, where he was to stay for the rest of his life." But for this gentleman, being a lawyer for an insurance company didn't really capture his sense of self. Shortly after he began this vocation, he wrote to a new girlfriend, "I should like to make a music of my own, a literature of my own, and I should like to live my own life." And he did so. In fact, two of them. For the rest of his life, the person we know as the poet Wallace Stevens led a double life. The money that made life comfortable came from the offices of insurance companies. The quality that gave it richness and joy came from writing poetry.

Like many who lead double lives, Wallace Stevens was troubled by the condition. He complained that working for the American Bonding Company made it impossible to get away, even on Saturday afternoons, to visit J. P. Morgan's collection of manuscripts on display at Columbia University's library, where he wanted to study the work of John Keats. At one point he said, "It seems insincere, like playing a part, to be one person on paper and another in reality."

But which was the reality? He had this to say about working in the insurance business: "I certainly do not exist from nine to six when I am at the office. Today was the anniversary [his first year with a new firm]; but tonight I could not write a single verse. There is no everyday Wallace, apart from the one at work—and that one is tedious. At night, I strut my individual state once more."

Wallace Stevens is one of a number of illustrious people who have led double lives. William Carlos Williams, a contemporary of Stevens, was a physician by day, a poet by night. Charles Ives left music to earn a living, like Stevens, through insurance. (Maybe something about the field of insurance encourages double lives.) But he gained a sense of self and later recognition from his music compositions. The actor Paul Newman is another—we know him through his films, but he expresses much of his self and his being through race car driving.

But double lives are not only for the illustrious. Let me describe a fellow I shall call George, a janitor at a school for children with learning disabilities. We met as I was moving from one house to another. He answered an ad I had placed announcing a refrigerator and stove for sale. But his interest was not alone in kitchen appliances. He asked of my new abode: "Have you gone completely through the attic and the basement?" When I expressed some curiosity at the question, he said that it quite often happened that people left old model trains or parts of trains when they moved from one house to another.

George, it turned out, spent his evenings and weekends on model railroading. On a janitor's salary, he had filled his basement with what he estimated to be $50,000 to $60,000 worth of model railroading equipment. He was also an officer in the model railroading society, and when he and his wife went on vacation they frequently went to model railroading conventions. During the workday his mind was often on model railroading, and he spent most evenings in the basement with his son. They were engaged in what some might have called playing with trains, but it clearly had a larger significance than that for him. It was a way of being special, of mastering a particular niche in the universe. It was perhaps his chief source of identity, the thing that made him distinctive as a human being. And it also organized his social life. He observed, apropos the model railroading conventions: "You meet the nicest people."

George and Wallace Stevens are only two examples of a phenomenon I believe to be important and increasingly familiar. Virtually any human activity has the capacity to become enough of a preoccupation for someone to consider it a core part of their life. You will all have your own examples, but I'll give you a handful simply to fill out the range. I have known a high school teacher so deeply into birding—searching out and identifying the names and call of birds—that many dawns and virtually all weekends are consumed with the activity. I know a Jewish lawyer who describes himself as "an Israel person." His time and identity are very tied up with the fate of Israel as a nation and a culture, and he sees his work as a necessary interference with that commitment. I know a secretary in New York who spends virtually all her savings beyond the necessities of life in attending a wide array of musical events. Her work is in a Manhattan office tower, but her life and her heart are at Lincoln Center. I also know a bailiff who sings operatic arias on the job and who is committed to the study of opera. The morning paper tells of a policeman who, much to the surprise of his colleagues, has just published a first book of poetry. I know a woman in Vermont whose gardens are so well known that people come from around the town to admire them. Her life is made full by the flowers she grows during the hours and hours she spends in the garden. And, of course, the world of games and sports, like the world of art and music, provides many examples:

while for most these activities are mere pastimes, for a few they become the central, organizing focus of their lives. This has been true of tennis and golf, of rock climbing and deep sea diving, of bridge and chess. And those who love old things can often turn that love into a double life. There are persons whose evenings and weekends are consumed repairing and displaying antique automobiles.

The key idea here—and the keystone of my topic—is that work, if it ever did, no longer provides a full sense of vocation. The special calling, the investment in something for its own sake, the commitment, constrained only by the demands of work and family, to an activity that is its own reward—that is my central concern.

It is important to be absolutely clear about what the subject is not. It is not what is normally thought of as "leisure studies," the study of hobbies or avocational pursuits. It bears a close family resemblance to be sure, for one and the same activity may serve some as a diversion or a time filler and others in the much more significant role I am interested in here. Rather than hobbies, these activities may be thought of as *preoccupations*—things so important to the self that it is hard to get them off one's mind and out of one's thoughts. But I admit that it is not easy to find a clear and sharp boundary. My criterion would be a social-psychological one: If the person himself or herself does not think of the activity in question as truly central to their life and their well-being, then it doesn't qualify as a preoccupation and won't necessitate a double life.

Do the activities from which double lives are constructed have any special attributes? I think they do. They must have enough complexity and enough detail to be able to capture one's interest and hold one's commitment. But that, of course, is a relative matter. The level of complexity is a function of the starting point—it perhaps depends on one's own level of intelligence. If the starting point is fairly low it may not require a great deal of complexity to leave plenty of room for most of us to expand our horizons without exhausting the material at hand.

I am thinking of central life interests (Dubin 1956) that fall outside the sphere of the family, the workplace, and religion. Clearly for some people it may be enough to express one's self through these major institutions. The mother or father of the year awards that are given in some communities may indeed go to those who have made their families a preoccupation, devoting all free time to family time. And there are many we know as workaholics, for whom work is not only an occupation but a preoccupation. And I am not talking, at least for these purposes, about those whose other life or double life is essentially a deviant one matched with a conventional cover—the classic double agent, the quiet officeworker by day who is a sneak thief at night, or those doing conventional jobs whose lives are preoccupied with deviant sexual practices of one kind or another. I am talking about the enormous variety of ways of giving individuality and distinctiveness to the self through pursuits that are legitimate, though not ones that every neighbor is going to be interested in. These are the activities that add infinite variety and color to life, that add diversity and range to human experience.

Double lives are not a new phenomenon. They can probably be found in some number in virtually every civilization, but certainly not in the same rates or numbers. For all but the leisure classes, preindustrial societies pretty much ruled out the level of involvement that is required to sustain a double life. Work was too hard and there was too much of it. One had to define one's self in relation to one's work because it consumed such a large portion of the waking hours. But a number of conditions have changed so as to make double lives a more prevalent phenomenon now than in the past.

Most important is the changing nature of work. Work for most people is less back-breaking than it used to be and less time-consuming as well. When the forty-hour work week replaced the forty-eight- or sixty-hour week, when clean and light industry replaced heavy industry, and when mechanical tools were developed and took much of the burden off the human body, both time and energy were freed up and available for allocation elsewhere. Sometimes, of course, this time and energy went into a second or even a third job, the economic pressures remaining despite improvements in the workplace. But often they were available for preoccupations.

Changes in values may have occurred as well. When a production society becomes a consumption society, there may be increased demand for goods and activities that allow more opportunity for individual self-expression.

Double lives may grow in importance as institutional networks weaken. If people have fewer children, weaker extended kinship systems, and less of a sense of rootedness in family or religion, they have lost important sources for the construction of social identity, and they may have as a result greater need for the kinds of identity I am describing.

If one of the important attributes of preoccupations is that they allow persons to develop a distinctive sense of self—a special identity and a special niche in life—then there are two further conditions of modern society that tend to favor the emergence of double lives. The first is sheer population density. It is easier to sustain the preoccupation or double life when others are doing it too. But if distinctiveness comes in part from the fact that few other people do it, only the largest areas may have enough of a population base to sustain the culture of the preoccupation. To take a distinctly nonrandom example, those who currently pursue jazz music as a serious preoccupation will find a culture of jazz in New York and to some degree in a handful of other major cities, but the number of talented professionals to listen to and learn from as well as the number of amateurs who share a high level of commitment is likely to be too small in out-of-the-way places. So cities, those breeding grounds of diversity and specialization, become a favorite home for those with a passionate commitment to activities other than work and family.

A second condition is the emergence of the photocopying machine and similar tools of communication. Many who don't live in large urban areas nevertheless sustain a strong preoccupation, in part through special-interest newsletters. Only a few preoccupations have such a mass following as to allow the regular appearance of articles about them in daily newspapers, though bridge, chess, and coin and stamp collecting may get attention in the largest dailies. But it is the inexpensive, do-it-yourself newsletter, now made much cheaper and easier to produce by xerography, that enables networks of those consumed with a given preoccupation to stay in touch and keep the network going. We might also expect that as television increases the potential for diverse programing made possible by cable, it may be possible for some preoccupations to be encouraged and reinforced through that medium.

When all of these conditions are present we have the potential for a flourishing of preoccupations—and of double lives. But it remains only a potential until individuals actually become preoccupied. What determines whether they will become preoccupied and what their preoccupation will be? It is too early to support generalizations in this area, and perhaps there won't be any. Perhaps the fact of a preoccupation and the object of the preoccupation are both functions of so many situational contingencies that it will be hard to generalize about them. Certainly some people simply fall into a side interest and don't realize until much later that it has become a preoccupation. Others may feel a lack in their lives, a real need for a deeper involvement, and may consciously throw themselves into the activity in question. It may be enough for some folks to dabble in this and that, giving the appearance of well-roundedness, but not letting any one thing or activity grow to the point of becoming a preoccupation. Others may find they have an all or nothing at all attitude: either the thing is worth doing wholeheartedly so that it becomes a major part of the self or it is to be dropped altogether, it being less painful to drop it than to sustain the activity at unsatisfactorily low levels of involvement.

All those preconditions, being expressed, it is nonetheless true that many preoccupations seem to have their roots in events of childhood or adolescence. They are often activities first undertaken at an early age. Not a lot of research has been done on the topic, but Dale Dannefer's study of old car enthusiasts lends support to this view.

Dannefer studied those who organize their lives around collecting, restoring, showing, and touring in antique automobiles, and they are a fine example of the phenomenon I am talking about. Here is his description:

The consciousness and the round of activities that typify the social world of old cars are sustained by a genuine and intense subjective attraction that can accurately be described as passionate. From the standpoint of participants, it is clear that the social network of car people exists for the sake of this passion. When the enthusiast—most often a male—climbs into his old car, it envelopes him and insulates him from the world. When he settles back into the seat, it comforts him. When he turns the key and the engine responds, it submits to him. When he puts it in gear and drives away, it serves and glorifies him. If it's a dependable car, it is anthropomorphized as a benevolent friend. If it is of massive size, it appears "damn near omnipotent"— especially if it is loud, or fast, or both. If it contains an engineering innovation, its cleverness is regarded as the product of superior knowledge. For many, it is a point of contact for treasured memories of the past and, so long as it is taken care of, it will remain so for the foreseeable future. These are some of the reasons that people find to become passionate about cars. (Dannefer 1980)

Half of the old car enthusiasts that Dannefer studied said they had been fascinated by cars since their childhood and youth. Their interest appears to have been a distinctly individualistic and private one. Only after becoming strongly committed did many of them learn of the existence of a world of car people with similar interests. Others in Dannefer's sample were late bloomers who often had a strong interest in cars when very young but did not pursue them as collectors until years later.

It seems at least plausible to me that all those special extracurricular activities that occur in the more affluent school systems—the camera clubs, language clubs, nature clubs, and the like that are offered sometimes to spell relief from training in the three r's—may also provide early experience in what may become the locus of a more lasting commitment.

The enormous range and variety of possible preoccupations make any classification scheme both much needed and much in doubt. How are we to know what the central qualities are, and what dimensions it is most important to isolate and identify?

The second dimension is whether the activity in question is privatizing, in the sense that it must be pursued essentially on one's own and may require isolation from others—poetry is a good example—or whether the activity throws one into the company of others, as do bridge and team sports. Many provide a mix of both, as when amateur musicians practice alone but get together with others for performances.

This dimension of range of involvement may be particularly important in the relationship between the person with the preoccupation and his most significant others. Some preoccupations may bind families, as all members join in the same activity. There are skiing families, golfing families, bowling families, singing families. But sometimes the preoccupation pulls one away from significant others. It may be what makes the person special *to* the family rather than *with* the family. And it may, indeed, by a source of aggravation to those outside the activity. The person's heart may be seen as not really lying with the others but with the preoccupation.

Another obvious basis of classification is cost. People who are poor may be able to afford a preoccupation, but they won't have much choice, for most of the activities we have discussed require a degree of financial as well as emotional investment. A relatively high level of affluence in a society will enable the kind of cost commitments that allow expensive preoccupations to flourish. But here again it is a relative matter. Those whose lives are lived through music can stand at the back or sit in the fifth balcony if necessary, and those who are invested in old cars don't have to work on the most expensive models.

I began this paper by discussing double lives, and I have drifted into talking about preoccupations. There is obviously an intimate relationship between the two, and I should like to end the paper by discussing that relationship. For some people, of course, work *is* their preoccupation, and they have no double life in the sense that I'm using it here. For others, work bears a variety of relationships to the preoccupation in question. Sometimes the work is chosen precisely because it fits in with the preoccupation that one is hoping to convert into an occupation: the legions of young actors, dancers, musicians, and writers who wait on tables in New York and Los Angeles are examples.

More commonly, people bend their occupation to fit their preoccupation. I've known firemen who love golf more than family life and who work nights in order to have the daylight hours free to pursue that passion. And there are, of course, many whose sense of identity is linked to place and who can move only so far because of it. Sailors and body surfers come to mind. In arranging their place of work, some place a high premium on access to their preoccupation. Is it only one subway ride away or does it require a change?

Many allow their preoccupation to become an occupation, as they leave what they do for money for what they think they love. When the preoccupation is turned into a way to make a living, it may well be a mixed blessing. One is then required to do what before one really loved doing for its own sake. Still, there are lawyers who have become professional photographers and stamp collectors, and art collectors who have become professional art dealers. I know a former pharmacist who loved books and book collecting and gave up pharmacy for it. He now owns two used book stores in New England, and summers find him on the roads of Vermont and New Hampshire, selling books out of an old car at various flea markets and small town celebrations. He says it's not as good a living, but he's happier selling books than packaging pills.

I have meant to do no more than raise a series of questions and observations about the passionate interests I have called preoccupations that for many lead to the living of double lives. The traditional image of a double life is that of a

Doctor Jekyll and Mr. Hyde. I am suggesting that double lives need not be organized in that stark a manner but may be the principal means by which people give expression to the self while doing paid work that provides only limited meaning and shape to their lives. If I'm right, double lives may increase in frequency as more people have more time away from work and find less meaning in work. A double life is an answer of a sort to the notion of worker alienation.

Perhaps my main theme is simply to suggest that although we know a great deal about how the world is divided up into levels of stratification, we still know little about how the world is divided into functional interests and pursuits. There is research on the so-called situs dimension as it applies to occupations, but that barely scratches the surface. If we spend relatively less time studying what people do and more studying what they really care about, we may come closer to learning how people construct workable identities. For Wallace Stevens, for George, and for legions of others, work and the workplace are not enough. What makes them distinctive and gives their life substance and character are activities they pursue elsewhere. These are labors of love in the truest sense.

REFERENCES

Dannefer, Dale. 1980. "Rationality and Passion in Private Experience: Modern Consciousness and the Social World of Old-Car Collectors." *Social Problems,* 27, no. 4: 392–93.

Dubin, Robert. 1956. "Industrial Workers' Worlds: A Study of the Central Life Interests of Industrial Workers." *Social Problems* 3.

‖‖‖‖‖ Labors of Love in Theory and Practice: A Prospectus

ELIOT FREIDSON

Few would deny that work is a basic human activity, not only because it produces the resources for survival, but also because it is the distinctively human method of gaining such resources and because it contains within it the potential for creativity. Nonetheless, most of what has been written about work through the ages is hostile in character. It is mostly seen as an arduous and joyless necessity or at best as a moral duty that will eventually yield rewards, if only in heaven (see Tilgher 1958; Anthony 1977). Few are the writers who have seen intrinsic virtues in work itself. But human society cannot survive without at least some people working. Must that work always be an unpleasant necessity, something to be merely minimized? Or can it be in itself creative and satisfying?

The most powerful and influential characterization of the everyday work of capitalist societies is no doubt that of Karl Marx, who stressed its alienated character. To him the labor of workers under capitalism does not allow self-fulfillment and runs counter to generic human nature. Forced by economic necessity rather than voluntary, it is not intrinsically satisfying: it is characteristically alienated. But he believed that work could and should be otherwise.

Powerful and influential as Marx's analysis is, it shares the weakness of the philosophical tradition from which he draws in that it asserts no really coherent positive ground on which its critical position can rest firmly, Bender's (1972:116–25) culling notwithstanding. What is the nature of labor that is not alienated, that is truly part of the nature of humanity, that is self-fulfilling, that is voluntary, intrinsically satisfying? Marx, who argues that theory should be wedded to practical action, does not concern himself with the conditions under which such labor becomes possible. Can a viable political economy be constituted in which unalienated labor is the norm? These critical questions are ones on which Marx and for that matter all self-styled critical writers with whom I am familiar are silent. Surely it is important to consider whether it is possible for the world of productive work to be otherwise.

Some of the elements necessary for an answer to those questions have been suggested. Hannah Arendt (1959) has attempted to provide some of the missing philosophical foundation for analysis by distinguishing between what she calls labor, which is a function of biological and economic necessity, and what she calls work, which is intrinsically and especially human in that it is creative rather than merely reproductive. Her conception of labor is related to Marx's analysis of alienated labor, and her conception of work is in some sense the obverse. And she relates work and labor to political participation in society. More recently Csikszentmihalyi, studying "people . . . who choose to expend energy for goals that carry no conventional material rewards" (1975:3), has explored in some depth the psychology of "peak experience" and the intrinsic gratifications of some kinds of activities, and Schwalbe (1986) has attempted to develop a reasoned theoretical conception of the social psychology of "natural" as opposed to alienated labor. In turn, Lawrence Haworth (1977) has attempted to address the issues involved in the organization of a society and economy that would permit and advance unalienated, creative labor. He argues the desirability of a society organized around the performance of creative work rather than around the consumption of goods and suggests that the institutions of professionalism can provide a viable source of organization.

But such discussions are scarce. The bulk of the literature on work has been concerned with the fact that people do not have work, that they are unemployed, and that when people do have work, it is characteristically unsatisfying. Both are important observations (though there is some debate as to the truth of the latter). But they do not help us understand unalienated work and the circumstances in which it becomes possible. The documents of Studs Terkel, for example, deserve our sympathy and attention, but they do not in themselves provide much aid in clarifying either the theoretical or the practical issues of developing less alienating forms of work and of creating less exploitative methods of managing work. Analyses of unemployment are even less helpful: based on official statistics, they are hostage to the assumptions and definitions underlying the categories and methods of those statistics. Official unemployment does not necessarily mean lack of work so much as lack of officially defined and recorded income from officially recognized work. Recent studies by writers such as Pahl (1984) rescue us both from sentimental complacency and from accepting received concepts of employment and unemployment.

On the whole, the impetus of discussions of work today has been overpractical. There has been little interest in tackling the underlying conceptual issues. The focus has been on the immediate problems of providing work and income to those who lack it and of providing rights to official employment benefits to those who, like homemakers, work without them. The importance of those problems cannot be deprecated, but as legitimate and necessary as a problem orientation may be to dealing with work today, many practical problems cannot be dealt with effectively without conceptual guidance.

At some quiet points in history, it is possible to deal with problems incrementally, step by step, tinkering with extant institutions on a purely practical basis, unconcerned with the underlying assumptions and distinctions. When such a method works it is because those institutions are still basically viable. When, however, quite basic changes are taking place in the foundation of a political economy, incremental and manipulative strategies of practical action may not provide even temporary solutions because of the essential weakness of those institutions. In such times, even if we are not able to create new concepts for as-yet-unrealized new institutions, we can at least sharpen our consciousness by making explicit the limitations of the concepts and theoretical assumptions that characterize our present-day institutions. That is what I hope to begin doing here for the concepts of labor and work.

In this paper I will suggest in a very preliminary way some of the conceptual distinctions that I believe are necessary to clarify the generic nature of work and its relation to economy and society. I shall do so by seeking to delineate a special kind of work whose characteristics bring into sharp focus the problems of analysis. I refer to the kind of work about which Marx and most other writers have been silent—the opposite of alienated labor. For that type of work I will use the phrase labors of love. In contrast to alienated labor, labors of love are voluntary. Being freely chosen, they can be part of the worker's nature and allow self-fulfillment. They imply motives for undertaking work that are not in the immediate and obvious sense self-interested, that are beyond economy. I shall ask, How are labors of love distinguished from other kinds of labor? To answer that question requires examining the concept of work or labor itself and contesting its conventional attachment to economy and exchange. When I do that, however, I must ignore the vast body of empirical material on blue-collar and white-collar work that we use to advance and sustain our present-day concept. The development of new concepts requires new empirical data. I shall conclude, therefore, by suggesting several major sources of empirical data on productive activities with only an indirect relationship to the market that can, if studied closely, stimulate the development of concepts that can embrace both alienated and unalienated labor.

FACETS OF WORK

The concept of work is intrinsically ambiguous and relative in all but one usage—when it refers to any activity that consumes energy. Should we wish to be objective and consistent in a positivist sense, work as the expenditure of energy is about the only conventionally recognized definition we can use. But that usage reduces human activities to the merely physical. The only difference between running a four-minute mile and operating a drill press is the amount of energy expended. Running a four-minute mile or, for that matter, a ten-minute mile, engaging in sexual intercourse, playing chess, and operating a drill press all expend energy and all are work.

But while the expenditure of energy is an element of work that is too important to ignore, it is perhaps not always a necessary and certainly never a sufficient criterion of work in the social world, where its social meaning is critical. In addition to the amount of energy, the type of energy-consuming activity has been used by a number of writers to distinguish various kinds of work. Of historic significance is the distinction between mental and manual labor (see Sohn-Rethel 1978), which implies a distinction between little and much physical effort as well as between clean and dirty work and dignified and undignified work. Work that is manual is unpleasant and to be avoided as much as possible: it is an arduous necessity since expulsion from the Garden of Eden. Work that is mental or intellectual, on the other hand, is not really work because it does not involve extensive physical effort. The social meaning of that distinction extends into issues of status or prestige, with manual labor being regarded as contemptible and those who perform it of low status, and mental labor being admirable and those performing it of high status. Rattansi (1982) argues that in his late work Marx gave up the idea of abolishing the division of labor and settled for the abolition of the separation of mental and manual tasks and an acceptance of leisure as the sphere in which freedom could be exercised. Indeed, that which is defined as work, whether manual or mental, is sometimes given lower status than not to be working at all. Those who spend their time in pursuits that are defined as leisure rather than work are the blessed.

Once we distinguish between work and leisure, however, we must jettison the use of the criterion of energy expenditure. All activities consume energy, and some leisure activities like sports can consume far more energy than most kinds of work, even manual labor. Thus, the only viable criterion for distinguishing leisure from work and various types of work from each other becomes the social meaning of activities, their value and the context in which they are undertaken. The same activity can be leisure, or nonwork, in one context and work in another.

However, leisure is not merely the obverse of work. As deGrazia's critical analysis (1962) indicates, it, too, is a very complex concept. Consider that not to be working is sometimes called being unemployed and examine the shifting meaning of the words *labour, unemployment,* and *work* in Williams's *Keywords* (1983). Even though unemployment has sometimes been described genteelly as being temporarily at leisure, free, or at liberty, the leisure, freedom, and liberty it entails are neither voluntary nor desired. One uses the term *unemployment* to represent the position of someone who wants to be working but is not able to. Not working in that sense is an unwanted curse, offering not leisure but enforced idleness.

Furthermore, and most important in the context of present-day societies, unemployment represents a circumstance in which one does not receive the material necessities of life in exchange for one's labor. What is received is provided by other means. An exchange does not take place. Leisure activities, on the other hand, presuppose the existence of some acceptable means of obtaining the material necessities of life: leisure does not itself generate such necessities by being tied to an economic exchange. And as we know, prestige and other social meanings are attached to the various sources that provide the support for leisure. Leisure based on earned wages is distinguished from that based on investment income, on inherited wealth, on unemployment benefits, or whatever (cf. deGrazia 1962:368–72).

It may appear at first glance that since the same activity can be work in one context and leisure in another, we can disregard the activity entirely as a criterion and consider work to be solely the means by which one gains a living. But because a living can be gained by inheritance, qualifying for state benefits, and other means that no one would want to consider work, we cannot accept such a simple solution. It remains necessary to consider work to be an activity, not a mere status, but, unlike leisure, an activity connected with gaining a living. The activity itself may not distinguish work from leisure, but its connection with the necessities of life can. And since few if any real individuals produce all their necessities themselves, such activities are embedded in a system of social relationships involving the *transfer* of labor, materials, and products within it. The living that people gain is a function both of their relations to each other in that transfer or distribution system and of the magnitude and substance of the resources involved in those transfers.

EXCHANGE, ECONOMY, AND OFFICIAL CATEGORIES

If we were to concern ourselves solely with the conventions of our own time, we would be free to define work by its relationship to income gained by an exchange. We would use the terms *exchange* and *economy* freely and unself-consciously. But those terms and their conventional assumptions would greatly handicap both practical and theoretical efforts to deal with the idea of labor for love or the antithesis of alienated labor. Exchange theory and economic theory sustain their elegant simplicity by assuming that every activity has a material quid pro quo. If a relationship does not involve an obvious exchange of money or goods in return for labor or other goods, if one person transfers goods or provides services to another without receiving anything tangible in return, then those subscribing to the theory must hypothesize that there really was an exchange but that it was intangible, involving "psychic goods" or the like. When an exchange is not empirically observable, therefore, an exchange must be invented if one is to hold on to the theory that assumes it. There is no comfortable room in economic or exchange theory for altruism: no transfer of labor or goods is possible without mutual gain; no transfer can be unilateral, made for the love of the person or for the love of the activity. There is no give without take.

Both economic and exchange theory are attractive for their parsimony, and they are useful for a variety of questions if only because they force us to look closely for reciprocities. But when employed to analyze an issue like labors of love they must stretch themselves past the limits of usefulness, becoming meanspirited and unimaginative by employing (sometimes very imaginatively!) no other resource than committed reductionism. And of course, once one admits psychic or, for that matter, cultural goods, income and capital as legitimate coinage, one enters a world of metaphor and symbolism entirely different from the material world of money and goods upon which the power of the theory has been demonstrated: it is a world in which apples are treated as if they were artichokes. While metaphors and analogies can sometimes be intellectually fruitful devices, they can also be seriously misleading.

In all, I suggest that the assumption of exchange and market relations implicit in conventional notions of work runs a high risk of obscuring more than it clarifies when we grapple with the problem of labors of love. Market relations may be seen to involve transfers of goods or services produced by labor, but not necessarily *exchanges*. Work or labor should not, therefore, be defined generically by its relation to making a living. Under most circumstances today in our world work is part of an economic exchange and by definition has exchange-value. But if we wish to conceptualize labors of love, we must develop a more catholic conception of work that is based on what writers since Adam Smith have called use-value. Work must be conceived of generically as an activity with use-value that need not have any exchange-value at all.

However, virtually all the official information we have is predicted upon the connection of work with exchange-value. What is work? who are members of the active work force (that is, the working population) and who members of the inactive work force? who is employed and who unemployed? These distinctions are arbitrarily established by reference to the official marketplace. Such conventions seriously limit the universe of work and workers about which official information is collected and made available for analysis. We all know that homemakers in many countries are not officially counted among those employed and that what they do is not considered to be work by official definitions. There is justification for such limiting definitions: after all, homemakers do not enter into a wage contract that formally specifies working hours, activities, and compensation, and so they have a rather different relation to those who provide them with their living than do conventional wage earners. But over the past decade or two we have learned enough about homemakers and their work to make us loath to exclude them from consideration as genuine workers. And we have also learned enough about underground and informal economies (for example, Handy 1984; Pahl 1984; Redcliffe and Mingione 1985; and Ferman, in this volume) to recognize that a much greater variety of arrangements surrounding work exists in our world than the official economy concedes, and that if we wish to explore the full range of economic relationships we cannot rely on the guidance of either official information or on the arbitrary concepts that organize and select it (see Miles and Irvine 1979: 113–29). We need more comprehensive sources for understanding generic characteristics of work that are beyond the official economy of our time.

EMPIRICAL SOURCES FOR NEW CONCEPTS

Thus far I have dwelt on semantic and logical aspects of the concept of work, a mode of analysis that is fairly common but of limited value standing by itself. Logical, semantic, and theoretical analysis can make little or no connection with practical reality unless it is based on an informed sense of empirical plausibility. It consistently relies on producing empirical-seeming examples to test itself or to demonstrate its relevance to worldly affairs. The practical value of the analysis is limited by the content of the empirical examples it relies on. It is likely to be considerably strengthened by expanding the universe of empirical data from which to draw examples and by which to test its capacity to make sense of the real world. Labors of love are not conventional in ordinary circumstances of work in the present-day world: work is, if not thoroughly alienated in character, then at least tied to getting a living. Where can we find the empirical grist from which to grind out new concepts?

When we deal with labors of love we must look outside the conventional economy for empirical examples, to areas of experience in which activities are not self-evidently attached to gaining a living or to exchange. In the crudest sense we must look at areas of life in which people are believed to perform activities that may otherwise be called work or labor, but that are done for something other than money: we must look for instances of unpaid labor. But not all unpaid labor is relevant: it must be voluntary rather than forced, free rather than slave. Furthermore, it must be free of the assumption that it will gain a return in the form of a living, even if not a cash payment. Thus, we would not look at forced or slave labor, which is not done voluntarily, nor at the home-maker, who, although working voluntarily, must assume, like the slave, that the master or breadwinner will provide the means of subsistence.

The most obvious universe in which to find empirical examples of labors of love is populated by volunteer labor. The characteristics of such labor are only dimly perceptible to us in our present state of knowledge, and its boundaries are very unclear. But we do know there is a great deal of it. We need think only of Red Cross volunteers during catastrophes or of those engaged in the postrevolu-tionary mass public health campaigns conducted by countries like Cuba and China. What makes those examples visible is the fact that they are mobilized on a large scale by the state or by a large, officially recognized organization. Indeed, many kinds of volunteers have quasi-official status, as we see in the case of ambulance or emergency vehicle crews, firefighters, auxiliary police officers, and those leading and staffing civic enterprises (see, for example, Greenberg 1984; Kramer 1981; Kaminer 1984; Daniels 1988). But outside that visible and semiofficial pool of volunteer workers there are others about whom we know very little.

Insofar as we are concerned with delineating the generic characteristics of labors of love and the conditions under which they are undertaken, empirical study of the entire variety of forms of volunteer labor is essential. However, if we want to ask how it is possible to conceive of a society in which the *central* form of labor is unalienated and voluntary—and look for empirical examples of unpaid labor today that are relevant to the question—much of the volunteer labor that is easily visible does not provide what we need. This is because it does not often have the characteristics of work upon which a viable society must depend—work that requires more than everyday skills and that is regular and sustained over time. The mass mobilization of volunteers that is characteristic of the present day is typically short-lived and requires little skill. Furthermore, most sustained programs that use volunteers have had to contend with a charac-teristically high turnover and absentee rate (see, for example, Oldham 1979). Low skill and unpredictable effort are not an adequate foundation for a viable society: labor with such characteristics can only supplement the work which provides the real foundation of goods and services. Where, then, can we find empirical examples of labors that are skilled, regular, sustained over time, unpaid, and part of a functioning division of labor?

In English, the word *volunteer* tends to be used to designate people who are unpaid participants in some purposive program that is often organized as a social movement or a campaign. In contrast, the word *amateur,* while also used to designate people who are unpaid, has no necessary implication of participation in an organization or a movement. It can be applied to isolated individuals as easily as to participants in a program. Although in some contexts it implies a lesser degree of skill than *professional,* in general it refers to people who work without payment, its root as a word referring literally to labor of love. All who cultivate or practice a particular skill without the assumption of material gain— those called amateurs or hobbyists—are likely to be worthy of far closer study than has been done until now (see Stebbins 1979). However, these studies should not be conceived of as studies of leisure. Rather, at least some amateurs should be studied as people engaged in work or labor which, because unpaid and performed during leisure, nonpaid work hours, is therefore described as leisure.

This is not the place to elaborate on the themes suggested by amateur work, but we can note that it has been seriously underestimated as a productive source of goods and services. This is so not only in the context of Jonathan Gershuny's idea of a self-service, do-it-yourself postindustrial economy (Gershuny 1978), but also in the context of the history of the development of scientific and scholarly knowledge. A great deal of the sustained, specialized, complex intellectual labor that created the modern academic disciplines of the liberal arts and sciences was performed by amateurs in their free time rather than by people who made their living at it. Charles Darwin, after all, and a host of lesser but nonetheless important scholars and scientists of the nineteenth century were, strictly speaking, amateurs. Most often they were people with inherited wealth, but some of them earned their living by one (respectable) means or another. It was only after the modern university developed that scientific and scholarly labors were professionalized and amateurs either absorbed or excluded.

However, in addition to the arenas in which unpaid volunteers and amateurs work there exists another of some magnitude in which essentially unpaid labor requiring elaborate skill predominates: there, we find people who may *not* be called either volunteers or amateurs. I refer to those working in the visual, literary, and performing arts. Their circumstances vary from one nation to another, but in economies that are not closely organized by the state, the vast majority of art workers are for all practical purposes unpaid. This is distinctly the case in the United States, where few authoritative academies, protective sinecures, or public financing programs assure a living to artists. There is a large and complex set of art worlds containing quite varied enterprises, both paid and unpaid (see Becker 1982). Even though the vast majority of art workers do not gain a living from their artistic work, however, it cannot be denied that they perform highly complex, skilled activities over a prolonged period of time and are involved in a professional rather than an amateur work career. Most do wish to be able to make their living by their art, but most are not able to and must work for the love of the activity itself while gaining their actual living in some other way (see for example, Wassall, Alper, and Davison 1983). The arts both in the United States and elsewhere are in fact a vast laboratory for the empirical study of sustained, highly skilled labors of love (see Freidson 1986).

THE QUESTIONS

Now that I have located some of the areas of present-day life in which empirical forms of unpaid labor can be studied with conceptual profit, I can conclude by suggesting some of the basic questions that should be asked.

First, there is the question of subsistence, or material gain. While labors of love by definition do not depend for their performance on gaining a living, no one can survive without a living. The question for those who perform skilled and sustained labors of love is, What are the means by which they actually gain their living and what is the relation of those means to the labors of love themselves? How are the free time and energy to practice labors of love obtained? Does the means of gaining a living influence the labor of love? Some means, such as having a private income, are ostensibly mere sources of support, with no relationship to the unpaid work one does, its frequency, intensity, and quality. Other means, such as domestic (Simpson 1981:192–98), state, private foundation or other forms of patronage (Haskell 1980), may hinge on approval of the amount and kind of unpaid work done, creating a major contingency for the worker that may be exploitative and therefore alienating. Still others may do paid work that is closely related to the labor of love, requiring the use of the same or related skills—for example, teaching the skills of that labor to others. And yet other kinds of paid work can have no relationship at all to the skills of the labor of love, being merely the work one must do in order to gain the resources to allow one to use one's free time for the labor of love (see Wheeler, in this volume). Such work may be chosen because it can be scheduled so as to leave particular amounts of time or blocks of time free; or for its uncommitted, casual character, easy to leave whenever one wishes. Knowledge of the full range of sources of support for unpaid work can allow us to imagine methods by which a viable society can sustain various specialized labors of love.

Second, I might observe that since labors of love are by definition neither organized nor driven by the conventional marketplace, a critical problem of analysis is to discern the other means by which they are organized into sustained activities. Since the market, like the state, plays some role in most activities in advanced societies, careful analysis of both is essential for delineating the boundaries markets create beyond which labors of love go. In the case of the arts, Moulin's (1967) now-classic study of the French art market and Menger's (1983) study of composers and their audiences, not to speak of the Whites' (1965) study of painters in an earlier time in France, show us those boundaries and allow us to understand the position of those who must work unpaid outside them. The recent study of Moulin, Passeron, Pasquier and Porto-Vazquez (1985) shows how one may attempt to delineate the universe of artists both inside and outside the official institutions.

What may not be problematic for conventional occupations may very well become an enigma to be fathomed in the case of labors of love. Where the market does not operate normally, what functions as an analogue to the marketplace in mediating relationships and establishing use-value, and how does it work? What motivates workers if not income or the immediate anticipation of income? How does recruitment and training take place in face of the fact that there can be no realistic assumption that learning the skill is an investment in human capital that will pay off in later earnings? And in the absence of gaining an income, how does commitment to perform the work regularly—commitment to a career—get established and sustained over time? How is the work organized both as an individual activity and as one activity embedded in a larger work-world composed of a division of labor and an array of sustaining and collaborating persons and institutions (Becker 1982)?

That question brings me to a final point bearing on the strategy required to reach an adequate understanding of the characteristics of labors of love and of the prerequisites for their existence. Adequate understanding requires that we focus on the everyday forms of labors of love, and on average rather than extraordinary workers. In the case of the arts, the experience of the unsuccessful, who never arrive at the point of actually making a living from their art, is much more important than the experience of the successful, because it is they, not the successful, who must labor for love throughout their career, never receiving significant economic rewards. The extraordinary could not be what they are without legions of average, even mediocre colleagues populating and participating in the institutions from which they gain their recognition. As Becker (1982:231) put it, "If we bothered only about the *very* best . . . we would never have the facilities ready for those worth bothering about when they did appear, for you cannot maintain those organizations with such sporadic use." Furthermore, if we are concerned with a *socially viable* form of unalienated labor, we must be concerned with the form it takes among ordinary people who have no extraordinary gifts of talent, energy, dedication, or whatever. Societies are not sustained by extraordinary people. It is in the close and sympathetic study of the everyday, modest, and uninspiring that we are most

160   ELIOT FREIDSON

likely to find the empirical resources for moving us beyond the seriously limited economistic conception of labor that handicaps our thinking about both present and future (Bouvier 1983).

REFERENCES

Anthony, P. D. 1977. *The Ideology of Work,* London: Tavistock.
Arendt, Hannah. 1959. *The Human Condition.* Garden City, N.Y.: Doubleday.
Becker, Howard S. 1982. *Art Worlds.* Berkeley: University of California Press.
Bender, Frederic L., ed. 1972. *Karl Marx: The Essential Writings.* New York: Harper Torchbooks.
Bouvier, Pierre. 1983. "Pour une anthropologie de la quotidienneté du travail." *Cahiers internationaux de sociologie* 74:133–42.
Csikszentmihalyi, M. 1975. *Beyond Boredom and Anxiety: The Experience of Play in Work and Games.* San Francisco: Jossey-Bass.
Daniels, Arlene K. 1988. *Invisible Careers. Women Civic Leaders from the Volunteer World.* Chicago: University of Chicago Press.
Finch, J., and D. Groves, eds. 1983. *A Labor of Love: Women, Work and Caring.* Boston: Routledge and Kegan Paul.
Freidson, Eliot. 1986. "Les professions artistiques comme défi à l'analyse sociologique." *Revue française de sociologie* 27:431–43.
Gershuny, J. 1978. *After Industrial Society.* Atlantic Highlands, N.J.: Humanities Press.
DeGrazia, Sebastian. 1962. *Of Time, Work, and Leisure.* Garden City, N.Y.: Anchor Books.
Greenberg, M. A. 1984. *Auxiliary Police: The Citizen's Approach to Public Safety.* Westport, Conn.: Greenwood Press.
Handy, Charles. 1984. *The Future of Work.* New York: Basil Blackwell.
Haskell, Frances. 1980. *Patrons and Painters,* 2d ed. New Haven: Yale University Press.
Haworth, Lawrence. 1977. *Decadence and Objectivity.* Toronto: University of Toronto Press.
Kaminer, Wendy. 1984. *Women Volunteering: The Pleasure, Pain and Politics of Unpaid Work from 1930 to the Present.* Garden City, N.Y.: Anchor Press.
Kramer, R. M. 1981. *Voluntary Agencies in the Welfare State.* Berkeley: University of California Press.
Menger, Pierre-Michel. 1983. *Le Paradoxe du musicien: le compositeur, le mélomane et l'état dans la societé contemporaine.* Paris: Flammarion.
Miles, I., and John Irvine. 1979. "The Critique of Official Statistics." In *Demystifying Social Statistics,* edited by John Irvine, Ian Miles, and Jeff Evans. London: Pluto Press.
Moulin, Raymonde. 1967. *Le Marché de la peinture en France.* Paris: Editions de Minuit.
Moulin, Raymonde, Jean-Claude Passeron, Dominique Pasquier, and Fernando Porto-Vazquez. 1985. *Les Artistes: Essai de morphologie sociale.* Paris: La Documentation Française.
Oldham, Jack. 1979. "Social Control of Voluntary Work Activity: The Gift Horse Syndrome." *Sociology of Work and Occupations* 6:379–403.

Pahl, R. E. 1984. *Divisions of Labor*. New York: Basil Blackwell.

Rattansi, A. 1982. *Marx and the Division of Labour*. London: Macmillan.

Redclift, N., and E. Mingione, eds. 1985. *Beyond Employment*. Oxford: Basil Blackwell.

Schwalbe, M. L. 1986. *The Psychosocial Consequences of Natural and Alienated Labor*. Albany: State University of New York Press.

Simpson, C. R. 1981. *Soho: The Artist in the City*. Chicago: University of Chicago Press.

Sohn-Rethel, A. 1978. *Intellectual and Manual Labor*. London: Macmillan.

Stebbins, R. A. 1979. *Amateurs: On the Margin between Work and Leisure*. Beverly Hills: Sage Publications.

Tilgher, A. 1958. *Homo Faber*. Chicago: Henry Regnery.

Wassall, G., N. Alper, and R. Davison. 1983. *Art Work: Artists in the New England Labor Market*. Cambridge: New England Foundation for the Arts.

White, H. C., and C. A. White. 1965. *Canvases and Careers: Institutional Change in the French Painting World*. New York: Wiley.

Williams, R. 1983. *Keywords: A Vocabulary of Culture and Society*, rev. ed. New York: Oxford University Press.

I I I I I I I Forced Labor in Concentration Camps

LEWIS A. COSER

Concentration camps are peculiarly modern institutions. They are not remnants of an older order that will disappear with modernity and progress. On the contrary, they are the hellish creations of specifically modern political actors. They are the concrete proof of the insufficiency of any explanation that assumes some kind of straight and unilinear progressive history of humankind. We must understand them if we are to arrive at an assessment of the contemporary world uncontaminated by Panglossian illusions. I conceive of this paper as a modest effort to fathom an evil phenomenon which those who still cling to the ideas of the Enlightenment must come to terms with if they want to make sense of contemporary predicaments.

Concentration camps are prime examples of what Erving Goffman has called total institutions.[1] Yet they differ from other total institutions in one crucial respect. Whereas almost all others assert some moral or ideological claim that their inmates benefit from being confined there, concentration camps make no such claim. While prisons or mental hospitals are said to aim at the rehabilitation or resocialization of those who are confined there, concentration camps do not provide such moral defenses. They are amoral.

When it is objected that institutions assume the ideology of rehabilitation hypocritically and that it is only a smoke screen to hide the real purposes of the institution, one may observe with La Rochefoucauld that hypocrisy is always a tribute that vice pays to virtue. But in the case of concentration camps, no such hypocrisy can be detected. The sign over the main entrance of Auschwitz, *Arbeit Macht Frei* (Work Will Set You Free) was meant as macabre humor rather than as an attempt at moral or ideological justification. Even slaveholders

1. Erving Goffman, *Asylums* (New York: Doubleday, 1961).

in the United States found ideological defenders who claimed that slavery benefited the slaves. No justification of this sort was advanced by the masters of the camps. Concentration camps, as distinct from other total institutions, did not camouflage the purposes of the victimizers; they were to bring about the physical and psychical destruction of their inmates in the long run and their maximum exploitation through forced labor in the short run.

At first blush it would appear that the sociology of the concentration camp would reveal a simple dichotomous structure such as can be found in some other total institutions; that is, that concentration camps consist of two major strata, the victims and the victimizers, with none of the shadings and differentiations that one is accustomed to finding in other asymmetrical systems of power and status. As Ivan Denisovich, the hero of Aleksandr Solzhenitsyn's first great novel, discovers, "Those in the warm will never be able to understand those who must stay in the cold."[2] They live in a different universe, have dissimilar experiences, and speak a different language. But upon reflection, it turns out that concentration camps have a highly differentiated social structure so that simple dichotomous schemes fail to come to grips with their complex system of stratification. They have a unique, complicated rank order and hierarchical system that differ from all other known systems of stratification.

The world of the concentration camp is a world upside down. The guards as well as older prisoners assess newcomers to ascertain how they will have to be fitted into the existing scheme of things. Such assessments have little to do with the previous status of the new inmate. For example, lawyers and medical practitioners inhabit adjacent niches in the stratification systems of the outside world, yet they occupy vastly different positions in the world of the camps. Medical doctors have skills that are very much in demand, be it by the authorities or the inmates, and are hence highly valued, whereas lawyers have no function whatsoever and hence are assigned despised positions near the very bottom of the occupational structure.

It is probably true that the Davis-Moore functional theory of stratification[3] is not helpful for understanding the modern capitalist system, but it is of great use to comprehend the order of the concentration camps. In that world, people are indeed ranked in terms of their functional contribution to the system at large or to some segments of that system. Medical doctors possess skills that are highly valued by the authorities who are concerned with keeping at least some of the inmates fit for the work load that is imposed on them. This is obviously not the

2. Aleksandr I. Solzhenitsyn, *One Day in the Life of Ivan Denisovich* (New York: New American Library, 1963).

3. Kingsley Davis and Wilbert Moore, "Some Principles of Stratification," *American Sociological Review* 10 (1945): 242–47.

case in extermination camps but was a major factor in all other concentration camps both in Stalin's Russia and in Nazi Germany. Given the extreme deprivations in these camps, the death rates among inmates are obviously very high, yet a minimum of able workers is necessary if the commander of the camp is to reach the work quota imposed on him. Medical personnel have often stressed that they survived because they were given some privileges and status advantages denied to other inmates. At the same time, the prisoners also value physicians, who may well be able to treat them even though medication may be scarce or nonavailable. Many of the accounts and memories of former inmates stress that they managed to survive because they got some help from fellow inmates in charge of medical facilities.

The positions of other manual and nonmanual occupations are likewise utterly different in the camps from what they are in the outside world. By and large, in the outside world, people with manual skills are assigned lower position than white-collar workers. The reverse is true in the upside-down world of the camps. Those who have skills in the making of things rank higher than those who can only manage people. To be a tailor or a carpenter gives prestige in the eyes of both authorities and other inmates.

But more important still than the reversal of the order of stratification is the concomitant differential system of rewards and punishment. Inferior status in the camp is not only frustrating but implies low chances of survival. Social Darwinism, whatever one may think of it as a useful mode of explanation in the world outside the camps, operates completely in the world of the camps. Only the fittest, as defined by the concentrationary order, have a chance to survive, and fitness is largely measured in terms of usable occupational skills.

Solzhenitsyn puts it well: "In camp it was advantageous to be a medical assistant, a barber, an accordian player, I daren't go any higher. You would get along all right if you were a tinsmith, a glass blower, or an automobile mechanic. But woe on you if you were a geneticist, or, God help you, a philosopher, a linguist, an art historian, then you had had it. You would kick the bucket on general work in two weeks."[4] Or as he says elsewhere: "A lathe operator, a carpenter, a stovemaker, was not yet a fully fledged trusty, a shoemaker, however, and a tailor even more so, was already a high-class trusty. Tailor in camp sounds and means something like 'Assistant Professor' out in freedom. (And the reverse side is that in camp, the genuine title 'Assistant Professor' sounds derisive, and it is best not to call yourself that and become a laughingstock.)"[5] The Polish sociologist Anna Pawelczynska, herself a former in-

---

4. Aleksandr I. Solzhenitsyn, *The Gulag Archipelago 1918–1956*, vol. 2 (New York: Harper and Row, 1975), 265–66.

5. Ibid., 252.

mate of Auschwitz, offers some important observations on the sources of differentiation in the inmate population:

Certain necessary jobs arose in the camp, requiring special qualifications. A German prostitute could perform the function of *Kapo* (trusty) perfectly well, but she would not do office work or any other type of work requiring skill and intelligence. Obtaining of such a function offered better chances of survival, thanks to the lighter work load and the extra food. It also gave one a certain range of possibilities of authority which, depending on the person who had won that function, could be made use of either for the saving of oneself alone . . . or for the saving of oneself and others.[6]

In other words, to be engaged in special work, whether because of previously acquired skills or because one was learning new skills in the camp, allowed a person to gain a measure of credit that could be spent in an altruistic or in an egoistic manner. It turned out that even in the camps meritocratic criteria played a certain, if perverse, part.

Previous skill level, as has been seen, was a major cause of position in the camp's stratification system. But, in addition, access to tools was another key determinant of hierarchical position. As one former inmate puts it, "Already the beginning of work created a grotesque, farcical tragedy for many prisoners: the fight to have access to tools. There was a limited number of such tools in the camp and the quality varied a lot. Those who did not get ahold of tools were in danger of becoming 'conspicuous,' that is, to be considered shirking work."[7] In a perverse way, the position of inmates was partly determined by their relation to the means of production.

Just as in the world outside, where a rough indication of the relative position someone occupied was afforded by ascertaining whether he or she was engaged in blue-collar or white-collar work, so in the camps one's general position depended largely on whether one worked inside or outside the camps. This is similar, of course, to the key difference in slave societies between house slaves and field hands. Those who worked in the camp workshops lived much better than the majority, who worked outside. Inside workers didn't have to line up in the morning, and that meant they could get up and have breakfast much later than those doing outside work. Moreover, the insider's work was in a warm place or else a warm place was always handy, "and he usually worked not in a brigade, but as an individual craftsman, which meant he did not have to put up with nagging from his comrades, but only from the chiefs."[8]

In the examples so far, I have not yet made distinctions between the func-

6. Anna Pawelczynska, *Values and Violence in Auschwitz* (Berkeley: University of California Press, 1979), 106.
7. Eugen Kogan, *Der SS Staat* (Stockholm: Hermann-Fischer Verlag, 1947), 96.
8. Solzhenitsyn, *Gulag*, 252.

tional value of skills for the inmates and for the guards. Many skills benefited only the authorities, not inmates. Camp guards were often in a position to exploit the skills of inmates for their own purposes. Inmates were used to produce fine furniture for the guards, to work in their gardens, and to produce articles of various sorts that the guards would then send home to their families. The master race of guardians exploited the services of the inmates for their private benefits as well as for the maintenance and expansion of the concentrationary universe. In camps with women inmates, the sexual exploitation of females went together with the exploitation of skilled male expertise.

When one talks about the exploitation of the prisoners by the guards one has to be aware of the reciprocal dependency of the guards on some prisoners. One finds here an almost pure example of Hegel's famous dialectic of masters and slaves. As one observer remarks,

> Greed compelled [the guards] to cross the uncrossable line and to enter into contact with prisoners . . . . [Prisoners] became indispensable partners, who chose the most valuable goods for the SS officers. . . . In this way some of the SS officials came to depend on prisoners, who could in turn skillfully make demands of their own. A currency strong enough to buy the services of SS officials and prisoner functionaries had made its appearance inside the camp. New groups of interest arose, linking particular officials with prisoners who were no longer anonymous. . . . This activity considerably weakened the effectiveness of some SS officers.[9]

Their greed sometimes undermined their power.

Not all guards could be corrupted in this way. Differences between the guards in this respect stemmed in part from their social origin and in part from peculiar abilities to gain maximum advantage from their power position. While recruitment of guards for concentration camps seems to have been a negative selection process, it would be inaccurate to believe that all of them were recruited from depraved and criminal elements. The lowest strata in outside society certainly provided a major quota, but in addition guards were recruited from a variety of outside milieus. Although lumpen proletariat elements may have predominated, there were also physicians, teachers, university professors among the guards.[10] Like the victims, the victimizers had a rank hierarchy, but a hierarchy that differed considerably from that in the normal world.

I have not yet sufficiently dealt with the differentiated power structure among prisoners. Here again it makes little sense to simply speak of the powerless and the powerful. There were subtle gradations in the possession of power just as in economic status and chance of survival.

The Russian and German concentration camp authorities depended to a large degree on inmates in order to run the camps, to maintain order, and to ensure

9. Pawelczynska, *Values and Violence,* 105.
10. Ibid., 20.

discipline. There were nowhere near enough guards to run the camps single-handedly. Hence camp commanders depended on a layer of inmates who ran the day-to-day affairs of the camps. This inmate power elite was fed more, clothed more adequately, and lodged in barracks provided with amenities not available elsewhere. Recruitment for such power positions systematically favored criminal elements. In the Russian camps, thieves were usually in charge. They had the skill of ingratiating themselves with the authorities that other inmates lacked. But, above all, they had none of the scruples of other inmates. Power positions among inmates were hence largely allocated just as they were among the guards: by negative selection. The brutal, the vile, the unscrupulous, the sociopaths, that is, the very dregs of the outside population, were typically recruited into the top categories of those who ran the camps to the satisfaction of the guards. The criminals lorded it over most other categories of inmates since they possessed the trained capacity to beat, maim, even kill other inmates without scruples.

In some camps under the Nazis noncriminal inmates succeeded in wresting power and control from criminals. Such noncriminal members of the power elite of German camps were almost always members of the Communist party. They undoubtedly saved the lives of many inmates, but it should be stressed that their regime could at times be as horrid as that of the criminal elements. They favored members of their own party or fellow travelers over other inmates. When, for example, they received orders from the camp authorities to deliver a certain number of inmates to be transported to extermination camps, they would select nonpolitical inmates to be killed so as to be able to save the lives of members of their own group. They protected others from the oppressive regime of the criminals, but at the same time they were intent upon serving their own above all. To my knowledge, it was always an elite of the Communists rather than other political inmates that wrested the power over life and death from the criminals. Their strong discipline and sense of solidarity allowed them to disregard "dysfunctional" sentiments such as pity for the weak or sympathy for the especially afflicted. The Communist party claimed full control over the lives of its members, whether inside or outside the camps. This ironclad discipline allowed its members to hold positions of power and sometimes to displace the monopoly on inmate violence otherwise held by the criminals. They had to be even tougher than the criminals if they wanted to replace them. In the inhuman world of the camps only those who were possessed of a strong drive for survival would endure. Among the Communists, survival skills largely served group survival, whereas among criminals they were almost completely used so as to benefit individuals.

In his memoirs about the Siberian prison in which he was incarcerated in imperial Russia, Dostoevsky remarks that while all work in the prison was irksome and often painful, it was most difficult to bear if it had no utilitarian character at all and was hence utterly senseless. To move a pile of bricks from one place to another in the morning and then be forced to put it back again in the afternoon, Dostoevsky argued, is an almost unbearable torture. I have not come across a similar observation in the concentration camp literature, but it corresponds to my own experience. I was interned in a French camp during the first part of World War II as a German citizen, even though I was known to the authorities as an antifascist. My comrades and I did all sorts of backbreaking labor in these French camps. But I well remember that by far my worst experience was to help dig the foundations for a French aircraft factory at a time when the Nazis were already in Paris and would surely overrun the camp and the future aircraft factory in a few days. The senselessness of the situation is still most vivid in my memory. I saw it as a kind of moral torture, distinct from the other harsh types of work we had to do.

It would be a cliché, if not an understatement, to insist on the fact that labor in the concentration camp was alienated labor. This was so, of course, yet this type of forced labor had characteristics that Marx could not have observed in his Victorian world. Even if one is prepared fully to recognize the inhumanity of alienated labor as depicted by Marx, one must nevertheless stress that forced labor in modern concentration camps, just like forced slave labor, has distinct features. Even alienated factory workers, in Marx's time and in our own, are not completely devoid of a sense of workmanship. Even if they have no control over the work process, over their own product, or over their own rhythm of work, workers in modern industry can derive a minimum of pleasure and satisfaction from some aspects of their work. But even this is utterly lacking in the forced labor that characterizes the main routines of concentration camp inmates. In addition, of course, the rigors of work are alleviated for the modern worker by the expectation of the weekly or monthly paycheck. By contrast, there was no remuneration whatever, in cash or in kind, for the ordinary camp inmate. Privileged workers may have received some concrete benefits from their work, but the great majority of workers received no compensation whatever.

The camp authorities not only exploited the inmates but also subjected them to systematic degradation. They attempted by any means at their disposal to destroy the sense of autonomy and moral integrity of the inmates. They all too often succeeded—but not always. Groups of people possessed of a strong sense of moral values, be they orthodox Jews, Jehovah's Witnesses, Socialists, or Communists, were able to withstand to some extent the constant efforts to undermine their sense of moral integrity. When, in addition, people managed to make use of skills, whether acquired in the camp or outside, their chances of survival not only physically but also morally were increased.

Anna Pawelczynska offers an observation in regard to personal autonomy that I find deeply moving and entirely apt: "One could eat the desired piece of bread immediately. Or one could, though feeling hungry, keep part of it in one's pocket, conscious of freedom won: I am not eating it all, because I choose not to." This existential criterion is, however, immediately qualified when she adds, "This form of self-defense, however, was related to the tolerance of hunger, which varies widely among individuals."[11]

The system of forced labor that characterizes the concentration camp was largely successful in constraining the inmates to respond to the whip of the guards and the commands of the inmate power elite of trusties. But it was never completely successful. There always remained inmates who did not eat the desired piece of bread immediately.

The concentration camp is a peculiarly powerful total institution. It effectively strips most inmates of their previous persona and severs those bonds that formerly linked individuals to others in their significant environment. None of the roles that inmates occupied in the outside world can continue to sustain a sense of autonomy and effectiveness in the camp. The concentrationary universe creates a new order after it has obliterated the relevance of the old order to which prisoners once belonged. Only those with skills that are highly functional in this environment and those with a very strong sense of shared solidary values survive the world of the camps. The camps flourish on the severing of former bonds and the destruction of former skills among the inmates. Most of its inmates are transformed into hollow men. Those who are incapable of playing new roles that are valued in the concentrationary world are likely to die. Those who manage to learn new, functionally valued roles have some chance to survive physically, and only some of those survive morally. They are the salt of the earth.

11. Ibid., 128.

PART FOUR • THE POLITICS OF WORK AND UNEMPLOYMENT

I I I I I I I I The Split Society

SEYMOUR S. BELLIN
AND S. M. MILLER

Recent discussions about economic policy have usually involved one of two conflicting visions of social stratification in America. One thesis presages a trend toward increasing the polarization of society on the basis of the development of a two-tier labor market: a set of good jobs that pay relatively well, are secure, and afford opportunities for advancement and a second group that are relatively poorly paid, dead-end jobs (see especially Harrison and Bluestone 1988). In opposition to this segmentation (often discussed as a dichotomy) is a more sanguine perspective that foresees a trend toward a postindustrial society and a labor market composed increasingly of good jobs as a consequence of the shift from old, smokestack industries to high technology and service industries (see Etzioni and Jargowsky, in this volume). This paper examines the thesis of increasing polarization—the nature of the evidence and its implications for inequality—and suggests policy alternatives.[1] Advocates of the polarization thesis typically focus on two related issues: (1) the quality of jobs, especially new jobs, operationally measured by occupational earnings, and (2) the rate of unemployment and its distribution. The key question is, Will there be enough of the right kind of jobs?

WILL THERE BE ENOUGH JOBS?

Work remains a central value for most Americans, and the right to employment is a key issue in social policy deliberations. Although unemployment is an important influence on household economic welfare, two important aspects tend to be neglected. One is that an annual unemployment

We wish to acknowledge the comments of Ellen Rosen on an early draft of this paper.

1. The most influential statement of postindustrial society's occupational structure has been that of Bell (1971). Recently, Erik Olin Wright has developed a more critical view (see Wright 1985).

rate has to be at least doubled to estimate the number of people who have been unemployed at some time during the year. A 5 percent annual average unemployment rate means that more than 10 percent were unemployed some time during that year. Second, over a third of the variance in incomes among jobs seems due to differences in the number of hours worked during the year, not to differences in wage rates attached to jobs (Jencks 1972). Unemployment prospects and hours of work are important factors in the quality of jobs.

The official estimate of overall unemployment for 1988 was 5.5 percent of the civilian labor force, down from its postwar high of 9.5 percent in both 1982 and 1983. Many consider the official estimate an underestimate and point to the "real" unemployment rate, which in addition to those officially unemployed includes "discouraged workers," who have given up actively looking for a job, and those who are involuntarily working part-time. When the official unemployment rate was 5.4 percent in January 1989, the real rate estimate was 10.3 percent, a figure that can be lower or higher, depending upon assumptions used in classifying the behavior of individuals (*AFL-CIO News* 1989:14; Mishel and Simon 1988:19).

The official unemployment rate has moved upward since 1948. A comparison of economic growth rates from trough to trough and peak to peak (thus controlling for cyclical influences) reveals a secular rise in unemployment over a twelve-year period from 1969 to 1981 (peaks) and from 1970 to 1982 (troughs) (Podgursky 1984:20). The increases were from 3.6 to 7.4 percent and from 5.8 to 10.6 percent, respectively.

Although the unemployment rate declined after 1983, it is still higher than in postwar expansion periods: in 1967, the official unemployment rate was 3.8 percent; in 1973, 4.9 percent; in 1979, 5.8 percent; in 1987, 6.2 percent. The increase is due to the swelling in the number of job losers and the greater number of weeks that the unemployed remain unemployed. While in 1967, 15.1 percent of the unemployed were unemployed for fifteen weeks or more, in 1979, 20.2 percent had such unemployment durations, and in 1987, 26.7 percent. Moreover, the strains of unemployment increase with its longevity (*Economic Report of the President* 1988:86).

The great majority of the net increase in unemployment over the 1969–81 period is attributable to involuntary job loss. In particular, much of it is accounted for by an increasing number of once-stable workers who experience longer-term unemployment. They are often termed displaced workers or the new poor.

THE DISTRIBUTION OF UNEMPLOYMENT

The burden of unemployment—official or real—has not been equally distributed among all sectors of the population in terms of industry, occupation, or geography, and of such demographic characteristics as age, gender, and minority status. We turn first to demographic considerations.

Youth, teenagers in particular, have shouldered a disproportionate level of unemployment. In 1982, when the postwar civilian unemployment rate high of 9.7 percent was reached, sixteen- to nineteen-year-olds had an unemployment rate more than twice as high, 24.4 percent. In 1987, when the overall unemployment rate had dropped to 6.2 percent, the teenage rate was still more than twice as high at 17.8 percent (the real unemployment rate for youth was at least 50 percent higher than this official figure).

Unemployment is a much more severe problem for minority youth, especially for those of low education. In 1982, when white teenagers had an unemployment rate of 21.7 percent, their African-American counterparts had an unemployment rate of 48.9 percent! By 1987, the white youth rate had dropped to 15.5 percent while the African-American rate declined much more in absolute terms yet still measured 34.4 percent (*Economic Report of the President* 1988:292). The high African-American unemployment rate should be viewed as particularly disturbing because many out-of-school African-American youth are not considered actively looking for a job and are therefore not recorded as being in the labor force and unemployed. At least some of these out-of-labor teenagers are discouraged job seekers and should be designated as unemployed.

Gender differences in unemployment for post twenty-year-olds disappeared between 1979 and 1987 (1979: males–4.2 percent, females—5.7 percent; 1987: males and females both 5.4 percent). But differences between married men and single women who maintain families continued to be substantial. In 1979, the married male unemployment rate was 2.8 percent while the female householders' was 8.3 percent. In 1987, married men's unemployment rate had increased to 3.9 percent while the female householders' rate was 9.2 percent (*Economic Report of the President* 1988:292). Nonetheless, prime-aged men (those between twenty-five and fifty-four) contributed more than their share to the secular increase in employment compared to other age groups of men and all age groups of women (Podgursky 1984:20).

African-Americans and Hispanics continue to bear disproportionate burdens of unemployment despite gains in legal rights, affirmative action, and other antipoverty programs. The official unemployment rates for African-Americans reached its postwar high of 19.5 percent in 1983, when the overall rate was 9.6 percent. For all African-American males it was 20.3, and it dropped only to 18.1 percent for those males twenty years and over. African-American females had slightly lower rates for both groups (18.6 percent and 16.5 percent). The real unemployment rate was considerably higher so that a large section of the African-American population suffered unemployment. Despite the decline by 1987 in official unemployment rates, they were still high in that year: 13.0

percent for all African-Americans, 12.7 percent for African-American males, and 13.2 percent for African-American females.

Hispanic unemployment rates were higher than the overall average but substantially below those of African-Americans. The Hispanic rate rose from 7.5 percent in 1973 to 8.8 percent in 1987; unemployment among Hispanic teenagers grew from 19.7 percent in 1973 to 22.3 percent in 1987 (Mishel and Simon 1988; 19). The disturbing element in the trend is that unlike both the national and African-American unemployment rates, the Hispanic rates increased.

Education and occupation markedly affect African-Americans in their labor market experience. African-Americans with better-than-average education and white-collar occupations have much lower unemployment rates than African-Americans with limited education and blue-collar occupations. Black–white differentials in unemployment rates have diminished among white-collar, higher-educated African-Americans.

Geographic areas—regions, states, localities (both urban and rural)—differ in unemployment rates and trends (Shank 1985). One major consideration affecting area differences in unemployment experience is the diversity of their respective economic bases. Areas that are dominated by one or a few industries are much more economically vulnerable, dependent as they are upon the nature, history, and vicissitudes of those particular industries. For example, New England early developed a dependence upon labor-intensive, nondurable manufacturing, such as textiles. As a consequence of the shift of these manufacturing industries to the South, it has experienced an economic decline for much of this century. More recently, Michigan, Ohio, and Pennsylvania—heretofore dependent upon old, smokestack industries such as autos, steel, and heavy machinery—have suffered similar sharp declines as a consequence of the shift of industry to other regions and abroad.

Some regions, notably New England and to a lesser extent Michigan, have experienced a dramatic recovery in the past decade as a result of the development of high technology and the rapid growth of the services sector. The downturn in 1985 of the high tech field, despite the stimulus of military expenditures, has reduced optimism about the employment prospects of these cutting-edge industries (Miller and Tomaskovic-Devey 1983: chap. 6).

Old, smokestack industries have declined as high tech and service industries have expanded. As a consequence, unemployment has grown among workers in older manufacturing industries, while on the whole it has remained relatively low in many service industries (Miller and Tomaskovic-Devey 1983: chap. 6).

Discussions of the service sector often fail to conceptualize it in precise, consistent, convergent terms and lack classifications of service types that are useful for understanding labor market implications. Producer- and consumer-

oriented services, for example, not only have different functions but are subject
to different influences that affect employment characteristics (Stanback, Jr.,
and Noyelle 1982:8–9). Many official and semiofficial categories confuse
rather than aid analysis: in one instance, the construction industry was classified as a service industry rather than lumped with manufacturing, as is the more
frequent practice.

Occupations differ in the extent to which they are subject to unemployment.
Podgursky (1984) estimates the extent to which various broadly categorized
occupations contributed to the secular increase in unemployment from 1969 to
1982. Overall, blue-collar workers bore the "largest and most disproportionate
share" of the net increase in unemployment, whether measured from trough to
trough or from peak to peak (Podgursky 1984:23). In 1982, blue-collar workers
constituted 31.0 percent of the labor force but contributed 45.5 percent of the
secular increase of unemployment from peak to peak. While white-collar workers made up 51.3 percent of the work force, they accounted for only 27.6
percent of the twelve-year increase in unemployment. Service workers composed 13.5 percent of the labor force and constituted 16.5 percent of the
unemployment, a slightly disproportionate share.

Major occupational subcategories within white-collar and blue-collar groups
showed some differences. Among blue-collar workers during the twelve-year
period, laborers experienced relatively greater unemployment than operatives
and craftsworkers. Differences in unemployment rates between operatives and
craftsworkers were very small, though lower among craftsworkers (Podgursky
1984). Blue-collar and white-collar differences in unemployment rates are
pronounced whatever industrial classification is used (Osterman 1988:28).

Thus, despite the drop in unemployment rates in the middle and late eighties,
they continue high by historical standards and are particularly burdensome for
minorities, the young, and blue-collar workers. The costs of the national goal
of curbing inflationary tendencies have been largely borne by particular groups
of the total population.

Since predictions about unemployment rates are notoriously unreliable and
space is limited, we do not offer our conjectures about the future. Rather, we
discuss in the later policy section what might be done to lower unemployment
rates and possibly shift the distribution of unemployment. Our assumption is
that unemployment is an issue of policy, not of the structure of the labor market
alone.

"GOOD JOBS" AVAILABILITY

The polarization thesis rests primarily on the implications of
the following major developments: a shift of industries from goods to service-

producing sector; from sectors with higher to lower average earnings; from old, smokestack to high technology industries; from production in high to low wage/salary areas in the United States and from the United States to abroad; from effective competition from abroad; and from the deskilling effects of (new) technology.

Although this chapter focuses on the polarization thesis and the alleged disappearance of middle-level jobs, it should be noted that other models of the labor force are consistent with the hypothesis of growing *in*equality. In addition to the hourglass (reduction of middle-level jobs) image of polarization, there is the toad or squat base (relatively greater concentration of poor jobs), and the elongation of the earnings pyramid (relatively greater increments in compensation at the upper levels of the occupation pyramid compared with those at the bottom). Critics of these views offer a more sanguine perspective of developments in the labor market: they visualize a trend toward an onion or diamond shape, that is, the gradual substitution of better jobs for dead-end, poorly paid ones.

While considerable ambiguity surrounds the definition of a "good job" (see Jencks, Perman, and Rainwater 1988), recent debates about economic policy have focused especially on occupational earnings. This focus stems partly from availability of detailed data on wages over time and partly from the implicit assumption that income is the most salient criterion of a good job. Although this latter assumption is by no means firmly established, few could contest the policy significance of any marked proliferation of low-wage employment (the central contention of the polarization thesis). To what extent does existing research support claims of polarization?

A detailed early study of the changing distribution of earnings was carried out by Thomas M. Stanback and Thierry Noyelle for ten major occupational groups in eighteen industry categories (Stanback, Jr., and Noyelle 1982:29–39). Their analysis supports the polarization thesis for the period 1960 to 1975. They applied 1975 earnings data for the ten major occupational groupings to data on employment trends from 1960 to 1975. Standardizing the earnings data, they estimated the effect of changes of occupational composition alone on the distribution of labor force earnings. They showed that both the top two quintiles and the bottom two quintiles grew at the expense of three middle-earnings classes. Moreover, the bottom grew faster than the top.

They attribute much of this change in earnings distribution to the growth of the very broadly defined service sector, which expanded in their definition from 57 percent of the labor force in the early post–World War II period to about 70 percent in 1982 and accounted for about 80 percent of the net growth in the labor force in this period. Stanback and Noyelle showed that the six major subgroups of service industries were characterized by different rates; the overall

earnings distribution of the large increase in service sector jobs was very clearly
bimodal (Stanback, Jr., and Noyelle 1982:39).

For the period 1969–82, Robert Z. Lawrence found support for the polarization thesis in manufacturing as well as in the service sector (Lawrence 1984,
1985). His explanation stressed supply side factors: the effect of demographic
changes and the role of unions. The large baby boom cohort and the surge of
women into the labor force during these years depressed entry level job earnings. Although members of the baby boom generation will always be relatively
disadvantaged by their numbers compared to other age cohorts, Lawrence
expects them to improve their earnings as they age and increase the proportion
of middle-level earnings. The low level of unionization in the expanding service sector compared to manufacturing also contributes to its relatively low
occupational earnings.

Lucy Gorham studied the implications of employment changes between
industries for the polarization thesis during the period 1969–82 (Gorham
1984). Drawing upon Bureau of Labor Statistics (BLS) data on 136 Economic
Growth Sectors, she found not polarization but a relatively greater concentration of jobs at the lower tier, at the expense of the middle and top tiers.

Neal Rosenthal's detailed study of 416 occupations between 1973 and 1982
is at odds with all those reported above (Rosenthal 1985). His analysis supports
an onion or diamond model. Examining the effects of such factors as occupational composition on the distribution of employment earnings, his study revealed that the top tier gained about 2 percentage points and the middle tier lost
slightly. Rosenthal offered two possible explanations to account for the dispari-
ty between his findings and those of Stanback and Noyelle. One deals with
differences in data and methods between the studies. While Rosenthal acknowl-
edges that both sets of data may have limitations, he feels that his analysis is
superior because it examines detailed occupations and industries that may mask
contrary trends within broader categories. A second possibility is that the
tendency toward polarization was present in the earlier, 1960–75 period studied
by Stanback and Noyelle but dissipated during the following decade examined
by Rosenthal. This explanation, of course, would not provide a plausible
account of Gorham's findings.

The inconsistencies among these studies cannot be readily reconciled because of differences in concepts, units of analysis (industry vs. occupation), and
sources of data (U.S. Bureau of Labor Statistics household survey and employer reports). Moreover, occupational earnings and occupational composition as well as industry changes are subject to different, complex, and possibly
conflicting sets of influences.

In this connection, it is particularly useful to consider a study by Patrick
Walker, cited by Lucy Gorham. It addresses the question of polarization by

examining changes in the distribution of skill for different occupations between 1950 and 1978. The study covered 221 detailed BLS industries and measured skill levels in each industry by the General Educational Development and Specific Vocational Preparation rankings, which include earnings as one variable. His data showed that 197 of the 221 industries were becoming more bimodal in skill distribution and that bimodality of the U.S. economy had increased by one-third between 1960 and 1978 (Walker 1983:195). This evidence, based on criteria in addition to earnings, lends further credence to the thesis of increasing labor market inequality, if not polarization. Recent work by Barry Bluestone and Bennett Harrison provides additional support for this conclusion (Bluestone and Harrison, 1986; Harrison and Bluestone, 1988).

Stimulated by the analysis of Bob Kuttner (1983), Harrison and Bluestone contend that a U-turn in wages has occurred: inequalities in the distribution of wages declined from the early sixties to the middle seventies and have increased since then. This U-turn is characterized by a decrease in the relative number of middle-income jobs and an increase in low-wage and high-wage jobs. Their polarization thesis has undergone a number of criticisms (Blustein 1988; Leigh-Preston 1988; Kosters and Ross 1987) and, in a series of articles, monographs, and a book (Harrison and Bluestone 1988), they have striven to meet many of the objections (for example, dealing only with full-time, full-year workers rather than with all workers).

Some of these objections cannot be evaluated because what is best or desirable practice (for example, deciding whether to and how to specify a three-category classification of wage earners) is not a matter of agreed-upon, well-tested experience. Nonetheless, there appears to be increasing acceptance of the principal Harrison-Bluestone thesis of the declining percentage of jobs that are middle-income (Harrison and Bluestone 1988:221–22; Blustein 1988). At least two important criticisms remain. One is the argument cited earlier (Lawrence 1984, 1985) that polarization is a short-term phenomenon produced by demographic trends; but the continuation of polarization raises the question How short is short-term? Harrison and Bluestone contend that polarization is due to structural changes in the economy that, if not corrected, would continue to produce wage and other inequalities.

The other criticism is that Harrison and Bluestone conflate a low-wage trend with a polarization or increasing inequality trend (Osterman 1988:16–17, 181). Since real wages have not advanced since the early seventies—what has been termed a "wage depression" (Levy 1987)–taking wages in a later year as the base and adjusting wages in earlier years to deal with changes in the consumer price index confuses "a possible downward shift in the overall (real wage) average with a possible increase in the fraction of jobs on the bottom of the distribution" (Osterman 1988:181). The point is well taken.

Unfortunately, isolating the two influences introduces an anomaly. To get rid of the effect of overall declining wages requires using each year's average wage (usually the median) as the standard and allocating jobs into low, middle, or high earnings on the basis of their relation to that average. This annual shifting of the level of the standard (the average) means that the wage level that defines a low-income job could be lowered year after year so that fewer and fewer workers are in that category at the same time that a large number of workers were doing much more poorly than were low-wage workers in earlier years. The two influences cannot be cleanly and appropriately separated. The low-wage depression perspective can be a supplement or an alternative to the polarization thesis: the two can go together, as implied by Bluestone and Harrison, or one can be operative while the other is not.

The pattern of family income is less controversial and shows a decided tendency toward inequality and polarization. Not only is the Gini coefficient, which measures overall income inequality, rising but the share of income going to the bottom quintile has decreased while the share received by the upper fifth and the top 5 percent has increased. The distribution of wealth shows a similar trend (Harrison and Bluestone 1988:128–37).

A splitting rather than a homogenization of the economic components of the social structure seems to be occurring.

POLICIES FOR A SPLIT SOCIETY

Increasingly, trends affecting the occupational structure do not spring from the immanent and unavoidable structure of the economy; they are made or permitted by governmental actions and inactions. This is clearly the case with unemployment and, growingly, with inequalities in general.

The crucial perspective for an employment policy and for the reduction of inequalities is to reject, decisively, *the normalization of unemployment,* the acceptance of a high unemployment rate as full employment. Many conservative and not a few liberal economists argue for defining full employment as the level at which prices begin to rise rapidly. For them, "full employment" would be reached when unemployment dropped to a 6.5 percent or even 7 percent level. Contrast this with the policy view of the Kennedy years that 4 percent was an "interim" goal on the way to a lower unemployment target. Today, high-level unemployment is offered as "normal" and "acceptable"; "the noninflationary full employment rate" and "the natural rate of unemployment," concepts which economists use with increasing frequency, are ideological terms masquerading as technical jargon.

It is dangerous to legitimate this proposition that high unemployment is an unavoidable and justifiable price for the prevention or alleviation of inflation, or that it is natural. The language of economists becomes the dialogue of policy and obscures the fact that hidden ideology, values, and policy choices are involved in that terminology. What is noninflationary employment depends on what a society is willing to do to deal with inflation, for example, increase interest rates or lower the money supply; impose price controls on industries that are rapidly driving up their prices, as the Reagan administration did with some medical costs; subsidize the prices of key commodities in order to lower them; limit wage increases, and so on. We cite this variety of antiinflationary measures to indicate that an inflationary level is at least in part a product of governmental action and inaction in dealing with price pressures. The high-level-of-unemployment-as-full-employment-outlook asks that government not interfere with markets and that government do nothing to promote employment. This perspective assumes that high levels of unemployment are economically necessary and morally acceptable. Sweden has shown in the eighties that full employment, economic growth, and low inflation are compatible when government plays an active role in producing needed adjustments.

If the normalization of unemployment is rejected, what can be done to reduce unemployment rates and improve the availability of good jobs? We discuss these issues under five broad topics: overall economic growth, employment growth, improvement of jobs, reduction of barriers to employment, and microeconomic policies. Our particular concern is with so-called disadvantaged workers, the structurally unemployed, whose personal characteristics or low human capital or both supposedly are the causes of their unemployment.

General economic growth—more precisely, the rate of growth of gross national product (GNP)—is important to employment and unemployment. A high general growth rate brings down the overall unemployment rate as the economy expands. Less attractive workers become more attractive to employers as the supply of unemployed workers diminishes. Wage rates and other conditions of work increase. An improving economy is more likely to provide higher public benefits to the unemployed and those who cannot work; these expenditures are less of a burden in times of expansion, and taxes are more acceptable to the general public as their real incomes increase. An attractive scenario.

Unfortunately, achievement of a fast-enough rate of growth to absorb all those seeking employment is not likely under current conditions. As noted above, inflation fears curtail governmental policies to stimulate the economy to a level of what was once called tight full employment. Furthermore, more general growth is needed today to produce the same number of jobs that a lower growth rate once induced. In addition, employers are reluctant, even under tight supply conditions, to hire less attractive workers. Thus, macroeconomic policies that lead to high growth rates are needed and desirable. They are unlikely under today's conditions, however, to be strong enough by themselves to generate enough employment to absorb everyone who wishes to work. Other policies are also needed.

EMPLOYMENT GROWTH

In this section we deal with policies that are more directly and specifically aimed at increasing employment than are policies for general economic growth. The proemployment policies discussed are shorter hours, changes in the pattern of governmental expenditures, tax policies for employment, protectionism, and industrial policy. All of them will be treated only lightly. The intention is to show that the quality, nature, and extent of employment are subject to influence and that governmental policies to shape and reshape them are possible.

In the late thirties, the Fair Labor Standards Act attempted to reduce the standard hours of work by exacting a penalty rate for work beyond forty hours, the famous time-and-a-half payment for overtime. Office work generally operates a thirty-five-hour week (9 to 5 with an hour for lunch); the factory work standard is forty hours plus a short lunch break. No major statutory change to reduce the standard work week has occurred in the United States since the original effort. In France and West Germany, by contrast, limited efforts are under way to expand employment opportunities by reducing the work week. Reduction of hours of work receives very little attention in the United States, although a number of organizations and analysts advocate it [see the papers by Best and by Gans, in this volume].

The rate of growth in GNP has become the yardstick of performance of an economy. For many reasons, it is an extremely crude measure, especially for those concerned with employment growth. It is not the rate of growth in GNP that is all-important for employment; it is the *content* or composition of that growth that is crucial. Two growth rates and levels of GNP can yield quite different results in terms of the amount and kind of employment (as well as in terms of environmental damage and energy use). What is produced and how it is produced are central issues.

The best-known example revolves around the employment contrasts between military expenditures for Research and Development (R&D) and a similar level of governmental expenditures for civilian purposes. According to some analyses, military R&D expenditures not only produce less employment overall than do civilian expenditures, but are also less likely to yield jobs for workers with low levels of education.

Health-education-welfare spending at all levels of government provides a substantial number of the good jobs that are held by women and minorities.

Decreases in HEW-type spending and increases in military R&D outlays have negative results for women and minorities, for the R&D pattern of expenditures reduces their chances of obtaining professional and managerial jobs.

Governmental patterns of expenditures shape the content of GNP, the level and kind of employments, and who is employed. The question is not whether a government should shape the composition of national output, for that is unavoidable when more than 30 percent of spending channels flow through a government. Rather, the question is, To what objectives should the GNP be directed?

A great variety of governmental activities affect the content of output, what is produced and how. Tax breaks for investment in physical capital encourage shifts away from labor-intensive production arrangements. Governmental lending and concessions could lead to more or less use of labor. Subsidies to firms that increase their employment could make the employment of labor less expensive and thereby increase the number of jobs.

Two of the most frequently debated economic topics today—protectionism, or managed trade, and industrial policy—are about the content of GNP. Similarly, another debated measure—urban enterprise zones—seeks to affect where production takes place and who is hired. Indeed, state and local efforts to attract industry can be seen as striving to affect the location of industry and, thereby, who is employed. The general point is that many measures can and do influence the amount and kind of employment.

What kind of GNP is a fundamental question of any economy. By not openly addressing it, we are not avoiding it. We are only disguising the answers given to it.

Obviously it is not only the number of jobs that is at stake, but also the quality or, better, the qualities of employment. Even if one believes in the diamond modeling of the job world—that more middle-level jobs are being produced—one has to recognize the sizable growth in low-paying, insecure, low fringe benefit jobs. What can be done to improve jobs? The answer lies in what government can require of employers and what government itself could do to improve jobs.

The best known and probably most important way that the federal government can force the improvement of jobs is by raising the minimum wage. That may, as some argue, decrease the number of low-level jobs, though the evidence is inconclusive on how many. Certainly, substantial pay raises improve jobs.

Although the government requires firms with a certain number of employees to contribute to social security and unemployment insurance funds, other employee protection is not demanded of employers. By requiring that all or most jobs provide some minimum level of medical expense coverage or pension contribution the government could upgrade the sizable slice of the lower end of the job market, which provides few fringe benefits to employees.

Other regulatory devices could improve the job security of workers. The recent plant shutdown legislation provides for advance notification to employees of the closing down of a plant or the laying off of a high percentage of the firm's employees. It applies only to large employers and does not require the provision of aid to the community or to those laid off who may have worked in the plant for many years and have few economic alternatives. Employee rights legislation, which would curtail arbitrary practices and firing by employees, has failed to pass at the national level, although some states have such legislation. Employee rights laws provide the kinds of protection that unions offer their members. If unions continue to decline as a percentage of the labor force, the importance of employee rights legislation will grow, especially for marginal and immigrant workers.

On the question of what government itself could do to improve the conditions of employment, the most important step might be national health insurance that would cover everyone adequately. Employees would then have medical cost protection regardless of where they worked. Health protection inequalities among jobs would be reduced.

The Earned Income Tax Credit (EITC) could be improved so that it represented a larger addition to low-wage incomes than it now does. (The 1986 tax reform act did strengthen the credit, which, in effect, returns to low-wage earners their social security taxes.) The EITC, a form of negative income tax, although it is seldom discussed as such, indicates the possibility of allocating governmental supplements to low-wage earners so that they reach a decent income level.

Many people need financial aid during the work year. The improving and extending of unemployment benefits and public assistance (Aid to Families with Dependent Children-Unemployment) would lighten the pain of unemployment that is associated with many jobs. (In the 1980s, a decreasing percentage of the unemployed were aided by unemployment benefits compared to the 1970s.) An economy with many irregular, undependable jobs requires ways of compensating for these interruptions in the flow of income.

The approach of affirmative action is not to affect the total number of jobs or to improve them from the perspective of the worker but to affect who gets one or another job. That is, the most that these programs can accomplish is to improve the job prospects of those who are discriminated against, regarded as "disadvantaged" in the labor market, pushed to the end of the labor queue, or relegated to the less good segmented labor markets. The overcoming of barriers is a resorting process, not a job augmentation process.

Affirmative action continues to be important in leading employers to hire people whom they would not usually hire or hire for a particular position. Without the pressure of affirmative action, continued progress for minorities and women is unlikely.

Structural unemployment—whether rooted in the deficiencies of prospective workers, the mismatch of skills and/or requirements, or the production of a relative surplus population—is a problem that merits consideration even though it is often overstated as a cause of unemployment. Some of the issues that have been raised in connection with it should be addressed, if not in the way the human capitalists, who believe that education and training can overcome the shortage of jobs, would push us.

Many employers demand much higher educational and general qualifica tions than the ongoing tasks of a job require. The result is that many people are barred from positions that they could perform well. Frequently, the excessive requirements (of strength, for example) exclude minorities and women from many jobs. In the case against the Duke Power Company the Supreme Court ruled against tests that have little relevance to a job and that function to limit minorities in particular positions. A wider expansion of this principle and others could force employers to reduce excessive job requirements (credentialism) and open up positions to those now grossly underrepresented in them (Miller 1968).

The U.S. government could follow the French example and tax employers for education and training. The French government provides for the upgrading and adaptiveness of the labor force by making educational opportunities available to the employed as well as unemployed workers. Once operating at full steam, the program is intended to place 3 percent of the labor force in education and training programs each year. If education and training were part of all jobs, then the differences among jobs would shrink.

The programs that receive the most attention as ways of reducing unemployment are those which involve training, improving the job readiness and skills of disadvantaged workers. The large (though now-reduced) federal outlays are carried out under the Job Partnership Training Act (JPTA), earlier called the Comprehensive Employment and Training Act (CETA), and originating as the Manpower Development and Training Act (MDTA). The literature evaluating the employment effects of these programs is immense and often contradictory. Our guess is that many of the programs improve the competitive chances of many disadvantaged workers but that the total number of jobs is not increased (see Anderson, in this volume). Whether employment training can be the basic strategy for advancing the employment of disadvantaged workers does not rest on the issue of whether the individual programs are cost-effective. Rather, the issue is whether upgrading the supposedly low quality of "human resources," a barbaric term, is more important than increasing the total number of good jobs, if the goal is to achieve a pronounced decline in the number of disadvantaged workers. We believe that *the problem is a shortage of good jobs to a greater extent than it is inadequate training and development.* Thus, we believe that JPTA-type programs can be only a limited part of a proemployment strategy. This view goes counter to much received wisdom among economists and politicians.

The two main types of microeconomic policy, previously mentioned, are interesting for their recent contrasting political history. Protectionism, which was successfully painted as a self-defeating policy for many years, is now a real political possibility as a major economic policy in the United States. Industrial policy, which had great fanfare in the late seventies and early eighties, has been tossed, at least temporarily, into the dustbin once occupied by protectionism. It has been placed there by the improved economy, reduction of interest rates, and the rising ideology of less government and more free market outcomes.

Rather than discussing these two widely publicized types of microinterven-tion, we discuss a less important but very interesting development. Part of its interest lies in the fact that it presents measures as social policy rather than as economic policy. The measures represent a change in social policies and a surreptitious way of influencing employment and the economy, that is, they serve as a selective economic policy but are labeled as a social policy. Then, even Thatchers and Reagans can support them while continuing to advocate "free markets." Our term for this rapidly developing set of measures is social-policy-as-economic-policy.

On one hand, the national government is calling for less intervention in the market, a reduction of governmental activities that regulate economic ac-tivities: let the free market rule is the principle. On the other hand, some government policies seek to improve the employment prospects of disadvan-taged workers by providing subsidies to them or to employers who hire them. In effect, these are microeconomic policies for unemployed, hard-to-place workers.

Transfers, either directly or through the tax system, are ways of influencing the employability of particular groups of workers and of increasing direct employment. One approach, called transfer diversion, uses transfer payments to induce employers to hire individuals whom they might not ordinarily hire. A woman on AFDC, for example, becomes more attractive to a private employer if she continues to receive her AFDC payment while she is working; her welfare benefit during a specified period supplements her wage. At the end of the period, the employer is expected to retain the AFDC recipient at full salary, and the AFDC payment is discontinued (or the woman returns to AFDC).

The tax system is also used to promote the appeal of less attractive workers. In the Targeted Job Tax Credit (TJTC) program, employers can reduce their federal taxes by hiring those who meet the criteria of disadvantaged workers. The broader proposals for job vouchers would use the transfer or subsidy system to encourage employers to hire the unemployed and to train them.

These various schemes clearly increase the attractiveness of workers who have trouble in the labor market. Thus, they move them up the queue of potential employees. Whether this process of increasing attractiveness and employability increases the number of jobs is not clear: it may result only in a different sorting of workers at best, though that is not a mean achievement. (The recent TJTC experience suggests that employers are little influenced by the possibility of a tax credit.) On the other hand, reducing at least the initial costs of hiring workers may induce employers to expand their labor force. In this view, lower labor costs for some period may expand total employment. Our guess is that employers make decisions basically on their calculation of prospective demand and that the savings of transfers-subsidies are too small to affect the total level of employment. But they may have an impact—how much of one is unclear—on changing the outlook of companies so that they hire people whom they are usually reluctant to employ.

Our prediction is that more varied use will be made of transfers and tax rebates as proemployment measures. Macroeconomic policies will continue to be constrained by domestic and international economic and political considerations even if unemployment rates are high. Under these conditions, *intervention in the economy for purposes of employment will be pushed to the periphery of economic policies and to the core of social policies.* A fundamental question is, How much can be achieved through social-policy-as-microeconomic-policy?

Public employment is much more important in other nations than in the United States. Contrary to what one would conclude from the attacks on federal employment, only a fifth of public employees are on the federal payroll. State and local governments are the main public employers, and their employment has been increasing much more rapidly than that of the federal government. The prospect of continuing increases in public employment is low. Similarly, fast growth in employment in the not-for-profit sector, stimulated or supported by governmental expenditures, is not likely to continue unless there is a reversal in the recent slowdown in public outlays for social and educational programs.

Short-run, "emergency" public employment in periods of high unemployment continues to be a possibility. It can ease the economic plight of the jobless, and in addition, such temporary employees carry out much useful activity. But it is short-term, seldom produces upgraded skills, and does not contribute to a continuing expansion of employment.

IMPLICATIONS

Our suggestions for decreasing unemployment and improving employment point to a disturbing conclusion for contemporary sociological theorizing. To a major extent such theorizing is built around the theme of determinacy: that process and events proceed somewhat inexorably along pre-determined lines and that while there is variation in the ways that problems and tensions are met, technological and other forces strongly condition choices and lead to hard-to-change results. It is not only technological deter-minists and historicists anticipating the unfolding of stages who think this way. Much Marxist theory sees the determinants of class relations as lying in the laws of motion governing capital accumulation rather than in the political realm. And most forms of functionalism have this bias also. Even those who think in terms of the continuing impact of values on a society or community (for example, Digby Baltzell in *Puritan Boston and Quaker Philadelphia*) see an inexorable tendency growing out of its historically prior value outlook.

Our perspective clashes with this way of thinking about inevitability. Recent work on the adoption and application of technology strongly suggests that which technologies are utilized and how they are adapted will be a matter of social choices rather than sheer economic and technological necessities (Noble 1984; Sabel 1982; Piore and Sabel 1984). Government actively shapes produc-tion decisions and can do so in a variety of ways. When it is known what could be done to change outcomes, then not doing some things is as much a political act as is pursuing our desired outlooks. Societies are not in the grip of inev-itabilities: struggle, choices, decisions, and nondecisions occur. We are often in the condition of anticipatable unanticipated consequences, a case of quasi-intentionality, in which results are not clearly intended but are definitely not avoided (Ferge and Miller 1987:297–99).

If the United States has high rates of unemployment generally, very high rates among blacks, especially black youth, and high long-term unemployment rates among other groups ("the new poor" of "displaced" workers—those who once had good jobs and are now "skidders" forced to take much lower-paying jobs), these results are not happenstances. They are willed, at least in the sense that we have not striven to avoid such outcomes when they might have been avoided.

Social stratification is being created by acts of decision and nondecision. Therefore, to predict the future of social stratification one must not only under-stand economic pressures but also factor in political will to shape, combat, or avoid these pressures.

Struggles over economic policy are to a major extent about the politics of employment and unemployment—who shall be employed, doing what, at what wages? Sociologists have treated social stratification as being largely determined by occupation, income, education, and residence. Increasingly, these variables are affected by political decisions. Social scientists, therefore, are dealing with the politics of social stratification, the making of the social structure, not its unfolding.

Whether we have an increasingly split society depends, then, on what this nation does politically. The growing salience of a global economic order and context does not render the nation-state obsolete or powerless in shaping both external events and internal outcomes. At the least, sociologists should clarify the explicit and implicit stakes in the actions that are and will be taking place.

REFERENCES

AFL-CIO News. 1989. February 18, 34, 4.

Baltzell, Digby. 1980. *Puritan Boston and Quaker Philadelphia.* New York: Free Press.

Bell, Daniel. 1971. *The Coming of Post-Industrial Society.* New York: Basic Books.

Bluestone, Barry, and Bennett Harrison. 1986. *The Great American Job Machine: The Proliferation of Low-Wage Employment in the U.S. Economy.* Report to the Joint Economic Committee of the U.S. Congress. Washington, D.C.: U.S. Government Printing Office.

Blustein, Paul. 1988. "The Great American Jobs Debate: Is Anyone Telling Voters the Truth?" *Washington Post,* August 28, H1, H7–H8.

Economic Report of the President. 1988. Washington: U.S. Government Printing Office.

Ferge, Szuzsa, and S. M. Miller. 1987. "Social Reproduction and the Dynamics of Deprivation." In *Dynamic of Deprivation,* edited by Ferge and Miller. Brookfield, Vt.: Gower.

Gorham, Lucy. 1984. "U.S. Industry Employment Trends from 1969–1995 and the Implications for Economic Inequality." Master's thesis, MIT.

Harrison, Bennett, and Barry Bluestone. 1988. *The Great U-Turn: Corporate Restructuring and the Polarizing of America.* New York: Basic Books.

Jencks, Christopher, et al. 1972. *Inequality.* New York: Basic Books.

Jencks, Christopher, Lauri Perman, and Lee Rainwater. 1988. "What is a Good Job? A New Measure of Labor Market Success." *American Journal of Sociology* 93 (6):1322–57.

Kirkland, Richard I., Jr. 1985. "Are Service Jobs Good Jobs?" *Fortune,* June 10.

Kosters, Marvin, and Murray Ross. 1987. "A Shrinking Middle Class?" *The Public Interest.*

Kuttner, Bob. 1983. "The Declining Middle." *Atlanta Monthly,* July.

Laurence, Robert Z. 1984. "Sectoral Shifts in the Size of the Middle Class." *Brookings Review,* Fall.

———. 1985. "The Middle Class Is Alive and Well." *New York Times,* June 23.

Leigh-Preston, Nancy. 1988. "The Nation's Changing Earnings Distribution from 1967 to 1986: What Happened to the Middle?" *Working Paper No. 491.* Institute of Urban and Regional Development, Berkeley: University of California.

Levy, Frank. 1987. *Dollars and Dreams.* New York: Russell Sage Foundation.

Miller, S. M. 1968. "Breaking the Credentials Barrier." New York: Ford Foundation.

Miller, S. Michael, and Donald Tomaskovic-Devey. 1983. *Recapitalizing America.* Boston: Routledge and Kegan Paul.

Mishel, Lawrence, and Jacqueline Simon. 1988. *The State of Working America.* Washington: Economic Policy Institute.

Noble, David. 1984. *Forces of Production.* New York: Knopf.

Osterman, Paul. 1988. *Employment Futures.* New York: Oxford University Press.

Piore, Michael, and Charles Sabel. 1984. *The Second Industrial Divide: Possibilities for Prosperity.* New York: Basic Books.

Podgursky, Michael. 1984. "Sources of Secular Increases in the Unemployment Rate, 1969–82." *Monthly Labor Review,* July.

Rosenthal, Neal. 1985. "The Shrinking Middle Class: Myth or Reality?" *Monthly Labor Review,* March.

Sabel, Charles. 1982. *Work and Politics: The Division of Labor in Industry.* New York: Cambridge University Press.

Shank, Susan Elizabeth. 1985. "Changes in Regional Employment over the Last Decade." *Monthly Labor Review,* March.

Stanback, Thomas M., Jr., and Thierry J. Noyelle. 1982. *Cities in Transition.* Osmun Publishers.

Walker, Patrick. 1983. "The Distribution of Skill and the Division of Labor 1950–1978." Ph.D. diss., University of Massachusetts-Amherst.

Wright, Erik Olin. 1985. *Classes.* London: New Left Books.

I I I I I I I Brother, Can You Spare a Job? Work and Welfare in the United States

THEDA SKOCPOL

The United States recently marked the fiftieth anniversary of the Social Security Act of 1935, the federal law that established the enduring framework for modern public social provision in America. This act established the major programs of public assistance, unemployment insurance, and old-age retirement insurance that add up to America's peculiar and incomplete version of a modern "welfare state." With the exception of Medicare, Medicaid, and Food Stamps, which were added in the Great Society period, the framework established by the Social Security Act has remained largely unmodified. Yet the legislation that Franklin Delano Roosevelt signed on August 14, 1935, was proposed by a Cabinet-level Committee on Economic Security (CES) that saw this measure as but one part of a set of commitments by the federal government that would be needed to address "the problem of economic security for the individual" in the United States.[1]

If the policy planners of the CES were to return to our midst to look back over the evolution of public social provision since the New Deal, they would be highly pleased that "social security's" program of old-age insurance has expanded and become politically entrenched—to the point that not even the ultraconservative president Ronald Reagan was able to cut it back. But at the same time, the members of the CES would surely be unhappy that what they

This paper was originally presented at the Thematic Panel on "Work and the Welfare State" at the Annual Meeting of the American Sociological Association, Washington D.C., August 27, 1985.

1. *The Report of the Committee on Economic Security of 1935, and Other Basic Documents Relating to the Development of the Social Security Act,* Fiftieth Anniversary Edition (Washington, D.C.: National Conference on Social Welfare, 1985), 23.

"No, keep the dime. But Brother,
could you spare a job?"

Source: Cartoon by Kevin Wachs (WOX). From William A. Gamson and Kathryn Lasch, "The Political Culture of Social Welfare Policy," in *Evaluating the Welfare State,* ed. Shimon E. Spiro and Ephraim Yuchtman-Yaar (New York: Academic Press, 1983).

considered the federal government's most basic role—providing "employment assurance" to the American people—has never been institutionalized.

To the CES policy planners the huge expansion of welfare payments to the poor since the 1950s would be little cause for celebration. They would see this expansion as an indication of the government's failure to assure jobs to all able-bodied American adults. For the CES members believed that if everyone who could work had a decent job, only a modest residuum of truly dependent people would need or want outright public assistance. Essentially, the CES members adhered to one of the major perspectives that William Gamson has identified as constitutive of the "political culture of welfare policy" in America.[2] According to this perspective—which the CES members believed was widely held by the American people—the poor person is thought to prefer a job to a handout. The accompanying cartoon (borrowed from Gamson) captures the essence of this perspective.

Few people realize that the planners of Social Security placed such a great emphasis on the federal government's role in assuring jobs for all who needed

2. William A. Gamson and Kathryn Lasch, "The Political Culture of Social Welfare Policy," in *Evaluating the Welfare State,* ed. Shimon E. Spiro and Ephraim Yuchtman-Yaar (New York: Academic Press, 1983), 397–415.

them. Yet in their *Report of the Committee on Economic Security* (January 1935), the very first policy recommendation, preceding even the recommendation for unemployment insurance, was about "employment assurance." It read as follows:

> Since most people must live by work, the first objective in a program of economic security must be maximum employment. As the major contribution of the Federal Government in providing a safeguard against unemployment, we suggest employment assurance—the stimulation of private employment and the provision of public employment for those able-bodied workers whom industry cannot employ at a given time. Public-work programs are most necessary in periods of severe depression, but may be needed in normal times, as well, to help meet the problems of stranded communities and overmanned and declining industries. To avoid the evils of hastily planned emergency work, public employment should be planned in advance and coordinated with the construction and developmental policies of the Government and with the State and local public works projects.
>
> We regard work as preferable to other forms of relief where possible. While we favor unemployment compensation in cash, we believe that it should be provided for limited periods . . . without governmental subsidies. Public funds should be devoted to providing work rather than . . . relief.[3]

How was the federal government to implement employment assurance? In the mid-1930s, reformers devoted to institutionalizing such a commitment by the federal government thought in terms of an updated, expanded, rationally planned system of public works projects on which the unemployed could, if necessary, do useful work at public expense.[4] This took an old idea in American politics and transferred it from the local to the national level.[5] By the late 1930s, another idea of what the federal government could do had emerged and coexisted with this earlier conception. So-called stagnationist Keynesians both within and without the executive branch argued that federal spending on socially useful projects should be expanded when necessary to maintain the economy at "full employment equilibrium."[6] In this way, private investment

3. *Report of the Committee on Economic Security*, 23–24.

4. See National Planning Board, *Final Report, 1933–1934* (Washington, D.C.: U.S. Government Printing Office, 1934), secs. I and II.

5. Leah Hannah Feder, *Unemployment Relief in Periods of Depression: A Study of Measures Adopted in Certain American Cities, 1857 through 1922* (New York: Russell Sage Foundation, 1936).

6. Robert M. Collins, *The Business Response to Keynes, 1929–1964* (New York: Columbia University Press, 1981), 10–11, 51; Dean L. May, *From New Deal to New Economics: The American Liberal Response to the Recession of 1937* (New York: Garland Press, 1981); Richard V. Gilbert et al., *An Economic Program for American Democracy* (New York: Vanguard Press, 1938); Alvin H. Hansen, *After the War—Full Employment,* a National Resources Planning Board publication (Washington, D.C.: U.S. Government Printing Office, 1942); and National Resources Planning Board, *Security, Work, and Relief Policies* (Washington, D.C.: U.S. Government Printing Office, 1942).

and job creation would be maximally stimulated by federal deficit spending, and some of that spending could simultaneously be used to provide public jobs to workers in industries or communities with especially severe and persistent unemployment.

Still later, in the post–World War II period, some American "manpower economists" became attracted to ideas for "active labor market policies."[7] These would be policies tailored to particular industries or areas, policies used to train or retrain workers and to help them find jobs and if necessary relocate with public assistance so they could take those jobs. Ideally, such active labor market interventions could be closely coordinated with Keynesian macroeconomic stimulation and with projects offering temporary public employment. By the 1960s, therefore, at least three sets of recognized policy instruments—public employment, deficit social spending, and active labor market policies—were potentially applicable, singly or in combination, in the task of realizing a federal government commitment to employment assurance.

From the 1930s through the 1970s, repeated efforts were made to commit the U.S. national state to coordinating such policy instruments for employment assurance, yet every one of those efforts failed. The most notable efforts happened in 1945–46, 1967, and 1976–78:

• Around the end of World War II, the stagnationist Keynesian vision was embodied in the Full Employment bill of 1945. This called upon the federal government to guarantee jobs for all who were willing to work and to use public spending for stimulative purposes and, if necessary, to provide public employment. However, the bill was eviscerated in Congress and became merely the Employment Act of 1946. The 1946 law endorsed "high" rather than "full" employment; it no longer mandated public spending as a priority policy instrument; and it backed off from institutionalizing planning around an annual National Production and Employment Budget.[8]

• In what historian Bonnie Schwartz has called "the first major push for public employment since the Great Depression," Senators Joseph Clark and Robert Kennedy proposed in 1967 an Emergency Employment bill that would have given the secretary of labor $2.5 billion to assist public and private agencies to offer new work opportunities in health, education, and related fields.[9] But

7. See the discussion in Margaret Weir, "The Federal Government and Unemployment: The Frustration of Policy Innovation from the New Deal to the Great Society," in *The Politics of Social Policy in the United States,* ed. Margaret Weir, Ann Shola Orloff, and Theda Skocpol (Princeton: Princeton University Press, 1988), 168–80.

8. The evolution of the 1945 bill into the 1946 act is analyzed in Stephen Kemp Bailey, *Congress Makes a Law* (New York: Vintage Books, 1950).

9. Bonnie Fox Schwartz, *The Civil Works Administration, 1933–1934: The Business of Emergency Employment in the New Deal* (Princeton: Princeton University Press, 1984), 268–69.

even though this proposal came along with the Great Society's antipoverty efforts, the Johnson administration was opposed, and the legislation failed to pass.

- In 1976, the Humphrey-Hawkins Full Employment and Balanced Growth bill was introduced into the Congress. Like the Full Employment bill of 1945, this would have committed the federal government to guaranteeing jobs to everyone able and willing to work. Humphrey-Hawkins authorized $15 billion the first year for enhanced federal employment services and for temporary public-service jobs, and it required the president to submit every year a "full employment and national purpose" budget embodying plans to keep the unemployment rate below 3 percent. But two years later, in 1978, Humphrey-Hawkins passed as a mere resolution, with all the operative provisions excised, with the unemployment goal raised to 4 percent and with the goal of reducing inflation also mandated in the purely symbolic resolution that was enacted.[10]

Across the Western, advanced-industrial world in the post–World War II decades, the full employment welfare state came into its own, at least symbolically if not always actually. In this context, the United States stood out not only for its relatively high unemployment rates in the 1950s, 1960s, and 1970s, but even more for its passive governmental approach to managing the national economy. The variant of Keynesianism that held sway intellectually and in public policy practice after the defeat of the Full Employment bill in 1945 was "commercial Keynesianism."[11] This emphasizes the use of tax cuts and automatic stabilizers as tools of macroeconomic stimulation, rather than the use of increases in public social spending. U.S. policymakers officially aimed to fight inflation as much as to keep unemployment rates down, and social-welfare expenditures were not planned in coordination with macroeconomic management. Moreover, despite some minor efforts at manpower programs after World War II and again during the Great Society period, active labor market interventions have been much more extensively and effectively used in Sweden and several other West European nations than in the United States.[12]

10. See the discussion in Margaret Weir, *Ideas and Political Possibilities: Employment Policies in the United States* (Princeton: Princeton University Press, forthcoming), chap. 5.

11. This term comes from Robert Lekachman, *The Age of Keynes* (New York: McGraw-Hill, 1966), 287.

12. *European Labor Market Policies*, Special Report no. 27 of the National Commission for Manpower Policy (September 1978); Beatrice G. Reubens, *The Hard-to-Employ: European Programs* (New York: Columbia University Press, 1970); and Margaret S. Gordon, *Retraining and Labor Market Adjustment in Western Europe* (Washington, D.C.: Department of Labor, Office of Manpower, Automation, and Training, 1965).

In short, compared to most European welfare states in the postwar period, the United States has been profoundly reluctant both in political precept and in practice to use active governmental measures (spending, public employment, active labor market policies) to promote a full employment economy with decent jobs for all who want them. After the advent of Ronald Reagan's presidency, this reluctance became enshrined as official policy. From 1946 through 1979, lip service was paid to the goal of keeping unemployment rates down, and when they were rising or stubbornly high, pressures accumulated on the federal government to devise new measures to combat unemployment. Under Reagan, however, unemployment persisted for some years at 7 percent or above, yet the official goals of the administration were to reduce government's role in the economy and "unleash" private market forces through tax cuts and reductions in federal social programs. Nor was the Reagan administration isolated, for many members of the opposition Democratic party have endorsed these goals and the comprehensive anti–public sector rhetoric that accompanied them. The U.S. national government today is thus further than ever from pursuing the goal of employment assurance articulated by the planners of Social Security in 1935.

How can we explain the failure of the modern U.S. state to use public instrumentalities to pursue full employment assurance? I will eventually point out that the failure is not as complete as it might seem, because the U.S. federal government has always, in one way or another, functioned to distribute job opportunities to the local constituents of congressional representatives. But such "job creation politics" has not been explicitly debated that way at the national level, and it has never been possible to supplant congressional pork barrel with deliberate and selectively targeted national strategies. The peculiarities of administrative statebuilding in the United States since the nineteenth century have left national leaders without effective means to devise or implement explicit full-employment planning. And because of the nature of U.S. political parties, the great new waves of democratic electoral mobilization that came in the 1930s and 1960s ended up creating backlashes against potential commitments to a full-employment welfare state at the very moments when the balance of forces seemed to be swinging in that direction.

Before elaborating this argument centered on the U.S. state and political parties, let me briefly consider two alternative perspectives that might appear to account more straightforwardly for the absence of public employment assurance in America. Could we perhaps dismiss the entire issue on the ground that basic American values—and therefore public opinion in U.S. democracy—rule out the possibility of government taking responsibility for full employment? Or might we invoke the flip side of the variables that many political economists have used to explain Sweden's full employment welfare state, arguing that the American working class has been relatively weakly organized and thus business interests have held sway in the national political process, blocking possibilities for public employment assurance?

DO AMERICAN VALUES RULE OUT EMPLOYMENT ASSURANCE?

Arguments that basic American values rule out social-welfare activities have always flourished in periods of conservative reaction because it is easy enough for right-wing propagandists to invoke one possible reading—an antistatist reading—of values that surely are at the core of American culture. Americans believe in getting ahead through self-reliance and hard work—so we would all agree. Therefore, Americans do not want help from government, or so the right-wing propagandists attempt to conclude from the agreed-upon premise. But evidence from social history and modern opinion polling alike demonstrates that many Americans, including large majorities at times for which appropriate evidence exists, have held to a perspective more congruent with the core notion of the cartoon reproduced above. Americans have believed that simple "welfare" handouts, whether from private or public sources, were inappropriate (undeserved and demeaning) for those able to work. Yet they have also felt that public authorities had a special responsibility to help able-bodied people get jobs.

In short, many Americans believe that while people are helping themselves, government should also help the unemployed to acquire the jobs through which they can then get ahead through hard work. A complete review of the evidence on this point would take a lengthy paper of its own, but consider the following empirical findings, stretching from the nineteenth century to the late 1970s:

• In her research on the origins of urban political machines, Amy Bridges shows that nineteenth-century party politicians responded to demands for jobs from the unemployed. In New York City during the hard times of the 1850s, "mass meetings of the unemployed" discussed remedies; "private charity was declared both inadequate and degrading. Instead, unemployed workers demanded . . . [that] the city government . . . increase public works to provide employment, without partisan preference and with a guaranteed minimum wage."[13] By 1857, Mayor Fernando Wood responded positively to these demands, despite strong business opposition, and his organization gained electoral strength as a result. Similar developments occurred in Newark, Philadelphia, and Baltimore. In Bridges's words, "the depression of the 1850s brought demands for public works and public relief

13. Amy Bridges, *A City in the Republic: Antebellum New York and the Origins of Machine Politics* (Cambridge and New York: Cambridge University Press, 1984), 116.

[through jobs] . . . ; these demands won concessions from city governments and pressured politicians into a kind of pre-welfare-state-ism."[14]

- Social historian Alex Keyssar has studied unemployment and working-class responses to it in the state of Massachusetts. He documents that in every depression from the 1870s to the 1920s Massachusetts unionists "demanded that government offer direct aid to the unemployed by launching public works programs during depressions."[15] These demands spread upward from cities to state government to the federal government. In the depression of the 1890s, "the national executive council of the A.F. of L. sent a memorial to the President and to Congress asking for public works" and "similar demands were voiced in 1907–08, 1913–14, and most vociferously after World War I . . . [when, according to labor spokesmen,] a nation that sent men into battle had a moral and political obligation to make sure they had jobs when they returned home."[16] During this same period, the national A.F. of L. firmly opposed public unemployment insurance on the grounds that it would undermine workers' independence and subject them to the state. But the state's role in providing work for the unemployed was understood more positively, and the values invoked are revealing. According to Keyssar, "unionists stressed that public works programs were preferable to simple poor relief in three respects: they paid workers a living wage rather than a pittance; they permitted jobless men and women to avoid the demoralizing consequences of accepting charity; and they performed a useful public service."[17]

- According to a social historian who has looked at elite views toward unemployment during the same period covered by Keyssar's study of workers, by the time of the depression of 1913–15, "reformers were learning to recognize that the unemployed wanted jobs, not charity," and they were willing to support public works projects along with public labor exchanges and (as a last resort for those not given work) public unemployment insurance as a right, not a handout.[18]

- During the New Deal of the 1930s, of course, many governmental efforts to combat unemployment were launched—including the public employment programs of the Civil Works Administration, the Works Progress Administration, and the Public Works Administration—and many historians have documented the popularity of these efforts. Public opinion polling also started in this

14. Ibid., 123.
15. Alexander Keyssar, *Out of Work: The First Century of Unemployment in Massachusetts* (Cambridge: Cambridge University Press, 1986), 211.
16. Ibid., 212.
17. Ibid.
18. Paul T. Ringebach, *Tramps and Reformers, 1873–1916: The Discovery of Unemployment in New York* (Westport, Conn.: Greenwood Press, 1973), 178 and chaps. 5, 6.

decade. A poll conducted by *Fortune* magazine in July 1935 reported that three-fourths of the public agreed that "the government should see to it that any man who wants to work has a job."[19] And a 1939 Roper poll reported that 76 percent of the unemployed, 73 percent of blue-collar workers, 60 percent of lower white-collar workers, and 46 percent of upper white-collar workers agreed that the government should guarantee jobs to everyone.[20]

- In the 1960s, there was strong public support for the few targeted "active labor market" programs that were tried. In 1963–64, "a special survey done by . . . Gallup . . . demonstrated that three-fourths of the public favored Federal aid to 'depressed areas, that is, where unemployment has been high over a long period,' either at the present or an increased level."[21] And in 1967, even after a conservative electoral reaction had begun, 75 percent of Americans in a Gallup poll favored present or increased levels of federal funding for "retraining poorly educated people so they can get jobs."[22]

- In a mid-1970s survey of the U.S. urban workforce, including employed and unemployed respondents of all strata, Kay Schlozman and Sidney Verba found 77 percent agreeing that "the government should end unemployment."[23] Overall, only 30 percent agreed that the government should end unemployment if, in order to do so, it had to hire all of the jobless. Yet the proportions agreeing at each socioeconomic level were higher among the unemployed themselves, and about half of those unemployed at the lower levels would have the government hire all of the jobless.

- In a study (published in 1979) of public attitudes toward who should receive social services, Fay Lomax Cook found that, in general, respondents were loath to support public services for able-bodied poor adults, who were seen as responsible for themselves. But there was an exception if the services would help such people achieve independence. Thus, "when respondents feel they can help poor adults under 65 to escape their plight by providing them with education services, support is very high."[24] Cook did not ask directly about public employment opportunities, but the logic of her findings certainly would apply to job-training efforts.

- Finally, Robert Shapiro and his associates have explored American attitudes

19. Cited in Lloyd A. Free and Hadley Cantril, *The Political Beliefs of Americans: A Study of Public Opinion* (New York: Simon and Schuster, 1968), 10.

20. Cited in Kay Lehman Schlozman and Sidney Verba, *Injury to Insult: Unemployment, Class, and Political Response* (Cambridge: Harvard University Press, 1979), 220.

21. Cited in Free and Cantril, *Political Beliefs*, 11.

22. Cited in ibid., 12.

23. Schlozman and Verba, *Injury to Insult*, 202–05.

24. Fay Lomax Cook, *Who Should Be Helped? Public Support for Social Services* (Beverly Hills, Cal.: Sage Publications, 1979), 170.

toward public social provision in some detail. They find that "there has always been overwhelming support for work in place of welfare," even though the U.S. public is ambivalent about public works jobs.[25] These authors have compiled available findings from prior social surveys. In one telling question that has been posed since the 1950s, Americans have been asked whether they agree or disagree that "The government in Washington [or "the federal government"] ought to see to it that everybody who wants to work can find a job." Remarkably, during the 1970s agreement with this idea grew, reaching 74 percent in 1978.[26] Shapiro and associates also show that Americans are broadly supportive of job training programs for the unemployed, work requirements for people on welfare, and child care for working women—all measures that embody expectations that able-bodied adults should be helped to get ahead through work, rather than being left dependent on relief.

Although the evidence just sampled is only suggestive and does not represent all the evidence that could be marshaled, it seems sufficient to allow us to reject any notion that basic American values rule out government efforts at employment assurance. On the contrary, from the nineteenth century to the present, many Americans have called upon government to fight unemployment by using a variety of direct and indirect means to generate jobs for those who need work. Recurrently, moreover, the theme of government ensuring work or job training rather than providing relief has echoed through American politics. Thus the CES planners of 1934–35 *were* operating on value premises broadly shared by a substantial majority of their fellow citizens.

DOES POLITICAL CLASS STRUGGLE EXPLAIN THE FAILURE OF EMPLOYMENT ASSURANCE IN THE UNITED STATES?

If basic U.S. values have not ruled out a strong state role in employment assurance, perhaps the trouble has been in the balance of power between business and organized labor. Adherents of the most fruitful recent approach to the comparative study of Western welfare states—the working-class strength or social-democratic approach—would certainly direct our attention to the relative weakness of U.S. industrial unions and to the absence of a

25. Robert Y. Shapiro, Kelly D. Patterson, Judith Russell, and John T. Young, "The Polls—A Report: Employment and Social Welfare," *Public Opinion Quarterly* 51 (Summer 1987): 269. See also Robert Shapiro et al., "The Polls: Public Assistance," *Public Opinion Quarterly* 51 (1987): 120–30.

26. Shapiro et al., "Polls: Employment and Welfare," 274–75.

labor-based political party in U.S. democracy.[27] Given these weaknesses of working-class organization, the argument goes, U.S. capitalists have been able to use direct and indirect pressures to prevent governments at all levels from undertaking social-welfare efforts, and especially from undertaking labor market interventions or public works projects that would interfere with the prerogatives or profits of private businesses.

Unquestionably, political class struggle does partially help explain why the U.S. national state has not committed itself to full employment assurance. Swedish-style policies would probably have come about in the United States had American workers been as highly unionized as Swedish ones or had the modern Democratic party been a truly social-democratic party based in the organized working class. Moreover, American business groups have consistently pressured against the inception or extension of many welfare-state efforts. It would be pointless to deny that such business pressures—as well as the alternative public policy ideas championed by business-sponsored intellectuals—have had their effect on policy outcomes. For example, after the defeat of the essentially social-democratic stagnationist Keynesian ideas embodied in the Full Employment bill of 1945, commercial Keynesian prescriptions were instead put into effect. These policies had been partly developed and propagated under the auspices of two business organizations, the Committee on Economic Development and the U.S. Chamber of Commerce.[28]

Nevertheless, for several reasons it would be a mistake to attribute the failure of employment assurance entirely to the political class struggles of strong business versus weak labor. First, a focus exclusively on political conflicts of interest between capitalists and industrial workers deflects our attention from other partially socioeconomically grounded forces that have shaped and limited state activities in the United States. Agricultural interests in the South and West have always been very much a part of American politics, and regional and racial conflicts have been just as critical in shaping and limiting U.S. state activities in economic planning and labor market intervention as have conflicts between business and labor.[29] Moreover, business and labor groups have often united to work for or against governmental policies that would affect employment in

27. For overviews of this literature, see Michael Shalev, "The Social Democratic Model and Beyond: Two Generations of Comparative Research on the Welfare State," *Comparative Social Research* 6 (1983): 315–51; and Theda Skocpol and Edwin Amenta, "States and Social Policies," *Annual Review of Sociology* 12 (1986): 131–57.

28. Collins, *Business Response to Keynes.*

29. This theme is developed in several of the essays in Margaret Weir, Ann Shola Orloff, and Theda Skocpol, eds., *The Politics of Social Policy in the United States* (Princeton: Princeton University Press, 1988).

particular areas. As I argue below, the structure of the U.S. federal state and the character of U.S. political parties have especially encouraged local solidarities and interregional and racial/ethnic conflicts over economic interventions by the national government.

Second, the political class struggle approach applied to the case of the United States proves insensitive to the peculiar evolution of American political history. Any approach that focuses our attention on the rise of industrial unions fails to explain why U.S. party patronage democracy in the nineteenth century actually functioned as a precocious (albeit uneven) welfare state, distributing social benefits that included permanent or emergency jobs for many middle- and working-class men.[30] Ironically, America in the twentieth century may in many ways have retreated from the employment assurance efforts that certain nineteenth-century urban party machines were prepared to make for their popular constituents.

Finally, an approach that stresses political class struggle fails to explain the politics of employment assurance at those critical conjunctures in twentieth-century American politics—especially the mid to late 1930s and the 1960s—when U.S. business interests were politically vulnerable, when working-class and more broadly democratic forces were on the rise, and when many social-welfare policies that business strongly opposed actually did pass and become a permanent part of the federal government's activities. Why didn't employment assurance efforts become institutionalized as goals and programs at these conjunctures—when policies were actually proposed and debated, and U.S. public opinion (as we have seen) favored work over relief for the unemployed and the impoverished? A political class struggle approach alone will not explain the missed possibilities for national commitments to employment assurance during the special conjunctures of the thirties and sixties.

Thus, by paying attention to conflicts between capitalists and labor we can explain some features of modern U.S. social-welfare policies—especially in contrast to the social democracies of post–World War II Western Europe. Yet analysis from another perspective is also required if we are to understand fully why American democracy has not institutionalized full employment assurance as a goal and activity of the national state.

30. See Bridges, *City in the Republic,* passim; Martin Shefter, "Trade Unions and Political Machines: The Organization and Disorganization of American Working Class Life in the Late Nineteenth Century," in *Working-Class Formation: Nineteenth-Century Patterns in Western Europe and the United States,* ed. Ira Katznelson and Aristide R. Zolberg (Princeton: Princeton University Press, 1986), 267–72; and Steven P. Erie, *Rainbow's End: Irish-Americans and the Dilemmas of Urban Machine Politics, 1840–1985* (Berkeley: University of California Press, 1988), chap. 2.

204   THEDA SKOCPOL

THE POLITICS OF JOB CREATION
VERSUS EMPLOYMENT ASSURANCE
IN AMERICA'S FEDERAL DEMOCRACY

Many of the answers to the questions and puzzles I have posed lie in the history of U.S. state building and in the peculiar structures of U.S. federal democracy and party politics. As I cannot fully elaborate or prove my case in a short essay, let me make three bold propositions about how these matters relate to employment politics in major phases and key conjunctures of U.S. history. My propositions should be considered working hypotheses in need of further research and exploration. I lay them out here to provoke discussion and debate.

Proposition Number One: A "distributive" politics of job creation has always been an important part of public policymaking in the United States. But this kind of politics was explicit at all levels in the party-patronage democracy of the nineteenth-century and has become a nationally unacknowledged politics of local subsidies and regional competition in the U.S. state structure of the twentieth century.

Both social commentators and social scientists have often fundamentally mischaracterized American society and politics in the nineteenth century, suggesting that Americans back then were all hardy individualists and that governments did little to "interfere" in the economy or society. In truth, nineteenth-century America was the world's first mass democracy, and the polity was dominated at all levels by patronage-oriented political parties that were intensely competitive with one another and had elaborate organizations capable of getting out virtually all eligible white, male voters for incessant rounds of local, state, and national elections. These patronage-oriented parties specialized in distributive public policymaking—that is, they constantly looked for ways to generate divisible material benefits to pass out to their key cadres and supporters in as many states and local communities as possible.[31] Land grants, Civil War pensions, and tariff advantages were some of the distributive policies that characterized party-patronage democracy in the nineteenth century. But the most obvious distributions were of public jobs themselves. Thus national party managers distributed postmasterships and customs house jobs, and state and local party bosses distributed proliferating numbers of posts at those levels of government. Finally, as we have seen from Amy Bridges's work, urban political machines responded during crises to the demands of the unemployed for expanded public works projects to provide work for the jobless. All in all, it is

31. Richard L. McCormick, "The Party Period and Public Policy: An Exploratory Hypothesis," in *The Party Period and Public Policy* (New York: Oxford University Press, 1986), chap. 5.

fair to say that the central political organizations of nineteenth-century America, the parties, unabashedly worked at all levels to generate and distribute jobs in government or at public expense. Especially because it was dealing with such political parties, the emergent American working class learned to hope that government would provide work rather than charity.

In the twentieth century, however, patronage-oriented political parties have been on the defensive, as wave after wave of elite reformers from the Progressives on have sought, with considerable success, to weaken their organizations and reorient electoral democracy toward the expectations of upper-middle-class ideals of good government. Yet the politics of creating and distributing jobs has not disappeared. Rather it has survived in the operations of Congress at the federal level, and in the way congressional politics links up to local politics and regional interests.

The U.S. national state structure of the twentieth century has remained remarkably decentralized because national administrative structures have only rarely supplanted the powers of state and local governments, and because Congress, with its state and local constituencies, has used its committee system to retain great influence over both legislation and actual policy implementation.[32] Politically speaking, shifting congressional coalitions, often brokered through committee negotiations, are much more important than political party divisions as such in modern American politics. For public policy outcomes, this means that the bread-and-butter interests of many localities typically have to be brokered into most laws that get through Congress. Once laws are passed, individual congressional representatives will work with the federal bureaucracy to make sure that benefits are channeled to their localities.

The upshot of all this is that many modern U.S. public policies that appear to be about national problems—such as defense or health care or urban renewal—are really mechanisms for spreading federal subsidies to as many congressional districts as possible. Back home, each congressperson presents these policies as ways to generate or protect jobs for local people. But in national policy debates, they are not explicitly treated as employment assurance policies. And that matters, because if full employment were the explicit goal, alternative kinds of policies, more carefully targeted on selected areas of the country or aimed at helping people to move around more freely, might be preferred. As it

32. Background for this and the following paragraph comes from Stephen Skowronek, *Building a New American State* (Cambridge and New York: Cambridge University Press, 1982); Samuel P. Huntington, "Congressional Responses to the Twentieth Century," in *The Congress and America's Future,* 2d ed. (Englewood Cliffs: Prentice-Hall, 1973), 6–38; Morris P. Fiorina, *Congress: Keystone of the Washington Establishment* (New Haven: Yale University Press, 1977); and R. Douglas Arnold, *Congress and the Bureaucracy: A Theory of Influence* (New Haven: Yale University Press, 1979).

is, congressional brokering has repeatedly spent a lot of national resources on job creation for the middle classes and construction and defense workers across many, many localities. But people in especially depressed regions and localities (that is, inner cities) have been left in place, insufficiently helped to find employment. Yet those people do not feel even as entitled to ask for political help as the unemployed workers of the 1850s in New York City did—because U.S. politics in the twentieth century is not *openly* about job creation and distribution!

Proposition Number Two: Efforts at bureaucratic state building and administrative reform since the Progressive Era have not facilitated national economic planning for full employment. Actually, through their failures and half way successes, such efforts have created obstacles to the implementation of nationally coordinated public works, to Keynesian macroeconomic management through social spending, and to active labor market policies.

The reformist American elites who have worked since the Progressive Era to displace patronage-oriented parties and politicians from their formerly dominant role in American democracy have also had positive state building goals. Middle-class professionals, including social scientists, have always been prominent among such good government reformers, from the Progressives through the New Dealers to the New Politics reformers of the 1960s. These reformers have sought to create professional-bureaucratic agencies of government through which rational policies in the public interest could be pursued free from the clutches of mere politicians, especially those in Congress and in political party organizations. For our purposes here, the point to be made about efforts at administrative reform is that they have never succeeded in creating state capacities for national full employment assurance.

During the Progressive Era, reformers were determined to undermine patronage-oriented party politicians. Thus they favored the establishment of regulatory commissions free from political control but opposed new state activities that would allow politicians to channel money or jobs to popular constituents.[33] Working-class demands for public works to employ people during depressions met with a cautious response from reformers. Until city and state governments or federal agencies were reorganized under expert control, most reformers did not want them to have enhanced spending powers.

The one relevant reform that the Progressives did strongly favor was the establishment of a strong national system of employment bureaus, and had this

33. Skowronek, *Building a New American State,* part 3; and Martin Shefter, "Party, Bureaucracy, and Political Change in the United States," in *Political Parties: Development and Decay,* ed. Louis Maisel and Joseph Cooper (Beverly Hills: Sage Publications, 1978), 211–65.

succeeded it would have facilitated the later implementation of both public works and active labor market policies. But despite the setting up of a temporary federal Employment Service during World War I, this Progressive state building effort failed.[34] Local business and labor groups working through Congress dismantled the national system right after World War I, and the nation was subsequently left until the 1930s with no effective means to monitor or intervene in labor markets.

During the 1930s, of course, New Dealers resumed efforts to build new governmental agencies to serve the public interest—and many of their efforts were directly oriented to dealing with massive unemployment in the Great Depression. Throughout the New Deal and into the 1940s, however, there was an ongoing political struggle between New Dealers in the executive branch and Congress, with its ties to state and local interests. The struggle was over who would control enhanced federal spending and new federal activities; basically Congress won in the end. Key New Deal programs and failed efforts at administrative reform ended up enhancing federal and congressional controls at the expense of centralized national planning and coordination. Thus:

- Public employment agencies were established as a state-controlled federal system, rather than as a national system; and right after World War II, Congress defeated an attempt to maintain the nationalization of these services that had been necessary to implement wartime manpower policies.[35]
- The various emergency public works and public employment programs of the New Deal were constantly wracked by local objections to Washington's initiatives and requirements. Consequently, some of the most efficient programs, like the Civil Works Administration and the Public Works Administration, aroused opposition from local and state politicians and from Congress and ended up being dismantled or hobbled in their ability to fight unemployment in a nationally coordinated way.[36]
- What perhaps did the most to undercut the possibility of the permanent institutionalization of either public works or Keynesian social spending was the failure of the sweeping budgetary and administrative reforms that Roosevelt attempted to put through in 1937–38. Southerners feared too much federal intervention in their agricultural labor relations and in race relations, and southern congressional committee chairmen thus opposed efforts to strengthen the New Deal executive. Further, congressional representatives

34. I. W. Litchfield, "The United States Employment Service and Demobilization," *Annals of the American Academy of Political and Social Science* 81 (1919): 19–27.

35. See the discussion and references in Weir, "Federal Government and Unemployment," in *Politics of Social Policy in the United States,* 166–67.

36. Schwartz, *Civil Works Administration.*

generally, including liberals, were anxious to protect their branch's established ties to parts of the federal bureaucracy and their branch's controls over
the federal budgeting process. Thus Congress eviscerated Roosevelt's proposed administrative reforms.[37]

• In related moves, Congress step by step undercut and then abolished the
National Resources Planning Board that Roosevelt had hoped to make central
to long-range national economic planning for full employment. This happened during World War II, and it was just a prelude to Congress's defeat of
the Full Employment bill of 1945, which was a last attempt by New Dealers
interested in institutionalizing a commitment to employment assurance to
beef up the capacities of the president and executive branch to plan and
coordinate social spending and public works for that purpose.[38]

In the aftermath of the struggles between the executive and the Congress
during the New Deal and World War II, federal policies relevant to employment
proceeded on two tracks, neither well coordinated with the other. One track was
congressionally managed spending programs, which tended to be presented to
local constituencies as ways to bring jobs into particular localities, but not as
national strategies to combat unemployment as such. The other track involved
presidentially sponsored initiatives to combat either unemployment or inflation. These overtly national, macroeconomic strategies were devised by the
Office of the President and the Council of Economic Advisers, which were the
purely advisory bodies established after the New Deal administrative reforms
and the Full Employment bill had been emasculated. Yet, because these bodies
had little administrative authority and no capacity to control Congress, they
tended to gravitate toward passive, commercial Keynesian strategies that used
tax cuts and automatic stabilizers, rather than toward social spending or active
labor market interventions.[39]

As Margaret Weir shows in her important book about U.S. employment
policies from the 1960s to the 1980s, the established bifurcation—built into the
post–New Deal state structure—between congressionally controlled programs
and executive commercial Keynesian macroeconomic management meant that

37. Richard Polenberg, *Reorganizing Roosevelt's Government, 1936–1939: The
Controversy over Executive Reorganization* (Cambridge: Harvard University Press,
1966).

38. Marion Clawson, *New Deal Planning: The National Resources Planning Board*
(Baltimore: Johns Hopkins University Press, 1981); and Philip W. Warken, *A History of
the National Resources Planning Board* (New York: Garland Press, 1979).

39. Further discussion appears in Edwin Amenta and Theda Skocpol, "Taking Excep-
tion: Explaining the Distinctiveness of American Public Policies in the Last Century," in
The Comparative History of Public Policy, ed. Francis G. Castles (Oxford: Polity
Press/Basil Blackwell, 1989), 305–09.

it was hard during the War on Poverty of the 1960s for proponents of active labor market interventions to succeed.[40] During the sixties and early seventies, some manpower economists in the Labor Department wanted to devise new national approaches to unemployment, approaches that combined public employment with federally sponsored training programs and with the use of enhanced spending for the redevelopment of depressed areas. Under President Kennedy, however, the Council of Economic Advisers chose to use tax cuts to stimulate overall growth in the national economy, assuming that this alone would address unemployment.

Within the executive branch, the Labor Department economists could not sell their approach to the economic advisers or to presidents. Within Congress, the only kinds of manpower and spending programs that could get through were *not* programs that enhanced Labor Department controls over efficiently targeted training efforts. They were, instead, programs that would channel funds for administration by many local governments and agencies. President Johnson, moreover, was a president who thought in congressional terms, and he believed that the War on Poverty could best be fought by channeling some funds to many established local authorities and others (for example, Community Action grants) to newly mobilized blacks in the cities. Johnson did not support Labor Department ideas for targeted, centrally managed employment policies. Like other presidents, he relied on the Council of Economic Advisers for strategies to further national economic growth without specifically addressing structural unemployment as a national economic problem.

Proposition Number Three: The peculiarities of American political parties, and the internal contradictions of the Democratic party in particular, have made it impossible to translate upsurges of popular political participation in the 1930s and the 1960s into broad political alliances that could provide support for full employment policies. Instead, conservative backlashes occurred in each time period.

Whatever the difficulties of building and reorganizing the American national state in the twentieth century so as to facilitate full employment policies, one might still suppose that—if Americans really do prefer work to welfare— popular preferences for such policies would have prevailed, especially in the New Deal or in the aftermath of the civil rights revolution of the 1960s. Indeed, one can point to *potential* broad popular coalitions favoring employment assurance in both the 1930s–40s and the 1960s–70s.

In the 1930s, industrial workers were newly organized into increasingly powerful unions allied with urban-liberal Democrats, and masses of new voters were joining the Democratic electoral base. Moreover, during the New Deal, at

40. Weir, *Ideas and Political Possibilities.*

least initially, poor farmers in the South and Midwest were potential recruits to a Democratic–popular coalition that could have furthered a broad social program, including full employment planning and policies.

In the 1960s and early 1970s, American blacks were finally fully mobilized into the Democratic electoral coalition, and the potential was opened for an ascendant liberal coalition of workers, blacks, and some middle-class people as southern and farm-area conservative control of Congress was finally broken. However, in both these critical periods, the Democratic party was the key to any enduring pro-full-employment alliance. Yet the Democratic party's internal contradictions, as they played out within the U.S. federal state structure and electoral system, doomed possibilities for further reforms and triggered conservative reactions.

During the 1930s, the growth of urban-liberal forces within the Democratic party had to coexist with the entrenched conservative power of southern Democratic representatives of agricultural and racially segregationist areas.[41] For Roosevelt and the New Dealers never launched any concerted attack on the disenfranchisement of southern blacks. Ironically, as the national Democratic party grew, conservative southern committee chairmen in Congress gained increased strength, which they used to help undercut administrative reorganization and public works spending in the later 1930s and to help abolish the National Resources Planning Board and defeat the Full Employment bill in the 1940s.

Moreover, the conservative Democrats increasingly allied themselves in Congress with conservative Republicans, including many from midwestern farm areas that became increasingly opposed to further New Deal reforms after the mid-1930s. Such opposition developed once richer farmers had benefited from New Deal agricultural subsidies and once the American Farm Bureau Federation gained local administrative control of those subsidies and used its leverage to effect an antireformist alliance between southern planters and richer midwestern farmers. This came at the expense of the urban-liberal wing of the Democratic party, and the increasing Republican loyalties of many farmers after the mid-1930s prevented the development of a more progressive coalition inside the Democratic party between urban workers and midwestern farmers.

41. This discussion follows the lines of Weir, "Federal Government and Unemployment," in Weir et al., eds., *Politics of Social Policy in the United States,* 156–62, and Margaret Weir and Theda Skocpol, "State Structures and the Possibilities for 'Keynesian' Responses to the Great Depression in Sweden, Britain, and the United States," in *Bringing the State Back In,* ed. Peter Evans, Dietrich Rueschemeyer, and Theda Skocpol (Cambridge and New York: Cambridge University Press, 1985), 107–63.

Such a coalition would have no doubt sustained New Deal public works and facilitated social Keynesianism rather than commercial Keynesianism in the postwar period.

By the time of the Great Society and the War on Poverty in the 1960s, the grip of the congressional conservative coalition was finally relaxed, and there seemed to be new hope for a liberal Democratic party to complete an American version of the full employment welfare state. This was especially true because the civil rights revolution had finally brought most blacks into American democracy, and black opinion placed a high value on governmental efforts to further education and jobs, for many new black migrants to northern cities had not been able to find adequate employment. Organized labor and blacks could come together naturally and easily around employment assurance policies enacted by the federal government.

But once again the internal contradictions of the Democratic party—operating in the congressionally centered and administratively weak U.S. state structure— defeated progressive possibilities.[42] President Johnson, congressional Democrats, and state and local party leaders did not devise the War on Poverty as a self-conscious national full employment assurance strategy, as a way to create a universalistic social alliance including blacks. Instead, thinking in the usual terms of congressional brokering and broadly scattered subsidies to local interests, they decided to add new programs and subsidies for poor and black groups onto established or further subsidies for other locally based interests. Some monies for job training and public service jobs were channeled to black community groups in this way. The intention was to give poor blacks new, special resources, which it was hoped would help poor blacks get ahead in a growing economy and, in the process, add them onto established urban-Democratic coalitions.

But that was not what happened. In practice, economic growth did not prove sufficient to overcome the structural obstacles to employment faced by inner-city blacks; yet the channeling of new resources to them in a politically visible way helped trigger conflicts with other Democrats, including established city governments, white ethnic neighborhoods, and even some labor unions. In short, poverty was not overcome, and the northern Democratic party was thrown into turmoil. Soon many white working-class ethnics, as well as pre-

---

42. This discussion draws on Weir, "Federal Government and Unemployment," 180– 86, and Michael K. Brown, "The Segmented Welfare System: Distributive Conflict and Retrenchment in the United States, 1968–1984," in *Remaking the Welfare State: Retrenchment and Social Policy in America and Europe,* ed. Michael K. Brown (Philadelphia: Temple University Press, 1988), 182–210.

viously alienated white southerners, began switching to the Republican party, at least for presidential voting. This trend has continued (with a brief reversal for Jimmy Carter) from Richard Nixon to George Bush and in the 1984 election the Democrats did not get a majority of any white population group other than the Jews. The effect in the 1970s and 1980s has not been only on the presidency either, for even though liberal Democrats have survived a bit better in Congress, the presence there of avowed nonliberals in both parties has steadily grown— and the possibilities for new uses of federal power have correspondingly diminished.

Just as the upsurge of urban-liberal power during the New Deal helped once it was channeled into the Democratic party and the U.S. state structure—to spur reactions from the congressional conservative coalition of southern Democrats and Republicans, so in the current period the civil rights revolution and the upsurge of black political mobilization have functioned to unleash the right-wing anti-public-sector movement led and symbolized by Ronald Reagan. It is not coincidental that the policies and programs that were most successfully attacked during the Reagan presidencies were those launched by the Great Society, including the few federal job training and public employment efforts that remained. Nor is it coincidental that Reagan worked hard to debunk the idea that the federal government should be responsible for full employment. Finally, it is not surprising that the Reagan administration did all it could to trim the gains of the civil rights movement and reopen settled struggles between whites and blacks over affirmative action issues. For the Reagan forces under-stood full well that their ascendancy had grown out of the collapse of a potential broad Democratic coalition in support of enhanced social-welfare interventions by the federal government.[43]

Looking back to what may now be a concluded chapter in modern American political history—the New Deal and postwar era, stretching from the 1930s to the 1970s—I think we can see that a genuinely American full employment welfare state might have been established but wasn't. Much of the reason why such a full employment welfare state was not established lies in the structural obstacles inherent in the U.S. state and political party system, obstacles that I have attempted to analyze here. Yet these state and party structures were also transformed over time by reformers and political leaders. At times those leaders chose political strategies that were not optimal: for example, the strategy in the War on Poverty of attacking poverty in isolation from the economy as a whole and the strategy of mobilizing blacks in particular rather than creating new,

---

43. Brown, "Segmented Welfare System," makes this point especially forcefully.

broad social alliances that included their needs but ensured greater political support.[44]

For the future, if reformers or Democrats or any other forces in American politics get another opportunity to push forward (rather than merely defend) public social provision, they would be well advised not only to respect the structural obstacles of the U.S. polity but also to make better choices within its constraints. Choosing to work for national employment assurance appears likely to remain a potentially popular political choice, although it remains to be seen if any political leadership will soon be forthcoming to devise both the policies and the suitably universalistic political alliances needed to work for this goal. Nevertheless, even if little happens soon, the goal of full employment assurance itself—so clearly articulated in 1935 by the members of the CES— seems unlikely to fade away. For employment assurance accords with long-standing American values, and it would address the distresses of many groups and regions in our presently unsettled national economy. Sooner or later, there-fore, a politics of employment assurance—rather than one of welfare—will surely reappear on the American political scene.

44. For further elaboration of "universalistic" reform strategies that might work better than the tactics of the War on Poverty, see Theda Skocpol, "Targeting within Universalism: Politically Viable Policies to Combat Poverty in the United States" (Paper Commission for the "Conference on the Truly Disadvantaged," Northwestern University, October 19–21, 1989, sponsored by the Social Science Research Council and the Center for Urban Affairs and Policy Research, Northwestern University).

I I I I I I I I   Racial Tension, Cultural Conflicts, and Problems of Employment Training Programs

ELIJAH ANDERSON

This paper is based on fieldwork conducted over the past decade in Philadelphia inner-city black communities and on in-depth ethnographic interviews with individuals familiar with the culture of youth employment programs. Informants included current and former trainees, supervisors, and community people with a wealth of actual experience with employment and unemployment. In part, this is a conceptual discussion, informed by observations and my sense of what is true. The primary purpose here is to gain insights into the social context of employment-training programs geared to poor, unemployed, young minority males. While the account focuses on the training programs of the Carter administration, it has implications for our understanding of the effectiveness of training programs geared to the hard core unemployed more generally.

What follows, then, is not a highly systematic accounting of factors related to specific programs, but a general set of considerations of economic, political, cultural, and community factors that likely condition the effectiveness of youth employment-training programs. I believe that a great many of these programs failed in a basic respect: they failed to deliver on their implicit promise, what so many of the young participants wanted most: a meaningful job that paid a livable wage. The persistence and worsening condition of a ghetto underclass to this day speaks volumes of testimony to the failure of so many past and current job-training programs. The programs lacked significant political support and

The author thanks the following colleagues and friends for their helpful comments on this work: Victor Lidz, Harold Bershady, James Kurth, Fred Block, Eugenia Grohman, and Skip Gaus.

sufficient funding and were not well enough thought out to make an important impact on the eradication of persistent urban poverty; some program trainees think their time was wasted. While well-intentioned, the programs did not deal seriously with the social problem of educating, training, and placing young poor people. They failed to adjust effectively to the changing economy, from one based on manufacturing to one based increasingly on service occupations, and the implications of this change for training and employment prospects of trainees. Paying hardly any attention to these serious considerations, the many programs functioned as little more than stopgap measures to appease, to cool out or buy off problematic youth, measures that in effect led to their being retained in what amounted to human holding tanks. The programs were not designed to fundamentally alter the social and economic status of the participants, though some participants expected a great deal from them and were left disappointed.

The community to which the programs were geared—the ghetto underclass—accepted the meager benefits but with serious reservations; taking what they could get, many played along. To succeed, a training program must effectively train people to be competitive for existing and future gainful employment. For this, the training must be serious, it must understand the depths of the problem and appreciate its clientele, its relationship to the occupational structure.

With an eye to these issues, recruitment must be systematic, creative, and intelligent, involving early screening of problem trainees and the identification of those likely to succeed; and those who successfully complete the program must be effectively placed. Class and racial prejudice and intolerance directed toward black males in the training setting—and later in the work setting—must also be addressed. Enormously complicated by the supervisors' and employers' concerns about criminality, these factors were not adequately considered and ameliorated, and many trainees who felt their impact lost faith in such programs on this account alone.

The paper begins with a sketch of the on-the-job training during the 1930s and 1940s in which urban ethnic whites negotiated the labor market. In comparison, the social context of current job-training programs is then traced and described, based largely on interviews. The third section discusses the values held by and required of participants in youth employment programs.

THE EARLY DAYS OF ON-THE-JOB TRAINING

In the 1930s the New Deal instituted what could be called job-training programs. The Works Progress Administration (WPA), the Family Assistance Program (FAP), and other programs were initiated to alleviate the

216   ELIJAH ANDERSON

pain and suffering caused by the Great Depression. In post-Depression America, youth employment programs as we know them today did not exist. Rather,
employers often emphasized a form of on-the-job training.

During that era, many employers in labor-intensive industries relied on the
personal references of family members and trusted employees for their recruitment pool (Hareven and Langenbach 1978). The apprentice system, or an
approximation of it, was also of prime importance for industrial employment.
Various white ethnic group members, the primary source of labor in large urban
areas, tended to seek out their kind for invaluable on-the-job work experience
(see Hirsch 1978). Both the instructor/mentor and ethnic peers were genuinely
interested in seeing the employee "work out." And the man usually did work
out, for the extent to which he fit socially with a supportive work group usually
had much to do with his success on the job.

The following narrative of an eighty-two-year-old Irish American, a still-
practicing machinist and automobile mechanic, gives a glimpse of the culture
of on-the-job training in those years:

> In the thirties and forties the guys didn't go to any training program. No, they didn't.
> They studied, themselves. They had a certain natural ability. And they used that
> natural ability. In other words, I know a lot of fellows in the automobile business.
> They didn't go to any school. They didn't go to nothin'. But they learned as they
> worked. They didn't know if this car needed a carburetor, they didn't know if it
> needed points. They didn't know nothin'. But they found out. They'd say, "Yeah, I
> can fix your car. Bring it over here." Then they'd get busy and try this and try that, and
> finally they'd know how to do these things, see. They'd *learn on the job,* and the job
> wasn't supplied by the government [emphasis mine]. Guys [employers] gave 'em a
> break. They didn't know what else to do with 'em. What're you gonna do with 'em?
> You go out in the country, the country blacksmith, he was the guy that fixed the
> automobiles. He was a general mechanic. As a rule, a good blacksmith is just a very,
> very clever person, because he knows an awful lot about the material, the iron, steel,
> and so forth, tempering the iron, welding and all that. He knows all these things. But
> he learned it the hard way. He went in with his father when he was a little . . . so
> high. And he grew up in it. His father taught it to him. Now my father taught me a lot.
>
> Much of the skills in that day were passed on father to son or mother to daughter.
> Uncles and father would help the youngsters. If they didn't have that, somebody took
> them in to help out in a store. A boy would start by going with a store, and they'd start
> out by sweeping the floor, cleaning the place up, and they'd say in a year, "You can
> wait on customers," and after a while they'd ease up the system. They were taught
> things. Everybody seemed to be interested in something. They were interested in this
> thing. They'd come in and they took a hold.

The job training described above was common to various occupations, including carpentry, plumbing, and other skilled trades—occupations that to this
day are largely dominated by white ethnics. While blacks and other minorities
were occasionally employed and trained this way, they were often required to

accept the hardest, dirtiest, least demanding in terms of skills, lowest-paid occupations, which were essentially left over by whites who had preceded them (see Spear 1967; Davis and Haller 1973; Hirsch 1978; Hershberg et al. 1981). Blacks who were able to acquire an apprenticeship in occupations such as plumbing, masonry, or carpentry were not allowed to join unions or encouraged to practice their trades the way white ethnics were (see Marshall 1965). Those blacks fortunate enough to possess such skills were very often required to work independently, and at times sporadically, at less than union scale. The following comments of a seventy-year-old black wallpaper stripper are germane: "I learned masonry in North Carolina. Down there I could find work. Colored people often did this type of work. When I come to Philadelphia [at approximately thirty years of age], they [whites] wouldn't let me work. I couldn't find work even though I was qualified. So I went in business for myself, and started hanging wallpaper, made a living that way."

Some of the earliest organized job-training situations were developed in grade schools, YMCAs, and vocational high schools serving working-class youths. In shop classes boys were trained to run machines such as lathes, and girls were often taught sewing and home economics. At graduation a friend of the family, a relative, or a teacher would serve as a reference for the prospective worker. In this way schools, friends, and families provided important links to the workplace, informally shaping the work settings of the day along ethnic and cultural lines that reflected their neighborhoods, schools, and families (Hareven and Langenbach 1978).

Sometimes vocational instructors moonlighted at a local shop, where they could channel and place their able students in jobs. A person liked and trusted in one place was usually trusted in the other or at least given a break. Through these placements, the students often gained a trade for life and affirmation of themselves through work. Such channeling helped to create and support the peculiar racial and ethnic character of certain occupations. For the ethnic group members, these effective, informal "on-job-training" efforts were important steps between youth and adulthood. In part, they were effective at the time not only because there was a significant need for laborers and the workplace was highly receptive to them, but also because the new workers were heavily supported by those who sponsored them; they were part of a social system (see Hershberg 1981).

Such social connections and placements, in effect job networks, were crucial to the effectiveness of early employment-training efforts. People entering such relationships often did so on the promise that they would gain a job in return for their involvement. In just this way young men and women placed in comparatively rewarding employment positions could begin to develop what would become lifelong positive associations with work. In these circumstances, the

work ethic could be affirmed and reinforced, not only for the individual placed
in a meaningful job, but also for his not-yet-employed cultural peers, who could
closely identify with the worker and thus look forward to the day when they too
might have jobs.

When people were not pleased with their jobs or the way they were treated,
feelings of alienation and injustice could be generated and kept alive within
these groups. From the pressures of collective action, unions emerged (see
Hirsch 1978; Shelton 1986). In this way hope and expectations were fostered
and neighborhood solidarity was enforced. As these processes occurred, work
settings became resistant to incursions by rival ethnic groups and almost impen-
etrable for members of other racial groupings, particularly blacks (see DuBois
1899; Hughes 1946; Spear 1967; Clark 1973; Kornblum 1974; Hershberg et al.
1981). Such developments and the employment practices consistent with them
led to racial and ethnic competition, conflict, and dominance and to the subordination of certain people in certain jobs. This in turn gave rise to labels such as
the black job, the white job, men's work, and, of course, women's work.

MODERN JOB-TRAINING PROGRAMS

By the 1960s, especially during the days of the Kennedy administration, job training became more formal, and government-sponsored
programs were more firmly established. Bureaucratic rules developed and were
elaborated, and a variety of spin-offs such as the Job Corps were later instituted
(see Ginzberg 1980; Stromsdorfer 1980). In time, the racial and ethnic identities of both instructors and trainees in employment programs began to change
from white ethnics serving largely white ethnic constituencies to a sprinkling of
black and Hispanic instructors serving a racially and ethnically mixed group of
participants. The white ethnic presence in these programs declined, and hard-
core minority youths made up an increasingly significant portion of program
participants.

Once, the ethnic and cultural organization of a neighborhood was ethnically
compatible with that of the work settings into which the trainees moved. Later,
however, contrasting, if not conflicting, ethnic populations were expected to
work together. Although the work settings had formerly been receptive to white
trainees, they were not for blacks. Discrimination was a problem, to be sure,
but equally if not more important was the fact that the nature of the world of
work was undergoing a fundamental transformation (see Bluestone and Harrison 1982; Wilson 1978; Wilson 1987; Karsarda 1989).

Under these circumstances, the general effectiveness of conventional work-
training programs was severely tested and, because of the growing difficulty of
training and placing students, found wanting. Increasing automation of indus-

try changed or eliminated numerous labor-intensive jobs, and many jobs for which the students were being trained did not exist by the time they graduated.

In the face of widespread and increasing automation of industry, high-paying manufacturing jobs were vanishing from the economy, replaced by thousands of jobs that were either in emerging high-tech industries or were low-paying and service-oriented; increasingly, these jobs existed in the suburbs, beyond the reach of poor, inner-city blacks (see Kain 1968; Ellwood 1986). A certain technological and social match between traditional training and employment was being lost. The training programs were rapidly losing the ability to render to young people, particularly those with limited education, the skills that would gain them livable wages or make them competitive for newly emerging, technologically oriented occupations. It was in this context that so many job-training programs in effect became holding tanks for poor minority youth.

Clearly, the solutions for the employment problems of white ethnics often did not work well for blacks and other nonwhites. The availability of employment opportunities that had awaited the ethnic whites was declining just as large numbers of blacks and Hispanics were attempting to negotiate the labor market (see Doeringer and Piore 1971; Wilson 1980; Hershberg et al. 1981; Karsarda 1989). Moreover, the social connections to the workplace that had been critical to the successful employment efforts of whites were largely lacking for blacks and others. When they did exist, they were often negated by forces of racism and ethnic competition. As the director of a local training Center of Court Adjudicated Youth 14–18 commented, "From our experience over the last ten years [1979–89] of training youth, we have found that our white trainees, upon completion of training, obtain sponsorship to enter the higher paying union jobs. The black trainees usually do not find union sponsorship, go to work in small shops, are layed off when the work slows down." In addition to the major technological changes in the world of work, this lack of social connection and linkage between training and employment continues to be an important determinant of the ultimate effectiveness of job-training programs (see Granovetter 1973; Berg and Shack-Marquez 1985).

INSTRUCTORS AND TRAINEES

In many instances, instructors in the programs of the 1960s were ethnic whites—and some working-class blacks—who were fond of remembering how they "came up the hard way" and at times invoked the American "bootstrap theory" of social mobility (Hershberg 1981). Increasingly, however, many of the new trainees were young black men from urban ghettoes, people their instructors could readily compare negatively with their own success stories and label as "out to get something for nothing." To many working-

220   ELIJAH ANDERSON

class white ethnics, these young black men represented a threat (see Blumer 1958; Pettigrew 1980).

In earlier times, when mentors taught their protégés work skills or a trade, the mentoring process was often slow and guided by the cautious development of trust among participants. The tricks of the trade and other occupational secrets usually were divulged slowly to trainees considered worthy, likable, and able, evaluations that were made subjectively and at times arbitrarily.

When young black men were introduced into this type of job training, to be instructed largely by white, working-class instructors, the scenario became extremely complicated. A certain amount of tension between divergent cultural groups may be anticipated and perhaps dismissed as normal happenstance. But with the introduction of race and the resulting competition for access to jobs, many instructors were no longer able to view themselves as simply passing on skills and trades to deserving youth (see Bonney 1972; Wilson 1973; Kornblum 1974). Rather, the instructor, who may have been a master craftsman, might have sensed that his own group interests were threatened by the prospect of training young black men for occupations held by members of the instructor's own ethnic group. The instructor was likely to experience some difficulty, if not profound psychological dissonance, in teaching something so dear to him as his trade to people generally defined as outcasts making spirited assaults on areas of influence and privilege traditionally (and legally) reserved for others he might more readily identify as his own kind (see Blumer 1958; Goffman 1963; Higginbotham 1978).

Instructors at times resolved this dissonance by approaching minority trainees with ambivalence. Doubtful of the basic potential of ghetto youths, they often relied on racial stereotypes in their dealings with them. But also important, black trainees were often equally suspicious of their instructors, at times believing them to harbor prejudiced attitudes and approaching them only with hesitancy and caution. And what was ostensibly begun as an instructor–trainee relationship sometimes became a full-blown racial, ethnic, and class contest, a situation that does not foster effective job networks for such youths.

The social friction between instructor and trainee is just one problem among many that must be addressed if one is to gain insight into the more general issue of the effectiveness of job programs. In addition to the attitudes of teachers toward students, the attitudes of the trainees must be examined. In what manner are these attitudes expressed both in the job-training context and on the actual job?

SOURCES OF CONFLICT

In addition to what might be viewed as a problem of cultural background—the issue of ethnic or class friction or competition—there exists a more manifestly troublesome aspect of the social fit between instructors and trainees. The culture of the job-training program, and perhaps the culture of any school situation, clashes with the culture of the ghetto street. The hard-core unemployed, toward whom these programs are usually geared, are often the embodiment of this street culture. Even to the casual observer, their values appear to be very much at odds with the dominant, middle-class value system represented and often invoked by the staff of the program (see Liebow 1967; Hannerz 1969; Wellman 1977; E. Anderson 1978; Auletta, 1982).

Many of the program trainees are young black men who have generally either quit or socially "graduated" from a segregated inner-city high school unable to read, write, or compute. In these school settings, decisions are made for them and by them that negatively affect the scheme of their entire lives, particularly their future employability in an increasingly high-tech economy. Through the years since school, money and employment have been recurrent and serious concerns for most, and almost any income they have obtained is likely to have come from being serially employed in low-paying and unreliable service occupations, if not in the underground economy (see Anderson 1980). Some speak of having responded repeatedly to Help Wanted signs in the windows of various establishments but being rebuffed by prospective employers who treat them in stereotypical, distrustful, and fearful ways. After a series of such experiences, a youth becomes frustrated and increasingly discouraged. At such low points they may check into the job-training advertisements on bulletin boards at the local community center. For many inner-city youths enrolling in the training program is thus the course of last resort, entered into perhaps with hope but without much faith—or encouragement from successful role models—that this path will lead to a permanent, well-paying job with a future.

A central problem is that the hard-core unemployed are socialized and conditioned to be tough in their encounters with other men, particularly challenging authority figures who are white; their experiences have taught them to have little faith in whites generally. In the training context, their demeanor often adapts to this perceived reality. Sensitive observers report that this demeanor frequently evolves into a kind of self-conscious arrogance that is often a defensive display, particularly when the trainee is confronted by what he perceives as threats or challenges to his independence and manhood. Such displays and demeanor are enacted by many youths to conform to hip street roles, and they regard these roles as being absolutely necessary in their effort to maintain their manly dignity and survive the mean ghetto streets. Such concerns help shape the presuppositional background of the trainee—a different background from that of the instructor—and it creates conflicts with which the instructor is often not prepared to deal.

When he meets the job-training instructor, the youth is expected to suddenly defer training setting and discontinue many of the behavioral patterns gained through prior socialization—part of a subculture, really—that he has come to take for granted and to value. It may appear to him that he must now, in effect, humble himself in the face of authority that, whether assumed by a black or white person, to him is of dubious legitimacy. In addition, the value of changing his behavior is not completely clear to him, as he is skeptical that deference and the time spent in the training program will result in meaningful employment.

Other problems result from this clash of backgrounds. Certain manifestations of the culture of the hard-core unemployed carry over into the job-training setting and contribute to tensions between the instructor and trainee. Numerous trainees seem to have difficulty with the middle-class concept of time. From the perspective of the staff, many seem to lack interest in being—or are unable to be—punctual; many seem to take tardiness as normal happenstance, or they may be absent from class much of the time. Instead of an attitude of seriousness, many youths appear to take a cavalier attitude toward the program, appearing simply to be putting in time and thereby expressing a degree of alienation.

It is difficult to comprehend the social effects of long-standing and real ethnic, racial, and class hostility on the current job-training setting. This "outsider" class of youths—black ghetto street boys and young men—who by their life-style and demeanor often threaten white and even black instructors from the old working class, cause the instructors to maintain a certain social distance in self-defense. The teacher–student relationship, particularly in an employment-training program, requires a profound degree of trust if it is to succeed, but this needed trust is often sorely lacking.

Program trainees are sensitive and observant in this context and voice numerous complaints of insensitivity on the part of their instructors. For instance, some say certain instructors close and lock the door at the beginning of class, refusing to open it for someone who is five minutes late. After traveling ten miles by subway from the North Philadelphia ghetto, some youths are prepared to call the instructor's actions racist, if the instructor is white, or antiblack, if he is black. As one youth explains, "Five minutes ain't a whole lot of time." But the instructor is not inclined to see things this way. The instructor's attitude may be that this black youth fits into the category of a person trying to get something for nothing, without putting in the hard work. Indeed, some youths think fifteen minutes one way or the other is simply not that important or even that missing four or five days of school is of negligible import. Added onto issues of attendance and punctuality is the fact that the trainees have a chronic lack of money and, thus, of reliable transportation to the job-training site.

Under the Comprehensive Employment Training Act (CETA) many of the hard-core unemployed were likely to receive their carfare to the training site one day and spend it all in the next day or so. This population, not unlike those of the middle class or even the working class, has an unlimited list of "necessities" on which to spend money, from liquor to food. Once their money is spent, they often lack a means of transportation. Then, after repeated tardiness or absence from training sessions, they fall irretrievably behind (or so their aggravated instructors may unsympathetically judge and treat them); many then become unwilling or unable to participate further. Unfortunately, these issues are likely to become confused and interpreted simply as indicative of behavioral laxity.

Feeling readily discouraged and frustrated in this dominant cultural context, many youths become convinced that the instructor, in being a tough disciplinarian, is not all that supportive or interested in seeing them succeed; and they may be right. The instructor may respond, "Well, if this was a job and you were getting paid, then these are the real expectations. You must be on time, and you must come every day. If you don't come every day, or if you come late, then you're not going to keep that job for very long." Such a lecture makes good sense to the instructors. But to many young people in a training context, such invocations of discipline, attendance, and punctuality, delivered at times with an excessively sharp tongue, may easily be taken as clear evidence of prejudice. Insensitive to these perceptions, and often with a strong sense of commitment to discipline, the instructor may believe it more important to get the trainee back in line.

Significantly, it is not only white instructors who may carry such problematic attitudes into job-training situations. Increasingly, many of today's instructors are Hispanic and black and have often emerged from traditional working-class backgrounds. Here, instructors may think of themselves as having worked extremely hard and sacrificed much to get where they are. Having a heightened sensitivity to propriety and a rule-oriented "correct way," they may be inclined to be impatient and intolerant toward unemployed minority youths. Concerned with developing proper ethnic role models, such instructors manifest an over-zealous desire to turn out highly successful black and Hispanic workers, concerns which then may result in strong and at times arbitrary invocations of discipline in the training process. There is often a fine line between the appropriate invocation of discipline for effective training and the arbitrary manifestation of class and ethnic prejudice in the form of harassment.

As noted above, such actions may simply trigger defensiveness in a tough, street-wise trainee. Many trainees must indeed be taught or reminded of the importance of discipline, punctuality, and good attendance in the workplace, but at the same time, instructors must become aware of the special problems, cultural or otherwise, of the hard-core unemployed.

Ideally, the instructor would be able to recognize the cultural problems noted here and then display a certain sensitivity and patience in searching for creative and effective ways to teach and remind youths of their particular shortcomings with regard to the culture of the workplace. Both white and black instructors would learn to set their prejudices aside and to work to instill proper work attitudes and behavior patterns in their trainees. Moreover, there should be clear and identifiable rewards for both the trainees and their supervisors for effective behavior and attitudes displayed in the training context. In an ideal world, the trainees would feel that it is worthwhile to sacrifice time and effort and to relinquish the dearly held but more street-oriented values with which they started. And then, if employment-training programs were to be effective, they would deliver what trainees want most: gainful employment. Unfortunately, most programs fail miserably in this crucial respect.

The generalized American belief in pulling yourself up by your bootstraps appears at times to work against the credibility of government-sponsored job-training programs. Working for a living, the bootstrap ideal, and the avoidance of government handouts represent values that many black and other minority Americans share with others (see Anderson 1978). Many would like nothing better than to realize these values, and they work very hard at achieving them. But while such ideals and values have in the past worked for other groups, they seldom work easily for such youths today.

Presently, one striking difference for underclass black youths is that many of the manufacturing concerns or other companies where such youths might be employed are leaving the inner city for foreign lands or the suburbs. In the past when many ethnic whites negotiated the labor market, they not only tended to have supportive work groups, but also benefited from an expanding economy that actively sought their labor in exchange for livable wages (see Hershberg 1981). Such receptivity by the job market makes an enormous, though indirect, difference for the ultimate success of training programs and a prospective worker's commitment to the work ethic. The lowest levels of the emerging service-oriented labor market are receptive to young inner-city blacks and Hispanics, and often the jobs they receive commit them to a life of poverty. In this context, many youths view the required investment in certain types of job training against the uncertain or limited benefit as essentially a losing proposition. Further, such youths often face discrimination by prospective employers and coworkers because of their subcultural displays, including their skin color and styles of self-presentation (see Anderson 1980). And when possible, many employers prefer to hire more "trustworthy" newly arrived immigrants, older people, and women.

But some youths work hard despite these various obstacles and thus seem to manage to overcome. In their classes they achieve positive reports and outstanding records. Highly motivated to succeed, such individuals are imbued with self-confidence and a positive outlook, despite the large amount of distrust and discrimination they encounter. When such youths become involved in a job-training program, they often attain a measure of success. They appear to emerge from a family and social background that, while financially poor, places much emphasis on self-discipline, self-esteem, religious values, and a strong belief in the work ethic.

In addition to their families, at work fostering such values is usually an "old head" who has invested a significant amount of time and energy in the young boy's social and moral development, encouraging in him a certain positive outlook on life. In the traditional black ghetto, the old head was a man of stable means who believed in hard work, family life, and the church. His acknowledged role was to teach, support, encourage, and, in effect, socialize young men to meet their responsibilities regarding work, family life, the law, and common decency. Many young boys had confidence in the old head's ability to impart useful wisdom and practical advice about life. When the young boy's father was absent or otherwise ineffective, the old head, in the form of an uncle, a cousin, or a friend who served as self-conscious role model, would step in as a surrogate. Despite the poor employment situation and deteriorating local community life, they strongly believed in and supported the work ethic, common decency, and responsibility to family through their daily activities. With this support, the youth often develops a positive sense of the future and believes he can succeed, in spite of the broad social dislocation and obstacles he experiences in his daily life (see Anderson 1989).

As such young boys negotiate the training program, they very favorably impress certain teachers who take an interest in them. When these teachers learn of openings, they do not hesitate to recommend such youths for jobs. It is for these relatively advantaged individuals that the programs seem most effective. These young men tend to obtain jobs and move on to negotiate certain areas of the occupational structure. But, emerging as they do from backgrounds of persistent poverty compounded by racial prejudice and discrimination, such successful individuals tend to be rare. They owe much to the traditional old head.

But as meaningful employment has become increasingly scarce for young blacks and crime and drugs have become a way of life for many, the old head is losing his prestige and authority. With the expansion of the drug culture and its opportunities for making large sums of quick money, many street-smart young boys are reaching the conclusion that the old head's lessons about life and the work ethic are no longer relevant.

In place of the traditional old head, a new role model is emerging on ghetto street corners. This new old head is in many respects the antithesis of the traditional one. He is often a product of the street gang and indifferent at best to the law and to traditional values. For him, the work ethic does not exist; if he works at the low-paying jobs available to him, he does so grudgingly. More likely, he's employed, either part-time or full, in the drug trade or some other area of the underground economy.

On the street corner, his self-aggrandizement consumes his whole being, as he attempts to impress people through displays of material success like expensive clothes and fancy cars. And eagerly awaiting his message are so many young, unemployed black men, demoralized by a hopeless financial situation and inclined to emulate his style and values. As the director of a local Training Center for youth between fourteen and eighteen commented, "We are dealing with the constant pull of the street drug trade economy that offers greater and quicker financial rewards. In the last three months [August 1989], we have lost numerous trainees to the drug trade, including one arrested for being the Uzi 'trigger man' in a turf battle in which a Philadelphia high school teacher was shot."

It is not difficult for ghetto youth to become employed in the dealing of drugs, which can involve selling anything from marijuana to heroin to crack. Today, one does not have to be a full-time "professional" dealer to work in the drug trade. In the ghetto, youths as young as twelve have been observed working for major dealers; some have worked as lookouts, spotters, and messengers for what are to them huge sums of money. Or an older boy can begin with simple involvement on a part-time basis and develop a full-time business, at times for a small initial investment. Participation in the drug trade is often dependent on and the result of a serious, persistent need for money. As this need becomes satisfied, illegal activity at times becomes sanctioned by poor ghetto families. Older siblings, mothers, and fathers may wink their eye or simply look the other way as "unexplainable" money finds its way into the hands of a youth in the family. In these circumstances, the drug economy becomes in effect a temporary, if unreliable, answer to the dearth of jobs for young males in the inner city and the ineffective government-sponsored youth employment-training programs.

An important policy issue for those interested in increasing the effectiveness of youth employment programs is that of how to effectively compete with the underground economy and how to instill the attitudes and behavior patterns of successful individuals into other trainees. Initially, the programs must improve their reputations among the youth. Dramatically, they must deliver gainful employment to the youths. If they do not meet this fundamental requirement, young men will continue to treat them with disdain and regard them as the absolute last legitimate resort.

CASUALTIES OF THE PROGRAM

Given the realities of the employment arena, including ethnic and racial competition and prospective employers' persistent distrust of black youths—made even more complicated by the growing drug trade—placement appears to be one of the most troublesome aspects of the training process (see E. Anderson 1980). Yet it is this aspect that ultimately determines the effectiveness of the program. Unfortunately, too many trainees pursue the programs, graduate, and are then left in the same circumstances they were in before they became involved in the program. This process repeats itself far too often, lending credence to negative commentary about the programs within the minority communities. The comments of one former program participant are relevant:

As far as I know, no one [of his job-training cohort] got a permanent job. Like, I got a job for a year, right? What could I have done? That was money I made and spent on clothes, a little carfare. You couldn't make no moves [to get married, for instance, to by an automobile, or to rent an apartment] with it. Now with my program, the people made it for themselves. Now the director of my program went on to a multimillion dollar insulation program. He contracted his work out of Jersey, New York, and cities in this area here. Pittsburgh. He went to Reading, little cities and towns in Pennsylvania, Ohio, Delaware. But he did not take none of those people that was involved in his program. And he liked me! But he never invited me to do insulation work. Because he most likely wasn't confident in what they were teaching us.

And you knew it wasn't enough, because the extent of the weatherization program we went to was plastering holes, putting on the heat blanket, Mortite, caulking a window. That was the extent of the matter. But he took it further than that. He insulated all the pipes of people's homes. He contracted all the work in all these new buildings. So before anybody move into these houses he was insulating them.

What I'm saying is that the whole program was about somebody taking an interest in hiring these young people, to give them permanent jobs. That was the whole thing. That's what they were asking these companies to do. Yet and still this man took on a multimillion dollar program of his own. He started it without a dime. His name and a couple of his references got him maybe a million dollar loan from a bank [the accuracy of this figure is uncertain]. But he did not take no one with him. He took one of the instructors. He gave another instructor money to start his own glass block company. And these are now reputable companies. You look in the white pages or the yellow pages, and you'll see these companies.

This is a far cry from the system of the past in which instructors felt a personal stake in placing their trainees in a job. Today's instructors manifest an entirely different attitude, one that undermines the trainees' belief in the possible success of the program. This is indicated in the following interview with a twenty-one-year-old youth who had been involved with a program and had worked in a related job for a year but who felt he had really not advanced from where he started:

Boy, these programs were very misleading, 'cause they were very unsuccessful. Led the people to believe they would get permanent jobs. And they had the right people there. They had the motivators. They had the people there who talk good [convincing], the cons, and all that. But I told 'em when they talked to me like that. See, I don't take things at face value. When somebody tell me "I can get you permanent work," I want them to take it into parts. Tell me why you think that. Do you know somebody who's gon' give me permanent work?

The program was a waste of money, a waste of time, very misleading, and it got a very bad rep in the community. They got the community all involved. Now, this happened in '81 and '83. A number of the people wouldn't believe in it from the beginning. And the ones who do get involved will be involved only for the money, only if there's a salary involved. It's just a band-aid. Everybody lacks confidence in it. It was a political act. They hired all these young guys just to get them off the street. It would be to your advantage not to be involved. Because it takes up time, and time is money. You start off with confidence, but down the line you gon' be let down. I don't know anyone that took that [was involved in the program] that's now independent. If they were on welfare before they started the program, they got back on. The program is just a sham. It was just a political move. People playin' chess with other peoples' lives.

Youth employment programs need effective teachers who possess the sophisticated knack for discerning the unexhibited potential of trainees and who are able and willing to help the trainees find themselves. But at the same time, program staff must be willing and able to help place the youth in meaningful employment after they complete their training. The trickling out of talented instructors who can do this is critical to the effectiveness of employment programs.

Since national and local politics often play such an important role in the employment programs, funding is variable and at times unpredictable. As the programs receive decreasing or fluctuating funding, they become increasingly unable to attract and retain teachers who are effective in placing their students in decent employment. As the teacher's salary becomes uncertain or decreases, he or she may lose a sense of commitment to the program. The better instructors may seek better-paying jobs, often in the private sector, or they may retire.

Such people are important resources for the programs, in part because of their work skills and their teaching abilities, but also because of their connections with the private sector and their interest in placing their more able students. In the early days, it was just such individuals who served ethnic whites as effective links between vocational schools and the work setting. But these people are rare today, given the low salaries of instructors and job insecurity. Their absence bodes ill for the effectiveness of employment-training programs. Increasingly, attempts are made to replace such people with their aides, who then begin to teach but who are not as highly qualified as their former teachers. Equally important, they sorely lack their teachers' credibility and connections with the workplace. If former aides possessed such connections, it may be argued, they might take advantage of them for themselves.

Over time, many young people who participate in youth employment programs become frustrated and demoralized by their experiences. They simply become worn down by the routine of the program and, often because of their inability to make visible progress, become intolerant of the program and its staff. Progress for them is to feel they are gaining marketable skills that will give them a chance to compete effectively for a permanent, well-paying job. Lacking clear signs of progress, many become frustrated and resign from the program, at times in an attempt to retain a sense of manhood and independence.

On leaving, they are in effect shaken out of the program. Later, in discussing the program with any interested party, they often recall their worst experiences and characterize the whole program as a waste of time. In bad-mouthing the program to other members of the community, they seek affirmation and support in having been wise enough to quit. As they travel through the community, they seldom have anything positive to say about it. In effect, they often only draw the cultural boundary between the streets and the programs more strongly and clearly. Insofar as they have prestige on the streets, they then influence others to be loyal to the streets by rejecting the programs.

As frustration and disappointment grow, the program also loses relatively mature participants who have a measure of discipline and often the motivation to succeed at using the program to obtain a permanent job. As mentioned above, this is the initial goal of many of those entering the program. But when they fail to achieve this goal, the serious, and perhaps more intelligent, youths—those with a clear sense of options—move on, wanting no longer to tolerate what is viewed as abuse and tensions with the staff. For many, the main problem is the prominent failure of the program to deliver on its ostensible promise: a job paying a livable wage.

As they move on, the casualties leave behind in the program many youths who possess relatively little in the way of personal or social skills that would enable them to participate effectively in a job-training program. They leave behind those who are not so highly motivated, those with limited options, and the new recruits. Many participants are so poor they do not have enough food to eat or even a reliable residence; alcohol and drugs are also persistent problems for some.

Program directors might then complain that the pool they now have consists of too many "mental defectives, drug addicts, ex-cons, retarded people, illiterates." Such views, not only among staff but also among community people and prospective trainees, contribute to the stigmatization of the program and ultimately to its ineffectiveness.

On many occasions, the program advertises itself on the ghetto streets, where instructors and trainees, perhaps unwittingly, are at times under the watchful eyes of prospective trainees. Following are some comments of a black male, twenty-one years old, who only briefly considered becoming involved as a job-training participant:

> I was on the street once and one of the CETA supervisors sent one of the guys across the street to pick up some material. And because the store, the clerks, did not wait on him promptly, the supervisor came across the street and hollers at the guy like, "What the hell are you still waiting over here for? Get yo' ass across the street!" Now, I'm talking about seeing him do this in a store full of people, you know. I mean, the guy must've felt bad. And then the supervisor, after that, he turned around, and he laughed about it. That just shows you how they treat the workers.

In the foregoing incident both the supervisor and the trainee were black men, an indication that conflict and tension between supervisor and trainee are not simply or always a function of interracial relations but sometimes a function of hierarchy and attempts to promote discipline. Yet, importantly, such incidents do little to improve the community's image of the job-training program.

In addition, it is important to consider the reputation of work as it is commonly defined and emphasized by such programs. Often the jobs for which youths are being trained are thought of as dead-end and menial; it is difficult for the youth to perceive the possibility of real advancement through such work. The training is often perceived as conferring low status on a person, who frequently possesses an expanded sense of racial and personal pride (see E. Anderson 1980). This again raises the issue of strain or lack of social fit between the older instructors and the younger trainees. The instructors in the program share certain beliefs and values concerning work, work settings, propriety, and the work ethic. Many profess to believe in hard work for just rewards. As so many ghetto youths are mobile about town, they are readily able to view others of their color-caste riding trolleys, trains, and buses and dressed in pinstriped suits and carrying briefcases. They have come to see this role model, to wonder about him, and perhaps to desire to emulate him.

Yet these youths have little real chance of becoming a young professional if they are being trained to be a carpenter, and trained poorly at that. Common sense tells them that such jobs are closed to them and their kind; from their elders, they've heard the tales of discrimination, and many have experienced it firsthand. Hence, many youths approach the program with a limited amount of motivation. They are ambivalent about its value, even if they were to be successful in completing it. For ultimately, the program prepares the young people for jobs many have come to see as beneath them, and hence, the more they invest in terms of time and energy, the more they believe they condone what is in their estimation an essentially inferior social and economic position, not to mention the boredom and toil that come with it. Yet they want jobs badly.

The foregoing account illustrates how the earlier ethnic labor experience of the 1930s through the 1950s was very different from that of blacks and other colored minorities today. The job market was much more receptive to laborers in general during that period. Given the great need for labor in the manufacturing economy at the time, there was on-the-job training for most people in need of work, though the "better" and "cleaner" jobs tended to go to whites. This general receptivity inspired many to be highly motivated. Family and friends made up effective job networks that were often supportive on and off the job. These primary reference groups helped them to work out, in part because they were often representing people who had helped them find work through word of mouth, but also because they could often identify with those they were joining in the workplace.

Such supportive job networks do not generally exist for poor, unskilled, and distrusted minority youths today. Largely because of unrelenting distrust of young black males of the urban environment, individuals—black or white—do not readily go out of their way to help such youths. And the youths, beaten down by the specter of distrust and discrimination, often become resigned to their outsider status, becoming unwilling or incapable of recognizing and seizing opportunity even when it does exist. From both sides—instructors and trainees—there seems to be a profound lack of confidence in the ability of the trainees to make progress in the job market. Many who would employ black youths share this lack of confidence and often a prejudice that the hard-core unemployed and their culture are truly not compatible with the work setting. Such attitudes represent major obstacles to the sponsorship and subsequent employment of youths after they have completed job training and thus are important considerations for the effectiveness of training programs.

Moreover, participants in the programs at all levels often feel a high degree of uncertainty about the future of these programs. Yet the primary issue concerning the programs stems from their inability to place participants in gainful occupations. The largest complaint among black youths is that the programs fail to deliver permanent jobs. Jobs that many received were of the "make-work" variety and are not for those who view themselves as serious breadwinners for families. Such assessments fostered a common perception that the programs served as holding tanks for young poor people. It is chiefly because of this failure—and perceptions of it—that relatively few trainees have positive evaluations of the programs. When a trainee does obtain a job, he often feels he could have gotten it without having gone through the program (see Berg 1970). To be effective, programs must be result-oriented, and there must be some mechanism for accountability. After training, participants should be placed in gainful, rewarding occupations. A novel but perhaps effective solution to the problem of placement would be to guarantee a job to each trainee who successfully completes the program. Such jobs preferably would be those in which the person could clearly expect a degree of financial security or mobility for his honest and diligent efforts.

In this effort to solve what is too easily viewed by many as an intractable social problem, the private sector must become much more deeply involved. Along with the federal government, corporate America must play a more direct role in the training and placement of young people. The federal government should encourage corporate America to invest in the urban minority communities. Instead of shipping data-processing and light manufacturing jobs to places like Ireland and Singapore, as seems to be the latest corporate trend, the corporations should develop serious on-the-job training programs to employ the persistently poor of the urban environments of the United States. In this respect, corporations have a moral obligation to help the persistently poor—and their children—to greater life chances. But corporations must also consider the situation of the urban underclass from the standpoint of the well-being of the general society (see Wacquant and Wilson 1989). For the welfare of the urban poor impacts immeasurably, indirectly and directly, upon the quality of life of the country as a whole.

REFERENCES

Anderson, Bernard. 1981. "How Much Did the Programs Help Minorities and Youth?" In *Employing the Unemployed*, edited by Eli Ginzberg. New York: Basic Books.

Anderson, Elijah. 1978. *A Place on the Corner*. Chicago: University of Chicago Press.

———. 1980. "Some Observations on Black Youth Employment." In *Youth Employment and Public Policy*, edited by Bernard Anderson and Isabel Sawhill. Englewood Cliffs: Prentice-Hall.

———. 1989. "Moral Leadership and Transitions in the Urban Black Community." In *Social Class and Democratic Leadership: Essays in Honor of E. Digby Baltzell*, edited by Harold Bershady. Philadelphia: University of Pennsylvania Press.

Auletta, Ken. 1982. *The Underclass*. New York: Random House.

Becker, Howard S. 1972. "School is a Lousy Place to Learn Anything In." *American Behavioral Scientist* 16:85–105.

Berg, Ivar. 1970. *Education and Jobs: The Great Training Robbery*. New York: Praeger.

Berg, Ivar, and Janice Shack-Marquez. 1985. "Current Conceptions of Structural Unemployment: Some Logical and Empirical Difficulties." In *Research in the Sociology of Work*, 3:99–117. Greenwich, Conn.: JAI Press.

Bluestone, B., and B. Harrison. 1982. *The Deindustrialization of America: Plant Closings, Community Abandonment, and the Dismantling of Basic Industry*. New York: Basic Books.

Blumer, Herbert. 1958. "Race Prejudice as A Sense of Group Position." *Pacific Sociological Review* 1(1).

Bonney, Norman. 1972. "Unwelcome Strangers." Ph.D. diss., University of Chicago.

Clark, Dennis. 1973. "The Philadelphia Irish." In *The Peoples of Philadelphia*, edited by Allen Davis and Mark Haller. Philadelphia: Temple University Press.

Davis, Allen, and Mark Haller. 1973. *The Peoples of Philadelphia*. Philadelphia: Temple University Press.

Doeringer, Peter B., and Michael J. Piore. 1971. *Internal Labor Markets and Manpower Analysis.* Lexington, Mass.: D. C. Heath.

DuBois, W. E. B. 1899. *The Philadelphia Negro.* Philadelphia: University of Pennsylvania Press.

Ellwood, David T. 1986. "The Spatial Mismatch Hypothesis." In *The Black Youth Employment Crisis,* edited by R. B. Freeman and H. J. Holzer. Chicago: University of Chicago Press.

Ginzberg, Eli. 1980. *Employing the Unemployed.* New York: Basic Books.

Goffman, Erving. 1963. *Stigma.* Englewood Cliffs: Prentice-Hall.

Granovetter, Mark S. 1973. "The Strength of Weak Ties." *American Journal of Sociology* 78 (6):1360–80.

Haller, M., and A. Davis, editors. 1973. *Peoples of Philadelphia.* Philadelphia: Temple University Press.

Hannerz, Ulf. 1969. *Soulside.* New York: Columbia University Press.

Hareven, Tamara, and Randolph Langenbach. 1978. *Ameskeag: Life and Work in an American Factory-City.* New York: Pantheon Books.

Hershberg, Theodore, editor. 1981. *Philadelphia: Work, Space, Family, and Group Experience in the 19th Century.* New York: Oxford University Press.

Hershberg, Theodore, Alan N. Burstein, Eugene P. Ericksen, Stephanie W. Greenberg, and William L. Yancey. 1981. "A Tale of Three Cities: Blacks, Immigrants, and Opportunity in Philadelphia, 1850–1880, 1930, 1970." In Hershberg 1981.

Higginbotham, Leon. 1978. *In the Matter of Color.* New York: Oxford University Press.

Hirsch, Susan E. 1978. *Roots of the American Working Class: The Industrialization of Crafts in Newark, 1800–1860.* Philadelphia: University of Pennsylvania Press.

Hughes, Everett C. 1946. "The Knitting of Racial Groups in Industry." *American Sociological Review* 11:514.

Kain, John. 1968. "Housing Segregation, Negro Unemployment, and Metropolitan Decentralization." *Quarterly Journal of Economics* 82:175–97.

Karsarda, John D. 1989. "Urban Industrial Transition and the Urban Underclass." In William J. Wilson, ed., *The Ghetto Underclass. Annals of the American Academy of Political and Social Science* 501:26–47.

Kornblum, William. 1974. *Blue Collar Community.* Chicago: University of Chicago Press.

Liebow, Elliott. 1967. *Tally's Corner: A Study of Negro Streetcorner Men.* Boston: Little, Brown.

Marshall, Ray. 1965. *The Negro and Organized Labor.* New York: John Wiley.

Pettigrew, Thomas. 1980. "Prejudice." In *Harvard Encyclopedia of American Ethnic Groups,* edited by Stephen Thermstrom. Cambridge: Harvard University Press.

Shelton, Cynthia J. 1986. *The Mills of Manayunk: Industrialization and Social Conflict in the Philadelphia Region, 1787–1837.* Baltimore: Johns Hopkins University Press.

Spear, Allan. 1967. *Black Chicago: The Making of a Ghetto, 1890–1910.* Chicago: University of Chicago Press.

Stromsdorfer, Ernst. 1980. "The Effectiveness of Youth Employment Programs: An Analysis of the Historical Antecedents of Current Youth Initiatives." In *Youth Employment and Public Policy,* edited by Bernard Anderson and Isabel Sawhill. Englewood Cliffs: Prentice-Hall.

Wacquant, Löic, and W. J. Wilson. 1989. "The Cost of Racial and Class Exclusion in the Inner City." *Annals of the American Academy of Political and Social Science* 501:8–25.

Wellman, David. 1977. "Putting on the Poverty Program." In *Problems in Political Economy,* edited by David Gordon. Lexington, Mass.: D. C. Heath.

Wilson, William J. 1973. *Power, Racism and Privilege.* New York: Macmillan.

———. 1980. *The Declining Significance of Race.* Chicago: University of Chicago Press.

———. 1987. *The Truly Disadvantaged.* Chicago: University of Chicago Press.

———. 1989. "The Ghetto Underclass." Annals of the American Academy of Political and Social Science 501.

I I I I I I I I Work Sharing: An Underused Policy for Combating Unemployment?

FRED J. BEST

When unemployment rates are high many persons advocate a reduction of work time as a means of combating joblessness by spreading employment among larger numbers. This paper will discuss this concept by (1) providing a brief history of work sharing, (2) outlining leading proposals for sharing work, and (3) assessing the role of work sharing among other approaches to combating joblessness.

Debate over the viability of reducing work time to fight joblessness has risen and fallen many times over past decades. Unfortunately, attention given to this topic has generally taken the form of advocacy for and opposition to very specific approaches to sharing work. As a result, many people have come to view work sharing as taking only one particular form rather than as a generic concept. First and foremost, this paper will seek to encourage readers to think of work sharing as the general idea of reducing work time in order to spread employment, and second, to recognize that there are many approaches to this general objective.

Yet another hope for this paper is that it will provide an overview of the social and economic forces that will determine the viability of the most promising forms of work sharing. Proponents have all too frequently paid inadequate attention to the real economic costs and institutional constraints that can neutralize the proposed benefits and applicability of work sharing. Correspondingly, even highly trained and sophisticated opponents have frequently dismissed all work sharing as a "defeatist strategy" without paying adequate attention to specific proposals or the currents of social change that may determine the viability and advisability of such programs. Work sharing, like all prospective areas of public policy, will succeed or fail within a complex web of technical, economic, and social conditions. The last section of this paper will examine some of these conditions.

HISTORIC BACKGROUND

Although the idea of work sharing has always been controversial,[1] industrial societies have consistently applied policies to reduce and ration work time as a means of combating joblessness.[2] In a general sense, there are two basic forms of work sharing. The first type is usually restricted to specific firms and used as a short-term strategy for preventing layoffs and dismissals by temporarily reducing work time. For example, employers and employees in a given firm may decide to reduce the work week and earnings for a short period by 10 percent as an alternative to laying off one-tenth of existing workers. Interestingly, about one-fourth of existing collective bargaining agreements have formal provisions for such work sharing.[3] The second type of work sharing seeks to reduce work time among the employed in order to create jobs for the unemployed, thus distributing available work more evenly among a larger number of persons. This second type has been used to combat unemployment caused by long-range conditions that are likely to persist beyond the periodic downswings of the business cycle.

While efforts to gain more free time have been a concern of labor movements dating back to the eighteenth century, the notion of reducing work time in order to share employment made its most obvious appearance in 1887, when Samuel Gompers, the president of the American Federation of Labor, declared, "As long as we have one person seeking work who cannot find it, the hours of work are too long." To what degree such comments reflected the intent to combat joblessness as opposed to a desire to justify the reduction of work hours remains an open question. Nonetheless, this position was embraced as a major justification for a series of worker movements to shorten the work week between the late nineteenth century and the 1930s.

The Great Depression of the 1930s fostered the first widespread, explicit efforts to reduce work time in order to spread employment. As joblessness rose to crisis proportions, employers sought to ease the burden of unemployment by

1. For a sample of critical comments, see Lloyd G. Reynolds, *Labor Economics and Labor Relations,* 5th ed. (Englewood Cliffs: Prentice-Hall, 1970), 46–50, 576–83; and Paul Samuelson, *Economics,* 8th ed. (New York: McGraw-Hill, 1970), 552–53.

2. Martin Nemirow, "Work Sharing Approaches: Past and Present," *Monthly Labor Review* (September 1984):34–39.

3. Peter Henle, *Work Sharing as an Alternative to Layoffs,* Congressional Research Service, Library of Congress, Washington, D.C., July 19, 1976.

shortening work weeks as an alternative to layoffs in an era when there was no unemployment insurance and great aversion to the few available welfare programs.[4] The Hoover administration made such work sharing the centerpiece of its effort to control a staggering 20 percent unemployment rate.[5] Even though this general concept was endorsed by then-president of the American Federation of Labor, William Green, the work-sharing concept became unpopular among workers. Although workers accepted it as the best of undesirable options, they also regarded it as symbolic of a depression commonly thought to be the creation of the business community and the Hoover administration.[6]

After 1932, Franklin D. Roosevelt's New Deal made multifaceted initiatives to combat joblessness. Some of these included new forms of work sharing that were more palatable to workers. Social Security, a self-proclaimed hallmark of the Roosevelt administration, was passed in 1935 primarily to ensure retirement with dignity, but also to reduce the number of persons seeking jobs.[7] A more direct work-sharing policy dealt with limiting the workweek. The Black-Connery bill, which limited the workweek to thirty hours, passed the Senate but was defeated in the House in 1933.[8] Five years later, Roosevelt signed into law a more flexible work-limiting approach in the form of the Fair Labor Standards Act of 1938.[9] This act sought to spread employment by defining the standard workweek as forty hours and imposing a time-and-a-half overtime pay premium for hours worked over this standard workweek. While available data indicate that predepression collective bargaining followed by massive work sharing during the years immediately preceding passage of this act had driven the average workweek down to the neighborhood of forty hours,[10] this measure appeared to encourage new hiring as an alternative to overtime and has come to

4. Sar A. Levitan, *Reducing Worktime as a Means to Combating Unemployment* (Kalamazoo, Mich.: W. E. Upjohn Institute for Employment Research, 1964), 1–2.

5. "Share the Work," in *Passport to Utopia: Great Panaceas in American History,* ed. Arthur Weinburg and Lila Weinburg (Chicago: Quandrangle Books, 1968), 241–47; and J. W. Fagan, "Work Sharing during a Depression," *Industrial Relations* (September 1938).

6. Richard Lester, *Labor and Industrial Relations* (New York: Macmillan, 1951), 159.

7. Arthur S. Link and William B. Catton, *The American Epoch: A History of the United States Since 1880's,* (New York: Alfred A. Knopf, 1965), 414–15; and Juanita Kreps, *Lifetime Allocation of Work and Income* (Durham, N.C.: Duke University Press, 1970), 73–75.

8. Levitan, *Reducing Worktime,* 1.

9. Paul Douglas and Joseph Hackman, "The Fair Labor Standards Act of 1938," *Political Science Quarterly* (March 1939):29–53.

10. John Owen, "Hours of Work in the Long Run," *Work Time and Employment,* Special Report no. 28, National Commission for Employment Policy, Washington, D.C., October 1978, p. 37.

be regarded as the single most dramatic public policy to foster the sharing of employment (see table 1).

World War II and the subsequent years of economic progress fostered little in the way of overt work sharing but gave rise to conditions that have had important impacts on work time trends and the distribution of employment within the United States. First, the combination of tax law incentives for fringe benefits and occasional wage-price freezes gave rise to an ongoing, multidecade trend toward increasing fixed labor expenditures on retirement pensions, health care,

Table 1. Average Length of Workweek, Selected Years
and Industries, 1909–1978

Year	Total private	Manufacturing workers	Construction workers	Retail trade workers
		Average hours of work per week		
1909	—	51.0	—	—
1920	—	47.4	—	—
1925	—	44.5	—	—
1928	—	44.4	—	—
1929	—	44.2	—	—
1930	—	42.1	—	—
1932	—	40.5	—	—
1934	—	38.3	28.9	41.5
1936	—	34.6	32.8	43.5
1938	—	39.2	32.1	42.6
1940	—	35.6	33.1	42.5
1942	—	38.1	36.4	41.1
1944	—	42.9	39.6	40.4
1947	40.3	40.4	38.2	40.3
1950	39.8	40.5	37.4	40.4
1955	39.6	40.7	37.5	39.0
1960	38.6	39.7	36.7	38.0
1965	38.8	41.2	37.4	36.6
1970	37.1	39.8	37.3	33.8
1975	36.1	39.5	36.4	32.4
1978	35.8	40.4	36.9	31.0

Sources: Workweek data for 1947 to 1978 cited from *The Employment and Training Report of the President,* U.S. Department of Labor, Washington D.C., 1979, p. 322. Workweek data for years prior to 1947 from multiple sources cited from *The Statistical History of the United States from Colonial Times to the Present,* (Stamford, Conn.: Fairfield Publishers, 1965), 92, 94.
Note: Discontinuities of data collection method do not allow strict comparability of figures for years prior to 1947.

paid time off, and other nonwage compensation. This trend increased free time, particularly in the form of earlier retirements. More important, expenditures on such benefits are, for the most part, fixed so that their costs to employers for every hour of labor received increase as the job time of individual workers declines (see table 2). Thus, the increase of such fixed expenditures on fringe benefits has become a growing barrier to work time reductions.[11] Second, the growth of income maintenance programs such as unemployment insurance and welfare has tended to encourage many persons who experience difficulty finding employment to withdraw from the labor force.[12] Finally, many have suggested that social norms and some social policies discouraged women from holding jobs.[13]

During the recessionary downturns of the 1960s, alarm over worker displacement due to automation[14] and the influx of the large post–World War II "baby boom" generation into the labor force revived interest in limiting the supply of labor to reduce unemployment. Collective bargaining efforts sought to reduce the workweek,[15] promote earlier retirement,[16] and instigate more exotic policies such as the U.S. Steel Sabbatical.[17] Public policies also sought to reduce the supply of labor to match the availability of jobs. An effort by organized labor to discourage overtime by increasing premium pay to double-time was narrowly defeated in the early 1960s.[18] More important, programs were developed to increase the school years of youth and the retirement years of old age. These programs had many other social purposes, yet policymakers of this era freely acknowledge that an important goal of these programs was to reduce the size of the labor force.[19] The policies worked well. As an indication

11. Robert Clark, *Adjusting Hours to Increase Jobs,* Special Report no. 15, National Commission for Employment Policy, Washington, D.C., September 1977, pp. 30–42.

12. Melvin Reder, "Hours of Work and the General Welfare," in *Hours of Work,* ed. Clyde Dankert (New York: Harper and Row, 1965), 179–200.

13. Laurie Werner, "Where Are Women Now: Update from Eli Ginzberg," *Working Women* (December 1978):32–35.

14. For a range of discussion of this issue, see National Commission on Technology, Automation and Economic Progress, *Technology and the American Economy,* vol. 1, February 1966; and Robert Theobald, ed., *The Guaranteed Income* (Garden City, N.Y.: Doubleday-Anchor Books, 1967).

15. "McDonald Asks 32 Hour Workweek," *Wall Street Journal,* March 9, 1961, p. 11; "Shorter Work Schedules," *Wall Street Journal,* January 8, 1962, p. 32; and John L. Zalusky, "Shorter Workyears—Earlier Retirement," *AFL-CIO American Federationist* (August 1977).

16. Ibid.

17. "Sabbatical Becomes Major Goal," *Business Week,* October 13, 1962, p. 106.

18. Levitan, Reducing Worktime, 12–36.

19. Phyllis Lehmann, "Willard Wirtz: Candid Answers About Joblessness," *Worklife* (February 1979):2–5; and Kreps, *Lifetime Allocation of Work,* 73–75.

Table 2. Dollar Costs per Hour for Fixed Costs of Labor by Variations of Work Time

Weekly work hours[a]	1974 National average nonwage compensation[b] ($57.34)	Weekly fixed costs of labor[c]													
		$20	$30	$40	$50	$60	$70	$80	$90	$100	$110	$120	$130	$140	$150
60	.96	.33	.50	.67	.83	1.00	1.17	1.33	1.50	1.67	1.83	2.00	2.17	2.33	2.50
56	1.02	.36	.54	.71	.89	1.07	1.25	1.43	1.61	1.79	1.96	2.14	2.32	2.50	2.68
52	1.10	.38	.58	.77	.96	1.15	1.35	1.54	1.73	1.92	2.11	2.31	2.50	2.69	2.88
48	1.19	.42	.62	.83	1.04	1.25	1.46	1.67	1.87	2.08	2.29	2.50	2.71	2.92	3.12
44	1.30	.45	.68	.91	1.14	1.36	1.59	1.82	2.04	2.27	2.50	2.73	2.95	3.18	3.41
40	1.43	.50	.75	1.00	1.25	1.50	1.75	2.00	2.25	2.50	2.75	3.00	3.25	3.50	3.75
36	1.59	.56	.83	1.11	1.39	1.67	1.94	2.22	2.50	2.78	3.06	3.33	3.61	3.89	4.17
32	1.79	.63	.94	1.25	1.56	1.88	2.19	2.50	2.81	3.13	3.44	3.75	4.06	4.38	4.69
28	2.05	.71	1.07	1.43	1.79	2.14	2.50	2.86	3.21	3.57	3.93	4.29	4.64	5.00	5.36
24	2.39	.83	1.25	1.67	2.08	2.50	2.92	3.33	3.75	4.17	4.58	5.00	5.42	5.88	6.25
20	2.86	1.00	1.50	2.00	2.50	3.00	3.50	4.00	4.50	5.00	5.50	6.00	6.50	7.00	7.50

Source: Fred Best, "Individual and Firm Work Time Decisions: Comment," Work Time and Employment, Special Report no. 28, National Commission for Employment Policy, Washington, D.C., October 1978, p. 225.

[a] Standard workweek assumed to equal forty hours.

[b] Nonwage compensation defind as including life and health insurance, private pensions, social security, paid time off, miscellaneous fringe benefits, and unemployment insurance taxes (1977 Handbook of Labor Statistics, p. 217).

[c] Can be viewed to include all nonwage compensation (fringe benefits) as well as costs of supervisional coordination, record keeping, recruitment, hiring, training, and retraining.

of their success, the percentage of the average U.S. male's total life span given to the nonwork activities of schooling and retirement increased from 35.5 percent in 1940 to 43 percent in 1980 (see fig. 1).[20] Generally high economic growth coupled with the somewhat subtle employment distribution impacts of these policies tended to downplay overt discussion of work sharing during this period.

The ultimate entrance of the baby boom generation into the labor force, a dramatic increase of women workers, high unemployment, and limited job creation fostered by "stagflation" once again renewed open consideration of work sharing during the 1970s. During and since the recession of 1975, work sharing within individual firms has occurred independently of government intervention in much the same way it did during the 1930s.[21] Also, serious consideration and eventual action was catalyzed for "unemployment insurance–supported work sharing," a program used by European nations to provide partial unemployment insurance benefits to workers put on reduced workweeks as an alternative to layoffs.[22] California initiated such a program in 1978, and several other states have done likewise since that time.[23] Starting in 1977, a coalition of unions initiated a new drive to amend the Fair Labor Standards Act so that the standard workweek was redefined as thirty-five hours and the overtime premium raised to double-time.[24] Correspondingly, many unions, most notably the United Auto Workers, resumed their historic effort to reduce work time via collective bargaining.[25] Finally, a range of novel, volunteeristic proposals were put forth to share employment via public sabbaticals, expanded

20. Fred Best and Barry Stern, "Education, Work and Leisure—Must They Come in That Order?" *Monthly Labor Review* (July 1977):4.

21. Henle, *Work Sharing as an Alternative;* Edith F. Lynton, "Alternatives to Layoffs," Conference Report, New York City Commission on Human Rights, New York, April 1975; Robert Bednarzik, "Work Sharing in the U.S.: Its Prevalence and Duration," *Monthly Labor Review* (July 1980):3–12; and Sar Levitan and Richard Belous, "Work Sharing Initiatives At Home and Abroad," *Monthly Labor Review* (September 1977):19.

22. Levitan and Belous, "Work Sharing Initiatives," 16–18; and Fred Best and James Mattesich, "Short-Time Compensation Systems in California and Europe," *Monthly Labor Review* (July 1980):13–22.

23. Fred Best, *Reducing Workweeks to Prevent Layoffs: The Economic and Social Impacts of Unemployment Supported Work Sharing* (Kalamazoo, Mich.: W. E. Upjohn Institute for Employment Research, 1985), chap. 1.

24. Paul Rosenstiel, "The Union's New Tune," *The Nation,* December 31, 1977, pp. 720–23; and Bernie Cloff, "Unions Campaign to Shrink Worktime," *Business Week,* April 24, 1978, p. 30.

25. "Paid Personal Holiday," *Solidarity,* October 21, 1977, pp. 6–10; and "Statement of John Zalusky, Economist, Research Department, AFL-CIO," Joint Economic Committee Hearings, U.S. Congress, Washington, D.C., June 14, 1978.

Figure 1. U.S. Men's Lifetime Distribution of Education, Work and Leisure by Primary Activity, Actual 1900–1970 and Projected 1980–1900

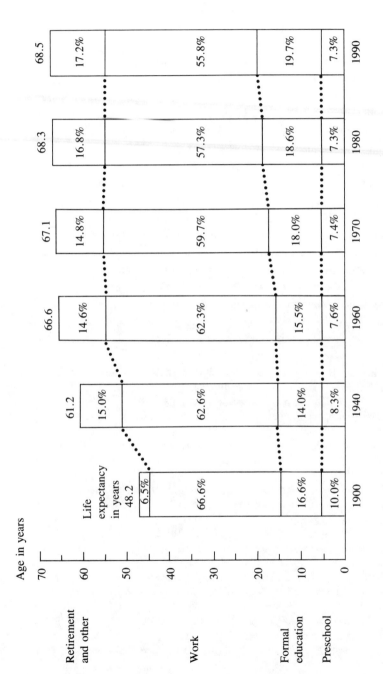

Sources: Work life expectancy figures (number of years in labor force) obtained from Howard N. Fullerton and James J. Byrne, "Length of Working Life for Men and Women, 1970," *Monthly Labor Review* (February 1976): 31–33; and Howard N. Fullerton, "A Table of Expected Working Life for Men, 1968," *Monthly Labor Review* (June 1971): 49–54. Life expectancy figures (at birth) obtained from *Statistical Abstracts of the United States, 1974* (Washington, D.C.: Bureau of the Census, 1975), 55. School years (completed for persons over 25) obtained from *Digest of Educational Statistics for 1975* (Washington, D.C.: U.S. Department of Health, Education and Welfare, Office of Education, 1975), 14–15. Projected figures of worklife and life expectancy from unpublished computations provided by Howard N. Fullerton, Bureau of Labor Statistics. Projected years of education are estimates derived from *Current Population Reports*, Series 20, nos. 243 and 293, and Series P-25, no. 476

part-time jobs, voluntary programs allowing workers to trade earnings for reduced work time, and nullification of legal barriers to work time reduction.[26] In parallel fashion, many European nations developed a serious interest in the potentials of fighting joblessness with work sharing.

Clearly, work sharing is not a new idea. Both private and public policies have promoted various ways of sharing and distributing jobs. In many cases, work sharing has been fostered by a number of social forces in conjunction with unemployment; and in many cases the work-sharing implications of social policies have been secondary but important considerations. Employment has indeed been shared and rationed within most industrial societies, and this has had a profound impact upon the nature of unemployment and patterns of work and leisure. The main issue concerning work sharing is not whether to use it. Work sharing is already a reality. The issues for the future are, How much work sharing should there be and what forms should it take?

ALTERNATIVE APPROACHES TO SHARING WORK

As noted previously, consideration of work time reductions as a strategy to combat unemployment has been hampered by a tendency to view work sharing in terms of only one of many approaches. When one reflects on the past, it becomes apparent that there are many ways to spread employment by reducing work time. This section will briefly outline and assess a number of specific approaches to sharing employment. Attention will be focused primarily on the various public policy levers that might be applied to foster work sharing, and only secondarily on the types of work time reductions that would be created by these policies. For example, a shorter workweek is one way of spreading employment. However, there are many ways to stimulate this and other types of work time reduction.

The Options

Some seventeen public policies designed to redistribute existing and prospective employment opportunities will be outlined.[27] In an effort to develop a framework for considering these options, I have grouped the policies into four major categories. The first is made up of policies that provide income subsidies to individuals in order to induce work time reductions or labor force withdrawal. The second category includes approaches that seek to limit work

26. Fred Best, *Flexible Life Scheduling: Breaking the Education-Work-Retirement Lockstep* (New York: Praeger Special Studies, 1981), pp. 169–73.

27. These seventeen policy options for work sharing are elaborated in Fred Best, *Work Sharing: Issues, Policy Options and Prospects* (Kalamazoo, Mich.: W. E. Upjohn Institute for Employment Research, 1981), pp. 59–186.

Table 3.   Alternative Work-Sharing Policies

Subsidized Work Time Reduction
   Larger and earlier retirement pensions
   Opportunities for prolonged schooling during
      youth
   Worker sabbaticals
   Midlife educational leaves
   Welfare and income maintenance programs
   Unemployment insurance–supported work sharing
Limitation of Work Time
   Restriction of overtime
   Reduction of the standard workweek
   Mandatory vacations
   Forced retirement
   Compulsory education
Long-Term Time–Income Tradeoffs
   Neutralization of tax incentives for selected fringe
      benefits
   Public subsidization of fringe benefits
   Tax incentives for work time reductions
   Encouragement of flexible benefit options
Voluntary Time–Income Tradeoffs
   Neutralization of payroll taxes
   Subsidies for work time reduction options

time over weeks or longer periods via legal restrictions and economic disincentives for prolonged work activities. The third category presents a number of approaches clustered by the common objective of fostering long-term partial forfeiture of pay raises resulting from economic growth or promotion for more time away from work. The fourth category comprises government efforts to encourage institutional options that allow individuals to exchange voluntarily portions of current earnings for work time reductions that might open jobs for the unemployed (see table 3).

Subsidized Work Time Reductions Many public policies have been proposed and implemented with the aim of effecting a redistribution of employment by providing financial incentives that make it easier for individuals to forego income-earning work time. While most of these programs were not intended primarily as a means of combating unemployment, advocates have commonly cited their alleged impacts on the distribution of work.

Larger and Earlier Retirement Options. Both public and private retirement pensions have been used, in part, to redistribute employment by encouraging the withdrawal of older workers from the labor force. In the United States today, public pensions financed through the Social Security Act provide retirement benefits to over 90 percent of the labor force starting at age sixty-two. Since 1970, over 50 percent of the labor force has been covered by private pension plans. Adjustment in the provisions of these plans can have considerable impact on the labor force participation of those at or near retirement age.

Opportunities for Prolonged Schooling during Youth. The extension of school years during youth has frequently been mentioned as a means of reducing the supply of labor and thus lessening unemployment.[28] Aside from extending compulsory school enrollment (a policy outlined later), time spent in school during youth can be prolonged by increasing educational opportunities through subsistence funds for students and accessible educational institutions. Presumably, young persons desiring education would respond to available resources by postponing entry into the labor force and thereby relieving competition for jobs.

Worker Sabbaticals. A number of proposals have been made for sharing employment through public worker sabbatical programs.[29] In general, these proposals would provide workers, after several years of consecutive employment, with some portion of their normal income during an extended period away from work. It is reasoned that such staggered withdrawal of a significant portion of the work force would require new hiring that would relieve the unemployment problem.

Midlife Educational Leaves. It has been suggested that competition for available jobs might be reduced by encouraging workers to return periodically to school in order to undertake educational programs that would update their skills, facilitate midlife occupational changes, or simply allow self-renewal and enrichment.[30] As in the case of worker sabbaticals, such extended leaves for

28. R. A. Hart and P. J. Sloane, "Working Hours and the Distribution of Work," paper prepared for the Organisation for Economic Development and Cooperation Conference on Collective Bargaining and Government Policies, Washington, D.C., July 1978, pp. 26–28.

29. Some examples of these proposals include, Dolores Melching and Merle Borberg, "A National Sabbatical System: Implications for the Aged," *The Gerontologist,* April 1974, pp. 175–81; James O'Toole, *Work in America,* (Cambridge: MIT Press, 1973), pp. 119–39; Donald Fraiser, "Social Security Sabbaticals: A New Dimension for the Social Security System," *Congressional Record,* August 22, 1974, pp. H8939–H8940; Robert Rosenberg, "A Pilot Program for Extended Leaves," Working Paper no. 10, Office of Research, California State Senate, Sacramento, December 1976; Jules Sugarman, "The Decennial-Sabbatical Plan," *CUPA Journal* 28(23):47–52; Otto Feinstein, "The Workingman's Sabbatical," unpublished paper, Wayne State University, December 1977; and Edward Lehner, "Towards Sabbaticals for Every Worker," *New York Times,* December 16, 1978, editorial page.

30. Feinstein, "Workingman's Sabbatical"; O'Toole, *Work in America,* pp. 121–52; and Barry Stern, "Feasibility of a Work Sabbatical Program," Office of the Assistant Secretary for Education, U.S. Department of Health, Education and Welfare, Washington, D.C., March 18, 1975, pp. 80–109.

midlife educational programs would make it necessary for employers to hire new workers to replace those who have temporarily left.[31]

Income Maintenance and Welfare Programs. While few commentators have suggested a linkage between income maintenance and work sharing,[32] it is well documented that increases in the coverage and benefit amounts provided by these programs tend to foster withdrawal from work and labor force participation. Consciously and unconsciously, industrial societies have developed and pursued income maintenance programs that encourage marginal workers to withdraw from work in favor of more competitive workers.[33] These income maintenance programs effectively subsidize work time reductions and have become powerful determinants of the way employment is distributed.

Unemployment Insurance–Supported Work Sharing. Another approach to work sharing entails the provision of partial unemployment insurance benefits to employees in work groups that experience workweek reductions in order to prevent layoffs or dismissals within a specific firm. As a rough illustration, if a firm were to reduce the workweek and pay levels of its employees 20 percent rather than lay off 20 percent of its workers, those employees working reduced workweeks would receive one-fifth of the weekly unemployment insurance they would have received if totally laid off. Thus employees on reduced workweeks would be partially reimbursed for lost earnings, and no workers would lose their jobs.[34]

With the exception of unemployment insurance–supported work sharing, most programs that subsidize the reduction of work time tend to be extremely costly and frequently inefficient as a means of transforming work time to employment for those who are jobless. However, many of these programs have been proposed and implemented for reasons other than the sharing of employment. While most of them may not be justified in terms of work sharing alone, their effects on the distribution of work may provide notable but limited opportunities for combating unemployment.

Limitation of Work Time A larger portion of current discussion about work-sharing concerns proposals to mandate legislatively limits to the amount individuals may work. Although many of these work limitation pro-

31. Hart and Sloane, "Working Hours," 25.

32. Manpower and Social Affairs Committee, "Unemployment Compensation and Work Incentives," Manpower and Employment Measures for Positive Adjustment, Organisation for Economic Cooperation and Development, Paris, April 26, 1979, Annex IV.

33. Reder, "Hours of Work and the General Welfare," 179–200.

34. Fred Best, "Short-Time Compensation in North America: Trends and Prospects," *Personnel,* January 1985, pp. 34–41.

posals have been combined with one another as well as with other types of work sharing, I will summarize each specific approach separately.

Restriction of Overtime. The idea of converting overtime hours into jobs for the unemployed has been applied in most industrial nations and continues to receive considerable attention as a potential employment policy.[35] To illustrate why many people find this approach attractive, the total number of overtime hours for U.S. production workers was estimated to be about 2.4 billion in 1974. If this overtime could have been transferred to persons seeking employment, about one million full-time jobs would have been created.[36] While some proposals have sought to reduce overtime by mandatory limitation, most seek to discourage overtime by requiring employers to pay higher rates to workers for overtime. For example, it is now frequently proposed that the National Labor Relations Act be amended so that overtime pay is increased from the current time-and-a-half to double-time in order to intensify disincentives to use overtime rather than hire new workers.

Reduction of the Standard Workweek. Mandatory premium overtime pay rates require the establishment of a standard workweek as a benchmark for the instigation of overtime. For example, the United States and many other nations have defined their standard workweek as forty hours, thus requiring that employees working longer than forty hours a week receive overtime pay. A leading work-sharing policy that is commonly combined with higher overtime pay is reduction of the standard workweek. This would result in overtime pay penalties going into effect sooner, creating an incentive for employers to cut the workweek and presumably hire additional workers.

Mandatory Vacations. Many European nations have legislated mandatory minimum vacations. For example, by the mid-1970s Belgium, Denmark, Finland, and France had statutes that set a minimum of three weeks' vacation for all workers.[37] Sweden ensures five weeks of paid vacation. It has been suggested occasionally that such mandatory vacation laws would reduce the size of the labor force and thereby combat unemployment.[38]

Forced Retirement. Over the last several decades, many organizations have

35. Alastair Evans, "Measures to Make Jobs Go Around," *Personnel Management,* January 1979, p. 34; Christian Tyler, "Unions' Crusade for the Shorter Workweek," *Financial Times,* June 2, 1978; Robert Taylor, "Work Sharing and Worklessness," *New Society,* November 23, 1978, pp. 452–54; Beatrice Taupin, "35 Heurs: Pas de Meracle," *Le Figaro,* May 15, 1979, pp. 1, 7; and John Conyers, "The Continuing Crisis of Unemployment," *Congressional Record,* September 18, 1978, pp. E5056–E5058.

36. Joyce Nussbaum and Donald Wise, "The Overtime Pay Premiums and Employment," *Work Time and Employment,* Special Report no. 28, National Commission for Employment Policy, Washington, D.C., October 1978, pp. 312–13.

37. Archibald Evans, *Flexibility in Working Life,* Organisation for Economic Cooperation and Development, Paris, 1973, pp. 67–68.

38. Hart and Sloane, "Working Hours," 26.

instigated policies that make retirement mandatory or almost mandatory at a predetermined age. In the United States, for example, evidence suggests that about 45 percent of employers providing private pension plans had such provisions in 1974.[39] Among other things, these retirement policies certainly influence the distribution of work among age groups and have, therefore, been viewed as potential work-sharing devices.

Compulsory Education. The United States and other nations have statutes requiring young persons to remain in school up to a specified age. Most of these statutes have been enacted to guarantee custodial guidance and a minimal level of educational attainment for all children and youth.[40] As a result, the minimum age for leaving school is relatively low, generally fifteen or sixteen years. Such compulsory education laws have work-sharing implications in that they attenuate competition for employment by delaying the labor force entry of young persons.

In overview, programs to spread employment among a larger number by imposing limitations on the workweek, workyear, or worklife appear to be costly, frequently unenforceable, and politically volatile because they constrain individual freedom. Increased overtime restrictions may have some potential for redistributing work, but problems would have to be overcome to ensure the avoidance of undue cost and inflexibility. Mandatory reduction of the standard workweek would be very costly to business if not accompanied by a commensurate or partial pay reduction, and politically infeasible with significant pay cuts. In today's era of intense international competition, the prospect of major labor cost increases would be strongly resisted. Expanded vacations could also be costly and would be unlikely to create new jobs unless vacations were greatly prolonged or intricately scheduled. Finally compulsory retirement and schooling laws would be extremely unpopular, occasionally illegal, and probably impossible to enforce.

Long-Term Time-Income Tradeoffs It has been proposed that work time be reduced gradually over the course of several years by the forfeiting of portions of pay raises made possible by economic growth or promotions. If economic growth trends continue, the resulting decline of work time would presumably make it necessary for employers to hire more workers in order to maintain potential economic output.

My updating of computations made in 1966 by Juanita Kreps and Joseph

39. Dorothy Kittner, "Forced Retirement: How Common Is It?," *Monthly Labor Review* (December 1977):60–61.

40. Robert Havighurst and Bernice Neugarten, *Society and Education* (Boston: Allyn and Bacon, 1975), 197–98.

Spengler indicates rather remarkable increases of free time could be gained by foregoing a portion of moderate economic growth.[41] Based like the original computations on projections of "slow economic growth" prepared by the U.S. Bureau of Labor Statistics, my updated figures illustrate how much free time the average American worker might gain if one-third of expected real growth were exchanged for more leisure. The number of hours worked per year would decline from 1,911 in 1976 (the base year for the most recent computations) to 1,598 by the year 2000. Thus, the average worker could have a thirty-three-hour workweek or eleven-week paid vacations or a thirteen-month sabbatical every seven years or retirement at age fifty-six (see table 4). These figures are now somewhat dated, but they underscore the potential of long-term time-income tradeoffs for reducing work time.

While these figures indicate tremendous potential for long-term work time reductions, they also raise questions of how public policies might encourage such time-income exchanges. Following are four possible approaches:

Neutralization of Tax Incentives for Selected Fringe Benefits. Tax systems within the United States and other nations allow lower taxation or waiver of taxes for selected fringe benefits. For example, the dollar value of private health insurance in the United States is essentially tax free, while wages and salaries are taxed.[42] As a result, employee interest groups and employers seeking to optimize compensation expenditures have placed heavy emphasis upon increasing tax-free benefits as opposed to other goals, such as added free time. Public policies that neutralize these tax differences might encourage greater emphasis on the exchanging of potential pay raises for free time by (1) removing disincentives to foregoing income for time, and (2) reducing the multidecade trend toward increasing the fixed labor costs associated with fringe benefits, which discourage employers from initiating work time reductions of all types (see table 2).

Public Subsidization of Fringe Benefits. Since the fixed costs of labor, most notably nonwork, hour–related benefits such as health care and life insurance, are significant barriers to work time reductions, it can be expected that relief of these costs to employers would reduce the disincentives to work sharing.[43] Thus, national health insurance and kindred developments would presumably

41. Fred Best, "The Time of Our Lives: The Parameters of Lifetime Distribution of Education, Work and Leisure," *Society and Leisure,* May 1978, pp. 95–124. The original study was Juanita Kreps and Joseph Spengler, "The Leisure Component of Economic Growth," in *Automation and Economic Progress,* ed. Howard Bowen and Garth Mangum (Englewood Cliffs: Prentice-Hall, 1966), pp. 128–34.

42. Clark, *Adjusting Hours,* 33–34.

43. Joseph Garbarino, "Individual and Firm Work Time Decisions," *Work Time and Employment,* Special Report no. 28, National Commission for Employment Policy, Washington, D.C., October 1978, pp. 195–200.

Table 4. Projected Growth of Productivity and Possible Use of Potential Free Time, 1975–2000 (Bureau of Labor Statistics "Slow Recovery" Projections, 1972 Dollars)

| | Computation of potential free time | | | | Possible uses of potential free time | | | | | | | |
| | | | | | All GNP growth to free time | | | | One-third GNP growth to free time | | | |
Year	Actual & projected adjusted GNP (billions)	Actual & projected total U.S. population (millions)	Actual & projected GNP per capita	Potential hours per year released from work per worker	Workweek (hours)	Vacation (weeks)	Sabbatical (months)	Retirement (years)	Workweek (hours)	Vacation (weeks)	Sabbatical (months)	Retirement (years)
1975	$1,191.7	213,540	$ 5,581	—	39.0	3.0	—	65.0	39.0	3.0	—	65.0
1980	1,557.8	222,769	6,993	385.0	31.1	13.9	17.6	53.3	36.4	6.4	5.5	61.3
1985	1,865.5	234,068	7,970	572.4	27.3	17.8	23.7	49.2	35.1	7.9	7.9	59.7
1990	2,210.9	245,075	9,021	728.5	24.1	21.7	30.2	44.9	34.0	9.2	10.0	58.3
1995	2,547.1	253,784*	10,036	837.0	21.9	24.5	34.8	41.8	33.3	10.2	11.6	57.3
2000	2,885.8	262,494	10,994	940.5	19.8	27.1	39.0	39.0	32.5	11.0	12.9	56.4

*Interpolation.

Sources: Actual and projected adjusted GNP: GNP for 1975 from *Statistical Abstract of the United States, 1976,* p. 394. Projections for 1980 and 1985 from "slower recovery" computations by Charles Bowman and Terry Morlan, "Revised Projections of the U.S. Economy to 1980 and 1985," *Monthly Labor Review* (March 1976); and 1990, 1995, and 2000 projections computed by extrapolation of a linear regression based on data and projections from 1965 to 1985. GNP figures adjusted to compensate for .25 percent potential GNP exchanged for free time in BLS projections. Actual and projected GNP per capita is the dollar value of average adjusted GNP per person in U.S. population. Potential hours per year released from work per worker is the number of hours per year per worker that could be subtracted from 1975 annual workhours if 1975 per capita GNP were held constant and potential per capita economic growth is exchanged for free time.

Notes:

Workweek: The average hours of work per week for the average worker.

Vacation: Total vacation time per year per worker. Potential increased vacation time is added to an estimated 1975 average vacation time of three weeks.

Sabbatical: The amount of extended free time possible every seven years if all potential free time gains are allocated to a sabbatical. 1975 annual vacation time is maintained.

Retirement: Average retirement age for worker aged 21 who allocates all potential free time toward earlier retirement. A 10 percent increase was made over other forms of free time for interest returns on deferred income.

250

make it easier for employers to reduce work time and lessen the cost of hiring new employees.

Tax Incentives for Work Time Reductions. Realignment of specific tax provisions to make paid time-off-the-job tax free in the same way other fringe benefits are could provide a powerful incentive to increase this benefit and thereby reduce work time. If all equivalents of paid time-off-the-job—whether they be shorter workweeks, longer vacations, or sabbaticals—were made tax free in the same way health care programs are, workers would receive a kind of bonus for paid time taken in lieu of other compensation. This would presumably encourage both employers and employees to reduce work time over the long run.

Encouragement of Flexible Benefit Options. Available data indicate that the willingness of workers to trade current or potential income for work time reductions depends on the types of prospective free time to be gained. Certain types of free time, such as vacations and long weekends, appear to be more popular than other types (see table 5).[44] Thus, policies that increase the variety of long-term time-income tradeoff choices are likely to maximize the long-term reduction of work time. One approach to maximizing such choices would be to encourage flexible benefit option programs. Such programs, which have been called cafeteria benefit plans, allow individual workers to choose among different combinations of benefits to suit their personal needs.[45] Removal of statutory restrictions[46] on such plans presumably would encourage work time reduction by allowing individuals to choose between desired forms of paid time-off and other benefits.[47]

In sum, it appears that proposals for encouraging long-term time-income tradeoffs for purposes of sharing work may have potential. With the probable exception of national health care, these approaches are relatively uncostly, have the capacity to foster significant work time reductions, and would presumably be

44. Fred Best, *Exchanging Earnings for Leisure: Findings of an Exploratory National Survey on Work Time Preferences,* Research and Development Monograph no. 79, Employment and Training Administration, U.S. Department of Labor, Washington, D.C., 1980, pp. 70–103.

45. Elizabeth Fowler, "More Companies Tailor Benefits to Each Employee," *Sacramento Bee,* July 10, 1983, p. 11; and John Greenwald, "A Variable Menu of Benefits," *Time,* June 27, 1983, p. 54.

46. Bruce Keppel, "Cafeteria Style Benefit Plans Stalled by IRS Warning," *Los Angeles Times,* April 15, 1984, pt. V, p. 3.

47. J. B. Chapman and Robert Otteman, "Employee Preference for Various Compensation and Fringe Options," *Personnel Administrator,* November 1975, pp. 30–36; and Stanely Nealey, "Determining Worker Preferences among Employee Benefit Programs," *Journal of Applied Psychology* 48(1) (1964):7–12.

Table 5. Stated Worker Preferences Toward Exchanging Portions of Current Income for Alternative Forms of Free Time

Value of tradeoff	Shorter workday vs. pay	Reduced workweek vs. pay	Added vacation vs. pay	Sabbatical leave vs. pay	Earlier retirement vs. pay
Nothing for time	77.0	73.8	57.8	57.9	64.0
2 percent of pay for time	8.7	11.6	23.2	24.4	17.6
5 percent of pay for time	5.8	—	8.5	8.0	8.1
10 percent of pay for time	—	7.6	6.2	4.8	5.9
12 percent of pay for time	5.5	—	—	—	—
15 percent of pay for time	—	—	—	4.8	—
20 percent of pay for time	—	4.5	2.2	—	4.4
30 percent of pay for time	1.6	—	—	—	—
33 percent of pay for time	—	—	2.0	—	—
40 percent of pay for time	—	.9	—	—	—
50 percent of pay for time	1.5	1.6	—	—	—
Total percent	100.0	100.0	100.0	100.0	100.0
Total respondents	954	953	952	951	951

Source: Data cited from results of a national random survey conducted in August 1978 (Fred Best, *Exchanging Earnings for Leisure*, Special Research Monograph, Office of Research and Development, Employment and Training Administration, U.S. Department of Labor, Washington, D.C., 1980).

Note: Column spaces are frequently blank for many tradeoff options because questions dealing with different forms of free time did not always have parallel exchange options.

Questions:

Workday: What is the largest portion of your current yearly income that you would be willing to give up for shorter workdays? (A) nothing; (B) 2 percent (1/50) of your income for 10 minutes off each workday; (C) 5 percent (1/30) of your income for 25 minutes off each workday; (D) 12 percent (1/8) of your income for 1 hour off each workday; (E) 30 percent of your income for 2 hours off each workday; (F) 50 percent (1/2) of your income for 4 hours off each workday.

Workweek: What is the largest portion of your current yearly income that you would be willing to give up for shorter workweeks? (A) nothing; (B) 2 percent (1/50) of your

(continued)

Table 5.   (*Continued*)

income for 50 minutes off 1 workday a week; (C) 10 percent (1/10) of your income for 4 hours off 1 workday a week; (D) 20 percent (1/5) of your income for 1 full workday off each week; (E) 40 percent (4/10) of your income for 2 full workdays off each week; (F) 50 percent (1/2) of your income for 2 full workdays off each week.

Vacation: What is the largest portion of your current yearly income that you would be willing to give up for more paid vacation time? (A) nothing; (B) 2 percent (1/50) of your income for 5 workdays added paid vacation each year; (C) 5 percent (1/20) of your income for 12.5 workdays added paid vacation each year; (D) 10 percent (1/10) of your income for 25 workdays added paid vacation each year; (E) 20 percent (1/5) of your income for 50 workdays added paid vacation each year; (F) 33 percent (1/3) of your income for 87.5 workdays (17.5 workweeks) added paid vacation each year.

Sabbatical: What is the largest portion of your current yearly income that you would be willing to give up in exchange for an extended leave without pay every seventh year? (A) nothing; (B) 2 percent (1/50) of your year income for 7 workweeks' paid leave after six years of work; (C) 5 percent (1/30) of your year income for 17.5 workweeks' paid leave after six years of work; (D) 10 percent (1/10) of your year income for 35 workweeks' paid leave after six years of work; (E) 15 percent (1/20) of your year income for 52 workweeks' (1 workyear) paid leave after six years of work.

Earlier Retirement: What is the largest portion of your current yearly income that you would be willing to give up in exchange for earlier retirement? (A) nothing; (B) 2 percent (1/50) of your year income for earlier retirement at a rate of 5 workdays for every year worked until retirement; (C) 5 percent (1/20) of your year income for earlier retirement at a rate of 12.5 workdays for evey year worked until retirement; (D) 10 percent (1/10) of your year income for earlier retirement at a rate of 25 workdays for every year worked until retirement; (E) 20 percent (1/5) of your income for earlier retirement at a rate of 50 workdays for every year worked until retirement.

responsive to the long-term goals and priorities of the labor force. Ultimately, the success of such efforts depends on the time-income tradeoff preferences of workers and the transfer of aggregate work time into new jobs.[48]

Voluntary Time-Income Tradeoff Options for Individuals
Indications are that many workers would be willing to exchange some part of their current earnings for more free time (see table 5).[49] This has caused a number of persons to suggest that volunteeristic programs might be developed that allow individuals to trade current earnings for more free time, thereby opening job time for those who are unemployed or in danger of being laid off. In response to a severe budget cutback, Santa Clara County in California instigated a program that allowed workers to trade 5 percent of current income for 10.5 days of added paid vacation, 10 percent of earnings for 21 days, and 20 percent for 42 days off. Some 17 percent of the ten thousand county employees

48. Best, *Work Sharing*, 28–44.
49. Best, *Exchanging Earnings for Leisure*.

requested and used one of these tradeoff options during the program's first year of operation. As a result, layoffs were prevented and many employees obtained work time arrangements that they wanted.[50] Other, similar programs have actually created new openings for job seekers.[51] Such programs have catalyzed interest in public policies to encourage employers to provide voluntary time-income tradeoff options to workers.[52]

Neutralization of Payroll Taxes. It is commonly agreed that payroll taxes cause barriers and distortions in the upward and downward adjustment of work time. In the United States, for example, employers must pay payroll taxes for employees for unemployment insurance and social security up to a specified ceiling of yearly individual income. For example, the 1985 taxable earning ceilings for unemployment insurance and social security were $7,000 and $39,600, respectively. These and other ceilings encourage employers to employ fewer workers for longer hours in order to maximize the number of hours of work received that are not taxable. Removal of such ceilings and instigation of a consistent tax rate for all levels of annual pay would remove one barrier to both short- and long-term tradeoffs of income for reduced work time.

Subsidies for Work Time Reduction Options. Government subsidies to attenuate increased employer costs resulting from work time reductions and possibly to provide incentives for implementing options for such reductions would be another means of encouraging time-income tradeoff options. It has been suggested that such incentives might be conditional on the creation or saving of a given portion of jobs with the foregone work time.

To summarize, the notion of sharing work through voluntary time-income tradeoff options is a new, relatively unexplored concept. Preliminary assessment suggests that it may have the potential for fortuitously combining the desire for more time off the job evidenced by a significant portion of today's employees with incentives from the government in order to effectively redistribute employment to those in need of work. Since this exchange of unwanted work for unwanted "leisure" would be essentially voluntary, the resulting redistribution should be beneficial to all. The principal issues to be resolved

50. "Santa Clara Time–Income Tradeoff Options Demonstrate New Approach to Work Time Reform," *NCAWP Newsletter,* National Council for Alternative Work Patterns, Washington, D.C., Spring 1978, p. 6.

51. "Statement of James Hooley," *Leisure Sharing,* Hearings of the Select Committee on Investment Priorities and Objectives, California State Senate, November 1, 1977, pp. 128–35.

52. James Mills, "Leisure Sharing," *State Government,* Spring 1979; and Fred Best, "Voluntary Work Time Reduction: Promising Answer to Social, Economic Transitions," *Work Times,* Summer 1983, pp. 1, 6.

are whether ample jobs could be created in this fashion, whether costs and administrative complications would be acceptable, and whether the policy tools available to government are adequate to stimulate significant creation of trade-off options by employees.

Assessing the Options

A rough comparison of all seventeen work-sharing options is presented in figure 2, which broadly summarizes and cross-references the costs and benefits of each proposal. Each option has been assessed for its likely impacts on (1) cost and productivity, (2) job creation and preservation (replacement of foregone work time with new employment), (3) degree of participation and effect on aggregate unemployment, (4) equitable distribution of costs and benefits among employees and employers, (5) flexibility of implementation and termination, (6) ease of administration and regulation, and (7) secondary social effects.[53] Each area of impact has been broadly categorized for each work-sharing approach as either poor; fair or neutral; excellent or good. These assessments represent the best judgments of the author, and readers may wish to reevaluate proposals for themselves.

If all criteria are given equal weight, only two of the seventeen options appear particularly promising. They are unemployment insurance–supported work sharing and incentives to encourage voluntary time-income tradeoff options for individuals. Eight other options that may merit varying degrees of continued attention include pension systems to encourage earlier retirement, financial aid to encourage longer schooling, worker sabbaticals, adult educational leaves, welfare and income maintenance programs, neutralization of tax incentives for selected fringe benefits, tax incentives for work time reductions, encouragement of flexible benefit options, and neutralization of employer payroll taxes. In most cases, these marginal work-sharing approaches would be promising only with specific modifications or in combinations with other policy options. In two cases, specifically, financial aid to encourage prolonged schooling and income maintenance programs, there is doubt that modifications would produce effective work-sharing programs. Indeed, these two options, and possibly others, were considered worthy of continued attention because of secondary impacts not directly related to the creation or preservation of jobs.

Clearly, the weight given to each of the criteria used in assessing alternative work-sharing policies is subject to much disagreement. Most notably, many work-sharing proposals have been advocated for purposes other than reducing joblessness. Specifically, many of these programs have the potential to increase

53. The criteria used to evaluate alternative work sharing policies is given detailed elaboration in Best, *Work Sharing*, 19–58.

Figure 2. Cross-Impact Analysis of Work-Sharing Policy Options

Work-sharing policy options	Productivity and price stability	Job creation and preservation	Level of participation	Targetability and equity impacts	Flexibility for termination and implementation	Administrative and regulatory viability	Secondary social impacts
1. Earlier retirement	Poor	Fair	Fair	Fair	Poor	Fair	Fair
2. Increased educational opportunity	Poor	Poor	Fair	Fair	Fair	Poor	Excellent
3. Worker sabbatical	Poor	Fair	Poor	Poor	Poor	Fair	Excellent
4. Mid-life educational leaves	Poor	Fair	Fair	Fair	Poor	Fair	Excellent
5. Short-time compensation	Excellent	Excellent	Fair	Excellent	Excellent	Excellent	Poor
6. Welfare and income maintenance	Poor	Poor	Excellent	Poor	Poor	Poor	Poor
7. Overtime restriction	Fair	Fair	Fair	Poor	Poor	Poor	Fair
8. Reduced standard workweek	Poor	Fair	Fair	Poor	Poor	Poor	Poor
9. Mandatory vacation	Fair	Poor	Fair	Poor	Poor	Poor	Poor
10. Compulsory education	Fair	Poor	Poor	Poor	Poor	Poor	Poor
11. Forced retirement	Fair	Poor	Poor	Poor	Poor	Poor	Poor
12. Equalization of tax incentives	Poor	Fair	Excellent	Poor	Poor	Fair	Fair
13. Subsidized fringe benefits	Fair	Poor	Excellent	Excellent	Poor	Poor	Excellent
14. Tax incentives for paid time-off	Fair	Fair	Fair	Excellent	Fair	Fair	Fair
15. Flexible benefit options	Fair	Poor	Fair	Excellent	Excellent	Poor	Excellent
16. Neutralization of payroll taxes	Excellent	Fair	Excellent	Fair	Poor	Fair	Fair
17. Subsidies for tradeoff options	Fair	Fair	Excellent	Excellent	Excellent	Fair	Excellent

Assessment criteria

Key:
Poor
Fair or neutral
Excellent or good

leisure for those seeking more time away from their jobs, address social ineq-
uity and ease economic hardship, relieve time pressures confronting dual-
earner households, increase opportunities for education and retraining, and
improve transitions between work and retirement. Thus, many might argue that
several of the work-sharing options given second-level status in this paper merit
more serious consideration.

WORK SHARING IN THE OVERALL SCHEME OF THINGS

Analysis indicates that the best work-sharing policies, applied
in the most effective ways possible, are not a panacea for the unemployment
problem.[54] Work sharing does not hold the promise of replacing existing employment policies. Work sharing, like other approaches, has some unique
characteristics that make it acceptable and applicable where other employment
policies are resisted and ineffective. Thus, work sharing at its best may hold
some promise as a weapon in the arsenal of approaches that could help reduce
unemployment.

While interest in work sharing is likely to be minimal in coming years, these
policies should not be ignored as solutions for local joblessness and yet unforeseen growth in unemployment. Demographic trends reducing the number of
new entrants into the labor force have combined to reduce unemployment.
However, these trends do not preclude the loss of work within specific firms
and communities. Nor do they preclude the possibility of a general economic
downturn or the prospect of reducing work time in response to technological
change.[55] In some fashion, unemployment is likely to become a problem again.
When this happens, the most promising forms of work sharing could provide a
valuable supplement to existing employment policies.

54. Ibid., 19–186.
55. Historically, technology change has created more jobs by increasing the demand
for lower priced goods made possible by increased productivity. At the same time,
reduced worktime has also historically occurred with increased technological innovation, both as a dividend for increased productivity and a means of maintaining full
employment.

| | | | | | | | Planning for Work Sharing: The Promise and Problems of Egalitarian Work Time Reduction

HERBERT J. GANS

One of the biggest questions about the future of the American economy is its ability to create new jobs and to maintain the old ones for its labor force. The major reasons for this question are by now familiar: the emergence of a competitive world economy in which high-wage countries lose jobs to low-wage countries; and the coming of computers (and eventually robots), which are eliminating jobs everywhere. Consequently, no one can tell whether enough jobs will be available for American workers in future decades.

This paper discusses what role work sharing—the policy to reduce work time so that more jobs are created or saved—can play over this period. My paper was planned from the start to supplement Fred Best's (in this volume) and complement it in three principle ways.

First, it deals only with deliberate work sharing policies specifically instituted to reduce unemployment in an *egalitarian* fashion. I emphasize "egalitarian" to distinguish work sharing from other work time reduction policies, notably involuntary part-time employment and premature retirement, which are favored by employers. While these can also reduce joblessness, they do so in an unequal fashion because they may victimize some workers.

Second, the paper focuses particularly on the problems of bringing about work sharing, describes some recent European experience in doing so, and applies that experience and other data to the distinctive political and economic situation in the United States. Third, it treats work sharing as a possible future policy about which we know virtually nothing so far. Since it may be many

The research reported in this paper was supported by a 1984 Research Fellowship from the German Marshall Fund of the United States.

years before the economic and political times are ripe for the implementation of work sharing, sociologists (and of course others) have an opportunity to conduct policy-relevant research to help answer some important questions that could help avert some missteps and mistakes if and when work sharing becomes a reality. Consequently, throughout the paper I will suggest salient topics for study but without constantly saying that they deserve study.

THE CONTEXT

Any discussion of work sharing must begin with *the* prior research issue: assessing whether the job effects of the world economy and automation will actually be serious enough to make deliberate work sharing necessary. In the late 1980s, the very possibility of this happening might seem absurd to many, for the official unemployment rate has ranged between 5 and 7 percent in recent years, and closer to the former figure most of the time. Furthermore, many economists are predicting a labor shortage for the 1990s when the so-called baby bust is expected to reduce sharply the number of young workers.

In reality, however, the employment picture looks far less optimistic. The labor force participation rates of blacks and other minority males continues to decrease, and once workers who have left, or never entered, the labor force because they are discouraged about the chances of finding a decent job are counted, the actual jobless rate is nearly double the official one. In addition, some of the many low-paid service jobs created in the 1980s may not be permanent; and even the labor shortage of the 1990s is not guaranteed, for new immigrants willing to work long hours at low pay may be invited, legally or illegally. Consequently, *actual* unemployment rates may remain in double digit figures.

Since most Americans, other than those in depressed areas, are aware only of the official jobless figures, unemployment is currently not a serious political issue. However, in the longer run, the loss of U.S. jobs to foreign workers is likely to continue as long as major wage differentials remain—and even if the differentials with Southeast Asia should begin to disappear, new industrializing countries (for example, in Latin America and Africa) will outbid Southeast Asia for low-wage jobs. (Moreover, sometime in the future, many of the hundreds of millions of workers in the People's Republic of China may be offered on the world labor market.)

To be sure, in the long run, some of the low-wage work now done overseas will be sufficiently automated so that it can be done in the United States, once transport costs are considered. Others of the foreign jobs will be taken by new illegal immigrants to the United States who are willing to work for very low wages; but immigrant low-wage labor remains a short-term proposition since the children of immigrants, legal or illegal, will be Americans and will ask for "American" pay and "American" working hours. Consequently, the very long run outlook is for a probably permanent shortage of jobs—and this without even considering the long-run impact of automation.

During the 1980s, there has appeared to be agreement that computers and related forms of automation both create and eliminate American jobs, in manufacturing and also in a number of services.[1] The disagreement is mostly over how the gains will compare to the losses and what will happen in the long run. Thus, researchers should try to develop alternative scenarios.

The scenario I find most credible suggests that initially new labor-saving technologies create such a burst of new opportunities and demands that they produce a net gain in jobs even as they begin to eliminate the ones for which they were introduced. Later, when these technologies and the new opportunities they have spawned are institutionalized, the loss of jobs continues but no new jobs are created, and indeed, the new technology will then begin to eliminate some of the new jobs it produced during the initial phase.

The eventual research task is to determine whether this or some other scenario will be played out, but the initial task is simply to estimate how many and what kinds of jobs will be gained and lost in the foreseeable future. So far, such estimates have been based on economists' mathematical models and projections from available data (for example, Leontief and Duchin 1986). As the actual experience with computers and robots increases, however, sociologists may be able to undertake case studies of firms and industries and judge from the processes and effects they can observe what might happen elsewhere in the future. I side with those who believe that unless current industrial, capitalist, and world competitive trends change, total job loss is eventually apt to be massive (Leontief 1983; Draper 1985; Shaiken 1986).[2] At the same time, *involuntary* part-time employment, which is only a somewhat lesser evil, will also be massive.

Consequently, deliberate work sharing in the United States will surely be needed eventually. However, even at best, work sharing can be only one policy among many to deal with joblessness (see Best, in this volume). In addition, the United States is going to have to deliberately create jobs in ways that have never

1. However, there is even disagreement among economists over whether U.S. manufacturing unemployment has actually declined. The prime debate has been between Lawrence (1983) and Bluestone (1984).

2. There is also an urgent need for a study of the science and art of projecting, for example to determine what factors (other than available data, method, and ideology) result in optimistic and pessimistic projections.

been tried before. Here too are opportunities for needed research: thorough case studies and social histories of the public experiments and demonstration projects in job creation that have taken place in America ever since the New Deal, as well as of the private, civilian bursts of job creation associated with the 1980s. Also useful are studies that identify past obstacles to deliberate job creation, and ways in which these have been or could be overcome. In recent decades, the most effective job creation machinery has come out of the Pentagon, even though more civilian jobs—and productive ones—could have been created for the same amount of public money (Melman 1970: chap. 8).

However, private industry, the voting citizenry—and the corporate funders of congressional election campaigns—have so far supplied political support mainly for what I call military Keynesianism. Concurrently, the citizenry has been sufficiently ambivalent about the governmental creation of civilian jobs that the opponents of government participation in the economy could successfully oppose it. Further efforts must be devoted to understanding why people are ready or resigned to pay taxes for weapons and under what conditions they would be more willing to pay them for the improvement of public works and public services. Reluctance to pay taxes for these in fact increases in bad economic times when the jobs are most needed, although it is possible that when the working and middle classes themselves need created jobs in large numbers, their political ambivalence will decline.

Nonetheless, it is also possible that their political ambivalence will not decline sufficiently or that they will lack the power to force the government to undertake the needed job saving and creation measures. In that case, the United States could become polarized not only between good jobs and bad (see Bellin and Miller, in this volume), but also among people with full-time jobs, those with part-time ones, and those without jobs, with the full-time workers making up less than half the population.

This polarization is already present between the so-called underclass and the rest of the population, but it has so far taken mainly racial forms. If that polarization should begin to be viewed as concerning jobs, and if and when it becomes serious enough to be visible, the fully employed could use their political influence to obtain, not jobs, but public programs defending them against political and other unrest generated by their less fortunate fellow citizens. After all, in bad times the employed have often perceived the unemployed as their enemies. This scenario is made more reasonable by the fact that the jobless are frequently even less active politically than when they are employed (Schlozman and Verba 1979; Buss and Redburn 1983). In addition, bottling up unrest remains both easier and cheaper than serious job saving and creation. Work sharing is neither easy nor cheap, but it would help to prevent the possibility of a society divided into occupational haves and have-nots.

THE CHALLENGES OF WORK SHARING

The rest of my paper treats both the possibilities and problems of work sharing in America, drawing to some extent on existing experience in a number of West European countries.[3] I shall not survey their specific activities because the details would require a book of their own, and one that would be out-of-date as soon as it was written. Suffice it to say that most countries have undertaken mixed egalitarian and inegalitarian kinds of work time reduction.[4]

During the early 1980s, however, the primary emphasis in work sharing was the reduction of the *average* workyear or workweek. For example, Belgium, the Netherlands, and some other countries have been in the process of moving away from the forty- to the thirty-eight-hour and thirty-six-hour week, and some West German labor unions struck for a thirty-five-hour week. There has also been talk, outside the governments, of long-range plans for an average thirty-two-, twenty-eight-, even twenty-four-hour week—at which point the entire labor force operates on what is in effect a part-time basis.

Before any of these plans can be implemented, in Europe or the United States, a number of issues and problems must be dealt with. My discussion will focus on five sets of these.

Can Work Sharing Work?

The first issue is understanding the effectiveness of work sharing. An early result of the application of work sharing in Europe was the discovery that a given reduction of working hours did not create or save the equivalent number of jobs. In bad economic times, private firms as well as

3. I spent part of my German Marshall Fund Fellowship in Western Europe in the spring of 1985, talking with researchers on worktime reduction, sociologists of work, economists, union officials, political leaders, and others, mainly in Holland, England, West Germany, Belgium, and France. I am particularly indebted to my Dutch colleague and friend Leon Deben for his help with the Dutch and Belgian interviews and initial data collection. Before and after my European trips, I have also collected data through correspondence and hope to return to Western Europe for further field-work when changes in work-sharing policy and practice occur. I should note that I have tried whenever possible to cite English publications and reports in this paper.

4. For a review of mid-decade developments in the ten European countries then involved in some work-sharing activities, see Kaeding (1986:45–62). Since then, the amount of such activities and news about them have declined considerably. The best way of keeping up with European and English work-time reduction innovations are the reports of the European Trade Union Institute and of the Commission of the European Communities in Brussels; the newsletter "News," of the European Centre for Work and Society in Maastricht, Holland; and the *European Industrial Relations Review*, published in London. A particularly useful review, but not in English, is the *Internationale Chronik zur Arbeits-marktpolitik* (International chronicle on the political economy of labor markets), published by the Wissenschaftszentrum für Sozialforschung in Berlin.

public agencies look for a variety of ways of cutting costs and increasing productivity, and work sharing has generally been instituted under such conditions. Indeed, agreements to initiate it have often been accompanied by a variety of ancillary policies, ranging from the reduction or elimination of teabreaks (White and Ghobodian 1984: chap. 7) to increased automation to cut the need for labor.

Consequently, the number of jobs saved and created by work sharing depends in part on various labor-saving policies that are negotiated at the same time; and one set of studies must determine which ancillary policies have the fewest negative effects on job maintenance and creation. This must accompany more basic studies of the number of jobs created and saved by the various kinds of work sharing schemes described by Best (in this volume) in various workplaces and industries, one eventual aim being to create a model of which kinds of work sharing are most effective in different industries and occupations. Needless to say, such empirical work cannot now be done in the United States. Instead, historians should attempt to estimate the job effects of the many instances of work time reduction, deliberate and otherwise, that have taken place in the United States at various times over the last century.

Systematic empirical work to determine the job effects of deliberate work sharing is just beginning in Europe. Indeed, so far the most often cited data are those assembled by the Dutch government (for example, Dutch Department of Social Affairs and Employment 1985). Generally speaking, about 30 to 40 percent of the reduced work time turns into new full-time jobs, although the replacement ratio goes up to 75 percent when worktime is reduced in public agencies (Dutch Department of Social Affairs and Employment 1985; Visser 1986:38–40). In other words, when the average workweek is reduced 10 percent, from 40 to 36, 3 to 4 percent of the total time, not 10, turns into jobs added—or saved from elimination. A 5 percent reduction in work time appears at best to halt the increase in joblessness.

These figures are only suggestive, for they will vary in different economies and polities, on whether employers can obtain labor-saving tradeoffs during negotiations with unions and governments, and on other factors. Moreover, early figures derived from a small European country cannot be applied to the United States. Still, these data indicate empirically that work sharing can be only a partial solution to joblessness—even though reducing the unemployment rate by 3 to 4 percent is not an insignificant achievement.

Some Political Obstacles – The West European Experience

The second problem is the political feasibility of work sharing, for despite its seeming attractiveness work sharing does not so far have much political support. Indeed, European observations suggest that the absence of support could be built partly into the policy itself, at least under present economic arrangements.

The historical evidence indicates that in good economic times, workers support the reduction of workhours and the extra leisure time that comes with it, while employers find it a useful policy for holding on to their workers. Even in the late 1970s, when rates of joblessness were already rising, polls indicated that workers still said they were ready to give up some work time to obtain more leisure, both in the United States and in Western Europe (see Best, in this volume, table 5; Engfer, Hinrichs, Offe, and Wiesenthal 1983).[5]

Once double-digit unemployment arrived in several West European countries, however, and work sharing was suggested as an antiunemployment policy, workers' attitudes and behavior seem to have changed. Several of my European informants indicated that workers now preferred additional income—and the freedom to buy further leisure time with their own money instead—although in hard times, they also wanted the freedom to put off that purchase. These workers were not particularly enthusiastic about lower work time in order to reduce joblessness among their fellow workers, although they accepted fewer hours in some instances. For example, in 1984, the West German printers and steelworkers engaged in a bitter strike to bring the workweek down from 40 to 35 hours, but after they lost the strike, obtaining only a 38½-hour week, it appeared that they had struck mainly in support of their union leadership, not of work sharing (Hinrichs, Roche, and Wiesenthal 1984:13–19).

Unions in Belgium and Holland have encountered similar reluctance among their members. As I noted earlier, during hard times the employed may feel threatened by the jobless, although we do not yet know how this varies with economic and political conditions, workplaces, and workers. Thus, older workers might support work sharing more if the jobless were their children and other relatives. Conversely, they seem to feel less supportive when the jobless include a large number of immigrants, especially those with dark skin. These are, however, almost always the first victims of unemployment in West European countries, as they are in the United States.

Moreover, most work-sharing schemes have involved some loss of total income, and workers are probably unhappier about the income loss than about the idea of work sharing. As a result, the Dutch unions decided to alternate years of work time reduction with years of wages increases, and the thirty-six-hour workweek that was achieved in some industries in 1986 seems to have been connected to the wage increases obtained in 1985.

5. However, even in good times, workers have also—but not always—expressed an unwillingness to participate in work sharing to help the jobless (Visser 1986:46–47).

Employers have so far been ambivalent about work sharing. Generally speaking they are not enthusiastic because the policy normally increases their costs. Even if workers are paid less in total wages, firms must hire more people, and both the hiring process and the overhead connected with a larger total work force increases the total cost of production. As a result, the thirty-six-hour week has been achieved most easily when employers are able to make a tradeoff.

In Holland and Belgium, the most successful deal was fewer average hours for the workers in exchange for more operating hours for the firm, and specifically, allowing firms to add new shifts. This deal is attractive to capital-intensive manufacturing firms that want to keep their machinery going twenty-four hours a day seven days a week. Some have gone as far as to offer twenty-four-hour-a-week jobs to keep the machines going on weekends, attracting mostly young people, who are willing to work two shifts of twelve hours each.[6] Such tradeoffs are not helpful to most firms, including labor-intensive ones, however. Still, if the early European experience is typical, the long-term success of work sharing depends on developing the right tradeoffs for all varieties of employers, at least when their cooperation is needed to reduce unemployment.

Governments also have been ambivalent supporters. On the one hand, they have initiated the most radical work time reduction arrangements, for example, the thirty-two-hour weeks instituted by the Dutch government for entry-level jobs in public agencies.[7] On the other hand, governmental decisions have reflected the diversity in the political arena. Most socialist parties are enthusiastic, except when they encounter worker opposition; but even conservative parties and governments (or center, center–left, and center–right coalitions) have at times gone along with work sharing, no doubt because of double-digit unemployment rates. In fact, in 1982, the center–right Dutch government pressured the unions to go along with work sharing.

The voting public seems to have been mostly quiescent so far. In 1986, the Dutch socialists failed to win the election despite a 14 percent unemployment rate and the Labor party's promise to move more rapidly on work sharing and other jobs policies. The unemployed who would have been the main benefici-

---

6. The scheme also attracted home buyers in need of extra money, but they, like some of the young people, also held other jobs during the week so that the weekend shift did not always create extra jobs (Denys, Hedebouw, and Lambert, 1985)

7. The thirty-two-hour week was only temporary, and the young workers subsequently worked the normal full-time week of thirty-eight hours. Meanwhile, the government also saved some money. However, I describe this scheme mostly to show that in Western Europe governments can frequently take the lead in implementing new policies and act as role models for the rest of the country. In the United States, the federal government currently follows innovations adopted by private enterprise.

aries are, however, virtually as inactive in electoral politics in Holland as in the United States.

The only regular supporters of work sharing have been union leaders, who have favored it both for ideological reasons and for the larger total membership it brings them. As a result, centralized unions in which the leadership is powerful have been more supportive of work sharing so far then decentralized ones, in which incumbent workers have used their influence to express their ambivalence.

Work time reduction issues are discussed annually in the Netherlands when union contracts are renegotiated, and in late 1986 some of the large employers decided to move from the now nearly universal thirty-eight hours to thirty-six hours. Others rejected further reductions, however, and the most comprehensive analysis of Dutch work sharing concluded in 1986 that "a further general cut beyond 38 weekly hours in the near future seems unlikely. . . . Given the wage interests of the employed and the counterpressures of employers, its potential as a solution is limited" (Visser 1986:6, 52). Meanwhile, the Belgians, who had also begun to move toward the thirty-six-hour week, then decided to stay with the thirty-eight-hour week, mostly because other economic problems are more critical. The Thatcher government turned down any further movement in English work sharing beyond thirty-nine hours in 1984, and by the mid-1980s West Germany and France appear to have stopped around a thirty-eight- to thirty-nine-hour average as well. Interestingly, Sweden has so far eschewed workweek reductions, but it has kept both its unemployment rate and the annual numbers of hours worked lower than anywhere else in Europe (or in the United States), the latter by instituting long vacations, parental leaves, and other methods of indirect work sharing.

Nevertheless, it is premature to suggest that work sharing in Western Europe is finished. On the contrary, if economic conditions require work sharing, the gradual but slow movement toward the shorter workweek could be resumed. At this writing, however, almost all countries are resorting to the inegalitarian work time reduction policies favored by employers, such as involuntary part-time employment for the young and involuntary early retirement for fifty-five-year-olds.

Implications for the United States

The preceding observations provide only a background for the U.S. situation. For one thing, the United States lacks any kind of effective jobs policy, other than military Keynesianism (see Skocpol, in this volume). Also, as I noted earlier, the official rates of unemployment have remained so low that political support for a government jobs policy has not been very strong, except in the depressed economic regions. However, they have so far been outnumbered by the highly populous areas, where there are enough jobs, at least for whites. The Republican party has never viewed the unemployed as potential constituents, and the Democrats know that the unemployed still interested in voting for a major party must choose them whatever the party's policy.[8]

In addition, interest in work sharing is still virtually nonexistent. The national AFL-CIO was long committed to the seniority principle, accepting job loss for younger workers rather than work sharing. Despite signs of some interest in work sharing among a few AFL-CIO leaders and staffers, the older union members, now in the majority, may not favor giving up seniority for work time reduction. The UAW has been in favor of work sharing in principle for many years but is hampered by the seasonal nature of auto production. There is also some evidence of opposition from middle management and supervisory levels (Best 1985:27).

Actually, most workers and employers do not even know that work sharing exists. Even the program of spreading *temporary* layoffs among all workers, with unemployment insurance funds paying the lost wages—a standard feature of jobs policy in most West European countries for decades—is only just beginning in the United States. Called unemployment insurance–supported work sharing or short-time compensation, by the mid-1980s it had been adopted by fewer than a dozen states (MaCoy and Morand 1984).

In a media-saturated society, introducing and familiarizing people with a new policy can take place fairly quickly, and if all other conditions were favorable, it would not be difficult to familiarize people with work sharing. Currently, however, no constituencies are interested in beginning the process. The United States lacks powerful unions and a labor party, and the West European "social partnership," in which labor and management nudge each other toward a mutually acceptable policy, is absent here.

The presently unemployed are a potential constituency but are not likely to become a real one because they know they lack the power to initiate change. If unemployment increases sharply, does so across the country, hits large numbers of young white males, and threatens many more, a worker constituency might come into existence. Another political constituency includes old workers who might like shorter work times but who all put job security first during hard times.[9]

One major research area is the identification of other potential constituencies

8. Only Michael Harrington and the tiny Democratic Socialists of America have consistently supported work sharing.
9. However, in October 1986 the senior citizens' lobby, which does not exist in Europe, was able to end federal legislation requiring retirement in the United States at age seventy, eliminating what little work-sharing potential this law has had in recent years.

for work sharing, the conditions under which they would emerge, and the incentives they need to support the policy. For instance, I wonder to what extent and when the giant manufacturers and sellers of consumer goods would become concerned about rising unemployment and interested in work sharing, since increasing joblessness would mean that fewer people can buy their goods. Also, given the right incentives, perhaps some old workers would be prepared to divide their jobs with young people who would eventually replace them, a scheme that has been tried in several European countries. Other incentives might interest more Americans in the four- to six-week vacations now standard in Western Europe—at least those who need not maximize their working hours and incomes so as to be able to buy a house, send their children to private colleges, or pay for medical expenses not covered by insurance.

Even so, whatever the process, it appears that in the United States the federal government would have to exert most of the political effort to bring about work sharing, which means that national politicians would be required to expend political capital on a new policy rather than share that expenditure with labor and management, as in Western Europe. Thus, it becomes especially important to identify as many potential constituencies as possible as well as the conditions under which they would reduce the politicians' risks.

Judging by past experience, there are yet other political objections to work sharing that would have to be overcome. For one thing, it can be perceived as a pessimistic policy insofar as it assumes a static economy in which the unemployment has to be shared. As a result it is vulnerable not only to the general American optimism about future economic growth, but also to cargo-cult politics, which promises a return to past patterns of such growth. President Reagan was hardly the first American politician to demonstrate the appeal of cargo-cult politics.

Work sharing is also vulnerable to liberal and Left arguments that object to the rationing of work at a time when public works and public services are badly needed in the United States and when poverty must be reduced both here and in the Third World. Such arguments are valid if the needed public funds can be found, and, as I noted earlier, work sharing can never be more than one policy against joblessness.

Actually, it is possible that given the dearth of constituencies and the abundance of political and other obstacles, the best time to initiate work sharing in the United States is in periods of prosperity, when it is instituted for reasons other than increasing employment. This would coincide with recent historical processes, for the average workweek declined most sharply in the United States (and elsewhere) during the postwar affluence. The job-saving and job-creating benefits would, however, persist in bad times, since work time normally does not return to past levels.

If work sharing is in fact best initiated in good times, the previously mentioned historical studies are needed of the earlier instances of work time reduction in the United States, at various periods across the country and in individual
industries, occupations, and even workplaces. The research should focus on the
job effects but also treat the economic, political, and other conditions that
produced the reductions.

The Money Problem

A third problem, itself a political obstacle, is the likelihood
that work sharing also means some income reduction for the workers involved.
While it is easy to favor reducing work time without cutting paychecks, the
resulting increase in labor costs is probably not going to be economically
feasible, except when work sharing is instituted in periods of prosperity. Because so much of the political risk of introducing work sharing falls on the
government in the United States, however, it is also hard to imagine that
politicians who need to be elected or reelected will support a policy that
requires them to vote explicitly to reduce their constituents' paychecks, especially in hard times.

Consequently, ways must be found to cut work time while maximizing
worker income. Perhaps the most feasible solution is to exchange work time
reductions for tax benefits. An additional possibility, probably less feasible, is
to tax profits obtained from automation and return them either to the jobless or
to participants in work-sharing programs. In all instances, the funds must be
large enough to satisfy the workers, yet small enough not to upset the employers (or the general public, which has to pay for them one way or another); in
any scenario savings are realized in unemployment insurance and welfare
benefits.

A long-range money problem also deserves to be put on the research agenda:
the possibility that if work sharing and work time reduction generally proceed
too far people will not earn enough money to live on, so that the historic tie
between work and income will have to be severed (Macarov 1980). For example, if the average workweek were to decline to twenty-four hours someday, it is
not at all certain that workers would earn a sufficient amount for even a scaled-
down version of the American standard of living. Even now, many American
households must work seventy to seventy-five person-hours a week to obtain
sufficient income, and the forty-eight person-hours of two breadwinners will
not be enough.

One solution is a change in families or households that increases the number
of breadwinners. Immigrants normally turn to this solution in order to save
money to send home or to put away for their own futures, but they treat it as a
temporary measure. It is hard to imagine Americans giving up the nuclear

family norm, but economic realities have forced changes in family or household structures before. In any case a more reasonable expectation—and proposal—is for government to step in with some income support for nearly everyone, perhaps with a demogrant, or what Roberts (1982), in a comprehensive analysis of this problem, has called a national dividend. This in turn means that eventually, work sharing will lead to pressure for some redistribution of income and wealth. However, the same pressure is likely to be generated by other work time reduction schemes, by the shortage of jobs itself—and in fact by any set of events that reduces the ability of large numbers of people to earn a living.

West European analysts have already been debating such scenarios, partly because European unemployment rates are high, but also because unemployed and unemployable people there are paid higher unemployment insurance and welfare benefits than are paid in the United States. As a result, Western Europe must think about income and wealth distribution much earlier than the United States, where benefits are far lower, of shorter duration, and more punitively administered.[10]

Problems of Implementation

A fourth group of issues surrounding work sharing involves determining how it is best implemented. Some of the implementation questions are themselves political, for while work sharing probably has to be instituted at the national level, at the same time it must be decentralized enough to be workable across industries and occupations. If one judges by the West European experience, the first issue is to determine what kinds of deals must be struck with employers and workers to make the policy attractive, and then to figure out the various costs and benefits of these deals, since they are likely to result in other alterations in the economy. To quote Visser once more: "The major breakthrough . . . of recent years was not the abandonment of the 40 hour week, but the disconnection of working and operating hours and its inherent multiplication of different hours-regimes and contractual forms. This has added in important ways to the ongoing decentralization of Dutch industrial relations" (Visser 1986:50).

Visser is referring only to manufacturing firms in a very small national economy. The complications multiply in the United States because of the diversity inherent in a continent-size economy. Although these complications might seem insurmountable, the fact is that working hours have been reduced

10. In Western Europe, welfare benefits have been about 60–70 percent of the median income, whereas in the United States the average welfare benefit (including foodstamps) is less than 25 percent of median family income, rising to about 40 percent of median income in the two or three most generous states.

regularly in the United States over the last century, and the last major reduction, from the forty-eight or more hours before the Great Depression to the forty hours after the end of World War II was in part the result of government action in 1938. If federal legislation called for the thirty-six- or thirty-two-hour week, or the forty-six-week workyear, both private industry and public agencies would find ways of obeying the law.

The critical issues are deciding, first, what kind of legislation would be most desirable in terms of the needs of the workers, employers, and the economy, particularly the maintenance of productivity; and second, what kind of flexibility and exclusion would have to be built in for industries that cannot go along, such as seasonal ones, as well as for workers, notably many of the self-employed. In addition, other flexibilities must be built in for small firms, which have more difficulty with work sharing than large ones.

Third, organizational and legislative planners must figure out how to discourage a variety of dysfunctional consequences, for example, the likely increase in moonlighting as work time decreases. This could be harmful if people take up jobs that would otherwise be available for sharing, thus adding to unemployment; but it might also be useful if the moonlighters could add job-producing stimuli to the economy. Studies of present-day moonlighting would suggest the effects it now has, and whether legislating against it would be useful or would simply drive such work more deeply into the off-the-books economy.[11]

Fourth, existing experience with short-time compensation schemes in the United States indicates that they succeed more easily when old workers are willing to share with young ones, so that the latter need not lose their jobs (Lammers and Lockwood 1984:72–75). In order to turn work time legislation into work *sharing,* workplaces now marked by seniority or other forms of hierarchy require democratization—although this requirement already appears to be necessary for the maintenance of productivity, worker morale, and other reasons.

Fifth, organizational planners must also figure out how executives and other high-level staff can participate in work sharing. So far, the West European countries have treated the policy as one suited only for production and lower-level clerical workers, but if and when work sharing becomes more widespread, such practice will be neither desirable nor politically possible. Executives tend to think that they cannot share their jobs with others, particularly in firms with pyramidical hierarchies, and researchers must discover whether they are correct. If they are, then the challenge is to figure out organizational alternatives in which high-status workers can share the work time of low-status workers, but without impairing the functioning of the organizations. Studies of

11. A more general study should seek to guess at the job-creating potential of the off-the-books economy.

whether and how top-level decision making can be shared would help to indicate how much large workplaces can be democratized.

ISSUES OF TIME, FAMILY, AND IDENTITY

A fifth question about work sharing, one that comes up if work time is reduced significantly, is how people will spend the extra leisure time. Moreover, should those with shorter work hours fail to ask how they will use this time, others will ask for them. Virtually all proposed reductions in work-time in America have been met by anxiety, mostly on the part of higher status groups, about what the "lower orders" would do with their extra hours; to what extent they would spend them "wastefully" in taverns, gambling dens, or in front of the television set, or whether they would choose "prosocial" activities that please or do not threaten higher status groups.

The question has a fairly obvious cultural and political class agenda, but since it will surely be asked, researchers might as well begin to study, historically and sociologically, how people who have obtained extra spare time have chosen to spend it. For example, areas of study might include the ways people have spent newfound leisure time when the workweek was cut from forty-eight to forty hours after World War II, and from forty to thirty-five in many offices over the last decade. A directly related study should estimate what new leisure industries they have encouraged and how many jobs have been created in *them*.

While I doubt that most people will have trouble filling up a few extra hours a week or long vacations, I also doubt that they will necessarily choose leisure. A sizable number will search for additional productive activities, including moonlighting, even if the financial gain is minimal.[12] Others may devote the extra time to familial activities. Some social planners have in fact suggested that young parents should be the initial beneficiaries of work time reduction—supported with generous family allowances—although researchers should also determine how many young parents are willing to spend the extra time with their young children.

THE PROMISE OF WORK SHARING

My analysis has so far treated work sharing as most analysts have treated it: as a policy full of problems, some not easily solved. There is, however, another perspective on work sharing, one that stems from a long tradition of utopian thought. In this tradition, work sharing is the ultimate goal

12. For example, many of the New York longshoremen who are paid their full annual incomes in exchange for being replaced by automation sell small goods from the trunks of their cars (DiFazio 1985:103). However, they spend even more time in grandfatherly baby-sitting activities.

of modern industrialism, the vision being that machines do the strenuous, dirty, and boring work as well as work requiring long hours. As a result, human beings can spend their lives working in the occupations and avocational pursuits of their choice for a smaller percentage of their total waking lives (for example, Bellamy 1888; Brown 1970).

Whatever the difficulties of work sharing, it would not do to lose sight of the utopian vision—or to treat it as merely utopian—for whenever work time reduction has taken place during periods of prosperity it has reflected that vision, even if not always by intent. In short, work sharing can and must be thought about also as a positive policy that eliminates the unpleasant and unnecessary and above all the harmful aspects of work even as researchers, planners, and then politicians figure out how to deal with its problems.

One way to legitimate and support that vision would be for researchers to start thinking about some components and consequences of such a vision. Probably the first question must be to determine how much of the vision can ever be feasible; for example, how much work time can be reduced and how much wealth can be increased and redistributed so that all people can earn enough income. Also, on the assumption that not all dirty and harmful work can be automated, scenarios might be developed to see how people can be recruited and properly rewarded for doing undesirable but necessary jobs.

Moreover, if we assume that the workweek would decline to twenty-four hours someday, thereby turning everyone into a part-time worker, it is relevant to ask whether work can, and should, remain a major supplier of social usefulness, self-respect, and identity. What could realistically replace work—or would people hold on to these social and emotional functions of work whatever their hours, for example, by inventing new nonwork activities that would make them feel productive, useful, and respected.[13]

Furthermore, what might family and community life be like with a universal twenty-four-hour workweek? Some Dutch academics with whom I spoke were already talking personally about a future in which each "partner" put in that kind of workweek, with the remaining time being devoted to family and personal pursuits. However, what might less-than-happy families or those lacking the academic's time-consuming personal pursuits do? Could there be a revival of the family farm, automated enough to eliminate the strenuous work, or would many people copy the increasingly widespread practice of spending as much

13. It would also be interesting to consider what will happen to the so-called Protestant but actually universal work ethic and to look at how workaholics would be treated. Would they be celebrated as people who might produce more jobs for others, damned as deviants who hog work that could be shared, or stigmatized as manifesting an antisocial addiction to work? Still, the most significant issue is what, if anything, would replace work as a factor in stratification and as a sorter of people into classes.

time as possible in weekend or summer houses, thus decentralizing community life yet further? Or would the reduction of work lead to yet more individualistic living and other arrangements before and after children are raised? Needless to say, many other possibilities could be considered and explored.

ON RESEARCH ABOUT WORK SHARING

In all but the last part of the paper I have suggested research that would be useful in the eventual planning for work sharing, because there is enough lead time before anyone in the United States is likely to take a serious interest in it. Such research will probably not be funded, of course, partly because of the topic and partly because the research methodology cannot always be strictly scientific as that term is defined nowadays. Some questions may be amenable to the usual empirical approaches, but many require the identification of deviant cases, present and past, which must then be used as indicators of behavior that might someday be associated with work sharing. Yet other studies require projections from such data to an uncertain future and many will have to rely on educated guessing.

Consequently, researchers who involve themselves with the kinds of questions I have raised probably have to believe in the desirability and viability of work sharing. They may also have to endure some skepticism from their colleagues. Still, they might discover some years later that what they have done will suddenly be in great demand, as did the handful of social scientists who studied poverty before it became a hot topic in the mid-1960s and again 20 years later.

To be sure, utopian visions and scenarios do not lend themselves to conventional policy research, and at first hearing may in fact sound like science fiction. Still, such visions and scenarios should be taken seriously, and I think they can lend themselves to thought-experiments that may also feed back on our understanding of current questions of work, family, community, and the like. In addition, they require sociologists to think about visions of future ways of life, a not-undesirable departure for a discipline that is today too often mired in the immediate present or in the timeless world of abstract theories and sociological "laws." Sociologists should not become utopianists, but some of us could do worse than figure out what is realistic in the societies of utopian writers, or better still, construct the outlines of better societies ourselves.

REFERENCES

Bellamy, Edward. 1888. *Looking Backward: 2000–1887*. Boston: Houghton Mifflin.
Best, Fred. 1985. "Work Sharing: An Underused Policy for Combating Unemploy-

ment?" Paper presented at the 1985 Meeting of the American Sociological Association.

Bluestone, Barry. 1984. "Is Deindustrialization a Myth?" *Annals of the American Academy of Political and Social Science* 475:39–51.

Brown, James Cooke. 1970. *The Troika Incident: The Coming of a Viable Human Society*. Garden City, N.Y.: Doubleday.

Buss, Terry F., and F. Stevens Redburn. 1983. *Shutdown at Youngstown: Public Policy for Mass Unemployment*. Albany: State University of New York Press.

Denys, Jan, Georges Hedebouw, and Magda Lambert. 1985. *Nieuwe Vormen van Arbeidstijdregeling* (New models of worktime arrangements). Hoger Instituut vor der Arbeid, Katholieke Universiteit Leuven, mimeo.

DiFazio, William. 1985. *Longshoremen: Community and Resistance on the Brooklyn Waterfront*. S. Hadley, MA.: Bergin and Garvey.

Draper, Roger. 1985. "The Golden Arm." *New York Review of Books,* October 24, pp. 46–52.

Dutch Department of Social Affairs and Employment. 1985. "Dutch National Report for the OECD/MAS Evaluation on 'Measures to Reduce Working Time.' " The Hague: The Department, mimeo.

Engfer, Uwe, Karl Hinrichs, Claus Offe, and Helmut Wiesenthal. 1983. "Arbeitszeitsituation und Arbeitszeitverkuerzung in der Sicht der Beschaeftigen" (The workers' view of worktime conditions and reductions). *Mitteilungen aus der Arbeitsmarkt- und Berufsforschung* 16:91–105.

Hinrichs, Karl, William K. Roche, and Helmut Wiesenthal. 1984. "Working Time Policy as Class-Oriented Strategy: Unions and Shorter Working Hours in Great Britain and West Germany." *Arbeitspapiere Aus Dem Arbeitskreis,* no. 7. Paderborn, West Germany: Arbeitskreis Sozialwissenschaftliche Arbeitsmarktforschung.

Kaeding, Klaus. 1988. "Adaptations in the Labour Market with regard to Reductions in Individual Working Time." In Commission of the European Communities, *Social Europe No. 1.* Brussels: The Commission.

Lammers, John C., and Timothy Lockwood. 1984. "The California Experiment." In *Short-Time Compensation: A Formula for Work Sharing,* edited by Ramelle MaCoy and Martin J. Morand. New York: Pergamon.

Lawrence, Robert Z. 1983. "The Myth of Deindustrialization." *Challenge* 26:12–21.

Leontief, Wassily. 1983. "Technological Advance, Economic Growth and Distribution of Income." *Population and Development Review* 9:403–10.

Leontief, Wassily, and Faye Duchin. 1986. *The Future Impact of Automation on Workers*. New York: Oxford University Press.

Macarov, David. 1980. *Work and Welfare: The Unholy Alliance*. Beverly Hills, Cal.: Sage Publications.

MaCoy, Ramelle, and Martin J. Morand, eds. 1984. *Short-Time Compensation: A Formula for Work Sharing*. New York: Pergamon.

Melman, Seymour. 1970. *Pentagon Capitalism: The Political Economy of War*. New York: McGraw-Hill.

Roberts, Keith. 1982. *Automation, Unemployment and the Distribution of Income*. Maastricht, Holland: European Centre for Work and Society.

Schlozman, Kay L., and Sidney Verba. 1979. *Injury to Insult: Unemployment, Class, and Political Response*. Cambridge: Harvard University Press.

Shaiken, Harley. 1986. *Work Transformed: Automation and Labor in the Computer Age*. Lexington, Mass.: Lexington Books.

Visser, Jelle. 1986. "New Working Time Arrangements in the Netherlands." Amsterdam: Sociologisch Instituut, Universiteit van Amsterdam, mimeo.

White, Michael, and Abby Ghobodian. 1984. *Shorter Working Hours in Practice*. London: Policy Studies Institute.

IIIIIIII **PART FIVE • THE FUTURE OF WORK**

I I | I | I | I   The New Work Force Meets the Changing Workplace

ROSABETH MOSS KANTER

A popular cliché about the design of American work systems holds that the problems of work can be solved by a shift to a more participative, entrepreneurial workplace. This shift, the argument runs, would solve two problems. It would create more opportunity for the ambitious "new work force," and it would restore international competitiveness by tapping new sources of creativity and enterprise.

Limited workplace reform, in that view, is all that is needed to respond to the growing expectations of the changing work force. The desires of the labor force for meaningful work and the desires of employers for greater innovation and productivity could be satisfied simultaneously—a happy situation, indeed.

This paper views the situation more pessimistically—or, at least, sees it as more complex and difficult. It is in the nature of social systems that solutions, particularly limited ones, beget new problems as the impact of a limited change begins to be felt in other parts of the system. And chipping away at one part of a structure may cause cracks in other parts.

Just as Daniel Bell identified the "cultural contradictions" of capitalism (1976), I attempt here to identify three "organizational contradictions" engendered by attempts to implement participative–entrepreneurial management principles (see also Kanter 1989). I argue that efforts to give employees more opportunity to contribute new ideas raise questions about how pay is determined and how the payroll should be divided. Second, I question whether or not the new entrepreneurial management modes are compatible with the command

279

orientation and bureaucratic-hierarchical trappings of today's organizations. And third, I suggest that the very spread of the new forms of work threatens equal opportunity goals. If the new workplace emphasis on greater involvement makes earnings dependent on initiative, then the time demands of work could increase. If this occurs, then those who shoulder the burden of out-of-work responsibilities (primarily women) could be excluded from "equal opportunities."

In short, while workplace reform has the potential to fulfill many of the expectations of the new work force, it also points to more fundamental problems in the design of organizations. The ideal-typical twentieth-century bureaucracy could be showing cracks and strains, tensions and contradictions that point to the need for a new concept of the corporation.

This paper is by necessity speculative. Although I have summoned evidence to support my analysis, the issues dealt with in this article hover under the surface of observable phenomena. By definition, these issues cannot be visible to the actors who experience only parts of them. It is the task of sociologists to find the wider patterns, the larger implications contained in the fragments of new experience that begin to present themselves in times of rapid change.

I will first provide some background on the new work force and the changing workplace. Then I will explore the three principal tensions arising out of the confluence of work force and workplace.

BACKGROUND: WORKPLACE REFORM

In the 1970s, the corporation was under attack for being unresponsive to the needs, values, and abilities of a changing work force. The profile of the American work force had changed in important ways since the mid-1960s, in both demographic characteristics (female and minority participation, age, and educational attainment) and in expectations (more career-minded, more rights conscious, and more concerned with meaningful work) (Kanter 1978).

Beginning in the early 1970s, many analysts pointed to a growing mismatch between the characteristics of the work force and the ability of the workplace, as then typically constituted, to satisfy the new expectations. One labor economist argued, in a book appropriately subtitled *The Great Training Robbery,* that the payoff from education was declining because of a growing scarcity of desirable jobs (Berg 1970); too many jobs were too narrow to use the skills and capacity of the workforce.

Furthermore, promotion opportunities—one of the major sources of increase in pay, challenge, and influence in a large corporation—were thought to be declining. Increased competition from a larger number of aspirants, an aging work force postponing retirement, and a slower growth economy prevented the organizational pyramid from expanding to accommodate all those seeking the better jobs. Even recently, popular management publications have made dire predictions about the problems about to occur as the baby boom generation reaches middle management, only to find their route upward blocked by bosses who would not step aside. Commentators wondered how these newcomers would assassinate their bosses.

The old workplace, then, was seen as inhospitable to the new work force. At the same time, there were signs that the corporate workplace was beginning to change in ways that would better suit the new work force. The impetus for these changes was only partially a response to the existence of new employee characteristics and attitudes, except where these were made the subject of government decrees, as in the case of equal employment opportunity. Even among the most progressive companies, for whom workplace reform was a long-standing interest predating popular concerns, change was as much or more a response to business concerns and competitive pressures as a recognition of employee needs, though these companies had in place more mechanisms than their counterparts for collecting data on workforce changes.

For example, General Motors was influenced to begin a Quality of Work Life program with the United Auto Workers in 1972 because of its experience with much higher productivity and quality in plants that had experimented with degrees of worker involvement in the 1960s; the bottom-line benefits to the company were clear. The program was helped along by adverse publicity from the wildcat strikes at the Lordstown Vega plant and then given a real boost by the success of Japanese cars in the U.S. market after the second energy crisis (Kanter 1983). Indeed, the speed of workplace reform in the United States was significantly increased after the discovery of the importance of certain human resource management practices in Japanese firms.

While it is very difficult to document the real extent of use of new forms of workplace organization across American corporations, there are indications from company surveys that new workplace practices such as these have been spreading since the 1970s and even beginning to be seen as normative (Goodmeasure 1985; Levering et al. 1984):

- employee involvement programs, including, but not confined to, quality circles and problem-solving teams in which employees are vested with more responsibility for and authority over changes that will improve performance; in some cases, they participate in organizational governance or sit on task forces making recommendations or decisions in areas well beyond the employees' usual jobs;
- "matrix" organization structures and project team-based organizations;

- organizational restructuring to reduce layers of the hierarchy, often layers in the middle, which significantly enlarge job scope, create closer communication with the top, and give greater responsibility without waiting for promotion;
- programs to stimulate innovation and entrepreneurship, such as internal venture funds that allow people to start businesses within the umbrella of the large corporation;
- flextime, part-time work, and job sharing, to allow people to exercise more choice over hours worked in order to accommodate nonwork interests or responsibilities.

As practices like these spread, they do indeed better match the needs and expectations of the new work force, enabling them to use skills, find meaningful work, and balance work and family responsibilities. *But each problem solved creates new strains.* As the new forms spread, they begin to conflict with other, often unexamined premises about corporate organization. As new forms take hold, they can pose challenges to the legitimacy of still other corporate practices, reaching further into fundamentals and becoming more threatening to those who benefit disproportionately from the status quo.

Because the pace of social change is uneven, some organizations are much further along in facing these problems than others. The most reform-minded, or progressive, are much likelier to experience these contradictions and dilemmas because of their longer experience with workplace changes. Other corporations are only at the beginning stages of implementing new workplace practices.

As stated earlier, I identify here three principal dilemmas or strains stemming from new workplace practices:

- the impact of greater employee participation on the legitimacy of pay systems—raising questions about how pay is determined and how the payroll is divided;
- the impact of the desire for innovation and entrepreneurship on the legitimacy of management controls;
- the tension between equal opportunity for women and the increasing absorptiveness of work.

My observations are drawn from several sources; ongoing fieldwork on the problems caused by change in major corporations (Kanter 1989), including detailed documentation of over thirty "change episodes"; a survey of 1,618 member organizations of all sizes of the American Management Association (Goodmeasure 1985); a comparison of 45 companies nominated by experts as innovative in human resource areas with a matched control group of 40 similar companies, including a survey on implementation of new work practices (Kanter and Summers 1984); access to in-company surveys and expert commentary; and the literature.

STRAIN NO. 1: PARTICIPATION AND PAY

The new work force has more education, at all levels; expects a greater voice in decisions at work; and wants opportunities beyond the job to use skills. At the same time, the new workplace is characterized by a requirement of higher levels of employee effort and mechanisms to stimulate this effort. For example, in the American Management Association company survey, it was discovered that almost half used cross-training and about one-third had quality circles, project teams, or the heavy use of task forces—all mechanisms for giving employees opportunities to participate beyond the job and to get involved in innovative activities. As employees contribute beyond the job, then rank and job definitions should become less important as determinants of how much employees contribute. At this point, the legitimacy of traditional distribution of pay is called into question—and with this, the legitimacy of the traditional hierarchy.

Such questioning is a major change. Employees have always expressed great concerns about pay, but the basic premises of the system appear to have been accepted. Employees wonder about the fairness of the distribution of rewards but not about the basis for determining how much each job is paid in the first place. For example, one in-house survey of twelve thousand employees of a large manufacturing company showed a prevalent feeling that poor performance was tolerated, especially in the upper ranks, and high agreement that "who you know" counts for more than "what you know." But there was little indication that anyone challenged the setting of pay levels.

Traditional pay systems are based largely on the cost of hiring (market forces) later rationalized into grading systems based on levels of responsibility (internal equity). While there was generally a small merit component in the traditional system, increases in pay largely came with promotion, thereby contributing to the dramatic emphasis on upward mobility in American corporations. (Just as the Eskimos have many words differentiating types of snow, indicating their preoccupation with it, so corporations have a proliferation of labels for people who are fortunate enough to be upwardly mobile, particularly at a rapid rate: fast-tracker, high-flyer, giant, boy wonder, superstar, waterwalker, and so on.) Extraordinary top executive compensation has always been justified as the cost of attracting someone with the required skills who was willing to take risks. That is why we have seen the occasional anomaly of top executives in failing companies being paid more than those in prospering ones—such a recent national hero as Lee Iacocca is a notable exception.

In the large, corporate bureaucracy, pay was by and large determined by rank. Each job was rated according to a number of features to decide what would be fair compared to the rating of other jobs. Generally, such factors as the number of subordinates and level of decision-making responsibility would be primary, thereby encouraging people to accumulate large staffs and to reserve decision authority for themselves. The basing of pay on hierarchical ranking created an incentive to maintain and then increase the hierarchy.

But the legitimacy of traditional systems is beginning to erode. The introduction of new work systems in response to the new labor force and the pressures on U.S. industry to become more competitive in an international marketplace both drive forward, giving people enlarged opportunities to contribute and then rewarding them for that contribution. Intensely competitive situations require organizations to engage more of the effort of their work force and, along with this, to find new ways to create incentives for increased performance.

Six new pay issues are emerging to rattle the iron cage of bureaucracy. *These challenges all move pay away from a status basis toward a contribution basis,* wreaking havoc with hierarchy in the process. The important issue is not how many organizations actually use each alternative, but the fact that so many alternatives and experiments coexist (see Lawler 1981). Each begins from a different premise, but in total they underline dilemmas for established notions of organization.

Pay-for-Performance

Merit pay, or pay-for-performance, is by far the most common new pay principle in American organization, generally the first one adopted when compensation systems are modernized to reward contribution. The idea is simple. People are paid a base salary defined by the ranking of their job in the overall salary structure—how much the organization feels it must pay to get someone to do that job, with some adjustments for internal equity, to ensure that comparable jobs have similar positions in the structure. Then, increases to base pay—the annual or semiannual raise—are determined by judgments about performance and contributions. Increases are calculated as a percentage of base pay. If people are asked to contribute more, they supposedly get more.

Merit pay is an essentially conservative approach to the allocation problem. It accepts—indeed, builds on and thus preserves—the status and category distinctions already defined by the organization. In its most common form, it retains, even enhances, the power of superiors over subordinates, as they dole out raises based on their judgments of contribution. In its individualistic bias, merit pay is also consistent with traditional corporate ideology, which holds the individual responsible for his or her fate.

But when the merit component of pay moves beyond a very small increment, there can be radical implications. When a merit pay system creates wide enough ranges, it is entirely possible that paychecks can reverse hierarchical statuses, with subordinates being paid more than their bosses. And if it builds on real contributions to enhancing organizational achievements, rather than on supervisors' subjective assessments of whether a person does an established job well, then it moves one step closer to loosening the shackles of bureaucracy and challenging the hierarchy.

For example, one public sector pay-for-performance system established remarkably broad pay ranges for jobs with bases of $40,000 to $100,000 (field interviews). The total range is now 40 percent away from a midpoint established in comparison with normal pay identified by an external salary survey. People can dip 20 percent below or rise 20 percent above, depending on performance against specific, quantifiable objectives. One result is that job category and official hierarchy have much weaker meaning as determinants of earnings. The top of the range is more than the chief executive is making, and at least two people are paid more than he is.

The impact of a system like this on productivity and entrepreneurship can be considerable. Its impact on work relationships is more subtle. After all, people don't wear their paychecks over their name badges, authority relationships cannot have the same meaning when people know that they outearn their boss.

The maintenance of an authority relationship depends on a degree of inequality (Marcus and House 1973). If the distance between boss and subordinate—social, economic, or otherwise—declines, so does automatic deference and respect. The key word here is *automatic*. Bosses can still gain respect by their competence and their treatment of subordinates. But power in the relationship has shifted. The situations are more equal.

The boss is thus forced to move from a relationship of authority to one that is more collegial. But there are positive implications for the boss as well. If the subordinate can earn more than the boss while staying in place, then one of the incentives to compete with the boss for his or her job is removed. Gone is the tension that can be created when an ambitious subordinate covets the boss's job and will do anything to kill off the boss. In short, if some of the authority of hierarchy is eliminated, so is some of the hostility of hierarchy.

Some organizational precedents exist for situations in which people in lower-ranked jobs are paid more than those above, but it is not a comfortable situation for most traditional corporations. Star scientists in R&D laboratories may earn more than the administrators nominally over them. Hourly workers can make more than their supervisors with the addition of overtime pay or because of union-negotiated wage settlements. But there is evidence from surveys that traditional corporations consider these situations a source of problems (Steele 1982). They do not want the gaps between hierarchical statuses to be closed. If merit pay is meaningfully implemented in organizations, then it can meet resistance from those who wish to maintain traditional relations.

Performance Bonuses

Performance bonuses create a variety of income-earning opportunities for the enterprising by adding special incentives for specific contributions. And these bonuses further loosen the relationship between pay and job status.

High technology firms are particularly dependent on the contributions of individual innovators who could sometimes just as easily leave to start their own firms. So entrepreneurial incentives are a particular necessity in these organizations.

For example, a 1983 random sample of the 105 Boston-area firms employing scientists and engineers compared the high tech ones dependent on R&D for new product development with their more traditional, established counterparts. The high tech firms tended, on average, to pay a lower base salary but offer more financial incentives of other kinds, such as cash bonuses, stock options, and spot awards—independent of job levels. Furthermore, the most successful firms did more of this (J. Schuster 1984, 1985).

Entrepreneurial Pay

The third challenge revolves around entrepreneurial pay—how to share the returns with people who provide added value to the organization by creating something new. The attempt to provide the new work force with entrepreneurial opportunities within an established corporation, including the higher income-earning opportunities that entrepreneurs have when they start their own businesses, has led to a very different kind of compensation system operating within some traditional corporations (Kanter 1989). In a style that is pay-for-performance to its fullest extent, special venture participants can earn a return, just like founder-owners do, on the marketplace performance of their product or service. While this alternative is still relatively rare (only 6.9 percent of the 1,618 AMA member organizations surveyed had special venture funds or entrepreneurial opportunities—Goodmeasure 1985), interest is growing.

Typically, such schemes allow people to start a business with the support of the parent company. They are paid a base salary, generally equivalent to their former job level, and they are asked to put part of their compensation "at risk"; their percent "ownership" is determined by the part they put at risk. Sometimes the return is based solely on a percentage of the profit from their venture; sometimes it comes in the form of internal "phantom stock" pegged to the parent company's public stock price.

Pay-out may occur at several intervals in the development of the venture, and not simply after the seven to twelve years it can take to earn a profit in a new venture. "Milestone bonuses" for meeting established targets may be used, with further incentives added for timeliness—if you're late, the payoff goes down.

Entrepreneurial pay, like other forms, threatens hierarchy. It is embarrassing, in the words of a senior bank officer, when people can earn more than their bosses. It is equally tense in the other direction, when lower-level employees get a 6.8 percent increase while their manager gets a 30 percent bonus for results that they know they helped create. People are getting angry and are beginning to push harder for a more equitable arrangement.

Gainsharing

The fourth response to the new work force and the new workplace gives workers at the lowest levels a direct return on their contributions, as a group rather than on an individual basis. In theory, gainsharing is a simple idea. Employees should share in the gains from contributions they make to improving the company's performance (Graham-Moore and Ross 1983; Bullock and Lawler 1984).

In practice, the term *gainsharing* refers to a cluster of programs with some features in common: sharing with groups (as against individuals), based on explicit formulas with objective measures (as against subjective judgments or flexible criteria), and always involving at least the hourly work force (as against only salaried managers and professionals). The unit whose performance is measured may be the whole organization, subdivisions of it, or single facilities. What's important is that the whole group benefits from overall performance.

Gainsharing programs come in three major variants—Scanlon, Rucker, and Improshare—though many companies develop versions of their own. All of the plans are compatible with the presence of unions, and all are found in both union and nonunion environments.

Scanlon plans are the best known and most elaborate version of gainsharing, with a long and honorable history extending back to the 1930s. Their features are the following:

- A focus on the overall organization as the key unit for determining performance.
- A carefully defined and relatively complex system of committees and groups that provide involvement of employees in decision making and implementation of suggestions.
- A firm belief in the need to reflect a total philosophy of management through the plan and its components, so that each element is articulated with every other.

- An elaborate process involving discussion and education of the work force, commitments from management (and union, if any), and a secret ballot with at least 95 percent in favor required before going forward with the plan.

Data on how many organizations use gainsharing and how many employees participate in programs are difficult to come by. Eleven percent of the 1,618 organizations in the AMA membership survey had some sort of gainsharing in operation (Goodmeasure 1985). A survey of high tech firms showed that over half had cash or stock awards for individuals, but only 6 percent had gainsharing or group profit-sharing (Spratt and Steele 1982). Bullock and Lawler (1984) estimate that the total number of implemented plans range from five hundred to one thousand, but they found only thirty-three cases described in enough detail to study. On the other hand, interest seems to be going up. Timothy Ross, head of an institute devoted to studying gainsharing, estimates that several thousand companies have some sort of gainsharing, involving probably millions of employees, but says that he cannot be more specific about the number because "gainsharing is being used now as an umbrella concept to also mean profit-sharing and pay-for-performance, and people will have to define their terms before we can even begin to make an accurate count. But in just the private companies the institute alone is working with now, we're probably talking about forty to fifty thousand right there" (1986, personal interview).

Unfortunately, there is little hard evidence to explain why gainsharing plans work. Bullock and Lawler (1984) speculate that plans "change the culture of the organization . . . transform(ing) individuals, working on their own tasks and largely unaware of how their jobs interface with the whole of the organization, into groups of employees which suddenly have a much broader understanding of and commitment to the total enterprise." Although there is some disagreement in the literature—for example, scholars such as Geare (1976) argue that money is the primary motivator—most gainsharing experts believe that employee participation is the key to effective change (M. Schuster 1984; Bullock and Lawler 1984).

I will go one step further. For gainsharing plans to work, a particular organizational structure and corporate culture are required, including open discussion of the plan to gain employee acceptance; establishment of cross-unit teams or task forces to develop the plan; and adoption of suggestion systems. Gainsharing programs also require open communication about company goals and performance. If employees' pay is based in part on profits, they need to know where the company stands and how their percentage is calculated.

Pay for Skill

A fifth variant on traditional pay practices was designed specifically with the new workforce in mind, and it too challenges conventional hierarchical assumptions: pay for jobs mastered (Lawler 1977; Tosi and Tosi 1986). Pay for skill provides individual incentives for employees to upgrade their performance rapidly—while creating strong teams that are virtually self-managed.

The system used by one manufacturing company is heavily team-based (field interviews). Teams have responsibility for all aspects of production: operating the machinery, working with suppliers, inspecting the product for conformance to quality standards, and keeping records. With this kind of responsibility, it clearly helps every member of the team to have highly skilled colleagues capable of fully sharing the load.

New employees are hired by the work team after extensive interviewing, and a training coordinator (also a team member) develops a five-year career plan for how the new employees will progress in skill. This planning is important to the team because other team members will have to provide coverage for the employee's job while he or she is attending training programs. (In one plant, the work team hired some temps because they planned to have two people out for personal computer training.)

Pay grows as the newcomer moves from entry to full team member. Small pay increments are given for time served through the first two years, but the real increases occur as the new team member progresses through as many as several dozen "skill blocks." The skill blocks move from general orientation (learning the plant, operating hand tools, and so on) to on-the-job and classroom training to learn all aspects of one, and then two, production processes. The multiskills requirement adds such skills as machine maintenance, quality control, and—one of the payoffs in terms of self-management—problem solving and leadership skills.

This skill building may occur within five years. By contrast, under the former system in the same plant, it took five years just to move from sweeper to helper to process operator for one process, with no training or responsibility for problem solving.

All in all, pay for skill is a clever approach. It stresses individual responsibility but does not have the drawbacks of other pay-for-performance systems that pit team member against team member in contention for the highest ratings. Because there is no limit to the number of people who can reach the highest pay levels, there is little formal inducement to maintain a monopoly of skills or withhold training from newcomers in order to preserve a superior position. It creates a community of nominal peers with a broad range of skills who decide among themselves how best to deploy those skills.

A system like this also runs counter to the goal many neo-Marxist critics attribute to modern corporations: to deskill jobs so as to keep some people confined to lower pay levels and to make it easier to accommodate turnover, ensuring that a reasonable proportion of the work force is always new and thus always paid at lowest rates (Braverman 1974). Both of these effects of deskilling keep the total wage bill low. How does an organization economically justify doing the opposite? Because of a work environment that better utilizes human skills, productivity improves and more than saves the additional costs of higher average wages on the shop floor. To do this, a new organization structure is required, one that challenges conventional notions of hierarchy.

Comparable Worth

As more and more women have entered the work force without closing the pay gap between women and men, activists have picked up the comparable worth banner (Livernash 1980). Comparable worth as an employee rights' issue is compatible with other new pay issues that arise from changes in the work force and the workplace. But its threat to the legitimacy of hierarchy is even greater.

Most of the ferment in pay reflects attempts by employers to improve organizational performance while controlling fixed payroll costs. And that's all. Organizational change is often not a goal, even if it is an unintended side effect, and it is often resisted by managers. The fact is that various forms of contribution-based pay also tend to shape up the hierarchy, challenge traditional authority relations, and weaken the meaning of organizational status—that's a source of trouble to most corporations. The threat of comparable worth, in the eyes of many executives, is the massive organizational readjustments it may entail, even more than the cost of equalizing pay across certain jobs.

Performance or contribution-based pay would seem to be highly compatible with the principle behind comparable worth: to ensure equivalent pay for jobs that create equivalent value for the organization. If we adopt a comparable worth principle, measures of status—the market price to hire for certain positions, the standing of the job in an organizational hierarchy, the social status of typical job incumbents—should be less important than the contributions made to carrying out organizational purposes.

Organizations are gradually coming to accept the necessity of gearing pay to performance and giving employees a cut of the extra value they produce. But they are also trying to confine this to rather minor changes, so that jobs do not have to be repositioned in a status structure.

Recall that merit pay comes as a percent increase above a predetermined salary level defined by job status. Incentive pay for special contributions is offered as a bonus above base salary. The return to internal entrepreneurs who build new ventures may be calculated with the preventure salary in the equation. Even gainsharing may be distributed as a function of wage level.

Clearly, some organizations see the development of a new pay policy as an occasion for making organizational changes. Jobs may be reevaluated to adjust the level of base pay, the supervisory ranks may be trimmed as employee teams take on more responsibility, a new venture structure goes along with opportunities to earn entrepreneurial returns. But—and this is an important point—organizations do not necessarily have to reconsider the relative positioning of jobs in the hierarchy in order to have contribution-based pay. They can preserve some of the old status order while overlaying the new contribution principle.

The old status order is at the heart of the comparable worth issue. And that's why comparable worth—a principle that should be swimming in the mainstream of the movement to reward contribution—is instead felt to be one of the ultimate challenges to the calculation of pay. If pay-for-performance systems rattle the hierarchy, comparable worth threatens to shake it to the core.

Overall, the new pay issues make clear the difficulty of maintaining a traditional command-and-control hierarchy once actual contribution becomes the basis for the distribution of pay. The emerging participative-entrepreneurial incentives for increased performance satisfy a number of the expectations of the new work force, but their existence also makes it harder to sustain the authority or the privilege of position.

The second strain involves a more basic incompatibility between the management systems required for innovation and entrepreneurship and those associated with continuation of already-established organizational operations.

STRAIN NO. 2: INNOVATION VERSUS MANAGEMENT CONTROLS

The new work force expects greater meaning, a feeling of making a difference. This feeling comes from the desire to innovate. For example, one highly placed executive in a well-regarded company, who was successfully climbing the management ladder, commented in an interview that the only thing he felt he would really be remembered for in the corporation and that he would remember about his work was a special assignment in which he had an opportunity to propose a major reorganization of a function.

The new workplace is also designed around a theoretical value on entrepreneurship and innovation—the theme of well over half of four hundred major corporate meetings included in a 1983–85 data base that is still being developed. Economic pressures have caused organizations to become more interested in new products, new services, and new systems. And this interest is compatible with the desires of the work force to make creative contributions.

But it is very difficult to accommodate this goal within the large corporation geared to stability, control, and maintenance of ongoing operations (Stevenson and Gumpert 1985). In those organizations that have deliberately established workplaces along entrepreneurial principles, there is growing tension between the existence of such pockets of change and the traditional hierarchy.

Because of characteristics of the innovation process itself, the creation and exploitation of new products, new processes, or new systems has four special requirements and unique situations (Kanter 1983; Quinn 1985; Van de Ven 1986; Kanter 1988, 1989). An understanding of the requirements of innovation makes clear why entrepreneurship challenges the legitimacy of the classic command-and-control hierarchy (Kanter 1985).

1. *Uncertainty.*   The innovation process involves little or no precedent and has no experience base to be used to make forecasts about results. Hoped-for timetables may prove unrealistic. Anticipated costs may be overrun. Results are highly uncertain (Quinn 1985). This situation thus requires:

- Committed, visionary leadership willing to initiate and sustain effort on the basis of faith in the idea.
- The existence of "patient money," or capital that does not have to show a short-term return.
- A great deal of planning flexibility, so that the original concept may be adjusted to the emerging realities.

But these requirements can run counter to those aspects of administrative management that may require instead:

- Detailed analysis in advance of resource commitments (for example, in one company the list of the *analyses* to be done itself runs ten pages).
- Fairly rapid returns on investment or a very high probable revenue base from the activity (for example, packaged goods companies uninterested in project ideas with projected sales of under $100 million/year). (Dean [1974] describes the "mismatch" between the pace of innovation and management's time horizons.)
- High-level sign-off on a "plan" and agreement to a set of procedures or steps, with the expectation that they will be followed without deviation—measuring managers on adherence to plan rather than on results.

2. *Knowledge-Intensity.*   The innovating process is knowledge-intensive; it relies on individual human intelligence and creativity. New experiences are accumulated at a fast pace; the learning curve is steep. The knowledge that resides in the participants in the innovation effort is not yet codified or codifiable for transfer to others. Efforts are vulnerable to turnover because of the loss of this knowledge and experience. This situation thus requires:

- Stability among the participants involved in an innovation effort, especially the venture manager or visionary leader.
- A high degree of commitment among all participants as well as close, team-oriented working relationships with high mutual respect, to encourage rapid and effective exchange of knowledge among participants.
- Intense and concentrated effort focused inward on the project.

The need for different types of structures may depend on whether the innovation is primarily concerned with the generation of new knowledge or the reformulation of existing information. For example, Kazanjian and Drazin (1986) argue that the implementation of a manufacturing innovation required both the creation of knowledge and the integration of current knowledge from the manufacturing organization. In this case study, the company established a separate unit staffed with a team of people from inside and outside the organization to generate new knowledge. At the same time, the organizer of the innovative process built multiple bridges to the manufacturing division, assuring access to existing manufacturing knowledge. The degree of separation of an innovative unit and the need for linkages from it to the layer organization may depend on the balance between new knowledge and the integration of existing knowledge.

These requirements for new knowledge may run counter to those aspects of administrative management that instead allow:

- Regular turnover of managers because of a lock-step career system that ties rewards to promotions and thus requires job changes.
- Bureaucratic assignment of managers or personnel without regard to their degree of belief in the effort or their compatibility with each other.
- Reporting requirements that disrupt project activities and distract participants by asking them to prepare special analyses for upper management or attend meetings unrelated to advancing the work of the innovation team.

3. *Competition with Alternatives.* In the innovation process, there is always competition with alternative courses of action. (The pursuit of the air-cooled engine at Honda Motor, for example, drew time and resources away from improving the water-cooled engine.) Furthermore, sometimes the very existence of a potential innovation poses a threat to vested interests—whether the interest is that of a salesperson receiving high commissions on current products or of the advocates of a competing direction. Indeed, observers point to political problems as one of the major causes for the failure of corporate entrepreneurship (Fast 1976). This situation thus requires:

- Champions or sponsors who will argue for the course of action, who will sustain the vision (Galbraith 1982).
- Coalitions of backers or supporters from a number of areas willing to lend credence (and resources) to the project.
- Sufficient job security throughout the organization that innovations are not seen as position-threatening.

These roles and the need for job security act as a constellation of roles and conditions rather than as singular conditions (Kazanjian and Drazin 1986).

These requirements may be difficult to meet if people have been selected, trained, promoted, and rewarded in an administrative mode which encourages instead:

- Cautious, conservative stands that involve betting on sure things only (for example, in one company requiring risk analyses, a preference for no-risk new products).
- Interdepartmental rivalry and competition for scarce resources or rewards, with each area having to "defeat" others to ensure its existence, and rewards based only on individual performance.
- Lack of confrontation or constructive arguing out of differences, but resorting to underground sabotage instead.

4. *Boundary Crossing.* The innovation process is rarely if ever contained solely within one unit. First, there is evidence that many of the best ideas are interdisciplinary or interfunctional in origin—as connoted by the root meaning of entrepreneurship as the development of "new combinations"—or they benefit from broader perspectives and information from outside of the area primarily responsible for the innovation. Second, regardless of the origin of innovations, they inevitably send out ripples and reverberations to other organizational units, whose behavior may be required to change in light of the needs of innovations or whose cooperation is necessary if an innovation is to be fully developed or exploited. Or there may be the need to generate unexpected innovations in another domain in order to support the primary product, like the need to design a new motor to make the first Apple computer viable. This situation thus requires:

- Enlarging the focus of participants in the innovation process to take account of the perspectives of other units or disciplines. (What I call kaleidoscope thinking is at the heart of the creative process in innovation—the use of new angles or perspectives to reshuffle the parts to make a new pattern, thus challenging conventional assumptions.)
- Early involvement of functions or units that may play a role at some later stage of the venture or innovation effort.
- A high degree of commitment to the innovation by functions or players outside the innovation-producing unit.
- A high degree of interaction across functions or units—and thus more interunit teamwork.
- Reciprocal influence among functions.

But these requirements can run counter to the typical administrative-bureaucratic pattern, which instead fosters:

- Narrowing of focus via an emphasis on specialization, single-discipline careers, and limited communication among functions or disciplines.

- A preference for homogeneity over diversity, for orthodoxy over new perspectives.
- Measurement of functions or units (or divisions) on their own performance alone, so that rewards drive behavior that maximizes unit-specific returns rather than partnership contributions to the projects of other units.
- Structural arrangements and reporting systems that separate (segment) functions or units and assign each a set of steps in a process assumed to be linear rather than reciprocal and interactional.

Overall, then, it is not surprising that research on the problems of new corporate ventures tends to attribute failures to such common factors as the requirements for inappropriate planning/analysis and pressure for faster results; turnover on the venture team and lack of committed leadership; the politics of gaining sponsorship within the corporation (or the perils of getting the wrong sponsorship); and interfunctioning conflicts that either slow the process down or steer the project in an inappropriate direction (Von Hippel 1977; Block 1982, 1983; Hobson and Morrison 1983; Fast 1976; MacMillan, Block, and Narasimha 1984; Quinn 1985).

The Tension between Command and Mutual Adjustment Systems

Traditional corporate management works to hold things in place, preventing deviation from established practice, once rules are made. It is compatible with a command system in which every person and every function knows its place. When this type of management results in high degrees of compartmentalization of responsibilities and limited contact between a large number of differentiated statuses (distinctions of level, of function, of unit), I have referred to it as *segmentalism*—an approach to organizing and managing that discourages change, even in the face of obvious problems (Kanter 1983).

But the entrepreneurial process requires instead more reliance on the particular persons involved, closer working relationships, the ability to depart from tradition, and a governance system that is one of continual negotiation and mutual adjustment among all participants with something to contribute to the effort. This approach to organizing can be called *integrative*—an emphasis on bringing people together rather than separating activities or people—and the governance system a partnership or *mutual adjustment* model.

A single proposition in organizational theory holds that under conditions of low uncertainty and high predictability about both inputs and outcomes, it is effective to manage by rules, paperwork, and other impersonal means administered through clearly established centers of command. But under conditions of high uncertainty and low predictability, it is more effective to manage by personal communication and negotiation—in part because of the sheer inability to issue enough commands to cover every contingency.

Thus entrepreneurship requires a system of management by mutual adjustment rather than a system of management by command. Management by mutual adjustment, in turn, relies on integrative organizational conditions: a close working relationship among all participants, mutual respect fostered by the absence of status differences, overlapping responsibilities, and concern for joint goals. It is partnership-oriented and allows for temporary alliances among equals instead of the submersion of parties in a hierarchy—for example, joint ventures versus acquisitions, borrowing or renting assets rather than owning them.

All established organizations clearly need both systems. They need a *command* system for those areas where repeating the past is necessary, where predictable products or services are to be turned out reliably and uniformly according to an established blueprint, and where efficiencies are to be gained through a learning curve derived from numerous repetitions. And they need a *mutual adjustment* system wherever innovation is desired, problems need to be solved, and new techniques or methods are sought.

The maximizing of both efficiency and innovation is required for an organization to be adaptive (Lawrence and Dyer 1983). Even in a fairly new company developing new products in a growing market, both systems play a role. Mitchell Kapor, the young founder and first CEO of Lotus Development Corporation, a highly successful software firm, acknowledged this need for two simultaneous management systems:

> To be a successful enterprise, we have to do two apparently contradictory things quite well: We have to stay innovative and creative, but at the same time we have to be tightly controlled about certain aspects of our corporate behavior. But I think that what you have to do about paradox is embrace it. So we have the kind of company where certain things are very loose and other things are very tight. The whole art of management is sorting things into the loose pile or the tight pile and then watching them carefully. (*Boston Globe*, 1/27/85)

Organizations in which administrative command systems dominate sometimes establish a separate system for entrepreneurship and innovation and run, in effect, two organizations side by side. One example is the parallel organization concept at use in the employee involvement or quality of work-life programs in many companies—a second, participative organization of temporary task forces added to the operating organization with its clear specification of roles and responsibilities and its numerous distinctions between functions and levels (Stein and Kanter 1980). While full-blown parallel organizations were used by only 8.5 percent of the 1,618 organizations in the AMA survey, well over a third had a more limited variant in the form of quality circles (Goodmeasure 1985). Another example is the establishment of new venture units in large corporations that operate by different principles from the organization running established businesses, like GM's Saturn subsidiary or the separate organization that developed the IBM personal computer.

But there is an uneasy coexistence between the two forms in the same organization. The very existence of the parallel organization challenges the legitimacy of the established hierarchy by posing an alternative, by giving people a taste of freedom from bureaucratic constraints. If the innovating unit is kept separate—to preserve its autonomy, acknowledge its special management requirements, and keep it from contaminating the parts of the organization devoted to routine operations—then it can soon draw fire as a privileged elite, threatening to the maintainers of the routinized organization and a target of resentment for other participants. Pressure mounts to dissolve it, to absorb it back into the established hierarchy and subject it to the established rules. Among the cases I have examined, this drama was played out in the entrepreneurial divisions of two computer companies and a pharmaceutical firm, and it has been a common fate of new venture units (Fast 1976). Perhaps this is why under 7 percent of the organizations in the AMA survey had internal venture funds for entrepreneurial opportunities (Goodmeasure 1985). On the other hand, if the entrepreneurial process is carried out alongside the command-and-control process for ongoing operations, then there is the likelihood of behavioral spillover from the mutual adjustment mode, which undermines traditional authority relations in the hierarchy. Once having tasted the freedom to participate in decisions, work across organizational boundaries, and envision alternatives, workers find it difficult to accept management by command. But as attractive as participative-entrepreneurial management may be to some segments of the new work force, it is less so to others because of the connections between the workplace and other societal institutions.

STRAIN NO. 3: EQUAL OPPORTUNITY FOR WOMEN VERSUS TIME DEMANDS IN DESIRABLE POSITIONS

As organizations move to more participative and entrepreneurial modes, creating a new workplace of high involvement and rewards for special contributions, another tension is introduced. This one does not involve so much a challenge to the legitimacy of established hierarchies as it does a challenge to the ability of organizations, as presently constituted, to fulfill another goal of the new work force: career success for women.

Ironically, the new workplace itself may impede progress toward meeting equal opportunity goals—unless organizations, together with the wider institutions of society, change in profound and fundamental ways.

The new work force contains an ever-greater proportion of women with ever-greater education and ever-greater aspirations. But the very people who are pressing for higher level positions carry with them heavier out-of-work demands, particularly centering around family responsibilities. Accumulated evidence indicates that women still do the bulk of the family work, even if men bear an increasing share.

At the same time, relatively few of the new workplace systems involve flexibility and time off or direct support for family responsibilities. If anything, the major thrust is in the opposite direction. Most of the new workplace systems *increase* the absorptiveness of work. The chances to earn performance bonuses or share in productivity gains or get funding for special entrepreneurial ventures or participate in innovations—all of these increase, rather than decrease, the time demands. The most desirable jobs all seem to take the most time, as Jencks (1985) found when he related hours of work to job satisfaction.

The modern corporation is what Coser (1974) called a "greedy organization." As new work alternatives take hold, they make it more so, at the same time that a large group in the work force wants it less so. Despite the career consciousness of the younger generation of women, a conflict between the demands of work and the demands of family still exists, and there is evidence that women's career ambitions begin to taper off when women enter their thirties and express a desire for children. The careers they have been educated to want, however, do not accommodate less than fully committed—and to a certain extent, even overburdened—people.

There is also evidence that the amount of leisure is dropping faster than the increase in hours worked, indicating, in part, that out-of-work responsibilities have not declined as workhours go up. A Harris survey of 1985 identified a steady and inexorable decline in leisure. Since 1973, the median number of hours worked by Americans (in paid work) increased by 20 percent while the amount of leisure time available to the average person dropped by 32 percent. Among the groups with the longest hours of work are those in the most "desirable" occupations: entrepreneurs in smaller businesses, especially retailing, at 57.3 hours per week; professionals, at 52.2 hours per week; and those with incomes over $50,000, at 52.4 hours per week. Clearly, the best jobs are the most time-demanding.

Such a situation holds not only because of what the corporation imposes on employees, but also because employees themselves seek under options to get access to more challenging and interesting work or to participate in organizational problem solving.

When work is more interesting, people take it home. In one organization, secretaries on a task force found themselves carrying piles of paper home for the first time in their career (field interviews). The task force was exciting, its mission interesting, and suddenly they had a project with goals that required reflection beyond the time permitted in the office. It is also common to see members of quality circles using their lunch hour to hold meetings, because they are committed to the goals of the group.

In addition, more challenging, more entrepreneurial, more participative positions carry with them the requirement for more communication and interaction. I have already pointed to the intensity of innovation—the requirement of a cohesive team that exchanges new knowledge frequently, as it is developed. Furthermore, groups take longer to do certain kinds of work than do individuals, even if the quality of the solution is higher. One needs more time for meetings in a participative-entrepreneurial workplace, where job territories overlap, people might report to more than one manager, and projects require the coordination of a number of people, each with specialized responsibility. Management tasks too are different under a more participative system. People need to spend more time selling ideas rather than commanding. They need to spend more time with subordinates explaining the goals, keeping them up to date with timely information, and making sure they understand where their places fit into the whole task.

Especially in high ranks of management—the levels women aspire to but in which equal opportunity goals are least likely to have been met—evidence suggests that most of an executive's time is spent communicating, often in short fragments on a large variety of topics (Mintzberg 1973).

In the emerging corporation, sheer communication, and therefore time demands, are up (Kanter 1989). One electronics firm in a fast-paced business with a great deal of need for communication across diverse entities established its own in-house helicopter service to link seventeen New England facilities. Concerned about travel time and costs, the company established an elaborate teleconferencing system to allow people to communicate without traveling (field interviews). But instead of reducing travel costs, the teleconferencing capacity actually increased them because when they found they could communicate more easily more people found even more reasons to get together.

Finally, when I asked successful innovators in my studies for *The Change Masters* (Kanter 1983) what their accomplishment cost, their answers were revealing: gaining weight, getting a divorce, getting in trouble with the family. The best-selling account of the development of a new computer at Data General, *The Soul of a New Machine* (Kidder 1982), widely used as an example of effective innovation in a high participation organization, documents the extraordinary lengths to which people will go to do highly absorbing work over which they have control: working sixty-, ninety-, hundred-hour weeks and going into the laboratory in the middle of the night when they had an idea. Of course, these employees were young males without families. But the fact that this work cycle is engendered by providing great opportunity for challenge and excitement may also eliminate the possibility that women can achieve in such jobs.

Therefore, we see a conflict between two kinds of change. Equal opportunity opens up hopes of higher positions for women, but new work systems (designed with many of the same liberal goals in mind) may increase the barriers to their getting them. There was for a time some evidence that organizations characterized by work systems with high participation and high involvement created more opportunities for women because of the values of the organization and the ways in which bureaucratic structures inhibited women concentrated in "stuck" (low mobility) positions from ever getting access to opportunity. But recent data from Silicon Valley show the paucity of women in significant positions in some of the most entrepreneurial companies in the country (Rogers and Larsen 1984). It becomes clear that women do not automatically do better in high participation environments unless there is also significant support for the additional responsibilities they bring with them.

A clear strain in the system shows here. As organizations loosen up and begin to operate on less hierarchical premises, giving more people an opportunity to participate in decisions, tackling challenging projects, and taking on exciting tasks, they absorb more of people's time and energy. If they are allowed to absorb more of the person without providing support for other responsibilities, either they will become more antagonistic to the family than they have been in the past or they will eliminate the prospect of ever reaching equal opportunity goals in the more challenging, higher-level, and better-paying positions.

Social and organizational change is fraught with dilemmas, tensions, and contradictions because of the impossibility of decoupling pieces of a system. A minor change there sends ripples through activities here. A problem solved here creates new, unanticipated problems there. Gradually, the structures that have supported one form begin to crack and crumble, even when only minor renovations are desired.

I have rejected the premise that the new work force itself presents the problem. Instead, I have argued that the new work force finds itself involved in a new workplace—created in response to forces such as global competition. This new workplace offers opportunities for greater employee initiative, for entrepreneurial effort, and for greater participation in problem solving. However, it cannot exist easily in the conventional command-and-control hierarchy of status and authority relations that has been the dominant organizational form in the twentieth century.

I have identified three principal strains. First is the shift from status to contribution as a basis for pay, as the new workplace attempts to improve performance and allow initiative to be expressed. Second, entrepreneurial management modes that take advantage of employee initiatives are incompatible with the command orientation and bureaucratic-hierarchical trappings of organizations. Third, the thrust of the new workplace is toward greater employee participation and making earnings dependent on initiative. Greater participation could so increase the time demands of work that those shouldering the burden of out-of-work responsibilities (primarily women) could be excluded at the time that the rhetoric offers them equal opportunity. All three strains represent the major tensions that organizations, particularly large corporations, need to manage as we enter the last decade of the century.

The cracks in the old system are showing. What will happen is still to be determined. We may see conservative keepers of the old way attempt to patch the cracks and fortify the walls against the new challenges, thereby shoring up an obsolescent system. Or we may witness the gradual crumbling of the traditional hierarchy and the reshaping of the work–family nexus.

REFERENCES

Bell, Daniel. 1976. *The Cultural Contradictions of Capitalism.* New York: Basic Books.

Berg, Ivar. 1970. *Education and Jobs: The Great Training Robbery.* New York: Praeger.

Block, Zenas. 1982. "Can Corporate Venturing Succeed?" *The Journal of Business Strategy* 3:21–33.

———. 1983. "Some Major Issues in Internal Corporate Venturing." In *Frontiers of Entrepreneurship Research,* edited by J. A. Hornaday, J. A. Timmons, and K. H. Vesper. Wellesley, Mass.: Babson College.

Braverman, Harry. 1974. *Labor and Monopoly Capitalism.* New York: Monthly Review Press.

Bullock, R. J., and Lawler, Edward E. 1984. "Gainsharing: A Few Questions, and Fewer Answers." *Human Resource Management* 23:23–40.

Coser, Lewis. 1974. *Greedy Institutions.* New York: Free Press.

Dean, R. C. 1974. "The Temporal Mismatch—Innovation's Pace Versus Management's Time Horizons." *Research Management* (May):12–15.

Fast, Norman D. 1976. "The Future of Industrial New Venture Departments." *Industrial Marketing Management* 8:264–73.

Fossum, John A., and Mary K. Fitch. 1985. "The Effects of Individual and Contextual Attributes on the Sizes of Recommended Salary Increases." *Personnel Psychology* 38:587–602.

Galbraith, Jay. 1982. "Designing the Innovating Organization." *Organizational Dynamics* 10:5–25.

Geare, A. J. 1976. "Productivity from Scanlon-type Plans." *Academy of Management Review* 1:99–108.

Goodmeasure, Inc. 1985. *The Changing American Workplace: Work Alternatives in the 1980's.* New York: AMA Membership Publishing Division.

Graham-Moore, Brian E., and Timothy L. Ross. 1983. *Productivity Gainsharing.* Englewood Cliffs: Prentice-Hall.

Hobson, Edwin L., and Richard M. Morrison. 1983. "How do Corporate Start-up Ventures Fare? In *Frontiers of Entrepreneurship Research,* J. A. Hornaday, J. A. Timmons, and K. H. Vesper. Wellesley, Mass.: Babson College.

Jencks, Christopher. 1985. "What Is a Good Job? A New Measure of Labor Market Success." Paper delivered at the Annual Meetings of the American Sociological Association, Washington, D.C.

Kanter, Rosabeth Moss. 1978. "Work in a New America." *Daedalus* 107:47–78.

——. 1983. *The Change Masters.* New York: Simon and Schuster.

——. 1988. "When a Thousand Flowers Bloom: Social, Structural, and Collective Determinants of Innovation in Organizations." *Research in Organizational Behavior* 10.

——. 1989. *When Giants Learn to Dance.* New York: Simon and Schuster.

Kanter, Rosabeth Moss, and David V. Summers. 1984. *The Roots of Corporate Progressivism.* Report to the Russell Sage Foundation.

Kazanjian, Robert K., and Robert Drazin. 1986. "Implementing Manufacturing Innovations: Critical Choices of Structure and Staffing Roles." *Human Resource Management* 25.

Kidder, Tracy. 1981. *The Soul of a New Machine.* Boston: Atlantic-Little, Brown.

Lawler, Edward E. 1977. "Reward Systems." In *Improving Life at Work,* edited by J. R. Hackman and J. L. Suttle. Goodyear.

——. 1981. *Pay and Organization Development.* Reading, Mass.: Addison-Wesley.

Lawrence, Paul R., and Dyer, Davis. 1983. *Renewing American Industry.* New York: Free Press.

Levering, Robert, Milton Moskowitz, and Michael Katz. 1984. *The 100 Best Companies to Work for in America.* Reading, Mass.: Addison-Wesley.

Livernash, E. Robert, ed. 1980. *Comparable Worth: Issues and Alternatives.* Washington: Equal Opportunity Advisory Council.

MacMillan, Ian C., Zenas Block, and P. N. Subba Narasimha. 1984. "Obstacles and Experience in Corporate Ventures." Working paper, New York University.

Marcus, Philip M., and James S. House. 1973. "Exchange between Superiors and Subordinates in Large Organizations." *Administrative Science Quarterly* 18:209–22.

Milkovich, George T., and Jerry M. Newman. 1984. *Compensation.* Plano, Tex.: Business Publications.

Mintzberg, Henry. 1973. *The Nature of Managerial Work.* New York: Harper and Row.

Quinn, James Brian. 1985. "Managing Innovation: Controlled Chaos." *Harvard Business Review* 63:73–84.

Rogers, Everett, and Judith K. Larsen. 1984. *Silicon Valley Fever.* New York: Basic Books.

Schuster, Jay R. 1984. *Management Compensation in High Technology Companies.* Lexington, Mass.: Lexington Books.

——. 1985. "Compensation Plan Design: The Power behind the Best High-Tech Companies." *Management Review* (May):21–25.

Schuster, Michael. 1984. "The Scanlon Plan: A Longitudinal Analysis." *Journal of Applied Behavioral Science* 20:23–28.

Spratt, Michael F., and Bernadette Steele. 1985. "Rewarding Key Contributors." *Compensation and Benefits Review* 17:24–37.

Steele, James W. 1982. *Paying for Performance and Position: Dilemmas in Salary Compression and Merit Pay*. New York: AMA Membership Publishing Division.

Stein, Barry A., and Rosabeth Moss Kanter. 1980. "Building the Parallel Organization: Toward Permanent Structures for the Quality of Work Life." *Journal of Applied Behavioral Science* 16:371–88.

Stevenson, Howard, and David Gumpert. 1985. "The Heart of Entrepreneurship." *Harvard Business Review* 63:85–94.

Tosi, Henry, and Lisa Tosi. 1986. "What Managers Need to Know about Knowledge-Based Pay." *Organizational Dynamics* 14:52–64.

Van de Ven, Andrew H. 1986. "Central Problems in the Management of Innovation." *Management Science* 32:590–607.

Von Hippel, Eric. 1977. "Successful and Failing Internal Corporate Ventures: An Empirical Analysis." *Industrial Marketing Management* 6:163–74.

I I I I I I I I   **The False Choice between High Technology and Basic Industry**

AMITAI ETZIONI AND
PAUL A. JARGOWSKY

THE TRANSFORMATION THESIS

Economists and public policy analysts suggest that a major transformation is now taking place in the U.S. economy. One of the seminal works on this subject is Daniel Bell's *The Coming of Post-Industrial Society* (Bell 1973). In it, Bell calls attention to the decline of basic manufacturing, once considered the cornerstone of the American economy: "The changeover to a post-industrial society is significant not only by the change in sector distribution" (that is, an ever-lower share of GNP in the manufacturing sector) "but in patterns of occupations, the kind of work [people] do" (Bell 1973:134). The two related trends march hand in hand: as the manufacturing sector declines, blue-collar workers are replaced by professional, technical, and clerical white-collar workers. As production of basic goods declines, a greater economic role is assumed by professional, technical, and clerical workers involved in the processing of information and the incorporation of innovations into the production of specialized goods and services.

"A post-industrial society," Bell writes, ". . . is a game between persons. What counts is not raw muscle power, or energy, but information. The central person is the professional, for he is equipped by his education and training, to provide the kinds of skill which are increasingly demanded" (Bell 1973:127). The central feature of the transformation to the postindustrial society, again in Bell's words, is "a changeover from a goods-producing society to an information or knowledge society" (Bell 1973:147).

Comments by Mark Benbick, Isabel Sawhill, and Marvin Kosters are gratefully acknowledged.

Bell's analysis has gained growing acceptance since its publication in 1973. Two developments in particular have served to buttress the America-in-transformation thesis. First, the steel, auto, and other basic industries have suffered greatly owing to increased competition from low-wage countries, growing obsolescence of the plants in these industries, and the increases in the cost of oil. While the oil price increases were anomalous in their severity, proponents of the transformation thesis hold that these exogenous shocks merely accelerated a trend already under way. With regard to competition from foreign countries, it is argued—by Peter Drucker, for instance—that low-wage countries have the comparative advantage in developed, mature, basic industries and that such countries will win an ever-increasing share of the world market in these industries.

The second development buttressing the transformation thesis is the growth in the United States of high technology industries. These are principally various types of information processing, such as computers and telecommunications, and the manufacture of highly complex equipment, such as guided missiles, space vehicles, and industrial robots, as well as biological engineering. These industries are information intensive in that they are characterized by a high level of research, development, design, and innovation and require highly skilled scientists and engineers and state of the art equipment. Industries with these traits are said to be those in which the United States has a comparative advantage. Not only is the United States moving toward an economy based on such industries, but, the proponents of industrial policy suggest, the move should be enhanced if not accelerated.

For example, Robert B. Reich and Ira C. Magaziner argue in *Minding America's Business* that government policies in recent years have been fighting the changes that are occurring, by "retarding capital and labor adjustments" rather than "easing the flow of capital and labor to the most competitive businesses within the industry or to related and highly competitive businesses outside the industry" (Reich and Magaziner 1982:203). Government should not only acknowledge the transformation, but encourage it: "It is essential that the United States seek to ease the transition of labor and capital out of declining businesses rather than simply postpone such shifts through 'voluntary' restrictions on trade and regulatory rollbacks" (Reich and Magaziner 1982:215).

What are the declining industries? Reich and Magaziner list "apparel, footwear, steel, automobiles, shipbuilding, color television receivers, and several other major industries," although they acknowledge that "certain businesses within these industries are salvageable" (Reich and Magaziner 1982:203). The high growth industries? The list includes "computers, semiconductors, aircraft, industrial machinery, pharmaceuticals, scientific instruments," and so on (Reich and Magaziner 1982:376).

Reich, in his book *The Next American Frontier,* discusses the possible modes of government intervention and their consequences. If economic policy is not adjusted to the changes that are occurring, he argues, we will "continue to endure a painful and slow economic transition" in which "a growing share of American labor becomes locked into dead-end employment" (Reich 1983: 255). In contrast, adaptive government policies lead to "a dynamic economy" in which capital and labor are shifted to reflect "the new realities of international competition" (Reich 1983:255). In Reich's view the stakes are high: "Either we will adapt to this new reality, or following our historical predecessors, the American ascendancy will needlessly come to a close" (Reich 1983:282).

A REASSESSMENT: THE TWO-TRACK SOCIETY

In contrast to the transformation thesis presented in the preceding pages, there is data to suggest that the information and high technology industries will not replace basic industries in the United States in the foreseeable future. By 1995 and beyond, basic industry will still be a mainstay of the U.S. economy. There will be a relative decrease in the share of jobs and GNP generated by basic industries and even an absolute decline in some industries. But, by and large, the basic industries will still generate new jobs, continue to account for a significant portion of the GNP, and be an important component of an integrated economy that includes both high technology, information-oriented industries and basic ones.

Furthermore, the dichotomy itself will break down as so-called basic industries will increasingly draw on high technology themselves, absorbing the new production, management, and distribution technologies being pioneered in the new high tech industries, while some high tech industries will engage in massive, routine, assembly line production.

To argue on behalf of basic industry is neither to deny the growth of high tech nor to favor protection for inefficient, outmoded factories and companies. Rather, we wish to emphasize the significant role basic industry will continue to play in providing employment and contributing to the GNP. To mistake the growth of high technology for an end to the industrial age, however, could lead to the adoption of policies that, if acted upon, could harm the U.S. economy, society, and security.

FUTURE EMPLOYMENT BY HIGH TECH
AND BASIC INDUSTRIES

One source of the misconception is the argument for proportional increases, which disregards absolute, base data. For instance, the fact that a new industry like bioengineering is projected to increase tenfold by 1995 is an argument based on proportionality. Often neglected is the fact that bio-engineering, minuscule to begin with, will still provide only a tiny fraction of jobs the auto industry or other paragons of basic industry will provide after a decade's growth. It is important to look not only at the rates of growth but also at job growth in absolute numbers and the resulting employment pattern if we are to gain a balanced picture of the implications of the high tech phenomenon for U.S. employment.

The basic trends evident over the last few decades are expected to continue. According to data compiled by the Bureau of Labor Statistics (BLS), agricultural employment dipped from 8.1 percent in 1959 to 2.8 percent in 1982, and is expected to drop to 2.0 percent by 1995. Mining, construction, and manufacturing also declined—from 31.6 percent in 1959 to 24.9 percent in 1982. By 1995, the BLS projects that these sectors will employ 25.7 percent— an increase of 0.4 percent over a thirteen-year period. At first, the small increase in mining, construction, and manufacturing seems to go against the basic trend, but it must be remembered that 1982 was the depth of a recession and a particularly bad year for basic industries. If instead we use 1979 as a comparison year, those three sectors will decrease from the 1979 level of 27.4 percent of total employment to the projected 1995 level of 25.7 percent—a decrease of 2.1 percent over a sixteen-year period (calculated from Personick 1983:26. Here and elsewhere in this paper we rely on the moderate growth projections of the BLS.)

These figures show that the basic structure of the economy is changing very slowly. For example, if the projected 1979–95 rate of decline in mining, construction, and manufacturing continued through the distant year 2050, those sectors would still account for over 18 percent of total employment.

To turn now to the other side of the thesis, the role of high tech, we run into a technical difficulty. Identifying just how many new jobs will be created in high technology industries is complicated by the lack of a commonly accepted definition of the term. Operating definitions are usually cast in terms of one or more of the following: (1) a high percentage of an industry's gross revenue or output dedicated to research and development; (2) a high percentage of scientists and engineers in the industry's work force; and (3) a high percentage of laborers characterized as highly skilled.

Several studies have attempted to isolate reasonable definitions of high tech industries and to analyze their employment patterns. The social scientists Donald Tomaskovic-Devey and S. M. Miller of Boston University identified three common definitions and those standard industrial classifications that currently satisfy them. Their analysis revealed that "strikingly few of the total number of new jobs in the seventies were created by the three sets of high technology industries. . . . All in all, the high technology industries produced jobs at about the same slow rate as manufacturing in general" (Tomaskovic-Devey and Miller 1983:58).

Another aggregate study was done by Robert Z. Lawrence of the Brookings Institution. He divided the U.S. industrial base into four segments: high technology, capital intensive industries, labor intensive industries, and resources industries. High tech industries were defined as those industries characterized by relatively high levels of R&D and technological innovation (Lawrence 1983). His high technology group is broader than the common use of the term implies, embracing about 35 percent of all manufacturing employment and including engines and turbine manufacturing, general industrial machinery, and chemicals, among others. The employment shares for his four categories within manufacturing employment are presented in table 1. While the high technology group as Lawrence defines it has been growing relative to the others, the other sectors have retained significant shares. Thus, if past trends are any indication, all four of the sectors figure to contribute major portions of total manufacturing employment in the near future.

It might be argued, however, that the high tech boom is only beginning and that the growth in the past decade is a poor indication of what we may expect. This calls for projections of future employment in high tech industries. The BLS, which makes specific industry-by-industry growth and employment projections, recently analyzed the job potentials of three separate high technology concepts. The narrowest focused on R&D expenditures and included only six industries: drugs; office, computing, and accounting machines; communication equipment; electronic components and accessories; aircraft and parts; and guided missiles and space vehicles. The broadest group relied solely on higher than average utilization of technology oriented employees. It captured forty-eight industries, including motor vehicles, some heavy construction, soaps and cleaners, radio and television broadcasting, some wholesale trade and others. A third group represented a middle ground between the two, excluding non-

Table 1. Share of Total Manufacturing Employment

	1960	1970	1980
High technology	.27	.30	.33
Capital intensive	.29	.29	.28
Labor intensive	.21	.20	.19
Resource intensive	.23	.21	.20

Source: Lawrence 1983, table 2, p. 140.

manufacturing industries such as broadcasting and trade, since "the exclusion of non-manufacturing industries is common in definitions of high tech industries." It also excluded motor vehicles and a few others, leaving twenty-eight industries (Riche et al. 1983:50–54).

Even if the broadest definition is used, the high tech sector is expected to employ only 14.1 percent of the labor force by 1995. The employment shares of the three high tech definitions studied (though not necessarily endorsed) by the BLS are summarized in table 2.

These groups have been further analyzed to determine the percentage of all new jobs projected by 1995 that each is expected to produce. The BLS projects that between 23.4 and 28.6 million new wage and salary jobs will be created in the economy as a whole between 1982 and 1995. Of those new jobs, the BLS estimates that

> between 1.0 and 4.6 million . . . will be in high technology industries. Growth in group I [the broadest group] will account for 16 or 17 percent of all new jobs, depending on the projection used, while growth in group II [the narrowest group] will account for 3 or 4 percent and group III [the intermediate group], 8 or 9 percent. The great majority of new jobs will be in industries other than high technology. (Riche et al. 1983:54)

Another attempt at aggregate projection of high tech employment was made by Data Resources, Inc. Their model used the BLS definitions of high tech discussed above. Their analysis projected that the number of jobs to be created in high technology industries over the next ten years will be less than half of the two million jobs said to have been lost in manufacturing in the last few years (*Business Week* 1983:85). Among the factors said to explain the small number of jobs to be created is the rapid rise in productivity in these industries due to their high rates of technological innovation.

We now turn to examine the specific industry by industry projections of the BLS. Personick (1983) sets out the industries expected to show the fastest growth in employment between 1982 and 1995 (table 3). Several of the fastest

Table 2. Employment by High Technology Industries under Three Definitions, 1959 to 1995

	1959	1982	1995*
Broadest definition	13.1	13.4	14.1
Intermediate definition	5.8	6.2	6.6
Narrowest definition	2.7	2.8	2.9

*Estimated; moderate growth projections.
Source: Riche et al. 1983:53.

Table 3.   Fastest Growing Industries in Terms of Employment: 1982–1995

Industry	Average annual rate
Medical and dental instruments	4.3
Business services	3.9
Iron and feroalloy ores mining	3.9
Computers and peripheral equipment	3.8
Radio and television broadcasting	3.8
Other medical services	3.8
Plastic products	3.5
Scientific and controlling instruments	3.4
Electronic components	3.2
New construction	3.1

Source: Personick 1983:29.

growing industries are indeed high tech, specifically, medical and dental instruments, computers and peripheral equipment, scientific and controlling instruments, and electronic components. The plastic products industry is included in some of the broader definitions of high tech, as is radio and television broadcasting. The latter, however, is usually excluded because of low levels of R&D. In addition, some subportion of business services is also high tech (data processing services). High tech industries do appear to be among the fastest growing.

A different picture emerges, however, when job growth in absolute terms is considered. The industries expected to have the greatest number of new jobs by 1995 are represented in table 4.

High tech industries do not appear on this list, which is mainly composed of traditional service categories. (Some subcategories of business services and perhaps other medical services might be considered high tech, but not the industries themselves.) In table 5 we see the high tech items from table 3 (fastest growing) in terms of the actual number of new jobs to be created for comparison purposes. Borderline cases of high tech industries are included. The largest of these high tech industries, electronic components, is projected to provide fewer jobs than one-tenth of the industry with the greatest number of projected new jobs, and little more than half the tenth-ranked industry in terms of new jobs (see table 4).

Most basic industries, even if their share of the total number of jobs is declining relative to computers and services, are still producing a great number of new jobs. Metalworking machinery, for example, lags far behind computers in terms of average projected annual rate of growth but is still projected to increase

Table 4. Industries with the Greatest Number of New Jobs by 1995

Industry	Number of new jobs	Percent of all new jobs
Retail trade	3,089,000	12.2
Business services	2,440,000	9.7
New construction	1,976,000	7.8
Eating and drinking places	1,583,000	6.3
Hospitals	1,461,000	5.8
Wholesale trade	1,149,000	4.6
Other medical services	1,024,000	4.1
Professional services	857,000	3.4
Education services (private)	514,000	2.0
Doctors' and dentists' services	502,000	2.0

Source: Personick 1983:30–32.

from 379,000 employees in 1979 (a nonrecessionary year) to 411,000 jobs by 1995. Even industries showing a decline in actual number of jobs should not be written off. The auto industry, although projected to employ more as it recovers from its severe decline in 1981–82, is not expected to return to its 1979 level of 991,000 employees. Still, the BLS projects that it will employ 862,000 workers by 1995, more than any high tech industry.

HIGH TECH OCCUPATIONS

A confusion of the growth in high tech *occupations* with the growth of high tech *industries* may lend credence to the idea that high tech industries will be the mainstay of the economy in the years ahead. These two

Table 5. New Jobs Generated by Fast-Growing High Tech Industries by 1995

Industry	Number of new jobs	Percent of all new jobs
Medical and dental instruments	114,000	0.5
Computers and peripheral equipment	266,000	1.1
Radio and television broadcasting	136,000	0.5
Plastic products	256,000	1.0
Scientific and controlling instruments	123,000	0.5
Electronic components	289,000	1.1

Source: Personick 1983:30–32.

related but distinct developments are often lumped together. For example, a recent *New York Times* article concerning the employment potential of "communications, electronics, computers and other areas of high technology" was accompanied by a chart showing the number of new jobs expected for data processing mechanics, computer operators, and so on (Serlin 1983). But many of these new high tech jobs are likely to be in basic industries as they computerize their production processes or in other non–high tech segments of the economy. Not paying adequate attention to this distinction could lead to calls for sunsetting basic industries like steel and autos because they are not high tech industries. Ironically, this would dampen potential sources of high tech jobs in computer operations and maintenance in these industries.

High tech proponents could reply that these new jobs in high tech occupations will be concentrated in high tech industries, so that the distinction is not as important as it would seem at first glance. While there are a greater-than-average percentage of computer operators and other high tech jobs in high tech industries, there is no close correlation. Many of the new jobs in high tech occupations will be created in basic and other non–high tech industries. For example, the BLS projects that there will be 338,038 computer programmers in the work force in 1990, but most of these jobs will be in industries other than high tech. According to the BLS analysis, only 9 percent will work for manufacturers of office, computing, and accounting machines. Three percent will work in communication and utilities, 7 percent in wholesale and retail trade, 3 percent in commercial banks, 6 percent in insurance, 9 percent in educational services, 8 percent in government, and so forth. The largest single concentration of programmers—23 percent of the projected 1990 cohort—will be in computer and data processing services. However, as the preceding list shows, they are by no means limited to or even concentrated in specifically computer-related industries.

Also, while high tech occupations do represent the fastest growing segment of the job market, these jobs will account for relatively few new jobs overall. A list showing the occupations producing the greatest actual number of new jobs is dominated by traditional and service-oriented occupations. In table 6 we show the fastest growing occupations as predicted by the BLS, the number of new jobs expected by 1995, and the percentage of the total new jobs this represents for each job category.

Almost all of the occupations listed in table 6 are high tech to one degree or another, the exceptions being legal and physical therapy assistants. Office machine repair is less high tech than the other occupations, but because of the increasing sophistication of office equipment it probably qualifies. Yet not a single one of the occupations on this list is going to be a major source of new jobs between 1982 and 1995. Computer systems analysis is the occupation

Table 6.   Fastest Growing Occupations

	BLS projection: 1982–1995		
Occupation	Percent growth	Number of new jobs	Percent of all new jobs
Computer service technicians	96.8	53,000	0.2
Legal assistants	94.3	159,000	0.6
Computer systems analysts	85.3	217,000	0.8
Computer programmers	76.9	205,000	0.8
Computer operators	75.8	160,000	0.6
Office machine repairers	71.7	39,000	0.2
Physical therapy assistants	67.8	22,000	0.1
Electrical engineers	65.3	208,000	0.8
Civil engineering technicians	63.9	23,000	0.1
Peripheral EDP equipment operators	63.5	31,000	0.1

Source: Silvestri et al. 1983:38–43.

projected to generate the largest number of new jobs of the fastest growing occupations, yet this category is expected to account for less than 1 percent of the new jobs to be created by 1995. The eight high tech items in the list of the fastest growing occupations taken together account for only 936,000 new jobs, less than 4 percent of the new jobs projected for 1995. Compare this with the list of the top ten occupations in terms of the actual number of new jobs created, as shown in table 7.

The occupations listed in table 7 are traditional, not at all high tech. The single largest area of expected growth, building custodians, accounts for more new jobs than the five fastest growing high tech jobs combined. The top eight from this list will create almost three million new jobs by 1995, almost six times the amount to be created by the eight fastest growing high tech jobs. Furthermore, only one high tech job appears in the top twenty job categories in terms of numbers of jobs created—electrical and electronic technicians, twentieth on the list, projected to generate 222,000 jobs by 1995.

A word of caution about the projections cited here: the Bureau of Labor Statistics, despite the fact that it is highly regarded and nonpartisan, cannot anticipate every swing in oil prices, technological innovation, or social change to come along. Moreover, the BLS is constantly revising its figures in light of new developments. But it is not the decimal points that concern us; rather, the general trends and the relative performance of one job category or industry versus others. We cite these projections as indicators of general trends, not as specific predictions. Major relationships can be expected to be roughly in line with the projections cited here.

Table 7.   Occupations with Largest Expected Absolute Growth

| | BLS projection: 1982–1990 | | |
Occupation	Percent growth	Number of new jobs	Percent of all new jobs
Building custodians	27.5	779,000	3.0
Cashiers	47.4	744,000	2.9
Secretaries	29.5	719,000	2.8
General clerks, office	29.6	696,800	2.7
Sales clerks	23.5	685,000	2.7
Nurses, registered	48.9	642,000	2.5
Waiters/waitresses	33.8	562,000	2.2
Teachers (elementary)	37.4	511,000	2.0
Truckdrivers	26.5	425,000	1.7
Nurses aides and orderlies	34.8	423,000	1.7

Source: Silvestri et al. 1983:45.

CONTRIBUTION TO GNP

Several basic industries are found on the list of industries expected to show the fastest growth of output between 1982 and 1995, such as railroad equipment and iron and feroalloy ores mining. Three clear examples of high tech industries do appear among the ten fastest growing industries, as shown in table 8 below. They are electronic components, computers and peripheral equipment, and drugs. Two other industries on the list might be considered high tech, depending on the definition used. Radio and television receiving sets, despite being a relatively routine manufacturing industry in some respects (think of mass production transistor radios), does have higher-than-average levels of R&D. "Communications, except radio and television" refers to the provision of those services, not the design, development, and manufacture of telecommunications equipment, which is a separate category. This involves the transmission of information and employs greater than the average number of technicians; thus, it sometimes qualifies as high tech. But the service side of communication, like the programming side of radio and television broadcasting, does not involve large R&D expenditures, scientists, and so on, and hence is more often than not excluded from lists of high tech industries (Riche et al. 1983:50). In the figures below, we will include radio and television manufacture but not communication services.

The combined expected output of the high tech industries in the fastest growing list above is about $157 billion out of a projected 1995 GNP of $3.7 trillion, or about 4.2 percent of the 1995 GNP. The motor vehicles industry alone is

Table 8.   Fastest Growing Industries, Output

Industry	Average annual rate of growth of output	1995 Output (billions, 1972 dollars)
Railroad equipment	8.2	2.8
Electronic components	7.6	52.9
Radio and television receiving sets	7.5	15.0
Computers and peripheral equipment	6.9	63.8
Communications, except radio and television	6.0	138.6
Motorcycles, bicycles, and parts	5.9	0.8
Iron and feroalloy ores mining	5.7	1.5
Drugs	5.6	24.7
Air transportation	5.5	32.9

Source: Calculated from the Bureau of Labor Statistics Economic Growth Model data base, moderate growth projections. Analysis by the authors.

projected to produce almost two-thirds the output of the four fastest growing high tech industries combined—$102 billion compared to $157 billion in 1995. Standard industries will still be producing large measures of the GNP, such as meat products ($43 billion), apparel ($27 billion), blast furnaces and basic steel products ($30 billion), eating and drinking places ($75 billion), other retail trade ($215 billion), and so on. And though there are more high tech industries than are listed in table 8—the exact number depending on the definition employed—everyone would agree that there are many more standard industries than high tech industries. As an approximation of an aggregate figure for the entire high tech sector of the economy, we may look at the total projected 1995 output for the industries that are included in the narrowest of the BLS high tech groupings. A translation of standard industrial codes used in the high tech industry study to the industrial sectors used in the 1995 model provided by Norm Saunders of the BLS shows the total output for all high tech industries is $211.7 billion (in constant 1972 dollars), or less than 6 percent of the projected 1995 GNP. In terms of GNP at least, it is clear that standard industries will continue to be a major part of our economy.

THE INTERMINGLING OF HIGH TECH AND BASIC

An additional point concerns the basic assumption of the post-industrial, information society ideal. It assumes that there is and will continue to be two essentially separate tracks, one high tech and one low tech (admitting, of course, a few intermediate cases). To some extent this is true now, but it is rapidly losing its force as many basic industries begin to make use of high technology in their production and management. They are employing ever-increasing numbers of computer programmers, technicians, and roboticists. They will also serve as the market for the high tech goods, such as robots, and services, such as sophisticated data management, as they modernize. Auto manufacturing, which together with steel is one of the paradigms of basic industry, is reaching a degree of technical sophistication that rivals or exceeds many computer manufacturing plants. In some factories, autos are assembled, welded, and quality controlled by robots, with as few as one human—a computer programmer—to oversee the process (Peterson 1983).

As an early review of Bell's *The Coming of Post-Industrial Society* put it, "'post-industrial society' is in fact not at all *post*-industrial, but assumes the continued existence and development of a highly automated and productive industrial system, the fruits of which give rise to and make possible all the other changes Bell envisions" (Olsen 1974:238). The basic points are that high tech and basic industries are more likely to move closer together than to separate and that the implied dichotomy, whatever its short-run validity now, is not a useful concept for long-term economic planning.

POLICY ISSUES

The evidence presented so far raises several policy issues that are in part subject to value judgments. Each deserves lengthy deliberation; hence we choose merely to raise the questions here.

Humanitarian Consideration

An economy that changes rapidly from basic industries to high technology, whether owing to interventionist industrial policies or to other reasons, may be inviting a great deal of suffering. Not everyone laid off by a basic industry may be able to switch to high tech even if high tech could provide the jobs. A great deal of study is needed (and is only beginning) of the social and psychic difficulties of unemployed blue-collar workers trying to switch to high tech. Those who advocate promoting high technology at the expense of basic industries must consider the possible ramifications of an ever-widening gap between the skills of the population and the jobs available, and the limits of retraining.

National Security

Raising the flag is a favorite stratagem of special interest groups who seek to protect their economic interests from foreign competition. Abuses of the national security argument have nearly destroyed its credibility. Mining interests declare that the United States needs to shore up its silver stockpiles; textile industry representatives argue that we need a domestic capacity to produce uniforms; and so on. Yet this should not lead one to the opposite extreme: to deny the relevance of national security considerations. We need to ask if an industrial base composed principally of high tech industries would be an advantage or a disadvantage in times of war or protracted international difficulties. Are there national security considerations a disinterested observer can recognize for the maintaining of a balance between high technology and basic industries?

Ramifications for Industrial Policy

An implication that follows from the data and arguments we have presented is that policies which seek to promote one sector of the economy over another may not result in a net increase in jobs or GNP. For example, tax credits that encourage the granting of credit to high technology industries may divert credit away from basic industries in need of capital to modernize their plants and equipment; at least, the relative cost of credit will be higher for the nonfavored industries, putting them at a competitive disadvantage. Are there ways to use tax incentives and other tools of industrial policy that are beneficial to a mixed economy? An example might be promoting the general amount of credit available for new investments and modernization in all sectors of the economy as opposed to high tech alone. Or should one avoid such policies altogether?

REFERENCES

Alexander, Charles P. 1983. "The New Economy." *Time*, May 30.
"America Pushes to High Tech for High Growth." 1983. *Business Week*, March 28.
Bell, Daniel. 1973. *The Coming of Post-Industrial Society*. New York: Basic Books.
Esfandiary, F. M. 1980. "Beyond Reindustrialism." *New York Times*, December 30.
Etzioni, Amitai. 1984. *Capital Corruption: The New Attack on American Democracy*. New York: Harcourt Brace Jovanovich.
Guiliano, Vincent. "Productivity in the Information Society: The United States as a Case Example." Unpublished paper.
Hawken, Paul. 1983. *The Next Economy*. New York: Holt, Reinhart and Winston.
Huntley, Steve. 1983. "High Tech: No Panacea for the Jobless." *U.S. News & World Report*, March 7.
Lawrence, Robert Z. 1983. "Is Trade Deindustrializing America? A Medium Term Perspective." *Brookings Papers on Economic Activity*, 1:129–71.
Naisbett, John. 1982. *Megatrends*. New York: Warner Books.
Olsen, Marvin E. 1974. "Review Symposium." *American Journal of Sociology* 80.
Osnos, Peter. 1983. "High-Tech Wizard Sees Brave New World in the '90s." *Washington Post*, March 6.
Personick, Valerie. 1984. "The Job Outlook through 1995: Industry Output and Employment Projections." *Monthly Labor Review*, November.

Peterson, Iver. 1983. "Is Talk of High Tech Jobs More Political Than Real?" *New York Times,* October 24.

Reich, Robert B. 1983. *The Next American Frontier.* New York: Times Books.

Reich, Robert B., and Ira C. Magaziner. 1982. *Minding America's Business.* New York: Harcourt Brace Jovanovich.

Riche, Richard W., Daniel E. Hecker, and John V. Burgan. 1983. "High Technology Today and Tomorrow: A Small Slice of the Employment Pie." *Monthly Labor Review,* November.

Serlin, William. 1983. "'High Tech' Is No Jobs Panacea, Experts Say." *New York Times,* September 18.

Silvestri, George T., John M. Lukasiewicz, and Marcus G. Einstein. 1983. "Occupational Employment Projections through 1995." *Monthly Labor Review,* November.

Toffler, Alvin. 1982. *The Third Wave.* New York: Morrow.

Tomaskovic-Devey, Donald, and S. M. Miller. 1982. "Can High Tech Provide the Jobs?" *Challenge,* May/June.

I I I I I I I I   Organized Labor and
the Welfare State

WILLIAM FORM

Ever since the Great Depression of the 1930s organized labor in the United States flexed its political muscles in the Democratic party to support the welfare state. Today, both labor and the welfare state are in trouble. The Reagan administration slowly eroded support for welfare activities, and labor appeared helpless to do much about it. This paper explains how this situation arose and suggests a new strategy for labor.

Historical evidence suggests that the goals and power of organized labor were not responsible for the growth of the welfare state. Labor influence on welfare legislation depended on how well it worked with organizations that had more focused welfare goals and how these organizations responded to labor. Changes in labor's relations with prowelfare organizations more than changes in its own strength have accounted for the fortunes of governmental welfare programs.

Both labor union growth and social security legislation were part of the New Deal's welfare program. A major change in organized labor's class composition occurred when the New Deal passed legislation that spurred the unionization of large manufacturing industries. First- and second-generation European ethnics in the Congress of Industrial Organizations (CIO) then became labor's bottom stratum, while older ethnic groups dominated the skilled labor aristocracy. Leaders of the American Federation of Labor (AFL) and of the CIO created separate political machines to pressure the Democratic party to continue its prolabor and prowelfare state course. But labor did not create an integrated political organization until a generation after the New Deal began—when labor's numbers and power were already declining. By this time, continuous

I am grateful to Joan Huber, Richard F. Hamilton, and Michael Wallace for their criticisms and suggestions for improving this paper.

prosperity had raised the economic well-being of both new and old European groups. But the urban underclass of blacks, Hispanics, and poor women continued to grow.

In the 1960s the federal government initiated programs to improve the economic opportunities of the poor, especially black youth. But organized labor did not vigorously support these programs and even actively opposed them in many communities. Moreover, labor failed to get prounion legislation passed. Labor's ability to promote welfare programs will decline unless it changes its political priorities. Paradoxically, labor's best strategy may be to increase its underclass membership and broaden its welfare state goals and deemphasize party politics.

LABOR'S THREE WELFARE STRATEGIES

The welfare state has been defined as a set of public policies and institutions that assures economic growth while it dampens class conflict (Galbraith 1969; Offe 1984). This essay ignores state management of the economy and focuses on the state's programs to assure the poorest third of the population a measure of economic security, a decent level of living, and equal access to education, occupations, and employment. These objectives can be accomplished by progressive taxation and income redistribution. Here I examine the role that labor plays in income redistribution efforts. Historically, it has used three political strategies: pragmatic unionism, social unionism, and class unionism.

In pragmatic unionism, organized labor defined the struggle as being limited to business and itself. Therefore, it focused primarily on building strong unions because its leaders believed that ultimately the welfare of the working class depended on trade union strength. Labor demanded little from government and even discouraged government intervention in labor–management disputes. Selig Perlman (1928) called this strategy "business unionism." All presidents of the AFL endorsed this strategy before World War II. Obviously, it did little to build a welfare state.

Social unionism aims to persuade government to help all organized and unorganized workers achieve economic security and social justice. In its most limited form, social unionism considers governmental welfare programs as supplements to labor's bargaining achievements. The United Automobile Workers' (UAW) two-way approach is illustrative: labor bargains with management for unemployment benefits and presses Congress to improve federal unemployment insurance programs (Jacobs 1983). Even though insurance programs help all workers, they disproportionately benefit union members.

Social unionism also fights for legislation that helps all workers: truth in advertising, antipollution, fair employment practices, and occupational health and safety. Some unions (for example, the UAW) have placed greater emphasis on such legislation while other unions (for example, the Railroad Brotherhoods or Building Trades) press harder for legislation that helps only the organized. Unions also vary in their involvement with coalitions that press for welfare state expansions. Most unions play minor roles, but a few occasionally head coalitions and furnish leadership, finance, and staff. Although scholars disagree on the extent to which American social unionism created the welfare state, they agree that labor actively supported it only from the early 1930s.

Class unionism explicitly assigns unions the task of building a workers' welfare state. In the social democratic version of class unionism, the capitalist welfare state is a phase in the transition to socialism. Labor parties, as creatures of unions, organize to guide the transition. In revolutionary class unionism, the welfare state is considered a bulwark of capitalism and it must be destroyed and replaced with socialism or communism. Class unionism stresses that political class goals outrank the union's economic goals. Most scholars agree that while class unionism has had little relevance in the United States, social unionism did help build a welfare state similar to those built by European social democratic parties (Greenstone 1977; Lipset 1977; Wilson 1979).

Historians (for example, Bauman 1972) have suggested that unions succeed in building welfare states when they (a) organize a broad range of industries, (b) avoid deep internal cleavages, (c) recruit members that resemble the entire working class, and (d) place higher priority on class welfare than union gains. I argue that these conditions were largely absent in the era of pragmatic unionism, appeared in the early stages of social unionism, have declined since, and must be restored to realize an expanded welfare state.

Pragmatic Unionism

The founding of the AFL in 1886 marked the end of class union experiments in the country. Gompers regarded the organization of all workers as a fruitless experiment and sought to organize only workers who had a natural affinity for organization and self-protection: skilled craft workers. The AFL strengthened local craft unions by linking them to autonomous national unions that were loosely coordinated at the national level. For over fifty years, union membership fluctuated with economic conditions but rarely rose above 10 percent of the nonagricultural labor force (Reynolds 1974:365).

When small industries dominated the economy and relied heavily on skilled labor, craft unions could exert considerable power in local labor markets (Montgomery 1979; Brody 1980; Jackson 1984). With the growth of large-scale industry, skilled male workers, mostly native born of English and German ancestry, became increasingly unrepresentative of manual workers in their occupations, employment sector, sex, ethnicity, and religion (Foner 1964:259).

Especially from 1890 to World War I, middle-class reformers, intellectuals, and socialists pressed parties and state and federal legislators to improve working-class welfare, and they met with some success (Rubinow 1934a,b). Reformers drew their inspiration from Germany, England, and other European countries that had already passed legislation for unemployment insurance, old age pensions, minimum wages, and family wage supplements. Although similar legislation was proposed in several states, the AFL did not support it. Up to 1932 most unions opposed compulsory unemployment insurance, regarding it as an ineffective invasion of the individual worker's rights (Wolman and Peck 1933:840). Up to 1937 the AFL also opposed federal minimum wage legislation (Ware 1934). Furthermore, from 1923 to 1973 labor annually opposed a constitutional amendment to grant women workers equal rights with men. The only social insurance program that labor backed was compulsory compensation insurance for job-related accidents. By 1915 almost all states had enacted such legislation (Witte 1934).

AFL officials argued that workers could best meet economic risks by individual planning and unfettered collective bargaining. The working class would become fully organized if government and the courts would not interfere with collective bargaining. Therefore, labor should push for legislation that limited court and government intervention in labor organizing and strikes.

Outside the labor movement a small and weak coalition of reformers struggled to enact federal welfare legislation. It was articulate, organized, not disreputable, and successful in some eastern and midwestern cities and states (Gilson 1934; Quadagno 1984). AFL officials branded the coalition as intellectuals, reformers, and socialists. Although craft unions were heavily enmeshed in both local and national politics (Greenstone 1977:31), they firmly opposed building a welfare state. Thus the welfare strategy of pragmatic unionism resembled the political instincts of small business and the middle class.

Antecedents of Social Unionism

The New Deal's early years marked the major expansion of the American welfare state. To assess the unions' part in this process, I first examine the social context of the AFL's earlier growth. From 1900 to 1930, AFL membership increased 2.8 times, from about 1 to 3.8 million members. This partly reflected labor force growth and growth of skilled workers. But semiskilled operatives increased even more, while unskilled laborers dropped slightly. The labor force in manufacturing peaked in the 1920s at about 30 percent and then began to decline.

Importantly, the number of manufacturing establishments declined 80 percent from 1910 to 1930, while their employees increased by half (U.S. Bureau of the Census 1960:P-1-10). But the foreign-born labor force grew by 50 percent. In 1910, 54 percent of manufacturing workers were either foreign-born or were children of one or two foreign-born parents. By 1930 the manufacturing labor force, concentrated mostly in the urban East and Midwest, predominantly comprised recent European ethnics. The percentage of black urban workers, 6 percent in 1910, expanded only slightly by 1930 (Edwards 1943:158).

The growth of AFL craft unions was uneven. While membership increased 2.8 times from 1910 to 1930, it increased only 1.2 times in chemicals, 1.8 times in mining, and 2.5 times in manufacturing. Where craft unions were strong, membership soared; for example, 4.7 times in transportation and communications and 5.9 times in building. Thus, although union membership was growing, it grew least in the expanding large-scale industries that largely employed recent ethnic groups and a rising minority of blacks (U.S. Bureau of the Census 1960: D 589–617). These conditions stratified working-class earnings. Hourly wage rates in the highly unionized construction industry in 1926 were 31 percent higher than in manufacturing. Even in manufacturing semiskilled and skilled workers in 1933 earned wage rates 40 percent higher than the unskilled (U.S. Bureau of the Census 1960: D 589–617, pp. 654–84). Work stoppages stabilized from 1900 to 1920 and then declined to 1932. With a few notable exceptions this was a period of low industrial unrest.

Although the AFL had a vocal socialist wing up to World War I, AFL officials embraced the political credo of nonpartisan voluntarism. However, rising anti-unionism in the Republican party after 1906 edged the federation toward the Democrats, but it maintained its official policy of nonpartisanship. Especially after World War I the AFL experienced increasing partisan tensions because some of its locals had worked out comfortable understandings with local Republican machines, while others backed Democratic machines. The federation continued its noncommital party stance in national elections. Although the Republicans won the 1928 presidential election, they had already lost the support of the urban ethnics and blacks to the Democratic party. Again in 1932 the federation refused to support the Democratic party openly. Thus, on the eve of the 1932 Democratic triumph, as the Depression deepened, the federation was losing membership, and most urban ethnics and blacks had shifted their loyalty to the Democratic party (Greenstone 1977:29–38).

The Era of Social Unionism

The economic crisis that faced the victorious Democratic party in 1933 is too well known to describe here. Between 1933 and 1938, to meet the crisis, Roosevelt and the Democratic party enacted the basic structure of the

American welfare state (see table 1). In 1934 they introduced unemployment insurance and the National Industrial Recovery Act. In 1935 they legalized the act's union provisions in the National Labor Relations Act (Wagner Act). They passed old age and disability insurance legislation in 1935, aid to dependent children in 1938, and federal minimum wage legislation in 1938. Organized labor played only a marginal role in this program, which was formulated and promoted largely by social scientists, intellectuals, Roosevelt's political advisors, and liberal members of Congress (Skocpol and Ikenberry 1983:99–122).

Table 1.   Dates of Welfare State Legislation and Labor Union Events

Welfare Legislation		*Union Political Events*	
1932	Norris-LaGuardia Act		
1934	Unemployment Insurance		
1934	National Industrial Recovery Act— Section 7a		
1935	Social Security Act (Old age and disability)	1935	Committee on Industrial Organization in AFL
1935	National Labor Relations Act (Wagner Act)		
1938	Aid to Dependent Children	1938	CIO expelled from AFL
1938	Fair Labor Standards Act (Minimum Wage)		
		1943	CIO sets up PAC
1946	Employment Act of 1946 (Full employment)		
		1947	Taft-Hartley Act
1950	Social Security Act to include totally disabled		
		1955	AFL-CIO merge; COPE established
		1959	Landrum-Griffen Act
1963	Equal Pay Act		
1964	Civil Rights Act, Title VII Equal Employment Opportunity Commission		
1964	Economic Opportunity Act (War on Poverty)		
1965	Department of Housing and Urban Development		
1965	Medicare and Medicaid		
		1968	UAW leaves AFL-CIO
1970	Occupational Safety and Health Act (OSHA)		

Under the protective umbrella of the Wagner Act, union membership almost tripled from 1933 to 1939 (Reynolds 1974:366). Unlike Western Europe, where unions, labor, and socialist parties pressed for welfare legislation, in the United States the New Deal pressed for union growth as part of its welfare state program. Thus, Roosevelt and the Democratic party were ahead of the AFL in promoting prolabor and welfare legislation (Greenstone 1977:48). The background of this unique situation requires elaboration.

During Hoover's administration, Congress, in response to growing labor unrest and rising Democratic representation, passed the Norris–LaGuardia Act (1932), which reduced judicial restrictions on labor organizing. In 1933, when Democrats took control of Congress, strikes per one million nonagricultural workers doubled[1] (Griffin 1929:38; BLS 1975:10). The Democratic Congress was well disposed to protect labor unions and pass the welfare legislation that Roosevelt initiated. Despite their ethnic and religious diversity, manual workers in the industrial East and Midwest converged to support the Democratic party. In turn, the party passed legislation that facilitated unionization of mass-production industries, in which European ethnics and black workers were concentrated. Despite some craft union opposition, a Committee on Industrial Organization was created in the AFL in 1936 to organize all workers in heavy industries, regardless of skill. Despite the committee's success, the AFL subsequently expelled these industrial unions, which then formed the rival Congress of Industrial Organizations (CIO). Thus, the CIO organized the ethnically heterogeneous work force in large-scale industries that the Democratic party had earlier organized politically. Greenstone (1977:37) observed that this historical process reversed Marx's prediction: political class solidarity was established before economic class solidarity.

Union Political Organization

I have argued that the basic structure of the welfare state was first erected largely without the political help of organized labor. The newly formed industrial unions and some craft unions then openly supported the program. Fearful of lagging worker support, these unions decided to create their own political organization to back the Democratic party and its prolabor welfare program. The dilemma that American labor faced in 1936 was to build a political arm without creating a labor party and yet avoid becoming a subsidi-

---

1. Piven and Cloward, (1971, chap. 2) claim that labor unrest forced the capitalist state to make concessions to labor. The strike evidence does not strongly support this claim. Strikes per million nonagricultural workers dropped steadily from 156 in 1915 to 22 in 1930. They rose to 36 in 1932, doubled in 1933, and remained stable throughout Roosevelt's first term. In 1937 the rate doubled again to 152 and then fell, never again to approach the 1915 and 1937 highs.

ary part of the Democratic machine. The traditional AFL solution of supporting any candidate favorable to labor did not work, and more had to be done to assure Roosevelt's reelection. Leaders of unions that later became the CIO formed a primitive political organization, Labor's Non-Partisan League. But not until 1943, five years after being expelled from the AFL, did the CIO build anything that resembled a permanent and effective political organization. Because many candidates it backed were defeated in the 1942 elections, the CIO organized a Political Action Committee (PAC) to reelect Roosevelt for a fourth term (Calkins 1952; Foster 1975).

PACs collected funds from union members to create a precinct network aimed at stimulating workers to register and vote for labor-backed candidates (mostly Democrats). The PACs were parallel to but independent of the Democratic party. Later the AFL, also responding to political defeats, created its own political arm, Labor's League for Political Education (LLPE). When the AFL and the CIO merged in 1955, they merged their two political organizations into the Committee on Political Education (COPE).

Labor's effectiveness in supporting welfare programs depended ultimately on the effectiveness of COPE in getting out the working-class vote for the Democratic party. Labor's first effective grass-roots political organization (CIO-PAC) was established in 1944, eleven years after the launching of the New Deal. And labor's first fully integrated political organization (COPE) emerged in 1955, twenty-two years after the New Deal began. By this time changes that would affect the future course of the welfare state had occurred in organized labor, the working class, and the Democratic party.

The peak of social unionism dated from the formation of the CIO-PAC in 1943 and continued, albeit abating, for another dozen years. From 1943 to 1955 the CIO sector of the labor movement resembled a cohesive social class more than any segment of the labor movement since the Knights of Labor. That is, CIO union members resembled unorganized workers socially and economically. They had buried most of their traditional ethnic and religious hostilities in order to support their unions. They were more united behind the Democratic party than in any period before or since. Political cleavages between CIO officers and the rank and file were small, and both supported the welfare goals of social unionism. All these conditions slowly changed after labor become politically united through COPE in 1955.

LABOR AND WELFARE STATE EXPANSION

After 1938 the welfare state continued to expand, but at a slower pace. Fearful that a depression might follow World War II, Congress passed the Employment Act of 1946, which pledged the government to maintain full employment. In 1950 the Social Security act was expanded to cover the totally disabled, and in 1963 Congress passed the Equal Pay Act, which required employers to pay women and men the same rate for the same job. In 1964 Title VII of the Civil Rights Act established an Equal Opportunity Commission to assure minorities and women equal access to all jobs. In the same year, the Economic Opportunity Act launched a war to eliminate poverty in America. In 1965, more than half a century after Britain had established a national health program, Congress passed Medicare and Medicaid to help the aged and poor defray medical expenses. In 1965 the Department of Housing and Urban Development was established to coordinate programs dedicated to improving housing for the poor and the physical environment of cities. Last, in 1970, under Nixon, Congress passed the Occupational Safety and Health Act (OSHA) to reduce work hazards. All this legislation, except for OSHA, was passed while Democratic presidents held office, and all of it received backing from organized labor. However, the objectives of most of the legislation have not been fully realized.

The course of the welfare state after 1950 differed significantly from its earlier course. Before 1950, social insurance legislation covered almost all citizens regardless of class. After 1950, welfare legislation aimed at reducing poverty and inequality of economic opportunity for minorities and women, groups that did not belong to labor unions. The failure of the welfare state to improve the well-being of the poor and to reduce economic inequality has been attributed to labor's faltering strength, increasing conservatism, and ineffectiveness in working with groups dedicated to helping the disprivileged.

Labor's Loss of Strength

With three marginal exceptions (Full Employment Act, Medicare and Medicaid, and OSHA), for almost a half century (1938–85), Congress enacted little legislation to advance organized labor's interests. On the contrary, in 1947, under Truman, Congress passed the Taft-Hartley Act, which severely restricted labor's jurisdiction over its members. During Eisenhower's second term, in 1959, Congress passed the Landrum-Griffen Act to increase federal monitoring of many of labor's activities. Beginning with Nixon's first term in 1969, the NLRB began tilting its decisions against labor. Ironically, even Democrat-controlled congresses failed to pass bills favorable to unions: for example, repeal of the Taft-Hartley and Landrum-Griffin acts and failure to pass the Davis-Bacon bill, which mandated contractors on federal construction projects to pay local community (union) wage rates.

This poor record seems inexplicable because the Democrats sometimes controlled both the presidency and both houses of Congress. Even as the most important block in the Democratic party, labor could not obtain its core legislative demands. It contributes more to the party than any other group; it operates the largest and most effective vote-getting machine in COPE; the AFL-CIO and the National Educational Association (NEA) have the largest delegations in the national conventions of the party; labor supports the most and perhaps ablest lobbyists in Washington; and labor has sometimes cooperated with the Democratic coalition even against its self-interests (Greenstone 1977; Rehmus et al. 1978; Wilson 1979).

Labor's strength peaked over forty years ago in 1945, when fully 36 percent of nonagricultural workers were members. Although membership grew in the 1970s, in 1985 only 20 percent of the nonfarm labor force was organized, and membership stabilized at about twenty million (Roberts 1984). More important, ideological and organizational conflicts grew. The AFL-CIO merger in 1955 probably increased cleavages in the House of Labor (Weber 1963). At varying times after the merger, one-third of all union members belonged to nonaffiliated unions: for example, Teamsters, United Auto Workers, Mine Workers, Railroad Brotherhoods, Electrical Workers, Postal Workers, and others. Moreover, the powerful NEA and other independent unions refused to affiliate with the AFL-CIO.

Other changes weakened labor's influence. While most of organized labor has been concentrated in a few eastern and midwestern states, job growth in the 1970s and 1980s shifted to the South and West. Moreover, recent economic recessions battered liberal ex-CIO unions more than ex-AFL unions. Thus, from 1980 to 1985 the Steel Workers lost one-half of its members and the UAW, one-third. Although the growth of politically liberal public sector unions (for example, the American Federation of State, County, and Municipal Employees) partially offset losses in the liberal ex-CIO unions, the conservative influence of ex-AFL unions (always dominant in the AFL-CIO) has grown even more as they expand into the retail and service sectors. Finally, although union membership tends to increase support for the Democratic party and liberal politics (Ra 1978), union members have increasingly defected from the party (Harwood 1982; Form 1985), even as the party itself has become more conservative.

Yet, growing union weakness does not satisfactorily explain labor's weakening influence on welfare legislation. Even with its shrunken membership, labor remains the largest, wealthiest, strongest, and best-organized sector of the Democratic party. Smaller groups with fewer resources, for example, milk and tobacco lobbies, obtain favorable legislation. Moreover, labor's leaders insist that COPE is still a powerful force because about 70 percent of the candidates it supports for office are elected. Despite union members' growing conservatism, labor lobbyists in Washington still support most welfare legislation. For example, in 1975 COPE selected twelve key pieces of legislation to evaluate the voting records of individual senators (RCIA 1976). Eight measures dealt with help for the needy: control of oil prices, appropriations to create one million jobs, voting rights, food stamps for the jobless, job safety, tax reduction, ending oil depletion allowances, and appropriations for emergency jobs.

Labor's Ineffective Coalitions

Labor's alleged failure to work effectively with the welfare coalition to get class legislation passed cannot be evaluated without more case studies. This argument assumes that a well-coordinated welfare coalition could push through legislation that would significantly reduce the proportion of families in poverty. Indeed, Reid (1982) and Davis et al. (1983) point to a trend of increasing inequality.

Greenstone (1977), the most eminent scholar of American labor politics, disagrees with the above portrait of welfare state politics. He claims that the welfare state expanded after 1960 because federal legislation continued to improve consumer well-being and that labor worked effectively with the consumer coalition to advance the interests of consumers. Even though labor suffered defeats in its own legislative program, it did succeed, with the help of other groups, to improve the well-being of consumers. Thus, unions served the class interests of all workers, including their members. Antipollution legislation, truth in advertising, federal aid to education, reapportionment, urban development, expansion of public utilities, and Medicare represent the expanding welfare role of government. Greenstone (1977:327) concludes that in advanced industrial societies traditional worker–employer class conflict has been replaced by a new form of class conflict, conflict between employers and workers as consumers. In this struggle, he concludes (and I agree) that labor has been an effective member of the consumer coalition. The question remains whether the coalition equitably advances the interests of all segments of the working class.

Two Welfare States or One?

Greenstone asserts that after World War II labor played an important role in creating the welfare state. After achieving large gains in collective bargaining, it turned to consumer legislation to increase further working-class well-being. Bargaining gains declined while consumer legislation gains increased to the point that consumer struggles supplanted labor–management bargaining as the main form of class struggle. Greenstone tends to equate the growth of consumer legislation with growth of the welfare state. Since in his analysis consumers represent the working class, as consumers advance their interests in the legislative arena, the working class also advances its interests, and the welfare state grows in size and importance.

In Greenstone's new class struggle, the class opponents of the working-consumer class are the economic authorities (Dahrendorf 1959), who own and manage large businesses. They oppose consumer legislation because they believe that they pay disproportionately for insatiable consumer demands, for example, social security expansion, pollution controls, truth in packaging. In Greenstone's analysis, all worker-consumers participate in this new form of class struggle. In the United States, labor aggregates the interests of various consumer groups and workers to support the Democratic party and its legislative program.

Altogether, Greenstone's class of economic authorities probably represents no more than 10 to 15 percent of the voters. Although their economic power is much greater than their numbers, in the American party system, where votes count, the consumer-worker class is so large that over time it erodes the veto power of the economic authorities. Since, by definition, legislation that supports consumer interests expands the welfare state, Greenstone's welfare state is bound to grow in response to pressure from many special interest lobbies from the Sierra Club to old age pensioners, downtown shoppers, steelworkers who want to keep dirty industries alive, and others. Although Greenstone's analysis may advance understanding of the political process, it ignores the diversity and stratification of consumers as a class—if indeed they constitute a class. He also neglects economic, status, and political conflicts among consumer groups.

I hold that once the basic structure of America's welfare state was laid down from 1933 to 1938, a new type of welfare struggle emerged. Organized labor was a double beneficiary of the original welfare state. It received governmental protection to organize and increase earnings through collective bargaining and it also received social insurance benefits extended to all citizens. Over time, organized labor improved its relative economic and political position, dividing the working class of manual and clerical workers into two economic and political strata (Form 1985). The most important welfare issue today is the fate of the poorer, politically weaker, and unorganized lower part of that class. In analyzing this issue, I distinguish two welfare states, one that benefits all consumers and another that benefits the disprivileged. The privileged position of union members may influence labor's welfare strategy.

Labor's Place in the Working Class

Even when we restrict the working class to manual workers, the social and economic gulf between union members and other workers runs deep. From 1970, the mean annual earnings of the unionized were almost two-thirds greater than those of the unorganized. Even when we control for most of the variables that affect earnings (for example, age, sex, marital status, chief earner, race, hours and weeks worked, skill, education, work experience, employment sector), the unionized earned 35 percent more than other workers, excluding fringe benefits. Freeman's (1981) survey of ten thousand firms showed that the average advantage in such benefits for unionized firms was over 2.4 times more than those of nonunionized firms, a proportion that far exceeds the wage gap. Other advantages of the union sector parallel their economic superiority. A higher proportion of the unionized are male, white, married, skilled, suffer less unemployment, and work in economically stable firms.

Although the above disparities are large, they do not reveal the full range of working-class stratification because nonunionized workers represent a broad spectrum. Thus, the mean annual earnings of nonskilled unionists are twice those of comparable workers in the economic periphery. The earnings relationship between the two is only marginally smaller when we compare full-time workers and major family earners (Form and Putnam 1985:21). Although the economic recessions of the 1970s caused high unemployment in unionized heavy industries, the earnings advantages of the unionized remained as large as ever. Most analysts fail to consider the devastating impact of the recession on workers who had no union protection or status advantages.

Today's urban working class is substantially different from what it was when the welfare state was launched. In 1933, first- and second-generation south and east European immigrants, some "older" American stocks, and a few blacks made up the unskilled and semiskilled proletariat. Members of the original CIO unions differed little from unorganized manual workers at the bottom of the economic, ethnic, and status ladders. Moreover, from 1870 until the formation of CIO unions before World War II, the American working class became more economically homogenized (Gordon, Edwards, and Reich 1982:100). After the war, it became increasingly stratified. Unionized workers in heavy industry steadily gained economic advantages over and sometimes at the expense of the unorganized (Kahn 1978). European ethnic neighborhoods disappeared in many cities as the second and third generations became economically, socially, and geographically mobile. Growing numbers of southern blacks, Hispanics from Mexico, Puerto Rico, and the Caribbean area, and Asian immigrants moved into the bottom of the urban working class. As the new underclass, these groups now compose 20 percent of the labor force and over one-third of all manual and service workers (Roberts 1984:26). They work in the lowest paying nonunionized industries and live in crowded, substandard housing in areas once occupied by European ethnics. And they suffer high unemployment, underemployment, and job discrimination. Neglected by the welfare state and unprotected by organized labor, they wait and wait for a new deal. In short, the United States today has two working classes. The upper one, mobilized by the first welfare state in 1933, has little to do with the underclass spawned a generation later (Wilson 1987). What has organized labor done about the new underclass? What agenda does labor have for it?

LABOR AND THE NEW WELFARE STATE POLITICS

The Erosion of Confidence in Labor

Consumer welfare politics appealed to the unions formed during the New Deal because it improved the memberships' economic well-being, but it has less appeal to today's working-class poor. Poor blacks, Hispanics, and women want secure, full-time jobs, better-paying jobs, and educational and occupational opportunities. They want an economic and social system that treats them fairly. These hopes could have been realized if post–World War II welfare state legislation had fulfilled its goals. But the Employment Act of 1946 did not produce full employment. Paradoxically, unemployment insurance enabled the nation to tolerate higher rates of unemployment and under-employment. The 1964 Civil Rights Act with its Equal Opportunity Act did not provide many blacks, Hispanics, and women equal access to desirable jobs in the secure economic sectors. The 1964 War on Poverty failed to reduce income inequality in the working class and society. The Department of Housing and Urban Development, created in 1965, as noted above, has not materially improved underclass housing. The 1965 Medicare-Medicaid Act unexpectedly raised medical costs so that some benefits were reduced. Finally, the OSHA of 1970 has been least enforced in small, economically marginal enterprises, which employ the bulk of the working poor. Unlike the successful implementation of the New Deal social insurance programs, post–World War II welfare legislation represents for the disprivileged unrealized national aspirations (see table 1).

Although organized labor supported most of this legislation, it did not convince disprivileged groups that it was firmly dedicated to their causes. Greenstone (1977:352) claims that labor supported Medicare, reapportionment, and civil rights legislation not because the bills benefited disprivileged groups but because labor needed their votes to support the Democratic party. Greenstone concludes that labor was not a special interest group or even a working-class entity. Rather, it was an organized constituency of the Democratic party. Although labor may have lacked sufficient power to convince the party to implement legislation that would guarantee full employment, it could, for example, help implement the Equal Opportunity Act. Labor strongly supported the legislation in Congress, yet failed to support, in fact even opposed, its implementation on the community and enterprise levels. The greatest strides in implementing the act occurred in the public sector (government and education) and in large firms where labor unions were relatively weak. Many ex-AFL unions opposed the hiring, training, and promoting of blacks, Hispanics, and women for skilled jobs. In heavy industry, where the ex-CIO unions predominated, minorities and women were absorbed in greater numbers, but even in the liberal UAW, their entry into the skilled jobs was painfully slow (Widick 1972).

Few union leaders have been willing to change seniority rules that keep minorities and women from achieving greater economic security. This situation indirectly retards the entry of women and minorities into union officialdom even in industries where they compose a majority of union members. Even though the AFL-CIO organized the Coalition of Labor Union Women (CLUW) in 1974, the latter experienced difficulties in attacking the seniority and officer representation issues. The Coalition of Black Trade Unionists (CBTU), organized in 1972 to help blacks become union officers, has had only modest success, confined mostly to unions in which blacks dominate the membership.

The War on Poverty and the war in Vietnam greatly fueled inflation, taxes, and the public debt. Only slowly and reluctantly did labor withdraw its support for the war, and it avoided confronting the war's inflationary aftereffects. Wage gains in unionized industries outstripped productivity increases during these years (Bell 1972:184). The War on Poverty could have been continued by increasing taxes on middle and high incomes, a strategy that labor opposed. Poverty remained a low saliency issue both for union officers and most members. Labor did support Medicare and Medicaid, but its support for OSHA was divided. Individual unions joined management to oppose OSHA when the costs of pollution control, for example, threatened marginally profitable industries. And labor could not affect the administration of OSHA in small, nonunionized firms.

Labor's cooperation with public welfare groups was not especially successful. Although blacks and Hispanics remained more loyal to the Democratic party than union members (Harwood 1982), COPE could not mobilize the former to vote in important elections. Feminists in the Democratic party began to define labor as uninterested in women's issues, if not actively antifeminist. Middle-class liberals in the Democratic party began to see themselves as left of labor and accused it of being more interested in party control than in welfare issues (Greenstone 1977:363).

Labor's changing moods about Democratic presidential candidates convinced many middle-class liberals that labor had become just another self-interested pressure group. Liberals criticized labor for supporting Humphrey, who they felt came out too late against the Vietnam War, for not supporting McGovern's peace platform, for weakly supporting Carter, and for prematurely supporting Mondale's presidential candidacy. Labor lost not only its reputation as the liberal coalition coordinator in the party, but also by 1980 the confidence of the liberal coalition itself. In the public mind, Big Labor had joined Big Business to support a heartless and uncaring Big Government. Whereas in 1936, 72 percent of adults approved of labor unions, only 55 percent did so in 1981. In 1976, 64 percent of Americans thought that unions had too much influence and 53 percent thought that ordinary workers had too little influence (Lipset and Schneider 1983:203–10). In the public mind, labor no longer talked for working people.

Rise of the Passionate Lobbies

The public's loss of faith in labor's ability to speak for the working class and its declining influence in welfare politics cannot be traced to loss of compassion on the part of labor leaders, but to their political priorities. Changes in the class system and in the working class after the Great Depression had spawned new welfare constituencies. Traditional liberals supported the new poor and labor still tried to coalesce these liberal groups in the party, but the liberal–labor coalition had come unglued. Neither labor nor the party has succeeded in coordinating the new passionate lobbies of blacks, Hispanics, women, consumer groups, peace activists, and environmentalists. None of these groups now feels that it has the wholehearted support of labor or the Democratic party. Black local union officials and black political leaders feel they have to force white officials to pay heed to black concerns. Blacks therefore trust only black legislators to understand the problems of blacks and put black priorities first. Unlike labor, black legislators have direct access to black communities, black organizations, and black lay leaders. These constituencies exhibit much more consensus and solidarity than do union members as such. The sense of deprivation, solidarity, passion, and determination that black leaders experience today parallels the psychology of labor organizers during the early New Deal. Moreover, when blacks organize political machines in black communities they help create new jobs for blacks and new leaders.

A similar scenario applies to the growing Hispanic communities. Though internally differentiated, Hispanics share a language and sense of fate. Unlike earlier ethnic groups that slowly assimilated, Hispanics continue to grow in number and self-awareness. Although the immigration of Hispanics may ebb, it will continue to be sufficiently high to keep their language and customs alive. If Hispanic loyalty to the Democratic party continues, like blacks, they will begin to assume party posts. Although fewer Hispanics than blacks are unionized, Hispanics are beginning to assert themselves in unions. As both minorities build their own networks, their solidarity and power will increase to the point where party and labor officials will need the minorities more than they need labor and the party. As these minorities mobilize in communities, labor unions, and parties, they may be better positioned to coordinate the liberal coalition than labor.

Women's lobbies may not be as well integrated as those of minorities, but women's ties probably are more extensive. Women are organized within labor (CLUW), within both parties, and to some degree within ethnic communities. Women's organizational networks transcend class and even political boundaries more so than do the networks between the different minorities. Moreover, no other group (certainly not labor or the parties) has such a vocal and talented intellectual elite. Women's groups have now developed such irreversible political momentum that labor and the political parties now actively seek women's support. But labor's past ambivalence makes women's groups cautious about cooperating.

Many consumer lobbies in Washington have developed so much political and financial strength that they do not need labor's help. Neither labor nor any other group can now integrate the many consumer lobbies into a single coalition. The Sierra Club, antinuclear groups, pure food groups, Ralph Nader's public policy lawyers, retired teachers' associations, and many other lobbies often operate independently. The knowledge, specialized staffs, and resources of these lobbies are too vast for labor to coordinate. Moreover, these groups often engage in direct action. They hire lawyers to sue violators of consumer legislation, and they sue government bureaus for failing to enforce the law. Many liberals who previously contributed money and time to political parties and labor now prefer to support consumer groups that get quick results. Court cases arouse passions, attract contributions, and provide free publicity. In short, today's consumer politics has little resemblance to the consumer-welfare politics of the 1950s and 1960s that Greenstone (1977) described. And it's not the kind of politics that attracts working-class passions.

The size of federal budget deficits dominates today's political scene. After President Reagan's first year in office, the defense budget soared while the social welfare budget has languished in some areas and dwindled in many others. The debate increasingly focused on the balance between defense and social welfare spending and on taxes. Labor might have been expected to develop clear policies on these matters, but confusion reigned. For example, President Reagan's first plan to simplify federal income taxes called for taxing all income, including fringe benefits that employers pay. In testimony before a congressional committee on the issue AFL-CIO president Lane Kirkland was deliberately vague. Members of industrial unions generally have substantial health insurance fringe benefits. They would have suffered least from the president's plan to tax only the first $10.00 a month that the employer pays. Other unions with less fulsome plans would have paid relatively higher taxes (*Wall Street Journal* 1985). In the defense area, an AFL-CIO poll showed that

70 percent of its members opposed cutting the defense budget. Yet labor's PACs tend to support congressional candidates who want to cut defense spending (*Wall Street Journal* 1984). Then public sector unions want a large federal budget while many private sector unions want to pare it. With some notable exceptions unions with members in the defense industries want large defense budgets at the same time other unions call for a reduction. Some unions want protective tariffs and other do not. In short, labor's heterogeneity inhibits consensus on the central issues of taxes, welfare, and defense. Unlike the passionate lobbies, labor cannot exercise its strong but undisciplined political clout.

Finally and most ironically, organized labor invented the PAC system, whereby individual solicitations are accumulated to finance the campaigns of candidates sympathetic to labor. Since labor lacked the resources of big business and since Congress passed legislation to limit organizational contributions, PACs enabled labor to raise enough funds to compete in the political marketplace. But business groups soon organized their own PACs, and now their campaign spending greatly exceeds that of labor and other groups. An anti-PAC lobby, coordinated by Common Cause, now seeks a law to limit PAC spending. Labor's stand on this issue remains to be seen.

To conclude, postwar welfare legislation that established national goals to help disprivileged groups called for labor to change its political agenda. Because labor's economic interests had changed, it was unable to focus its resources on issues of greatest importance to blacks, Hispanics, women, the poor, and new consumer groups. Consequently, these groups created lobbies that commanded the commitment, resources, and talents of their members. They grew while labor shrank; they expanded nationally while labor became regionalized; they elected their representatives to Congress, while labor did not; they targeted their legislation, while labor agonized over its priorities. Special interest lobbies attracted middle-class liberals who tired of labor's tactics in the Democratic party. Unable to aggregate the interests of the passionate lobbies or those of the working classes, labor played a weak trumpet on the issues of greatest national concern.

A PROGRAM FOR LABOR
IN THE MATURE WELFARE STATE

Most European unions have developed specific goals for the mature welfare state. They include (1) codetermination where management and labor share responsibility for setting and administering policies of work units, (2) jointly administered programs to improve the quality of work life, (3) expanded social ownership of the economy, (4) expanded social insurance programs, (5) guaranteed employment, and (6) tax reform to promote income equalization. Such social democratic programs appeal only to a small minority of American unions. Yet more than half a century after the onset of the New Deal, discouraged by recent Democratic defeats, American unions still struggle to define their political priorities and objectives. AFL-CIO president Kirkland once defined labor's strategy as simply one of influencing the Democratic party's choice of candidates for office. He reasoned that if more prolabor candidates are elected, labor's objectives would be more easily realized. However, this strategy does not specify labor's priorities nor does it respond to other party constituencies.

Discouraging as the current situation may appear, it holds some promise because it parallels some conditions of the early New Deal era. Blacks, Hispanics, impoverished women, and other working-class poor together represent large and growing constituencies that feel politically deprived and isolated. They are seeking ways to enter the political mainstream. As committed Democrats, they already represent its most prounion and most pro–welfare state constituency (Form 1985). Whereas a bare majority of union members voted Democratic in the past three presidential elections, 80 percent or more of blacks, Hispanics, and the poor identified with the Democratic party. Ironically, these groups are more prounion than union members themselves (Kistler 1984:99; Nie, Verba, and Petrocik 1979). Moreover, these groups are more self-conscious and cohesive than the rest of the working class, organized or unorganized. The groups are as ripe for unionization now as European ethnics were in 1933 when the New Deal began. Labor is being challenged to aggregate their potential political power. If it succeeds, the Democratic pro–welfare state coalition will be large enough to dominate the party and win elections.

Although the task is formidable, the time is propitious. While the bulk of the working class defines economic conditions as normal, blacks, Hispanics, poor women, and others suffer unemployment rates more than double the national average. When employed, they hold low-paying jobs in the expanding service sector. It would appear, then, that labor's first priority should be a massive drive to organize the services. Although not as easy to organize as the mass industries in the 1930s, Alan Kistler (1984:98), an experienced organizer, believes that this sector is inherently organizable. Large numbers of workers await organization in government, hospitals, schools, insurance companies, nursing homes, department stores, and shopping centers, especially in the South and West. Even if successful organizing campaigns turn out to be few in number, a massive and persistent drive will attract the attention and support of many liberals. It will convince service workers that labor is on their side.

Labor itself is partly responsible for its declining membership and it can reverse the trend. Freeman and Medoff (1985:229) cite evidence that one-third of the decline since 1933 is traceable to reduced spending for organizing. Since spending is a major determinant of the unionization rate, the drive for new members should take precedence over political spending for several reasons. First, organizing fits labor's basic goal: organize the unorganized. Second, organizing and administering labor contracts is what labor does best. Third, organizing produces what workers want most: higher wages and better working conditions. Fourth, most union members define organizing as nonpolitical and therefore more legitimate than political action. Fifth, organizing would counteract declining union membership and magnify labor's voice. Sixth, the drive would produce more union activists and officers among minorities and women. Seventh, unlike officers in other unions, those in service sector unions do not need to be persuaded to upgrade the jobs of minorities and women. Eighth, more organized workers would dampen trends in working-class stratification. Ninth, public attention would be diverted from labor's political activities to labor's more acceptable economic role. Tenth, and perhaps most important, organizing service workers would maximize both the prewar (social insurance) and the postwar (welfare targets) benefits of the welfare state.

I have stressed that prewar legislation emphasized social insurance while postwar social legislation aimed at full employment, elimination of poverty, better housing, equal employment opportunity, and occupational health and safety. Implementing postwar target legislation requires labor to apply pressure on Congress to provide funding. On the other hand, two targets, equal employment opportunity and OSHA, require constant union monitoring at the enterprise level. The successful organizing of the service sector would automatically expand labor's monitoring role to upgrade the skills of minorities and women and improve their working conditions. Such monitoring would obviously appeal to minorities and women because it simultaneously ties political action and economic benefits in the workplace, where they have most meaning. In effect, monitoring integrates party and plant politics, an outcome that class unionists seek but rarely enjoy.

The above program calls on labor to change its stance toward the Democratic party. In party conventions, labor has typically opposed the separate representation of groups (for example, women, blacks) in favor of a policy that integrates their interests. Yet labor itself may become a single-issue constituency if it continues to decline and if it deemphasizes the concerns of the passionate lobbies (Rehmus 1984:51). Labor's strategy to reveal its choice of Democratic presidential candidates early did not increase its popularity. A less conspicuous party role might actually increase its coalition building effectiveness. In the electoral arena, COPE might well redirect its energies to increasing the turnout of minorities and women for candidates that the latter select because, if elected, they would automatically support labor's general goals.

The growing minorities in the United States, the growing participation of women in the labor force, and the growing political involvement of these groups will, in the long run, increase their influence in labor unions and in the Democratic party. Perhaps, in this moment of history, labor would do well to hitch its fortunes to the issues raised by minorities and deemphasize its traditional commitments. Although the route may appear circuitous, it may be the fastest way to increase the well-being of the entire working class. If this strategy is not possible within the AFL-CIO, perhaps the time is ripe to form a new splinter trade union movement, comprised of liberal unions such as AFSCME, UAW, CWA, and the NEA. Along with women, blacks, Hispanics, and other liberal lobbies, the new coalition could have more political influence than the AFL-CIO. The historical evidence is not persuasive that a united labor movement is more politically effective than a divided one.

REFERENCES

Bauman, Zymunt. 1972. *Between Classes and Elites*. Manchester, England: Manchester University Press.

Bell, Daniel. 1972. "Labor in Post-Industrial Society." *Dissent* 19:163–89.

BLS (Bureau of Labor Statistics). 1975. *Analysis of Work Stoppages*. Washington: U.S. Government Printing Office.

———. 1981. *Earnings and Other Characteristics of Organized Workers, May 1980*. Washington: U.S. Government Printing Office.

Brody, David. 1980. *Workers in Industrial America: Essays on Twentieth Century Struggles*. New York: Oxford University Press.

Calkins, Fay. 1952. *The CIO and the Democratic Party*. Chicago: University of Chicago Press.

Cornfield, Daniel B. 1989. "Union Decline and the Political Demands of Organized Labor." *Work and Occupations* 16:292–322.

Dahrendorf, Ralf. 1959. *Class and Class Conflict in Industrial Society*. Stanford: Stanford University Press.

David, Henry. 1951. "One Hundred Years in Labor Politics." In *House of Labor*, edited by J. B. S. Hardman and Maurice F. Neufeld. New York: Prentice-Hall.

Davis, Garay, Carl Haub, and JoAnne Miller. 1983. "U.S. Hispanics: Changing the Face of America." *Population Bulletin* 38:3.

Davis, Mike. 1980. "The Barren Marriage of American Labour and the Democratic Party." *New Left Review* 124:48–84.

Edwards, Alba. 1943. *Comparative Occupation Statistics for the United States: 1870–1940*. U.S. Bureau of the Census. Washington: U.S. Government Printing Office.

Foner, Philip. 1964. *History of Labor Movements*. Vol. 4, *The Politics and Practices of the AFL, 1900–1906*. New York: International Publishers.

Form, William. 1985. *Divided We Stand: Working-Class Stratification in America*. Urbana: University of Illinois Press.

Form, William, and Claudine Hansen. 1985. "The Consistency of Stratal Ideologies of Economic Justice." In *Research in Social Stratification and Mobility*, vol. 4, edited by Robert V. Robinson. Greenwich, Conn.: JAI Press.

Form, William, and George Putnam. 1985. "Economic Cleavages in the American Working Class." *British Journal of Sociology* 36:1–33.

Foster, James Caldwell. 1975. *The Union Politic: The CIO Political Action Committee*. Columbia: University of Missouri Press.

Freeman, Richard B. 1981. "The Effects of Unionism on Fringe Benefits." *Industrial and Labor Relations Review* 34:489–509.

Freeman, Richard B., and James L. Medoff. 1984. *What Do Unions Do?* New York: Basic Books.

Galbraith, John Kenneth. 1969. *The Affluent Society*. Boston: Houghton Mifflin.

Gilson, Mary Barnett. 1934. "Unemployment Insurance." *Encyclopedia of the Social Sciences*. New York: Macmillan.

Goldfield, Michael. 1987. *The Decline of Organized Labor in the United States*. Chicago: University of Chicago Press.

Gordon, David M., Richard Edwards, and Michael Reich. 1982. *Segmented Work, Divided Workers*. Cambridge: Cambridge University Press.

Greenstone, David. 1977. *Labor in American Politics*. Chicago: University of Chicago Press.

Griffen, J. 1939. *Strikes*. New York: Columbia University Press.

Harwood, Edwin. 1982. "Union Political Action and Member Political Attitudes: A Parting of the Ways?" Unpublished manuscript. Department of Sociology. Macon, Ga.: Mercer University.

Jackson, Robert Max. 1984. *The Formation of Craft Markets*. New York: Academic Press.

Jacobs, David Carroll. 1983. "The UAW and the Campaign for National Health Insurance." Ph.D. diss., Cornell University.

Kahn, Lawrence M. 1978. "The Effects of Unions on the Earnings of Nonunion Workers." *Industrial and Labor Relations Review* 31:205–16.

Kistler, Alan. 1984. "Union Organizing: New Challenges and Prospects." *Annals of the American Academy of Political and Social Science* 473:96–107.

Lewis, H. Gregg. 1968. "Labor Unions: Influence on Wages." *International Encyclopedia of the Social Sciences*. New York: Macmillan and Free Press.

Lipset, Seymour Martin. 1977. "Why No Socialism in the United States?" In *Sources of Contemporary Radicalism*, edited by S. Bialer and S. Sluzer. Boulder, Col.: Westview.

Lipset, Seymour Martin, and William Schneider. 1983. *The Confidence Gap*. New York: Free Press.

Montgomery, David. 1979. *Worker's Control in America: History of Work, Technology, and Labor Struggles*. Cambridge: Cambridge University Press.

Nie, Norman H., Sidney Verba, and John R. Petrocik. 1979. *The Changing American Voter*. Cambridge: Harvard University Press.

Offe, Claus. 1984. *Contradictions of the Welfare State*, edited by John Keane. Cambridge: MIT Press.

Orloff, Ann Shola, and Theda Skocpol. 1985. "Why Not Equal Protection? The Politics of Public Social Spending in Britain, 1900–1911, and the United States, 1880–1920." *American Sociological Review* 49:726–50.

Perlman, Selig. 1928. *A Theory of the Labor Movement*. New York: Augustus M. Kelley.

Perlman, Selig, and Philip Taft. 1935. *History of Labor in the United States, 1896–1932*. Vol. 4, *Labor Movements*. New York: Macmillan.

Piven, Frances Fox, and Richard A. Cloward. 1971. *Regulating the Poor*. New York: Vintage.

Quadagno, Jil S. 1984. "Welfare Capitalism and the Social Security Act of 1935." *American Sociological Review* 49:632–47.

Ra, Jong Oh. 1978. *Labor at the Polls*. Amherst: University of Massachusetts.

Rattner, Ronnie Steinberg, and Alice Cook. 1981. "Women, Unions, and Equal Employment Opportunity." Albany: Center for Women in Government.

RCIA Leadership Letter. 1976. "Retail Clerks International Association." In *Labor and American Politics*, edited by Charles M. Rehmus. Ann Arbor: University of Michigan Press.

Rehmus, Charles M. 1984. "Labor and Politics in the 1980s." *Annals of the American Association of Political and Social Science* 473:40–51.

Rehmus, Charles M., Doris B. McLaughlin, and Federick H. Nesbit, eds. 1978. *Labor and American Politics*. Ann Arbor: University of Michigan Press.

Reid, John. 1982. "Black America in the 1980s." *Population Bulletin* 37:4. Population Reference Bureau.

Reynolds, Lloyd G. 1974. *Labor Economics and Labor Relations*. Englewood Cliffs: Prentice-Hall.

Roberts, Markley. 1984. "The Future Demographics of American Unionism." *Annals of the American Academy of Political and Social Science* 473:23–32.

Rubin, Beth, Larry J. Griffin, and Michael Wallace. 1983. "Provided That Their Voice Was Strong." *Work and Occupations* 10:325–47.

Rubinow, I. M. 1934a. "Old Age." *Encyclopedia of the Social Sciences*. New York: Macmillan.

———. 1934b. "Social Insurance." *Encyclopedia of the Social Sciences*. New York: Macmillan.

Schwartz, Arthur B., and Michelle Hoyman. 1984. "The Changing of the Guard: The New American Labor Leader." *Annals of the American Academy of Political and Social Science* 473:64–75.

Shapiro, David. 1978. "Relative Wage Effects of Unions in the Public and Private Sector." *Industrial and Labor Relations Review* 31:193–203.

Skocpol, Theda. 1980. "Political Response to Capitalist Crises: New-Marxists Theories of the State and the Case of the New Deal." *Politics and Society* 9:155–202.

Skocpol, Theda, and John Ikenberry. 1983. "The Political Formation of the American Welfare State in Historical and Comparative Perspective." In *Comparative Social Research*, vol. 6, edited by Richard F. Tomasson. Greenwich, Conn.: JAI Press.

U.S. Bureau of the Census. 1960. *Historical Statistics of the United States: Colonial Times to 1957*. Washington: U.S. Government Printing Office.

Wall Street Journal. 1984. "The AFL-CIO and Defense." November 1.

———. 1985. "Kirkland is Deliberately Vague on Overhaul Plans as AFL-CIO Splits Over Proposal to Tax Benefits." June 13.

Ware, Norman J. 1934. "Trade Unions: The United States." *Encyclopedia of the Social Sciences*. New York: Macmillan.

Weber, Arnold. 1963. "The Craft-Industrial Issue Revisited: A Study of Union Government." *Industrial and Labor Relations Review* 16:381–404.

Widick, B. J. 1972. "Black City, Black Union?" *Dissent* 19:138–45.

Wilson, Graham K. 1979. *Unionism in American Politics* New York: St. Martin's Press.

Wilson, William J. 1987. *The Truly Disadvantaged.* Chicago: University of Chicago Press.

Witte, Edwin C. 1934. "Workman's Compensation." *Encyclopedia of the Social Sciences.* New York: Macmillan.

Wolman, Leo, and Gustav Peck. 1933. "Labor Groups in the Social Structure." In *Recent Social Trends in the United States.* President's Research Commission on Social Trends. New York: McGraw-Hill.

I I I I I I I I   Comments and Observations
on the Nature of Work

STEVEN PETER VALLAS

During the past two decades American sociologists have de-
voted an enormous amount of attention to the nature of work as an institution.
Analysts have asked how technological change bears on the skills workers use
(see especially Spenner 1979, 1983; Attewell 1987, 1988; Zuboff 1988), and
why distinct forms of labor control evolve in different branches of the economy
(Burawoy 1985; Baron, Dobbin and Jennings 1986; and Cornfield 1987). They
have sought to understand how labor markets are organized, and how the
characteristics of firms contribute to the generation of economic inequality
(Baron and Bielby 1980). They have studied the social mechanisms that per-
petuate gender segregation and inequality at work (Cockburn 1983, 1985;
Milkman 1987; Reskin and Padevic 1988), the dynamics of worker participation (Zipp et al. 1984; Fenwick and Olsen 1986; Fantasia et al. 1988), and cross-
national differences in the organization of industry (Gallie 1978; Hamilton and
Biggart 1988).

While we have learned a great deal about work in these past decades, this
proliferation of research has been accompanied by an increasing balkanization
of the field. Quite apart from abiding theoretical differences among the various
camps, one finds little or no agreement as to whether the unit of analysis should
be the organization, industry, occupation, or underlying system of class relations. While advocates of the "new structuralism" have proposed ways of
reconciling such disagreements (see esp. Kalleberg and Berg 1987), their strategies seem mainly to catalogue the most relevant variables rather than to depict
their essential relationship. Hence the babel persists. Charged with understanding the division of labor within society, occupational sociology consistently

Much of the work reflected in these remarks was supported, intellectually and materially, by the Russell Sage Foundation, to which I am especially grateful.

343

falls short of its goal, not least because of the specialization and fragmentation internal to the field itself.

The present volume does not mean to provide a representative overview of the progress made in the various departments of occupational sociology. Readers seeking comprehensive reviews of the literature, handbook-style, are best advised to look elsewhere. These papers have a different aim: to explore forgotten terrain in the sociology of work, to redress important deficiencies in this field, and to move beyond routinized styles of research. I will use these closing pages to identify where I think the authors' contributions lie, to make some critical remarks on their arguments, and to offer some observations on the current state of our craft.

I

One of the classical themes in the sociology of work involves the effect of work on the person. Marx of course sought to theorize that relation in terms of alienation, Weber in terms of the "iron cage" that bureaucracy imposed on individual freedom. Members of the Chicago School took it as an article of faith that "the work men do is fateful" for their sense of self (Hughes 1958). Despite this theoretical legacy, however, as late as the early 1960s there were few systematic efforts to examine the link between work and personality.

Since that time our understanding of the relation between occupational conditions and personality has grown far more sophisticated, in large part due to the efforts of Melvin Kohn (1969; Kohn, Schooler et al. 1982), whose contribution to this volume takes stock of the progress he and his colleagues have made in this field. There is much to inventory. Kohn and his colleagues have amassed a solid foundation of research that shows how the "structural imperatives of work" affect specific facets of the worker's personality. As Kohn points out, these findings indicate that occupational conditions do indeed mold the worker's personality over time, as people learn or generalize from their occupational experiences to the social roles outside of work. The psychological consequences of work, we can be sure, do not stem from the selection of persons into given occupations (a favorite claim among epidemiologists); in fact, the effects of the job on the person are much more pronounced than any selection effects. Moreover, the job seems to mold the personality of men and women with roughly equal force, and in societies of quite diverse types. These conclusions rest on an unusually clear empirical foundation.

Erikson's paper on the question of worker alienation shares many of the same concerns addressed by Kohn but employs a different conceptual approach. Kohn (1976) has used the concept of alienation in his own research, but in the Durkheimian manner favored by Seeman (1959). By contrast, Erikson bases his discussion on Marx's definition of the term. In fact, one of the goals of Erikson's paper is to reorient research on alienation by demonstrating the theoretical power inherent in Marx's original approach.

While critical of many of the tenets of Marxist theory, Erikson agrees with the substantive thrust of Marx's philosophical anthropology. He therefore views labor as the fundamental nexus that shapes human consciousness. From this perspective it follows that when workers are denied any real control over their own labor and set to work for purposes they neither understand nor share, their creative powers will almost inevitably be stunted, their faculties narrowed and even mutilated by the needs of the production process. Forced to sell their freedom in order merely to live, workers bargain away little bits of themselves which even high wages cannot restore. Erikson wonders whether some of the most commonplace features of everyday life—its random violence, racial animosity, unthinking nationalism—may partly stem from workers' reduction to the status of commodities.

Erikson carefully avoids the pitfalls of traditional Marxist theory on the one hand and positivist (really, survey-based) research on the other. The problem with survey research, Erikson holds, is that it merely skims the surface of workers' consciousness, often accepting workers' own reports of their emotional functioning. (Might not our reliance on survey methods bespeak a profound alienation of the social scientist from the workers?) The problem with most Marxist research, by contrast, is that it typically imputes alienation to workers on the basis of their objective conditions alone. To speak of alienation in any strong sense, says Erikson, we must be able to identify some mark or wound registered deep in the worker's being. Our task is then to disclose the ways in which commodity production itself contributes to the sum of human despair and inhumanity that has been defined as a normal feature of modern life.

Despite the differences between Kohn's and Erikson's approaches—differences that may be most pronounced in the area of method—both emphasize mainly the structural aspects of work. One can hardly ignore the content or design of workers' jobs. The problem is that, taken too far, this structuralist emphasis risks portraying workers as passive objects or victims of the production process who cannot respond to the work structures they confront. We therefore lose sight of the ways in which workers collectively *act back on* the sources of their discontent, whether by fashioning social mechanisms for coping with boring work, for informally negotiating production demands, and at times even challenging the legitimacy of management's authority.[1] While Erik-

1. For studies of workers' modes of adaptation to boring work, see Roy 1959–60; Nash 1976; Burawoy 1979; and Molstad 1986. For examples of the literature on the informal negotiation of production standards, see Roethlisberger and Dickson 1939; Baldamus 1961; and Halle 1984. For analysis of workers' resistance, see Montgomery 1979, 1987; Brody 1980; and Costello 1985.

son does acknowledge such possibilities, they are peripheral to his analysis. And while Kohn alludes to the matter of coping and social support, he leaves little room for collective modes of conflict and adaptation. Clearly, if research on alienation is to build on the work of Kohn and Erikson, it will need to study more than the content of workers' jobs. In addition, it will need to explore the patterns of occupational community, solidarity, and industrial kinship workers form, which surely play a vital role in the link between work and personality.

II

The papers in the second section of this volume follow naturally from those in the first and invite us to relate workplace relations to their wider normative environment. The previous literature here is sparse. Only recently have organizational researchers taken the social environment seriously (and even here, only with respect to markets and interorganizational ties). Likewise, many occupational sociologists continue to do "plant sociology" (Kerr and Fisher 1957)—that is, to view the workplace as a closed system that can manufacture workers' attitudes out of whole cloth.[2] In contrast to this traditionally narrow focus, the papers by Cynthia Fuchs Epstein, Arthur Stinchcombe, and Rose Coser all insist, in varying ways, on the futility of studying work institutions in abstraction from the wider culture that gives them life.

Epstein criticizes both positivist and Marxist analysis of work on two interrelated grounds. First, they have failed to explore either the meanings workers attach to their jobs or the categories with which they experience their work. Second, they have viewed the workplace as an isolated compartment of social life, independent of the social order writ large. Using material gathered from her and Erikson's research on communications workers, Epstein sketches out an alternative perspective—one grounded in "action" theory, but which seeks to connect the cultural or intersubjective aspects of work to patterns of social inequality. We will not get far toward understanding the shifting boundaries between "men's" and "women's" work or the persistence of racial inequality, she implies, unless we focus our attention on the culture of the workplace and the work values that bind occupational groups together.

The paper by Arthur Stinchcombe addresses many of Epstein's concerns, though from a different perspective. Reaching beyond the "*new* structuralist" genre of research on firms, industries, and markets, Stinchcombe suggests that we have much to learn from the *old* structuralism, from Lévi-Strauss to Goffman.[3] He suggests, for example, that the oft-noted discrepancy between

2. For contrasting views on plant sociology, see Burawoy 1979; and Goldthorpe 1966; Sabel 1982; and Vallas and Epstein 1988.

3. For a penetrating analysis of Goffman's structuralism, see Gonos 1977. See also Kurzweil 1980.

formal and informal patterns of work behavior can usefully be reinterpreted as an instance of code-switching, as the same workers shift between different forms of discourse that are governed by different rules. Likewise, and even more important for our purposes here, Stinchcombe argues that the allocation of workers into particular occupations may in fact stem from an underlying "logic" whose principles lie deep within the cultural system. Thus whether we view men or women as appropriate occupants of certain jobs will rest on unconscious principles that function much like the elements in a myth. Implied in Stinchcombe's argument here is his belief that materialist or economic explanations of occupational segregation (see Cohn 1985) can take us only so far, and that we need to understand the symbolic rules and rituals that knit workplace behavior into the fabric of everyday life.

Like Epstein and Stinchcombe, Rose Coser also stresses the links between work and its wider institutional context. She is concerned with the relation between work and family, but from a vantage point that is different from most. Feminist scholars typically see little change occurring in domestic power relations, even when wives work for pay (see Hartmann 1976, 1981). Coser disagrees. In her account, husbands are increasingly willing to cede their traditional power, in effect trading it for the increased level of consumer goods and consequently the prestige that their wives' employment makes possible.

There is an element of irony involved here. According to Coser, the separation of work and home gave women control over the sphere of consumption and assigned them the task of enhancing the family's standing in the eyes of the community. Particularly among the upper classes, women performed a wide array of functions—voluntary activities in the church and community, support for the arts, moral guidance of the children—that were critical to the family's prestige. As industrialization expanded the range of consumer goods, however, such voluntary means of status-production could no longer suffice. Hence women's traditional function drew them into the labor market, setting the stage for decidedly *non*traditional, more egalitarian relationships between husband and wife. Thus while so many critics have derided status-seeking behavior, Coser finds that it has the unanticipated consequence of engendering greater freedom for women, and eventually for men.

Because Coser's analysis boldly challenges much current thinking about women, work, and class, it seems likely to provoke much debate. Some may object to her view that the function of women's work is necessarily different or more status-oriented than men's. Others will challenge her belief that women's paid employment alters the balance of power within the home so completely as she believes. Still others may wonder whether women's persistently low wages can have such pronounced effects on family prestige, or even whether prestige is the critical concern for working men and women. Despite such potential criticisms, however, Coser's paper begins to suggest an important point which, one suspects, increasingly applies to men and women alike: the meanings of work and family life and of production and consumption are much more intricately interwoven than our theories allow (Kanter 1976; Goldberg 1984; Freedman 1982).

III

Writers on work routinely employ certain stock categories— "blue-" versus "white-collar," "mental" versus "manual" labor, professionalism versus unionism, and the like—as the basis for their research. While these categories are sometimes useful, reliance on them has a way of taking its revenge. Too often, we begin to reify these concepts and to acquire a "trained incapacity" to observe subtle commonalities between apparently different forms of work—the junk peddler and the professor, the bartender and the priest—whose juxtaposition might yield useful insights (Hughes 1958:48). The papers in the third section of this volume begin to pursue the more imaginative analytic approach, exploring parallels that have often evaded the researcher's eye.

The paper by Ferman continues his pioneering research on the informal or irregular economy—labor performed outside regulated channels and which evades official detection. Some analysts have depicted the irregular economy as merely a sign of economic want or poverty—that is, as a "refuge from destitution" (see the discussion in Portes and Sassen-Koob 1987). Instead, Ferman views the irregular economy as a positive response to the bureaucratic structures that constitute the modern corporate economy. In his view, participation in the irregular economy grants workers greater power and flexibility over their economic lives. A rough equivalent of the medieval commons, the irregular economy enables workers to fashion self-styled alternatives to corporate structures and to at least partially overcome their separation from the means of production. Moreover, using bonds of kin and community as networks of exchange, the irregular economy also demonstrates the commingling of "values" in both the economic and cultural meanings of the term. Economic relationships, we are reminded, are inherently social ties (cf. Zelizer 1989).

The papers by Freidson and Lewis Coser extend the section's focus on the varieties of work and provide a useful contrast. Coser's paper looks at an *anti-utopia*—the social valuation of work in the concentration camp setting—in order to show the processes that allocate prestige (and even survival) under extreme circumstances. For his part, Freidson focuses on "labors of love"—a *positive* utopia that might help reshape the prevailing design of work. While these two papers are quite different in their content, their analytical strategy is nonetheless much the same: both papers seek to shed light on ordinary forms of work by examining work settings that are extraordinary or dramatically different from our own.

Freidson's paper is especially useful in that (as he himself notes) critics of work have seldom sought to imagine the coordinates of nonalienated labor in any detail. By focusing on labor undertaken as an end in itself, he hopes to demonstrate viable models that might lead beyond labor in its alienated form. Freidson looks to two quarters: voluntary work and the work of "amateurs" (for example, those artists, actors, and others whose tasks are faithful to the original meaning of the word). The latter cases provide us with examples of enduring systems of work undertaken for their own sake. Might not, he asks, *other* branches of our economy be recast in a similar mold?

Wheeler's concerns overlap those of Freidson. Wheeler explores the situation that results when workers lead "double lives"—that is, when they combine their routine occupational activities with a more passionate commitment to nonwork pursuits. There are many well-known figures who led such double lives. But for each Wallace Stevens or William Carlos Williams—we might add Alfred Schutz, a banker by day—there are thousands of unknown figures in much the same state: cab drivers who live for the opera, waiters whose souls lie in the theater, clerks who collect model trains. Although the prevalence of this phenomenon is unknown, Wheeler suspects that it has dramatically grown. He believes that the rationalization of labor and our society's increased emphasis on consumption weaken the attachment to work as a calling, while urbanization provides sources of identification that rival occupational life. Consequently, people are more likely to detach their selves from their jobs. According to Wheeler, many of our theories of work, which were premised on the centrality or primacy of production, have begun to show their age.

Wheeler is surely right to observe how little we know about this phenomenon. Yet he seems to go too far toward embracing a thesis we might call the declining significance of work under contemporary capitalism (cf. Dubin 1956). Quite apart from any romantic attachment to labor (Aronowitz 1985), there are two reasons for caution here. First, it seems likely that a large proportion of workers who lead double lives do so precisely *because* of their occupational commitments and pursuits. Students, for example, do indeed detach their identities from their present occupational roles, but primarily because of their anticipated commitments and career aspirations. Indeed, it seems likely that labor unionism would be more fully developed in many service occupations were it not for this future-orientation on the part of student employees.[4]

A second reason for caution in approaching Wheeler's analysis stems from

---

4. Thus Sabel (1982) coins the term *peasant worker* to refer to the distinct orientations toward work that prevail among immigrant workers, housewives, and students.

his interpretation of this detachment of the self from work. Most of the examples he gives relate to ordinary people (police, secretaries, custodians) who develop their aesthetic capacities through the opera, poetry and other gentle pursuits. Yet clearly, many nonwork preoccupations are remarkable not because they are so different from what we ordinarily call work, but precisely because they so closely resemble its traditional rhythms and reaffirm its cardinal values. As H. F. Moorhouse observes, "The more-or-less unexamined activities and ideological material of gardening, angling, cooking, boating, motoring, home-computing, sport and so on, all have plenty to say about labour and identity, skill and self, craft and commitment" (Moorhouse 1987:252). What Wheeler views as an autonomous embrace of nonwork activity may really comprise a muted protest against work in its modern, fully rationalized form.

IV

Earlier I noted that the papers by Rose Coser, Epstein, and Stinchcombe each stressed the cultural influences that impinge on both the allocation and the experience of work. The papers in the fourth section of the volume again focus on the relation between work and the wider institutions, but with an emphasis now on the specifically *political* factors that bear on work. This branch of occupational sociology too is poorly developed. Indeed, the connections between the state and the workplace have gone virtually unnoticed until the recent past (see Sabel 1982; Burawoy 1985). Given the pivotal role of the state in the provision of social insurance, the shaping of labor relations, the regulation of industries as well as the state's indirect influence as an employer, the absence of a genuinely political sociology of work is nothing short of astounding.

Bellin and Miller canvass the evidence on economic trends affecting the relative availability of "good jobs." In recent years, they note, there have been many claims of economic polarization, owing to a presumed proliferation of low-wage, insecure employment (see especially Bluestone and Harrison 1986; Harrison and Bluestone 1988). Reviewing available research on trends in unemployment, wages, and other labor market conditions, Bellin and Miller make a number of important points. First, they observe that discussion of polarization is too often couched in simplistic terms: many different models of development are consistent with a polarization effect (for example, an hourglass model, a pyramidal one, and many others as well). Second, while the evidence on occupational earnings does lend support to theories of polarization, however conceived, much of the research is hampered by serious methodological flaws. Third and most important, Bellin and Miller point to the impossibility of envisioning future economic trends in abstraction from the political context. In contrast to most analyses of labor market trends, Bellin and Miller show that economic outcomes are not self-generating: rather, they are produced and perpetuated by regimes that have the power to do things differently. Thus occupational trends are affected by military spending, subsidies, and tax laws (which directly impinge on capital investment); and the very structure and functioning of dual labor markets may owe much to political inputs (Sabel 1982). Thus Bellin and Miller provide a useful corrective to overly economistic conceptions of labor force analysis.

This emphasis on the political determination of economic structures is taken one step further by Skocpol, in her analysis of work and welfare in the United States. The question Skocpol asks is why the United States has made so few provisions for full employment and, alone among Western capitalist countries, lacks a national employment system. She criticizes two of the more popular answers to this question: perspectives that rely exclusively on cultural factors (for example, the thesis of American individualism and self-reliance), and those that invoke political class struggle (the relative strength of American capital in relation to labor). In her view, cultural explanations overlook widespread support for public works programs that would fight unemployment, while class struggle theories are unable to explain why labor's increased strength in the 1930s failed to produce a full-fledged national employment system. The answer, she contends, must be sought in two specifically political factors: the structure of the state and the nature of the American party system.

From the nineteenth century onward, Skocpol notes, the American state took on the character of a patronage system, whereby local political authorities maintained their power by controlling the distribution of work to loyal supporters. This system has continued into the twentieth century, in the guise of legislation that has little manifest connection to employment policy. This implicit system of patronage provides a powerful set of obstacles to the enactment of national employment legislation, inasmuch as congressional, state and local authorities resist any executive encroachment on their terrain. At the same time, American politics has been marked by the loosely coupled and often-contradictory structure of the Democratic party, which encompasses regional and racial groups whose perceived interests often conflict, and which has prevented the formation of alliances that might have generated a politics of full employment. The result, Skocpol shows, is a continuation of the segmented, half-formed system of employment policy that has traditionally characterized the United States. Complementing Bellin and Miller's stress on the political *choices* which enter into economic decisions, Skocpol emphasizes the structural *constraints* that limit or shape such choices, making some more likely than others.

To the extent that the United States *has* developed a strategy for full employment, the prevailing approach has been to rely on economic growth as a means of combating joblessness. Despite the apparently comforting state of the labor market as this volume goes to press, it may well be that this growth-oriented strategy for full employment is no longer viable. For given the internationalization of production and the widespread use of advanced technologies, the connection between economic growth and high demand for labor here at home has been gravely weakened. Responding to similar processes, workers' organizations in Western Europe have begun to favor strategies for full employment that might find application on these shores. Such strategies, which fall under the rubric of work sharing, are the subject of the papers by Best and by Gans.

Work sharing, Best informs us, refers to a large set of proposals all premised on the idea that unemployment can be reduced through reductions in working time (thereby distributing employment over a greater number of workers). The critical idea here is for the state to play a directive role in the allocation of labor time. While many will object to this idea as radical and unprecedented, Best points out that the state has long acted to "ration" labor time by restricting the use of child labor, setting standards for wages and hours, and by encouraging retirement at given ages. The issue then is not whether we should use work sharing, but how.

The paper by Gans underscores the relevance of work sharing less for its pragmatic value than for the insights and alternatives it invites us to weigh once we consider the full range of ways in which work can be redesigned. How can jobs be restructured into smaller modules that are more easily allocated among workers? Can workers share the jobs of their bosses? What cultural changes are implied in the reduction of labor time, and how will free time be used? The virtue of Gans's paper is that it begins to demonstrate the uses of such "utopian" thinking and to nurture a fuller, more open debate over the forms that "work" will take. The importance of job sharing, it may turn out, lies not so much in its pragmatic contribution as in the opportunity it provides for workers who wish to engage in alternative pursuits.

Whether or not a politics of full employment will reappear on the American scene, it seems likely that the issue of job training will continue to receive much discussion and debate. For this reason Anderson's analysis of the tensions and contradictions built into American job-training programs bears especially close attention. Anderson documents a major change in the nature of such programs from the pre-Depression years to the present. Then, little formal training was needed, as informal systems of labor recruitment, training, and control were in place. Typically, skilled workers recruited their fellow ethnics, generating social ties that firmly connected workers to the labor market (Tilly 1987). Given bonds of trust between members of the same or similar groups, little tension was likely to accompany the transmission of work skills and opportunities.

Following the end of World War II and the internal migrations it spurred, the American system of job training underwent a dramatic change. The informal system gave way to a formally administered one, while the new recruits belonged to a different racial group than their teachers and putative sponsors. The new arrangements, Anderson suggests, encouraged little of the sense of mutual support and sponsored mobility that had characterized the old system. Moreover, they encouraged many white instructors to see young blacks as a threat to their own group. Such instructors were poorly equipped to understand the culture of ghetto youth and often misconstrued their students' behavior. (Lateness may reveal more about mass transit, for example, than about students' values and commitment). The situation is made all the more complex because ghetto youth often reject the sense of time and work discipline that instructors impart, seeing such values as one more form of oppression. Given this intricate nexus of tension, misunderstanding, and distrust, the failure of job-training programs is all but assured.

Anderson's analysis is a rich ethnographic account of matters that have too often gone unnoticed among occupational sociologists. His piece reminds us that, amidst the outpouring of research on work arrangements, there has been little sustained attention given to questions of racial barriers on the job itself. The costs reach far beyond our journals, as equal opportunity policies are formulated on the basis of limited knowledge at best. If Anderson's analysis is any guide, research on racial disparities in the allocation of work would do well to focus not only on social networks, patterns of sponsorship, and ethnic succession, but also on the world views that people embrace in the course of struggle over economic rewards.

V

Many recent theorists have claimed that the present period marks a watershed in the capitalist economy, presaging qualitative shifts in the nature of work (Pahl 1988). Some see scientific and technological change as the driving force. Others stress economic and organizational processes involving the remaking of managerial authority (Heckscher 1989). Still others suggest that the future of work will be shaped by the relative powers of the combatants—especially corporate elites and the working classes. All agree that the older work arrangements that characterized mid-century America are fading into memory. What will replace them?

The paper by Etzioni and Jargowsky challenges one popular answer to this question, by refuting claims made on behalf of postindustrial society and its emerging high-technology industries. While these claims take many forms, each shares certain basic principles: manufacturing employment is withering away. Knowledge-intensive branches of production are vaunted into dominance, whether in terms of GNP or share of the labor force, as new classes take their place at the helm of the social order (cf. Bell 1971; Gorz 1982). Etzioni and Jargowsky summon an array of facts to challenge this body of assertions, and in so doing demonstrate three important points. First, there is little evidence that manufacturing employment is in fact falling away. Second, high technology industries and occupations are unlikely to absorb significant numbers of workers in the foreseeable future. (The fastest growing occupations are building custodians, cashiers, and truckdrivers and other job categories.) Third, the very distinction between "high" and "low" technology sectors obscures the increasing convergence of the two, as older branches of the economy invest in new technologies. The point, say Etzioni and Jargowsky, is that rumors of the death of manufacturing have been much exaggerated.

An increasingly popular conception of the future of work has been provided by Kanter, dealing with the organizational contradictions caused by changes in the structure of large corporations. According to Kanter, important changes have occurred in the American workforce, which harbors different values than did older generations (HEW Special Task Force 1973; Andrisani et al. 1978). Thus the promise of good wages and job security can no longer be counted on to motivate workers to produce. Instead, large corporations must offer greater opportunity, more challenging tasks and careers for a larger proportion of their employees than ever before. Even as they do this, Kanter suggests, corporations can expect to encounter serious strains and contradictions. For example, new systems of pay are increasingly based on merit or performance rather than on rank and will begin to collide against established hierarchies—especially when subordinates' pay rivals or even surpasses that of their bosses. The widening emphasis on innovation and entrepreneurial activities will run up against the older emphasis on certainty, short-term returns, and rule by command. And workplace reform generates increasingly "absorbtive" jobs which may tend to discriminate against those with heavy out-of-work commitments (such as often befall women employees). In these and other ways, efforts to further the cause of workplace reform will generate symptoms of strain that, unless dealt with adequately, may threaten the process of organizational reform itself.

No one could deny that modern corporations have adopted novel approaches to labor policy, in ways that previous generations of managers would not have believed. The very concept of personnel, for example, has given way to much broader departments that typically bear names such as Human Resource Management. Increasingly, large firms have begun to provide services that mirror those of government: there is a social service component (to deal with issues of alcoholism, drug abuse, and family needs and problems), a justice component (to address issues of equal opportunity), and an educational component (to provide training and other skills).[5] The question, however, is how we make sense of these and other changes in the structure of management.

Kanter's interpretation seems to make a number of assumptions which can be challenged on both empirical and theoretical grounds. The first point concerns the actual prevalence of workplace reform in the United States. This question has surrounded virtually every prior form of managerial control (from Taylorism to more recent incarnations) and is plagued by problems of both definition and data. However, a recent analysis by Russell (1988) provides important ground for skepticism as to the magnitude of the change that has purportedly swept across corporate America. According to Russell, only a minuscule proportion of even the large firms have made any determined efforts to reform their internal structure; and those that have (for example, by adopting the QWL process, or Quality Circle concept) have typically abandoned them after only a few years. We therefore have some cause to wonder whether Kanter's analysis is genuinely descriptive of reality.

A second point concerns Kanter's interpretation of the changes that *have* transpired. She suggests that the "new workplace" is less hierarchical, more egalitarian, and more conducive to the freedom that the new workforce seeks (cf. Zuboff 1988). But a more critical interpretation of these changes sees instead a new form of hierarchy—a means of restoring corporate hegemony and of transferring to workers the task of enforcing corporate goals (Fantasia et al. 1988; Grenier 1988). This is precisely what Edwards's (1979) concept of bureaucratic control identified: a system of labor control that powerfully weakened bonds of solidarity among workers by transmitting managerial ideology downward into the ranks. The question, then, is whether the new workplace of which Kanter speaks is really so fundamentally new.

Ultimately, it becomes impossible to address the question of the future of work without attending to the fate of the workers' movement. Many have sought to diagnose labor's decline (for example, Goldfield 1987), but Form brings a particular breadth of knowledge to the issue. His analysis aims to understand the historical relation between organized labor and the welfare state in the United States. Because American unions embraced a narrow form of pragmatic unionism that paid little heed to political action, the emergence of the American welfare state was chiefly the work of intellectuals and political elites. By the time labor had developed the political tools it needed to influence

5. To refer to this statelike function of management, Burawoy (1979, 1985) has coined the term *internal state* and later *factory regime*.

welfare legislation, important changes had begun to occur in the composition of the working class itself. Newer strata of black, Hispanic, and women workers flooded into the expanding service industries outside the house of labor. Representing the more affluent stratum of white male workers, labor unions increasingly acquired a defensive, sectionalist character bereft of broader social goals. The task of expanding rights and entitlements therefore fell to single-issue organizations that saw the labor movement as an obstacle to social change.

Form sees more than mere decay, however. He sees the possibility of a resurgence of the labor movement and renewed expansion of the welfare state. The strategy he offers toward this end is rooted in the poorer strata of workers, largely composed of racial and ethnic minorities. A resurgence of unionism here, he suggests, could not but address larger social questions of justice and politics.

One reader at least hopes that Form is right. His scenario does conform to the history of the American workers' movement, which has periodically grown through sudden breaks or ruptures with older organizational vehicles. Yet Form's analysis leaves a number of questions to be addressed. While he contends that divisions among workers need not limit their power—an assertion that seems to cut against the grain of his earlier work (Form 1976, 1985)—the validity of this claim is by no means clear. Indeed, one can argue that it was the politics of resentment among sectors of the white working class that opened the door to the recent attacks on the welfare state itself (see especially Rieder 1985). If so, then the need for political unity across racial lines may be more decisive than Form allows.

VI

Beginning with the appearance of models of "industrial man" in the early 1960s (Kerr et al. 1960), some of the most influential contributions to the study of work have been made by economists (Form 1979). This trend has only increased with the spread of transaction cost analysis and institutional economics. While there are numerous instances in which sociologists have challenged economic models (as with the critique of neoclassical economics and human capital theory), sociologists of work and industry have more commonly adopted economic premises and concerns (see Cornfield 1987). Should this trend continue, the danger is that research on work will lose sight of its *non*rational *supra*economic aspects. Hopefully, the present papers will help to redress this problem.

At various points in this volume the authors have spoken of the paucity of studies focused on the subjective experience of work and the cultural values that surround it. Relative to research by labor historians (Thompson 1967; Gutman 1977; Rodgers 1978; Joyce 1987) and anthropologists of work (Wallman 1979; Godelier 1980), occupational sociologists have paid relatively little sustained attention to the meaning of work and orientations toward it. As a result, the field has grown in a somewhat lopsided manner: We have accumulated a rich *materialist* understanding of the transformation of work during the twentieth century—this phrase is the subtitle of half a dozen recent books—but we lack even an outline for research on the *symbolic* importance of work during the same period (Zuboff 1983). Has a new set of work values emerged, as Kanter suggests, in marked contrast to the older, extrinsic orientation? Can we speak of the prevalence of a single, overarching "work ethic," despite prominent divisions of class, religion, ethnicity, and age? And how adequate *is* this distinction between intrinsic and extrinsic orientations to the reality it would describe? The fact that these questions have not been addressed may stem from the common assumption that cultural inquiry is by its very nature politically quiescent. Yet the opposite assumption seems more defensible: struggles for greater freedom and equality at work will require that we attend to such matters, and explore the ineluctably moral side of economic life.

A related theme that emerges in these pages concerns the adequacy of deterministic models of work structures. Implicit at many points in this volume—most clearly in the contributions by Epstein, Ferman, and Gans, but in other papers as well—is a latent dissatisfaction with hyperstructuralist models of work which view workers as little more than raw materials, shaped by (but never themselves shaping) work as an institution (Simpson 1988; DiFazio 1985). To say this is hardly to romanticize workers' capacity for resistance. Indeed, much of the literature on workplace relations shows that workers' responses to their jobs may act to trap them within subordinate roles (see Willis 1977; Burawoy 1979; Westwood 1982). The point nonetheless remains: we are not likely to understand how work structures emerge, persist, or change unless we take into account the ways in which workers act back on or negotiate their work situations.

A third point that emerges from the papers in this collection relates to the underdeveloped conception of politics that prevails within occupational sociology (see Burawoy 1985). It seems fair to say that sociologists have mainly focused on the myriad ways in which the organization of work and trade unions affect political life (see Montomery 1979, 1987; Sobel 1989). Yet (as Bellin and Miller and Skocpol remind us) the reverse is also true: Political institutions exert an autonomous influence on work structures. The question then becomes, How? In what ways and to what extent does the state itself shape the emergence of systems of managerial control over workers? Might not state policy help account for cross-national variations in the structure of labor markets? Might not political orientations condition workers' experience of their jobs? While a few scholars have begun to address such questions (Sabel 1982; Burawoy 1985), the latter require much more attention than they have received.

This lack of research on the relation between work and politics is not a random occurrence. Rather, it has a deeper source, stemming from our failure to view work as part of a broader ensemble of social relations. Caught up in what Kanter has termed the "myth of separate worlds," occupational sociologists have long viewed the family as foreign to the study of work. We continue to view the community as the rightful province of urban sociologists, and so rarely inquire into the links between work and community (Kornblum 1974). So too with the polity, with relations between dominant and minority groups, and so on. In all these cases, the structure of our own occupation impedes our grasp of the ways in which work is embedded in the wider social order. Increasingly, these divisions will need to be torn down. The development of the field requires that we transcend the division of intellectual labor we have ourselves devised.

REFERENCES

Andrisani, Paul J. et al. 1978. *Work Attitudes and Labor Market Experience: Evidence from the National Longitudinal Survey.* New York: Praeger.

Aronowitz, Stanley. 1985. "Why Work?" *Social Text* (Fall): 19–42.

Attewell, Paul. 1987. "The Deskilling Controversy." *Work and Occupations* 14 (August): 323–46.

———. 1988. "Big Brother and the Sweatshop: Computer Surveillance in the Automated Office." *Sociological Theory* 5 (Spring): 87–99.

Baron, James. 1984. "Organizational Perspectives on Stratification." *Annual Review of Sociology* 10:37–69.

Baron, James, and William T. Bielby. 1980. "Bringing the Firms Back In: Stratification, Segmentation and the Organization of Work." *American Sociological Review* 45 (October): 737–65.

Baron, James, Frank Dobbin, and P. D. Jennings. 1986. "War and Peace: The Evolution of Modern Personnel Administration in US Industry." *American Journal of Sociology* 92, 2 (September): 350–83.

Bluestone, Barry, and Bennett Harrison. 1986. "The Great American Job Machine: The Proliferation of Low-Wage Employment in the US Economy." *Report to the Joint Economic Committee of the U.S. Congress.* Washington, D.C.: U.S. Government Printing Office.

Bowles, Samuel, and Herbert Gintis. 1976. *Schooling in Capitalist America.* New York: Basic.

Braverman, Harry. 1974. *Labor and Monopoly Capital: The Degradation of Work in the Twentieth Century.* New York: Monthly Review.

Brody, David. 1980. *Industrial Workers in America.* New York: Oxford University Press.

Burawoy, Michael. 1979. *Manufacturing Consent: Changes in the Labor Process under Monopoly Capitalism.* Chicago: University of Chicago Press.

———. 1985. *The Politics of Production: Factory Regimes under Capitalism and Socialism.* London: Verso.

Clarke, Lee. 1988. "Organizational Sociology." In *The Future of Sociology,* edited by E. F. Borgatta and Karen S. Cook. Beverly Hills, Cal.: Sage.

Cockburn, Cynthia. 1983. *Brothers: Male Dominance and Technological Change.* London: Pluto.

———. 1985. *Machinery of Dominance: Men, Women and Technical Know-How.* London: Pluto.

Cohn, Samuel. 1985. *The Process of Occupational Sex Typing: The Feminization of Clerical Work in Great Britain.* Philadelphia: Temple University Press.

Cornfield, Daniel. 1987. *Workers, Managers and Technological Change: Emerging Patterns of Labor Relations.* New York: Plenum.

DiFazio, William. 1985. *Longshoremen: Community and Resistance on the Brooklyn Waterfront.* Introduction by Stanley Aronowitz. South Hadley, Mass.: Bergin and Garvey.

Dubin, Robert. 1956. "Industrial Workers' Worlds: A Study of the Central Life Interests of Industrial Workers." *Social Problems* 3.

Edwards, Richard C. 1980. *Contested Terrain: The Transformation of Work in the Twentieth Century.* New York: Basic.

Fantasia, Rick, Dan Clawson, and Gregory Graham. 1988. "A Critical View of Workers' Participation in the United States." *Work and Occupations* 15, 4 (November): 468–89.

Fenwick, Rudy, and Jon Fenwick. 1986. "Support for Worker Participation: Attitudes among Union and Non-Union Workers." *American Sociological Review* 51:505–22.

Ferree, Myra Marx. 1985. "Between Two Worlds: German Feminist Approaches to Working-Class Women and Work." *Signs* 10, 3 (Spring): 517–36.

———. 1987. "Family and Jobs for Working-Class Women: Gender and Class Systems Seen from Below." In *Families and Work,* edited by N. Gerstl and H. E. Gross. Philadelphia: Temple University Press.

Form, William H. 1976. *Blue Collar Stratification: Auto Workers in Four Countries.* Princeton: Princeton University Press.

———. 1979. "Comparative Industrial Sociology and the Convergence Hypothesis." *Annual Review of Sociology* 5:1–25.

———. 1985. *Divided We Stand: Working-Class Stratification in America.* Chicago: University of Illinois Press.

———. 1987. "On the Degradation of Skills." *Annual Review of Sociology* 13:29–47.

Freeman, Caroline. 1983. "The 'Understanding' Employer." In *Work, Women and the Labour Market,* edited by Jackie West. London: Routledge and Kegan Paul.

Gallie, Duncan. 1978. *In Search of the New Working Class: Automation and Social Integration within the Capitalist Enterprise.* Cambridge: Cambridge University Press.

Godelier, Maurice. 1980. "Work and Its Representations: A Research Proposal." *History Workshop* 10 (Autumn): 164–74.

Goldberg, Rhoda. 1984. "The Determination of Consciousness Through Gender, Family and Work Experience." *Social Science Journal* 21, 4 (October): 75–85.

Goldfield, Michael. 1987. *The Decline of Organized Labor in the United States*. Chicago: University of Chicago Press.

Goldthorpe, John. 1966. "Attitudes and Behaviour of Car Assembly Workers: A Deviant Case and A Theoretical Critique." *British Journal of Sociology* 17 (September).

Gonos, George. 1977. " 'Situation' versus 'Frame': The 'Interactionist' and the 'Structuralist' Analyses of Everyday Life." *American Sociological Review* 42 (December): 854–67.

Gorz, André. 1982. *Farewell to the Working Class: An Essay on Post-Industrial Socialism*. Boston: South End Press.

Granovetter, Mark, and Charles Tilly. 1988. "Inequality and Labor Processes." In *Handbook of Sociology,* edited by N. Smelser. Newbury Park, Cal.: Sage.

Grenier, Guillermo. 1988. *Inhuman Relations: Quality Circles and Anti-Unionism in American Business.* Philadelphia: Temple University Press.

Gutman, Herbert. 1977. *Work, Culture and Society in Industrializing America*. New York: Vintage.

Halle, David. 1984. *America's Working Man: Work, Home and Politics among Blue-Collar Property Owners*. Chicago: University of Chicago Press.

Hamilton, Gary, and N. Biggart. 1988. "Market, Culture and Authority: A Comparative Analysis of Management and Organization in the Far East." *American Journal of Sociology* 94 (Supplement): S52–94.

Harrison, Bennett, and Barry Bluestone. 1988. *The Great U-Turn: Corporate Restructuring and the Polarizing of America*. New York: Basic.

Hartmann, Heidi. 1976. "Capitalism, Patriarchy and Job Segregation by Sex." *Signs* 1 (Autumn): 137–69.

———. 1981. "The Family as the Locus of Gender, Class and Political Struggle: The Example of Housework." *Signs* 6, 3:366–94.

Health, Education and Welfare Special Task Force. 1973. *Work in America*. Cambridge: MIT Press.

Heckscher, Charles. 1989. *The New Unionism: Employee Involvement in the Changing Corporation*. New York: Basic.

Hughes, E. C. 1958. *Men and Their Work*. Glencoe, Ill.: Free Press.

Kallberg, Arne. 1988. "Comparative Perspectives on Work Structures and Inequality." *Annual Review of Sociology* 14:203–25.

Kalleberg, Arne, and Ivar Berg. 1987. *Work and Industry: Structures, Markets and Processes*.

Kanter, R. M. 1976. *Work and Family in the United States: A Critical Review*.

———. 1977. *Men and Women of the Corporation*. New York: Basic.

Karasek, Robert. 1979. "Job Demands, Job Decision Latitude and Mental Strain: Implications for Job Redesign." *Administrative Science Quarterly* 24:286–308.

Kerr, Clark, J. Dunlop, F. Harbison, and C. Myers. 1960. *Industrialism and Industrial Man*. Cambridge: Harvard University Press.

Kerr, Clark, and Lloyd Fisher. 1957. "Plant Sociology: The Elite and the Aborigines." In *Common Frontiers of the Social Sciences,* edited by M. Komaronsky. Glencoe, Ill.: Free Press.

Kohn, Melvin. 1969. *Class and Conformity: A Study of Values*. Dorsey.

Kohn, Melvin, Carmi Schooler, et al. 1982. *Work and Personality: An Inquiry into the Impact of Social Stratification*. Norwood, N.J.: Ablex.

Kornblum, William. 1974. *Blue-Collar Community*. Chicago: University of Chicago Press.

Kornhauser, Arthur. 1965. *Mental Health of the Industrial Worker*. New York: Wiley.

Kurzweil, Edith. 1980. *The Age of Structuralism*. New York: Columbia University Press.

Milkman, Ruth. 1987. *Gender at Work: The Dynamics of Job Segregation by Sex During World War II*. Chicago: University of Illinois Press.

Molstad, Clark. 1986. "Choosing and Coping with Boring Work." *Urban Life* 15, 2 (July): 215–36.

Montgomery, David. 1979. *Workers' Control in America: Studies in the History of Work, Technology and Labor Struggles*. New York: Cambridge University Press.

———. 1987. *The Fall of the House of Labor*. Cambridge: Cambridge University Press.

Moorhouse, H. F. 1987. "The 'Work Ethic' and 'Leisure' Activity: The Hot Rod in Post-War America." In *The Historical Meanings of Work*, edited by Patrick Joyce. Cambridge: Cambridge University Press.

Morse, Nancy, and Robert S. Weiss. 1955. "The Meaning and Function of Work and the Job." *American Sociological Review* 20:191–98.

Nash, Al. 1976. "Alienation and the Auto Worker." In *Auto Work and Its Discontents*, edited by B. J. Widick.

Pahl, R. E. 1988. *On Work: Historical, Comparative and Theoretical Approaches*. London: Blackwell.

Portes, Alejandro, and Saskia Sassen-Koob. 1987. "Making it Underground: Material on the Informal Sector in Western Market Economies." *American Journal of Sociology* 93, 1 (July): 30–61.

Reskin, Barbara, and Irene Padevic. 1988. "Supervisors as Gatekeepers: Male Supervisors' Response to Women's Integration in Plant Jobs." *Social Problems* 35, 5 (Dec.): 536–50.

Rieder, Jonathan. 1985. *Canarsie: The Jews and Italians of Brooklyn against Liberalism*. Cambridge: Harvard University Press.

Rodgers, Daniel T. 1978. *The Work Ethic in Industrial America, 1850–1920*. Chicago: University of Chicago Press.

Roethlisberger, F. J., and William Dickson. 1939. *Management and the Worker*. Cambridge: Harvard University Press.

Roy, Donald. 1959–60. "'Banana Time': Job Satisfaction and Informal Interaction." *Human Organization* 18:158–69.

Russell, Raymond. 1988. "Forms and Extent of Employee Participation in the Contemporary United States." *Work and Occupations* 15, 4 (November): 374–96.

Sabel, Charles. 1982. *Work and Politics: The Division of Labor in Industry*. Cambridge: Cambridge University Press.

Salaman, G. 1974. *Community and Occupation: An Exploration of Work/Leisure Relationships*. Cambridge: Cambridge University Press.

Seeman, Melvin. 1959. "On the Meaning of Alienation." *American Sociological Review* 24:783–91.

Shaiken, Harley. 1984. *Work Transformed: Automation and Labor in the Computer Age*. New York: Holt, Rinehart and Winston.

Simpson, Ida Harper. 1989. "The Sociology of Work: Where Have All the Workers Gone?" *Social Forces* 67, 3 (March).

Special Task Force on Work in America. 1973. *Work in America.* Cambridge: MIT Press.

Spenner, Kenneth I. 1979. "Temporal Changes in Work Content." *American Sociological Review* 44:968–75.

———. 1983. "Deciphering Prometheus: Temporal Changes in the Skill Level of Work." *American Sociological Review* 48:824–37.

Thompson, Edward P. 1967. "Time, Work Discipline and Industrial Capitalism." *Past and Present* 38:56–97.

Tilly, Charles. 1987. "Transplanted Networks." *Center for Studies of Social Change Monograph.* New York: New School for Social Research.

Vallas, Steven P., and Cynthia Fuchs Epstein. 1988. "Consent and Control in the Labor Process: The Limits of Job-Centered Analysis." Paper presented at the American Sociological Association meetings.

Wallman, Sandra, ed. 1979. *The Social Anthropology of Work.* New York: Academic Press.

Wilkinson, Barry. 1983. *The Shop Floor Politics of New Technology.* London: Gower.

Willis. Paul. 1977. *Learning to Labor: How Working-Class Kids Get Working-Class Jobs.* New York: Columbia University Press.

Wright, Erik Olin. 1985. *Classes.* London: Verso.

Zelizer, Viviana. 1989. "The Social Meaning of Money: 'Special Monies.' " *American Journal of Sociology* 95, 2 (September): 342–77.

Zipp, John F., Paul Luebke, and Richard Landerman. 1984. "The Social Bases of Support for Workplace Democracy." *Sociological Perspectives* 27, 4 (October): 395–425.

Zuboff, Shoshana. 1983. "The Work Ethic and Work Organization." In *The Work Ethic: A Critical Analysis,* edited by J. Barbash et al. Madison, Wis.: Industrial Relations Research Association.

———. 1988. *In the Age of the Smart Machine: The Future of Work and Power.* New York: Basic.

IIIIIII CONTRIBUTORS

Elijah Anderson is Professor of Sociology and Associate Director of the Center for Urban Ethnography at the University of Pennsylvania.

Seymour S. Bellin is Professor of Sociology at Tufts University.

Fred J. Best is President of Pacific Management and Research Associates, Sacramento.

Lewis A. Coser is Professor Emeritus at the State University of New York at Stony Brook and Adjunct Professor of Sociology at Boston College in Chestnut Hill, Massachusetts.

Rose Laub Coser is Professor Emerita at the State University of New York at Stony Brook, Adjunct Professor of Sociology at Boston College in Chestnut Hill, Massachusetts, and Visiting Scholar at the Henry A. Murray Research Center at Radcliffe College in Cambridge, Massachusetts.

Cynthia Fuchs Epstein is Professor of Sociology at the Graduate Center, City University of New York.

Kai Erikson is Professor of Sociology and Professor of American Studies at Yale University.

Amitai Etzioni is University Professor of Sociology at The George Washington University.

Louis A. Ferman is Professor of Social Work and Research Director, The Institute of Labor and Industrial Relations, University of Michigan.

William Form is Professor of Sociology at The Ohio State University.

Eliot Freidson is Professor of Sociology at New York University.

Herbert J. Gans is Robert S. Lynd Professor of Sociology at Columbia University.

Paul A. Jargowsky is Project Coordinator, John F. Kennedy School of Government, Harvard Unversity.

Rosabeth Moss Kanter is Class of 1960 Professor of Business Administration at Harvard University.

Melvin L. Kohn is Professor of Sociology at Johns Hopkins University.

S. M. Miller is Senior Fellow at the Commonwealth Institute and Professor Emeritus of Sociology, Boston University.

Theda Skocpol is Professor of Sociology at Harvard University.

Arthur L. Stinchcombe is Professor of Sociology, Political Science, and Organization Behavior at Northwestern University.

Steven Peter Vallas is Assistant Professor of Sociology at the School of Social Sciences, Georgia Institute of Technology.

Stanton Wheeler is Ford Foundation Professor of Law and Social Sciences at Yale University.

IIIIIIII Index

Swedes in Finland, 111

Taft-Hartley Act, 327
Targeted Job Tax Credit (TJTC), 188
Task forces, 283, 298–99
Tax rebates, 188
Tax Reform Act of 1986, 185
Taylor, Patricia A., 61
Taylorism, 355
Teams, 47, 281, 283, 289, 355
Teamsters Union, 328
Technological requirements, 59
Technology: high, *see* High technology;
  impact of, 89. *See also* specific types
Telecommunications, 305
Telephone operators, 95
Temme, Lloyd V., 45
Terkel, Studs, 150
Thatcher, Margaret, 187, 266
Threshold effects, 49
Tilgher, A., 149
Tilly, Charles, 352
Time demands of work, 280, 297–301
Time–income tradeoffs, 248–49, 253–54
Time and motion studies, 28
Time pressure, 37, 41, 48
Timing, 48–49
Toennies, Ferdinand, 25
Tomaskovic-Devey, Donald, 176, 307, 308
Tos, Nico, 61
Tosi, Henry, 289
Tosi, Lisa, 289
Total institutions, 162, 163, 169
Trade unions. *See* Unions
Tradition of opportunity, 95
Training. *See* Job training
Transaction cost analysis, 356
Transfer diversion, 187
Transfer payments. *See* Welfare
Transformation thesis, 305–06
Treiman, Donald J., 45
Trow, M., 88
Truman, Harry S., 327
Two-tier labor market, 173. *See also* Split
  society
Two-track society, 306
Tyree, Andrea, 81

Unconscious norms, 3, 112–15
Underemployed, 4, 12, 15
Underground economy. *See* Irregular
  economy
Underorganized, 15

Unemployment, 4, 8, 9, 10, 11, 12, 150,
  153; actual rate of, 259; distribution of,
  174–77; gender differences in, 175; hard-
  core, 221, 222; long-term, 189; normalization of, 181, 182; official rate of,
  174, 259; rate of, 173–74, 181, 182,
  259; structural, 186; work sharing and,
  235–57
Unemployment insurance, 185, 192, 194,
  199, 246, 267; work sharing supported
  by, 246
Unions, 12, 14, 15, 185, 209, 211, 262,
  348; decline of, 355; erosion of confidence in, 332–34; ineffective coalitions
  of, 329; loss of strength of, 327–29;
  political organization of, 325–26; welfare
  state and, 319–39; welfare state politics
  and, 332–36; working class and, 330–32;
  work sharing and, 266
United Auto Workers (UAW), 267, 281,
  320, 321, 328, 333, 339
Universities, 113
Urban enterprise zones, 184
Urbanization, 74
U.S. Chamber of Commerce, 202
U.S. Steel Sabbatical, 239
Used car salespeople, 111–12

Vacations, 11, 247
Vallas, Steven Peter, 29, 343
Van de Ven, Andrew H., 292
Van Houten, Donald R., 60
Van Kleeck, Mary, 78, 88
Veblen, Thorstein, 5, 72, 75
Verba, Sidney, 200, 261, 337
Veterans Disability Payments, 134
Vico, Giovanni Battista, 84, 85
Visibility, 72
Visser, Jelle, 266, 270
Vocational interest inventories, 108
Vocations, 143
Volpert, 44
Volunteer work, 6, 73, 156, 349; defined,
  156–57. *See also* Labors of love
Von Hippel, Eric, 295

Wacquant, Löic, 232
Wage depression, 180
Wagner Act. *See* National Labor Relations
  Act
Waite, Linda J., 77
Walker, Charles, 24, 113
Walker, Patrick, 179, 180